Child Abuse and Neglect

Kath hunny

Child Abuse and Neglect

Facing the Challenge

edited by
**Wendy Stainton Rogers, Denise Hevey,
Jeremy Roche and Elizabeth Ash**
at The Open University

B. T. Batsford Ltd · *London*
in association with
The Open University

First published 1989
This edition published 1992

Typset by Deltatype, Ellesmere Port
and printed in Great Britain by
Dotesios Ltd, Trowbridge, Wilts

Published by B. T. Batsford Ltd
4 Fitzhardinge Street, London W1H 0AH

A CIP catalogue record for this book is
available from the British Library

ISBN 0 7134 7177 8

CONTENTS

SECTION FOUR: RECOGNIZING AND RESPONDING TO SUSPECTED ABUSE

SECTION FIVE: THE EFFECTS OF ABUSE

SECTION SIX: RESPONDING TO CHILD ABUSE

ACKNOWLEDGEMENTS

The Editors and Publisher would like to thank the following for their kind permission to reproduce copyright material in this book:
Metropolitan Museum of Art, New York (picture of Joseph and Anna Raymond in chapter 1); Macmillan Education, Basingstoke (extract from 'Parenting in the 80s' in G. Pugh and E. De'Ath, *The Needs of the Parents*, 1985), © National Children's Bureau; Cambridge University Press (extract from R. Calam and R. Franchi, *Child Abuse and its Consequences: Observational Approaches*, 1987); Francesca Odell, Insight Photographers, London (photograph in chapter 7); Belfast Telegraph Newspapers Limited (photographs from archive, in chapter 12); *Nursery World* (M. Thornley, 'Fostering an Abused Child', 7 May 1987); Hodder and Stoughton, New Zealand (extract from K. Hume, *The Bone People*); Virago Press Limited, London (extract from J. Spring, *Cry Hard and Swim*, 1987); Macmillan, Basingstoke (extract from R. Holman, *Putting Families First: Prevention and Child Care*, 1988).

INTRODUCTION

Lou was what you might describe as 'a bit of a loner'. Brought up with several sisters, his boyhood artistic and theatrical interests prepared him badly for the public school he attended, and he emerged as a socially inept, long-haired young man, afflicted with a stammer and a range of obsessive symptoms which made it difficult for him to establish any lasting or serious adult relationships. In any case Lou's interest was in children, and from his early twenties he engaged in a series of intense liaisons with pre-pubescent girls, each lasting until the girl reached adolescence, only to be broken off abruptly by Lou, who would then go looking for another, younger girl. He established these relationships by filling his home with toys, books and other enticements, and taking trips to places like the seaside where he could meet children. He seems to have had an amazing capacity, once he had got a conversation started, to lure these young girls into his home. From his letters to them, it is clear that the relationships were more than platonic, as he would frequently mention kissing them. Over the years he built up a collection of photographs of the girls he befriended. At first they were posed in exotic costumes, but over time he asked them to wear clothes that were increasingly scanty and torn. Although he never managed to persuade any of them to pose nude, he had a large collection of 'artistic' pictures of naked young girls and spent many hours drawing copies of them.

Tom, on the other hand, is a pre-adolescent boy, who has been brought up by his elderly aunt, in conditions of severe social and economic deprivation. She has reared him strictly, beating him frequently, making him take cold showers, and dosing him with dubious patent medicines. Tom is a chronic school refuser; he smokes, lies, steals, tortures animals and carries a knife. He belongs to a gang of like delinquents, and his best friend lives rough on the streets. His fantasies centre on a life of crime. He has repeatedly run away from home, and on his most recent escapade he spent several nights away with a girlfriend.

What are we to make of Lou and Tom? If Lou were your next-door neighbour, or Tom a child you knew, would you be worried if nothing were being done about their problems? How far do we, as members of society, have a duty to protect children from people like Lou? Do we have an obligation to step in to help children like Tom?

And are these trick questions? Unfortunately yes, for as you may have recognized, Lou's full name is Lewis Carroll, and Tom's is Tom Sawyer. While from the perspective of today we would be likely to identify one as a potential child abuser and the other as probably an abused child, in their historical periods neither would have been seen or labelled in those terms. This is not just because the concept of 'child abuse' had not entered the vocabulary of the times. While Lewis Carroll's behaviour would have been considered somewhat eccentric, its meaning and assumed intent – to him, to the children concerned, and to the public at large – would have been quite different from what we would make of it today. Similarly Tom Sawyer's childhood was portrayed, in its time, as an adventure, not an example of socio-economic deprivation and abusive childrearing. Even though we may now wonder whether the children were being harmed, there can be little doubt that the adults of those times did not think so. [My thanks to Rex Stainton Rogers for suggesting these two illustrations.]

When, in the 1970s, 'child abuse' became a matter of increasing public and professional concern, the usual way to begin a book about child abuse was with the history of changing perceptions about the mistreatment of children (see, for example, Inglis, 1978; Jobling, 1978; Kempe and Kempe, 1978). Reviews like this usually started by remarking that child abuse is nothing new – parents have always whipped, starved, locked up and raped their children, worked them mercilessly, sold them and abandoned them. By this account, it is not that child abuse was not happening before, but that only today do we recognize it as a social problem, and want to do something about it. While agonizing over the amount of cruelty and neglect that still exists, this approach portrays current concerns about child abuse approvingly, as evidence that society has become much more caring towards children. Henry Kempe, generally acknowledged as the person who 'discovered' child abuse (although, to make it more acceptable he first termed it 'baby battering'), certainly saw it in these terms. For example, together with his wife Ruth, he began one of his standard texts on the subject like this:

> A book on child abuse could not have been written one hundred years ago. If an investigator from the 1970s were to be transported back to the nineteenth century so he could survey the family scene with modern eyes, child abuse would be clearly visible to him. In the past, however, it was largely invisible to families and their communities. Before it could be acknowledged as a social ill, changes had to occur in the sensibilities and outlook of our culture. (Kempe and Kempe, 1978, p. 17)

The reason that we began our review with historical case examples is that we wanted to convey in a rather different light the changes that have occurred between 'then' and 'now'. It may well be that we are now more caring towards children – we can afford to be, given that we are in general better off than our grandparents – but that is not, we believe, the point.

To understand why child abuse is now seen as a social problem, in a way even 50 years ago it was not, we need to go further than to recognize that the world in which we now live is a very different world – what people say, and think and do are different. The change is not just in the 'sensibilities and outlook of our culture' that allow us to see – to make visible – things that people could not see before. Our argument is that social problems like child abuse are not 'things that happen', but rather 'ways of making sense'. Such social problems have no reality as and of themselves; they are things that we have *made* real by the way we think and talk about them. In other words, child abuse is a product of the way we currently run society and construe our world.

This idea of reality being socially constructed is taken up and developed in several of the chapters in this book, starting with the first chapter, 'The Social Construction of Childhood'. In this, Rex Stainton Rogers develops an analogy between the social reality of 'self-abuse' in the nineteenth century and 'child abuse' in the twentieth. To the Victorian parent, to the childcare professionals of that age, and most importantly, to children themselves, the evils of self-abuse were self-evident. It was a 'sickness' to be feared and a habit to be controlled – by drastic measures if necessary (which included strait-jacketing children and even surgery).

Will people in the future look back at our preoccupation with child abuse, he asks, with the same puzzled disapproval as we now, with hindsight, regard the Victorian obsession with self-abuse?

This way of seeing child abuse as socially constructed becomes critical once we try to estimate how much child abuse is happening, an argument which Steve Taylor develops in chapter 3, 'How Prevalent Is It?' It is relatively straightforward to measure events within a natural science framework – we can all agree, say, on a child's birth weight or height. But measurement becomes problematic once we try to estimate events that are socially constructed, such as child abuse. For example, if we want to know how many children are sexually abused, our estimates will reflect the definition of sexual abuse we use. Would a child having her photograph taken, dressed like Alice in a torn and scanty frock, by an elderly bachelor who likes to kiss her, count as sexual abuse?

This problem of definition is taken up as a central theme in two other chapters. In 'Child Abuse in a Social Context', Martin Loney asks why we focus so exclusively upon definitions that blame individuals, generally parents, for the harm that comes to children. What about the harm done by government policies which condemn children to grow up in totally unsuitable 'bed and breakfast' accommodation? What about cuts in services and funds that prevent social workers being able to offer an effective preventive service? What about the way western consumerism is fed by exploiting child labour in the Third World? How many children die through the ill-health we know to be associated with poverty and deprivation?

To complement this, 'Labelling Children as Abused or Neglected' by Robert Dingwall, considers the psychological and sociological processes by which professionals decide which children are – and are not – being abused. He contrasts two strategies that could be used. First, professionals could adopt a pessimistic strategy that would treat all children who are seriously harmed as abused, based on the argument that they were not being looked after properly. The child rushed to hospital as the victim of a motor accident would, against this criterion, be an abused child, abused by careless driving or a failure to provide adequate safety devices in the car. This approach, Dingwall argues, would soon fill hospitals and Child Protection Registers to bursting – indeed, something like this did happen in Cleveland in 1987, when professionals there adopted a 'rather safe than sorry' strategy. To avoid such problems, workers more usually opt for an optimistic strategy – a 'diagnosis' of child abuse becomes a last resort, when all other explanations have had to be rejected. Like Taylor, Dingwall thus argues that the end result is that only some kinds of mistreatment tend to get labelled as child abuse, and only some kinds of parents tend to be suspected of abusing their children.

In this way child abuse as a social problem has become part and parcel of the way some sectors of society control others. By defining certain social conditions – such as being poor, young, unemployed, a single parent or a step-parent – as 'risk factors', and by defining certain forms of mistreatment as abusive – beating with a strap at home say, as opposed to beating with a cane in a public school – it becomes all too easy to justify intervening in the lives of some people yet not others. Targeting resources and services at those families in which children are seen to be most in need of 'protection' and 'preventive support' may be done with all the best intentions. But as Karl Asen points out in his chapter on 'Family Therapy', this kind of help may become counter-productive. And its effect is to stop us from questioning or trying to do anything about other equally serious kinds of mistreatment.

To bring this point home we have included a chapter which asks whether society itself can abuse children by putting their needs and potential for self-fulfilment a poor second to the demands of political sectarianism. 'Society as Child Abuser: Northern Ireland' by Ed Cairns explores some of the ways in which children growing up there may be harmed, not just directly as the victims of violence, but by pressures from the two communities that determine everything from the child's name, to his or her friends, schooling and potential marriage partner.

Gough (1987) suggests that definitions of child abuse have two things in common: that the child is harmed, and that somebody is responsible for that harm. Even this general definition, however, raises problems. There is no consensus about what is harmful to a child. This question is explored from a legal standpoint in Jeremy Roche's chapter 14, 'Children's Rights and the Welfare of the Child', but it is also the rationale for including several other chapters in this book. In particular, 'Childrearing in a Multicultural Society' by Wendy Stainton Rogers describes some of the alternatives to the Victorian-style nuclear family, illustrating that cultures differ in their assumptions about what children need, and to what ends childrearing should be directed. In some ways it acts as a foil to the chapter by Ed Cairns, because it points out that striving for individual success is a preoccupation of North European and white American culture, contrasted in particular with Eastern and Mediterranean cultures in which there is a much greater emphasis upon mutual endeavours and commitments within wide kinship networks.

This raises an important question about defining child abuse. Should we define it in relative terms, according to a child's cultural and social background? Or do we need, ultimately, to set some absolute criteria for what is abusive, come what may? Our solution to this dilemma has been to turn the question on its head, and to consider children's rights and entitlements rather than abuse. Our position is that there are certain resources, life-chances, standards of good treatment and respect to which all children are entitled as of right. We find it less easy to specify what these are, but have included two extracts which at least provide a starting-point for considering what they may be: 'The Demands of Parenting' by Gillian Pugh and Erica De'Ath, which describes the kinds of minimum conditions necessary to bring up children, and 'Setting Basic Standards' by Rachel Calam and Cristina Franchi, which sets out the rights that the authors see children as needing, following research into the effects of abuse on young children.

A focus on children's rights raises several issues. First, to what extent can the law act as a framework for resolving different rights. The chapter by Jeremy Roche and Wendy Stainton Rogers 'The Children Act 1989 – Better Protection for Children?' offers a review of the new Act as well as an investigation of the tension between effective child protection work and respect for family privacy. It concludes that only through working in partnership with families and working with and listening to children will some of these conflicts be resolved Nicholas Tilley, in 'The Abuser – Punishment or Treatment', explores some of the ways that a particular child's needs (for family life) may conflict with the rights of other children in the community to be protected from an abuser being left at large.

Finally, the social constructionist approach is elaborated in 'Taking the Child Abuse Debate Apart' by Wendy and Rex Stainton Rogers. They argue that one of the problems with current responses to child abuse is that professionals tend to be too single-minded. Like great reformers in the nineteenth century, such as Dr Barnardo and Mary Carpenter, they sometimes allow their crusading zeal to overwhelm their better judgement, rather than considering alternative understandings of what is going on, and what needs to be done. Reporting research conducted to elucidate alternative 'ways of making sense' (alternative social constructions, if you like) of child abuse, the authors show that currently there are at least three quite different discourses upon which people draw. One explains child abuse as the product of children's vulnerability, and the misuse of adult (predominantly male) power, and tends to favour removing children from their families if there is danger of re-abuse. Another more traditional account sees child abuse as what happens when parents are unable to cope with stresses like poverty, inexperience and social disadvantage, and favours keeping families together by providing support. A third views the mistreatment of children as a consequence of the way we construe children as 'property' and as 'objects' rather than as people – and favours policies that empower children to make their own choices. The authors argue that these alternative discourses can (and do) co-exist, both in people's thinking and in popular debate, conversations and so on. There is no single, right way to understand child abuse; it is a confusing and complex topic, and we will often 'be in two minds' about it.

Nevertheless, even when taking a social constructionist approach, history is still important. We cannot begin to understand the current situation – the way we think about child abuse, and the ways we respond to it – until we have traced back through the events that have led up to what happens now. It is important to know, for example, that in the United States the first attempts to tackle cruelty to children grew out of the legislation for the prevention of cruelty to animals. In 1875 there were no laws to protect children, and so when one little girl, Mary Ellen, was found to have been cruelly beaten by her guardians, it was as a mistreated animal that she was presented to the courts!

The main reason why animals got earlier and better protection than children was the enormous importance attached to the privacy of the family and the rights of parents (mainly fathers) to bring up their children as they saw fit. For example, in Britain in 1874 when attempts were being made to introduce welfare services to reduce the high levels of infant mortality among the poor, a noted reformer of the day, Whatley Cooke Taylor, said: 'I would far rather see even a higher rate of infant mortality prevailing . . . than intrude one iota further on the sanctity of the domestic hearth' (quoted in Inglis, 1978, p. 24).

This was, nonetheless, a time of reform. Not long before, historically speaking, young children of three and four years old frequently worked long hours in factories in Britain and the United States, and children not much older were employed in mines. Children were being hung for petty crimes – for example, in February 1814 at the Old Bailey sessions, five children were condemned to death: two boys aged 12 for burglary, and three boys aged eight, nine and 11 for stealing. Both in schools and at home, the accepted way to bring up children was by following the maxim 'spare the rod and spoil the child'. Susanna Wesley, the mother of the religious leader John Wesley, wrote about childrearing in terms which would have found broad agreement among most parents and teachers of her time:

> Break their will betimes; begin this great work before they can run alone, before they can speak plain, or perhaps speak at all . . . conquer their stubbornness; break the will, if you will not damn a child . . . make him do as he is bid, if you whip him ten times running to effect it . . . Break his will now and his soul will live, and he will probably bless you to all eternity. (Wesley, 1872, quoted in Jobling, 1978, p. 24)

Thus two assumptions underpinned the way that people perceived childrearing in the nineteenth century. The first was that parents knew what was best for their children, and had an absolute right to bring them up as they believed to be right. The second was that children needed to be forced to learn how to behave properly, and parents and teachers were justified in using physical punishment to ensure their compliance. These punishments were not cruelty, but for the child's own ultimate good. These assumptions added together created a situation where, when things went wrong, children could be seriously injured and even killed, without anybody being prepared to do very much about it. This does not mean that the majority of parents were cold or unfeeling towards their children – there is strong historical evidence of great love and affection in many families. But it did mean that when children were grossly mistreated within the privacy of the family, they had little protection and nowhere to turn for help.

However, towards the end of the nineteenth century, a number of reformers began to question the sanctity of family privacy when it came into conflict with children's needs to be protected from savage treatment. The Society for Prevention of Cruelty to Children was established in New York in 1871, and the National Society for the Prevention of Cruelty to Children (NSPCC) was set up in Liverpool in 1883. Members of these societies worked to introduce laws to protect children, which were passed in 1876 in the United States, but not until 1889 in England and Wales. Behlmer (1982) has noted that recently social historians have undervalued the enormous amount of work carried out by these philanthropists who both knew about – and were doing something about – child abuse, long before it came to be called by that name, or to be seen as a matter of wide public concern. It was not, however, until 'professionals' (notably doctors) became involved that cruelty to children came to be seen as a major social problem.

It took a long time for doctors to acknowledge that it was happening at all. For example, in 1888 West published a paper describing families of several children where severe swellings were to be seen on the long bones in the arms and legs, and bruises on the children's ribs, but he attributed these as probably being the result of rickets (a condition common enough at the time, due to poor diet and living conditions). It was not until 1946 that John Caffey, a paediatric radiologist, voiced an explicit suspicion that the evidence he was finding of multiple injuries at various stages of healing might not be caused by disease. But even he did not directly accuse parents. Silverman (1953) wrote that these kinds of injury might be due to 'parental carelessness' but it was not until 1955 that two doctors, Woolley and Evans, felt able to suggest that parents were hitting their children severely enough to break bones and cause severe bruising.

In the United States during the late 1950s, a number of other medical authors published similar conclusions to those of Woolley and Evans. In 1962, Henry Kempe, a paediatrician at the University of Colorado Medical School, gave a speech to a meeting of the American Academy of Paediatrics, in which he described a study, conducted with several colleagues, which had examined injuries reported to 71 hospitals and 77 district attorneys across the United States. Many of the 749 children involved had either died or been seriously injured. Kempe adopted a new and emotive term to describe what he believed was happening – 'the battered child syndrome'. This concept gained wide currency, in the United Kingdom and Europe as well as the United States, and there followed a major upsurge of concern among social workers and others working with children and their families about this newly acknowledged social problem. Papers about 'battered babies' soon began to appear in the British academic press (for example, Griffiths and Moynihan, 1963; Cameron et al., 1966), and in 1967 the NSPCC set up a Battered Child Research Unit to 'carry through a comprehensive programme of study and treatment of families where children have been battered, and to help build up an informed body of opinion on the "Battered Child Syndrome" ' (NSPCC, 1969). Between 1969 and 1973 members of this Unit published many articles in academic journals, and generally acted to publicize the problem and lobby for services to tackle it.

It is not surprising that since doctors had first identified and described the problem, 'child-battering' was seen as a 'syndrome', and consequently socially constructed as a *disease*. Underlying this terminology was the assumption that, like any other disease, the problem had a cause that needed to be found and 'treated'. Frude (1980) among others has argued that this was not an entirely helpful way to enable people to make sense of what has now become accepted as being a much more complex, multifaceted set of issues surrounding the mistreatment of children. More recently, for example, Blom-Cooper (London Borough of Brent, 1985) has criticized the way in which this ethos kept separate on the one hand the attempts of medical and social work professionals to work with families, and on the other the role of lawyers and the police in controlling adult behaviour and offering children legal protection.

Kempe and his followers, working within the disease model, tended to regard child abuse (as child-battering soon came to be known) as a product primarily of parenting under stress. Parents attacked their children, neglected them or allowed their disciplining to 'go too far' because they could not cope with the social and material privations of their lives, and had not the maturity and knowledge to nurture and care for their children. The solution, it was argued, particularly at a time which was dominated by Bowlby's ideas (see, for example, Bowlby, 1953) about the ill-effects of maternal deprivation, was to do everything possible to keep the abused child with his or her family, by pouring in resources and support, and then monitoring the child to make sure he or she was safe.

In the United Kingdom this strategy came into question in the aftermath of the death of Maria Colwell in January 1973. Maria, the fifth child of her mother's first marriage, had been fostered at four months old with an aunt and uncle. When Maria was five, she returned to live with her mother and stepfather, and her mother sought to have the care order (under which Maria had been supervised by the local authority since she was a few weeks old) revoked, and the local authority grudgingly agreed. There were worries about the move, but the local authority felt that if the matter went to court, they would lose. They relied instead on a supervision order, even though this gave them few legal powers to watch over the child. Maria lived with her mother and stepfather from 1971 until 1973, when she was killed by her stepfather; a pitifully thin and underweight little girl, she had been neglected and emotionally abused as well as beaten harshly on many occasions before she received the injuries that finally ended her life.

There followed a massive public outcry and the first major inquiry in the United Kingdom into a child's death at the hand of the parent. It is worth noting that much earlier, in 1945, there had been similar outrage followed by an inquiry by Sir Walter Monkton (1945) into the brutal killing of Dennis O'Neill by his foster father, which had led to considerable changes in the law regarding the placement and supervision of children 'in care'. Maria Colwell's death was not anything new, nor was it in fact that unusual. It was the inquiry, and the enormous publicity it received, which, as Blom-Cooper (London Borough of Brent, 1985) described it, forced the phenomenon of child abuse 'upon an unsuspecting and unprepared public'. Child abuse ceased to be the concern of a relatively small number of specialist professionals, and became a matter of major public interest, as is evidenced by the succession of child abuse inquiries that have followed on from Colwell in 1971, culminating most recently in the inquiries into deaths of Jasmine Beckford (London Borough of Brent, 1985) and Kimberley Carlile (London Borough of Greenwich, 1987). (See DHSS (1991) for a review of the reports of the inquiries up until 1990.)

Throughout the 15 or so years since Maria Colwell's death, newspapers and television reporters (with a few notable exceptions – see, for example, Phillips, 1987) have vilified the professionals whose job it was to protect the children that died. Social workers were the most frequently criticized, but health visitors and doctors too have found themselves exposed to calls for their dismissal or for disciplinary proceedings against them. The argument has usually been that they should have been able to see the signs that, with hindsight, seem so obvious; they should have had the courage to remove the child before the damage was done.

All this changed, of course, in 1987 when the events in Cleveland first hit the headlines. As documented by Nava (1988), this time the problem was portrayed as one of social workers, acting on the ill-informed edicts of crusading doctors, snatching children from innocent and unsuspecting parents. As many commentators noted at the time, this left professionals in a 'Catch 22' situation – damned if they tried to keep children with their families; damned if they tried to take them away. Underneath all the rhetoric, however, there were a number of important differences between responses to the deaths of children like Maria Colwell, and the removal of children from their homes in Cleveland, when there were concerns that they might have been sexually abused.

First of all, there is a difference in the way we react to physical abuse and neglect on the one hand, and sexual abuse on the other. Until the 1980s the distinction was not so marked, for both types of abuse tended to be seen as ways in which the normal and ordinary had 'gone too far': physical abuse was, after all, only the usual rough and tumble of family life and normal punishment that had 'gone a bit over the top'; incest was, after all, really just a matter of ordinary affection that had 'got a bit out of hand'. In any case, it was often assumed (although seldom actually voiced), that these things are endemic in certain kinds of families, and maybe do very little harm so long as a watchful eye is kept to make sure nothing really serious happens.

As the publicity about children being killed began to disturb complacency with regard to physical abuse, so too did new revelations about sexual abuse. Until the 1980s, in the United Kingdom at least, most people had assumed that this was usually, when it did occur, a sexual liaison between a father or stepfather and his teenage daughter – a transgression of taboos, maybe but not all that far beyond the bounds of decency. As with physical abuse, longstanding attempts to draw sexual abuse to public attention by, this time, feminists (particularly arising out of their work with women who had been sexually assaulted) tended to be dismissed and marginalized until professionals – once again doctors – became involved. In particular two paediatricians, Christopher Hobbs and Jane Wynne, published an influential paper in 1987, presenting evidence that child sexual abuse is something that is done to boys as well as girls, to small children of two and three years old (even babies) as well as teenagers, and that the repeated buggery of six- and seven-year-olds is something that happens far more often than most of us would like to believe.

Significantly, child sexual abuse is not, like physical abuse and neglect, something which tends to happen more in families that are socially and economically disadvantaged. Abusers are predominantly (although not exclusively) men, but come from all walks of life and all groups in society. Once the evidence began to accrue about the prevalence of buggery and of the potential long-term harm that may be done, wry jokes about the predelictions of some scoutmasters and vicars for little boys suddenly ceased to be funny. Once social workers started to take sexual abuse as seriously as physical abuse, and began to intervene into middle-class families, the whole ethos of intervention came to be seen in a new light.

The explanation that child abuse is what happens when parents crack up under the stresses and strains of poverty and unemployment could not apply here, for these abusers were as likely to be stockbrokers and teachers as they were to be teenage parents surviving on the dole. All of a sudden professionals and the public alike have had to reconsider what 'child abuse' means, and what we should do about it. The liberal democratic dilemma has become all the more marked. How far should we be prepared to intervene into family life by exposing parents and other caregivers to state scrutiny to protect children? To what extent are we prepared to accept that some children will die at the hands of their parents, some children will be secretly buggered and then bribed or coerced 'to keep the secret' as the price we pay for our civil liberties?

The majority of the chapters in this book were written when the events in Cleveland were in the public eye and the subject of the Butler–Sloss Inquiry (DHSS, 1988). As editors we have tried to maintain a balance between doing justice to the major changes in thinking and practice that have been emerging over the last few years, and at the same time not becoming so focused on issues like child sexual and ritual abuse that other kinds of mistreatment got lost. It is for this reason that we have updated the book for the second edition and stressed the social constructionist approach, since this seemed to offer the most useful way we could place child abuse within a broad context of different understandings. It is the reason, too, why we have taken care to extend beyond the usual definitions of abuse – physical, emotional and sexual abuse and neglect – to incorporate notions of deprivation and exploitation.

At the same time, we wanted to make sure that the book took on some of the practical aspects as well as the more abstract and academic. Our aim has been to provide a basic introduction which links theory and practice. To do this we began by commissioning Brian Corby to write a short review of the theory bases within which child abuse is understood today, and which inform practice. His 'Alternative Theory Bases in Child Abuse' offers a brief but comprehensive summary of theoretical frameworks as disparate as psychodynamics and feminism, learning theory and socio-economic analyses. In Section Two, Pamela Abbot's 'Family Lifestyles and Structures', and Adrian Ward's 'Caring for Other People's Children', suggest how some of the social changes that have been happening since the 1950s and 1960s – such as increases in single parenting and step-parenting, and the movement of women into the workplace and consequently the increase in daycare provision – have created new dilemmas for the task of bringing up children, and thus may contribute to children's vulnerability to abuse.

Geoffrey Watson's chapter on 'The Abuse of Disabled Children and Young People' focuses on how disability may increase children's vulnerability, and raises important questions about abuse as a failure to meet children's needs. In the Netherlands (see Jay and Doganis, 1987) *not* giving children sex education is classified as abusive; how then are we to sexually educate blind children while avoiding the accusation that we are sexually abusing them? How far is it abusive to use behaviour modification techniques to train children with learning difficulties, or 'difficult' children as in the notorious 'Pin-Down' regime in Staffordshire (Levy and Kahan, 1991)?

Another theme of our book, and indeed of the course for which it is written, is that as well as thinking about the topic and deciding what needs to be done, we cannot ignore what we feel about it. To respond to the challenges presented by child abuse, we need to gain some emotional as well as intellectual understanding of it. Consequently we have woven into the various sections short first-hand and fictional accounts of being abused, or having to cope with its aftermath. In Section Four this includes a short extract from Keri Hulme's prize-winning book *The Bone People*, which powerfully evokes the dilemma faced by somebody who has to decide whether to report a friend who is abusing a child. In Section Five we have included 'Fostering an Abused Child' by Mary Thornley, and an extract from Jacqueline Spring's novel, *Cry Hard and Swim: The Story of an Incest Survivor*, entitled 'Aquittal'. This is her attempt to explain what being sexually abused means to you when you are a child, and how it sets you apart from other children.

We have also included some extracts from a diary kept by a young woman when she was making the difficult journey, in her own words, from abuse victim to survivor. This woman contacted us when we first began to write the book and the course because she wanted to share her experiences in the hope that this would help other adults abused in childhood to seek solace and support. Her bravery, kindness and support to us became very important and we are grateful to be able to include some of her writings. These we believe are particularly important, as they remind us that overcoming the effects of child abuse is itself a task with its own dilemmas and problems. For this woman it was the conflict between her counsellor's advice to be angry and her religion's advice to be forgiving that she found most difficult.

Also included in Section Five is John Southgate's 'The Hidden Child Within Us', which draws upon the influential work of the psychoanalyst, Alice Miller, to describe some of the effects of the cruel ways in which we treat children, and our obligations as adults to become advocates for children. Southgate describes some of the stages through which an individual may need to progress to come to terms with his or her abusive experiences in childhood. Finally in Section Five are two chapters written by Denise Hevey and Helen Kenward, on 'The Effects of Physical Abuse and Neglect' and 'The Effects of Child Sexual Abuse'. These authors have combined their skills and expertise to produce chapters which retain the academic rigour needed to review research evidence, while illustrating the effects of abuse with short case studies. In this way we hope that readers will gain both information and some empathic understanding of the way children may be affected.

Two of the sections in this book are primarily practical. Section Four, about recognizing and responding, moves on from the extract from Keri Hulme's book and Robert Dingwall's examination of labelling, to a series of chapters which deal with the pragmatics. 'Recognizing Abuse' by Anne Bannister offers an introductory review of the main kinds of physical, behavioural and social indicators that should alert somebody to the possibility that a child may be being abused. 'The Investigation of Suspected Child Abuse' by Paul Griffiths tells us, again briefly, about the main stages in the processes of an investigation, and offers some advice about the principles of good practice upon which this should be based. Avril Osborne's chapter, 'Interagency Work in Child Protection', describes the procedural and organizational framework within which child abuse investigations and subsequent actions operate and are formulated, and Peter Dale's 'What Happens Next?' reviews the various outcomes of an investigation, and what this may mean for the child and family concerned.

We have included a chapter by Jo Tunnard – 'Supporting Parents Suspected of Abuse' – as an important component of this section. Although it covers the whole area of child abuse and how the wider family (such as grandparents) may usefully be included in protecting children, its position here indicates the importance we attach to recognizing that children need their families as well as to be protected, and that their needs are most likely to be met when professionals and parents can work together. Our last section consists mainly of shorter chapters. Our rationale here was that we did not want to cover the wide variety of ways of responding to abuse with just one bland review chapter, which in a book of this brevity would not be very informative. Instead we have invited five practitioners and two representatives from self-help groups to give us brief, personal accounts of the work they do, or examples of the kinds of provision with which they are involved. Necessarily these are not comprehensive, and describe only one approach or perspective within the broad category they represent. Elizabeth Ash's 'Individual Psychotherapy', for example, presents just one of the many ways that individuals may be offered counselling or therapy; Ray Wyre's description of the clinic he has set up to offer an alternative to prison for abusers is, at the time of writing, highly innovative in the United Kingdom, although such schemes are commonly used within the United States. Our aim was not to list the whole range of alternatives possible, but to give more specific – and we hope therefore more interesting – accounts of the possibilities that are on offer.

We end with Michele Elliott's 'Prevention and Protection'. This, like the other chapters in Section Six, offers a selective and personal account, in which she describes her work in helping children to develop strategies to stay safe, and to ask for help from adults when they feel threatened. It should be clear by this stage that we are not advocating (nor indeed, would Elliott herself advocate) that children should assume the responsibility for their own safety. But we do hope that by finishing with a focus on the empowerment of children, we may redress any imbalance elsewhere in the book, where the main 'voice' being heard is that of adults, albeit as advocates for children.

In updating the book for its second edition, we have made sure that recent references have been included, and that legal changes (most notably the England and Wales Children Act 1989) have been incorporated. What has surprised us somewhat in doing this has been just how little has actually needed to change over the last few years. While we have seen the events of Cleveland followed by Rochdale, the Orkneys, 'Pin-Down' and the scandals of sexual abuse in Leicestershire Children's Homes, the basic themes and ideas we have addressed remain just as important.

Overall we hope that this book will make available to as wide an audience as possible a clear and comprehensive introduction to something that is increasingly likely to touch all of our lives – as parents and neighbours, friends and the confidants of children as well as professionals and students. The book naturally reflects the biases and values that we, as editors, have brought to our work on child abuse and neglect. Our ultimate aim is perhaps best summed up by the statement with which Rex Stainton Rogers ends his chapter. If we are to offer to our children the opportunity for better childhoods, then this will be because we – and they – are able to participate in the construction of better childhoods.

> That we no longer hang children, burn them as witches or brand them as vagrants is not the victory of a few reformers, it is the victory of a whole society which has overcome the constructions that made such actions possible. The killings and maimings of children that our society still generates can also be consigned to the history book – by the same processes which have made possible the worlds in which we now live.

Tackling child abuse is not just a matter of investing more resources and ensuring better-informed and more skilled professionals; it will only happen when we reconstruct the way we construe children, and children construe themselves. As Lord Butler-Sloss has so powerfully argued (DHSS, 1988), children must be treated as people, not as objects of professional concern.

Wendy Stainton Rogers
Long Wittenham, December 1991

SECTION ONE

THEORIES, EXPLANATIONS AND MODELS

1 THE SOCIAL CONSTRUCTION OF CHILDHOOD

Rex Stainton Rogers

Lecturer in Psychology, University of Reading

'We live in a socially constructed world.' In this chapter I want to introduce you to the power of that idea and what it can do for our understanding of childhood.

A socially constructed world

If you accept the idea that childhood experiences mark us for life, you could trace my development as a social constructionist back to a holiday in Italy when I was about 11. It was my first time abroad and in 1953 holidays abroad were something few young people of my background experienced. In the bath I reached up to pull the safety toggle to switch on the light and – you've guessed it – called the maid instead! The knowledge I took for granted – that cords in bathrooms invariably switch on lights – proved wrong. But it wasn't only things that weren't the same in Italy, people weren't either, and that difference made me different. Finding out it was my eleventh birthday, an Italian family invited me to dinner. They generated a sense of occasion which made it quite unlike any birthday I'd experienced in England, 'killing the fatted calf' (looking back, I suspect literally) and plying me with champagne and liqueur. Needless to say, I also found out how mind-altering drugs change reality and I still have a vivid visual memory of their dog seeming to be walking up the wall!

Nowadays, like most adults, I seldom undergo such a dramatic sense of surprise. Experience has taught me to be a lot more cautious about what I 'know' and how matters 'must be'. My only certainty is that the world of things and people can be constructed in many alternative ways. I'm also pretty wise by now to the alternative ways in which I construct the world – I know it when sober and drunk, happy and sad, when I'm well and when I'm ill. Unless I'm very mistaken you could tell similar stories – you are that much of a social constructionist already. And, although you might not use my words, I don't think you would argue that this article, the word processor it was written upon, the language I wrote it in, are all socially constructed, that is, made through human activities and actions.

But what about childhood? Certainly there's an obvious sense in which the village children I can see from my window have been socially constructed – each life began in an unskilled human activity as old as *homo sapiens* itself! Equally, each has developed as a human being as children have always done, through their actions and the actions of others towards them. (This, by the way, is typical of social constructionist thinking: it isn't that we are determined *or* have free will, we are determined *and* have free will – we are both constructed and construct ourselves (cf. Berger and Luckmann, 1967).) They will continue to change throughout their lives by the same process of mutual influence in a shared world.

Just what is this shared world? Basically, it boils down to what we 'know'. For example, the children of Long Wittenham have come to understand that they 'have to go to school', that the human-made 'thing' down the road *is* a school, that certain activities belong in the classroom and others in the playground, and so on. The social world works because we share common understandings.

Indeed, so real can the socially constructed world seem that it often just gets taken for granted. It appears so normal, so right, so reasonable for children to go to school that they (and perhaps we sometimes) fail to imagine anything else.

To demonstrate the alternatives, social constructionists use a technique of challenge (or to use the jargon term, 'deconstruction'). What if I now call the school 'a camp', refer to the children as 'being conscripted', to schooling as '11 years of National Service'? Are you tempted to say I am being deliberately 'unrealistic' because I am not following the usual taken-for-granted rules for seeing the world? My answer would be that whether or not my reinterpretation is realistic can only be answered by posing a further question – 'in what reality?'. Different social realities (or world-views as they are often called) imply different taken-for-granted ground rules.

There are no hard-and-fast principles for defining when disagreements about how things are seen become significant enough to talk about them as different social realities. However, it is usually assumed that the more distant people are from one another (in terms of historical time, geographical location, culture or class) the more likely they are to have different world-views. It is also generally accepted that ideologies imply social realities, so that Marxists and capitalists 'see the world differently, (see chapter 2 for information about feminism as a world-view on children). Contrasted social realities can co-exist within a complex society and even battle 'inside our own heads'. (Chapter 4 explores some of the various constructions of child abuse voiced in our own society.)

When social constructionists look at childhood, it is to these different social realities that they turn. The interest is not just in learning about the constructions of childhood in history or in different cultures – it is also a technique that throws light on why we construct childhood as we do in our own time and society. In the next section I give an example of this approach.

What self-abuse may teach us about child abuse

Social historians tell us that many nineteenth-century parents put their children into protective devices to stop them engaging in 'self-abuse' (masturbating) (see Figure 1). To a social constructionist, understanding why these parents interpreted masturbation as 'self-abuse' and as something serious enough to need to be controlled in this way starts by assuming they were being realistic to their world-view.

So what was the social reality they were reflecting? Medical opinion at that time taught that masturbation caused a range of physical and mental problems including insanity! This was a risk doctors took seriously enough to use castration, clitorectomy and other surgical interventions to control masturbation (see Szasz (1970) for details and Mountjoy (1974) for a study of patents for anti-masturbatory devices). With that 'taken for granted' and in a society which was coming to accept that in the case of childrearing 'doctor knows best', what else should we expect a caring and 'realistic' parent to do but try to prevent masturbation by the best and latest means available?

If we now see this piece of social history not as a necessary response to the dangers of self-abuse by the child, but as an abuse *of* the child, this is evidence that our world-view (our reality) is different from theirs.

Of course, describing the eccentricities of constructed worlds which lie safely in the past or away from our social experience is usually a 'safe', even reassuring

Appareils contre l'onanisme.

40132.			40133.	
	Godet argent.		Godet métal argenté.	
40132. Ceinture contre l'onanisme, pour garçon.... depuis		120 »	depuis	90
40133. — — — fillette..... —		120 »	—	90
Ces appareils se font également en forme de caleçons hermétiquement fermés.				
40134. Moufiles en métal formant râpe, pour les mains.................... depuis				40
40135. Entraves pour les bras...			—	50
40136. —. — — jambes..			—	60

Figure 1. Anti-masturbation devices for boys and girls, from a trade catalogue of 1904

experience. Our world usually fares well from the implied comparison. But, by contrast, when a constructionist perspective is applied to our own taken-for-granted world (as in my 'deconstruction' of schooling) the effect can be distinctly unsettling.

What, we can ask ourselves, might a future century make of our efforts to respond to 'the best interests of the child'? Might they see 'child abuse' as a concept as 'loaded' and 'unrealistic' as we now see 'self-abuse'? Might they see some of our efforts as equally well-meaning and equally misconceived, even damaging? (It is already becoming possible to 'deconstruct' some disclosure techniques used in sexual abuse work as being heavy interrogation if not 'brain washing'.)

Self-abuse or child abuse then are not just simple descriptions of something children do to themselves or adults do to children, they are ideas coming from a particular way of thinking – in other words social constructions. As such they appear and may disappear as our construction of reality changes.

But social constructionism is more than a theory about words and ideas. It is also concerned with how we apply these constructs in the world – with what we make and what we do – how we *make them* real. Self-abuse became 'real' in this sense because caregivers spotted it, worried about it and acted on it. It was a 'thing' to be controlled *because* a society made devices to prevent it and because doctors were prepared to do almost anything to stop it. Finally, and most subtly, it became real because whole generations of children learned to see it that way, to hide it and to fear it and the consequences of its discovery. The anxiety and stress that created helped to convince both the 'sufferers' and outside observers that it truly was harmful – a classic self-fulfilling prophecy!

Different worlds, different childhoods

'Every social group with a distinct cultural awareness attempts to legislate what to them is a proper concept of children and adulthood' (Denzin, 1977, p. 17).

The kinds of arguments we have just looked at form the basis of the boldest of all social constructionist claims: that the child and childhood have no existence independent of the way our thinking and hence our actions bring them into being. This is a complex notion which gets a lot easier to handle if we look at concrete examples.

In the United Kingdom, 1988 saw the rejection by parliament of the 'Alton Bill' which tried to lower the time limit on abortion from 28 to 18 weeks. Some of the argument centred on whether a foetus is, as one pressure group calls it, 'an unborn child', and hence a *person* with rights (like the right to life). As our law stands at the moment it is not, but beyond 18 weeks a foetus has some legal protection, and once born it is a person whose life can be taken.

These issues and arguments are not new. Human groups and societies vary vastly in how they define the start of human life. Traditional Catholics take it from conception. By contrast, in many societies human status is only granted some time after birth. This usually goes along with an acceptance of infanticide and the absence of mourning and funeral rituals for very young children. The crucial time can vary between a few days after birth to two to three years of age (cf. Scheper-Hughes, 1987).

So, do we become a child at conception, at 18 weeks, at 28 weeks, at birth or some time after? The answer seems to be that it depends on whose definition of a child we are using – on how 'a child' is construed.

Some writers (e.g. de Mause, 1974) have tried to argue that there is a definite moral progression from those ancient or 'primitive' societies that operated an 'infanticidal mode' through to our present society which takes a 'helping mode'. But this is clearly a construction that relies on our social and legal definitions of child life. These, as we have seen, are contested by many in our own society (e.g. organizations like 'Life').

To highlight the dangers of taking for granted the moral superiority of 'our' construction of the child, some writers deconstruct contemporary western society as 'foeticidal' (i.e. foetus-killing). Others highlight the economic basis that constructs a childhood for some and denies it to others: 'For Americans, membership of the extended developmental period called *childhood* is an economic luxury, a luxury denied the urban poor and nearly all nonwhite racial and ethnic groups' (Denzin, 1977, p. 19).

Arguing the social construction of childhood
The idea that different world-views imply different childhoods is most powerfully expressed in a number of recent books on the social history of childhood. Aries's (1962) thorough and well-researched book *Centuries of Childhood* has been summed up as arguing that: 'Before the seventeenth century a child was regarded as a small and inadequate adult; the concept of "the childish" as something distinct from adults is a creation of the modern world' (dust-cover to the Penguin edition, 1973).

The analysis of historical material, both written and in the form of visual portrayal, can provide vivid images of what it was like to be young in earlier centuries, and of the kinds of social constructions of development that made such childhoods possible:

> Childhood as distinct from infancy, adolescence or youth was unknown to most historical periods . . . The worker's child, the peasant's child and the nobleman's child all dressed the way their fathers [sic] dressed, played the way their fathers played and were hanged by the neck as were their fathers. (Illich, 1973, p. 33)

Figure 2, taken from Schorsch (1979), shows the androgynous fashion found in early-nineteenth-century children's dress in the United States. This reflected the advice of the current expert on childrearing, Dr Strove, who said that it was of great importance *not* to alert children to the difference between the sexes!

Figure 2. Joseph and Anna Raymond, by the American artist Robert Peckham, *c.* 1840

Whether, as some writers have tried to suggest (e.g. Pollock, 1983), there are also continuities – ways in which childcare has *not* changed – the social construction-ists do seem to have hammered one lesson home with considerable force: that the experiences of the developing persons
– who made up the thirteenth-century 'Children's Crusade'
– who lived in the world of *Romeo and Juliet*
– who were pressed into the eighteenth-century navy
– who lived on the streets of war-torn Europe in 1945
– who are now working in Thai brothels
– who are 'starlets' in film, television or advertising
are fundamentally different from one another.

Their experiences are distinct too from those of children as typically presented in theories of childhood development. Indeed, a whole area of the social history of childhood is concerned with the recent and continuing impact of these theories and their construction of children and families (Riley, 1983; Rose, 1985). For example, Freud's theories and later Bowlby's concept of maternal deprivation fed what is often called, in a neat pun, the '*mal-de-mère*' syndrome (everything that is wrong with a child is its mother's fault). This had an enormous impact both upon women and upon child-centred social policy – for example, by justifying a lack of government support for nursery provision.

More generally, developmental theorists are accused of constructing theories which *presupposed* the superiority of the North Euro-American middle class to which they predominantly belonged and the greater desirability of its values and childrearing approach. These taken-for-granteds then became built into social policy practice – it was, for example, virtually unknown for 'middle-class' children to be adopted into 'working-class' families or white babies into black families, though the reverse was common enough.

Summing up these themes, the social constructionist argument is:

> both that childhood changes historically, which could be seen merely as a passive event, and that it is changed by people's actions. In other words, it is a political issue and one which, though it seems strange to need to mention it, involves children's actions as well as those of adults. (Hoyles, 1979, p. 1)

The social construction of better childhoods

As Hoyles points out, the concept of a socially constructed childhood is, amongst other things, a political theory, one concerned with social actions and outcomes. It *can* be taken very radically. The feminist Shulamith Firestone (1971), for example, sees the condition of children and women as very similar. To become 'fully human' children need to be liberated from childhood as women need to be liberated from femininity.

This is an interesting argument and one which is attracting increasing attention. Being socially constructed by those in power as 'child-like' (naïve, emotional, easily led, living for the moment) has been a significant taken-for-granted truth in the oppression of, and denial of human rights to, slaves, women and colonial peoples. If such groups can reconstruct themselves and be reconstructed as 'fully human' could not the same liberation come to children?

Perhaps? But other politicized writers see children's human rights as better thought about in terms of a right to protection than liberation:

> The child's capacity for acting upon the world, and changing it, will always be less than that of the adult. This cannot be 'equalised' by social transformation: even by *socialist* transformation . . . The child's right is thus not to a formal *equality* . . . but to a *relatively* protected space in which childhood can take place. (Fuller, 1979, p. 102)

What separates these two utopian visions are unanswered questions about whether what our society *construes* as the inevitable physical and psychological weaknesses and vunerabilities of the young *are* inevitable or are just more social constructions. Don't forget that social constructions are not just ideas. They are also what we make and do, so the liberationists have on their side arguments drawn from the experience of physically challenged people who can be disabled or enabled according to how we construct the physical world and the aids we do or do not manufacture. On the other hand, the protectionists see the vulnerability of the young in a rather different way: to lower a gas hob so that someone in a wheel-chair can cook a meal is enabling, to lower a gas hob in a family with young children runs the risk of being horrifically disabling!

However, I think I'd argue that the real power of social constructionism to point to better childhoods lies not in its ability to deconstruct our present world as a less than perfect one to grow up in, nor in any specific utopia it may open up to examination, but in the *idea of multiple realities itself*. In other words, we do not need to opt *either* for the uplifting of children to a 'fully adult' status (arguably hardly an enviable state anyway) *or* for the creation of a 'protected species' status from which children can subsequently become 'better' adults (with all the patronizing potential this view has). We do not need to do so because both constructions (and many others) already exist in our culture as viewpoints or 'discourses' about children.

Once frameworks for better childhoods come into being through political debate and argument they become part of the 'moral menu' potentially on offer to *all* in a society (including the young). Young people can construct their worlds around notions of their rights when, and only when, such concepts (and alternatives) are available both to them and the not so young with whom they must negotiate. If any truth exists in the notion that in our dealings with children we revisit our own childhood – with the roles reversed – then those children who are *au fait* with being seen as persons with rights will, in turn, become themselves adults who respect children's rights.

In opting for a menu of constructions of better childhoods (each containing its own utopia), we respect what we already have – a plural society in which ideas are allowed to argue with each other – and what we know of the people in this society – that they themselves can negotiate across realities (e.g. as parents or caregivers negotiating both 'freedom' and 'protected space' with young people). Many things, of course, can curtail or threaten such negotiation. These can encompass both individually enacted cruelties and neglects and corporatively enacted ones (like poverty and ignorance), as well as a dogmatic adherence to any singular view of 'their needs' or 'their rights' – arrived at without consultation and imposed without consent.

To negotiate with a less powerful person (whether a child or not) is not merely a liberal action of recognizing their humanity, it is to involve them in the very core of the human endeavour – the construction, deconstruction and reconstruction of the social world. *All* inputs change the potential future. That we no longer hang children, burn them as witches or brand them as vagrants is not the victory of a few reformers, it is the victory of a whole society which has overcome the constructions that made such actions possible. The killings and maimings of children that our society still generates can also be consigned to the history book – by the same processes which have made possible the worlds in which we now live.

2 ALTERNATIVE THEORY BASES IN CHILD ABUSE

Brian Corby

Lecturer in Applied Social Studies, University of Liverpool

Introduction

The aim of this chapter is to examine a range of theoretical perspectives which have relevance to our understanding of why and in what circumstances child abuse occurs. The approach I have adopted is to outline the basic principles of each perspective, using one or two theories as illustrations, and to consider their application to the problem of child abuse. The perspectives selected can be seen along a scale which starts with biologically based approaches, moves on to psychological and social theories and ends with a focus on political and philosophical considerations.

Ethological and sociobiological perspectives

These perspectives stem originally from the work of Charles Darwin (1859), the father of modern biology, who first put forward the proposition that all living creatures owe their survival to their ability to adapt to their constantly changing environment.

Ethology is the study by direct observation of animals in their natural environments. Darwin's evolutionary theory is used by ethologists as a guide to understanding the behaviours that they observe. Konrad Lorenz, the most famous proponent of this school of thought, devised the notion of 'imprinting' (Lorenz, 1970). He found from his studies of those animals that can walk or swim immediately after birth or hatching (such as ducks and geese) that they had an inborn tendency when very young to follow moving objects close to them. This usually turned out to be their mothers, but they could be imprinted to almost any moving object during a brief 'critical period' after birth, including in one famous experiment Lorenz himself. He theorized that the process of imprinting was instinctual and irreversible and that it had implications for behaviour later on in life, such as choice of sex partner.

Bowlby (1969), a psychoanalyst by training, borrowed these ideas derived from the field of ethology and applied them to human beings. He theorized that human babies also instinctively become attached to objects in early life, and that biological mothers are primed by their hormones to 'bond' to their infants. Bowlby argued that there is a crucially sensitive period, starting at the age of six months and lasting to five years, during which the infant has constant need of the presence of an 'attachment figure' (usually the mother). Poor attachment experiences – usually called *maternal deprivation* can, Bowlby argued, lead to severe personality disorders in children and adults in later life, including psychopathic and affectionless personality types (see Bowlby, 1988).

Others have applied Bowlby's thinking directly to child abuse. Kempe (1968 and 1978), the American paediatrician, who rediscovered child abuse in the early 1960s, has been foremost in this. He and his associates considered that much child abuse can be accounted for by the observation that many mothers who abuse their children have themselves suffered from poor attachment experiences or maternal deprivation. As a result they lack the ability to act as good attachment figures to their children. They hold unrealistic expectations of their children and expect them to be naturally rewarding. When these expectations are frustrated, they often resort to physical ill-treatment.

On this basis, Kempe argued that after adequate safeguards have been made for the protection of the children concerned, the focus of treatment should be on the parents, for example by providing them with the supportive 'mothering' relationship they have missed. Consistent with attachment theory, Kempe and others (Lynch and Roberts, 1977) have paid special attention to evidence of 'bonding' between mother and infant in the perinatal period in order to try to predict and prevent child abuse.

In the mid-1970s a 'new' theory based on the original Darwinian ideas emerged, that of *sociobiology*. This sought to reintroduce emphasis on the biological and instinctual features of human behaviour which was seen as lacking in the social sciences. Dawkins, in his book *The Selfish Gene* (1976), has argued that survival is the 'name of the game', and that all animals are programmed to preserve themselves and ensure the passing on of their characteristics by producing and rearing as many healthy offspring as possible. Although human beings are more complex than other animals and language gives them the capacity for abstract thought and reasoning, sociobiologists argue they are basically driven by the same forces.

Clearly child abuse poses some problems for sociobiologists, since if parents are all programmed to ensure the survival of their own genes then what drives them to maltreat their *own* children? The theory proposes that under certain conditions, particularly those of stress, abuse of offspring can be seen as consistent with the need for survival. Some animals (like rats and rabbits) brought up in stressful conditions, where food is in short supply, may even devour their young. If they do not rate the survival chances of their infants as very high, then the priority becomes to survive and breed again *themselves*, hopefully in a more benign environment. Similarly, where animals have several offspring, and conditions are harsh, they are likely to neglect the weakest so that the stronger ones can survive – the culling process.

Sociobiologists have also taken an interest in substitute and step-parenting. In the animal world there are clear examples of non-biological fathers grossly ill-treating their mates' young. How far these notions can be transferred to human beings is highly questionable, but for sociobiologists the message is clear – step-parents do not have a particular investment in the genes of these offspring and so have no investment in their chances of survival.

The psychodynamic perspective

All theories within the psychodynamic perspective are based on the work of Sigmund Freud, though many subsequent theorists have adapted and extended his original ideas, resulting in many schools of thought within the psychoanalytic tradition. In this section we will focus mainly on the original Freudian theory. Brief reference will be made to those who have been influential in developing this theory and to the critique of mainstream psychoanalytic practice by Alice Miller (1986), whose work is considered in more detail elsewhere in this book.

Freudian theory evolved over a period of 40 years or so from Freud's clinical work with mainly female middle-class patients who lived in late Victorian/Edwardian Vienna. His early work on hysteria (a condition where people experience symptoms like paralysis that have no observable organic cause) led him to believe that this psychiatric condition derived directly from the sexual abuse of his patients as children. These views were not well received, partly because sex was very much a taboo subject at that time and because of the implication that sexual abuse of children was widespread. Such a view was not acceptable in Freud's era and culture.

Within a year Freud changed his tack and began to argue that the experiences which were being related to him had not actually happened, but were wishful fantasies. If ideas about sexuality were not the result of violations by adults, then they had to come from 'within'. Hence Freud proposed a strong sexual element in children's thinking at a much earlier stage than had ever before been thought possible. He argued that a person's sexual drive (libido) was an instinctual force which motivated behaviour from birth onwards. Children were said to go through a series of five stages of psychosexual development each of which could be related to the most important source of gratification in their lives at the time (see Table 1).

Table 1 *Stages of psychosexual development as proposed by Freud*

Age	Stage	Source of gratification
0–1	Oral	Breast
1–3	Anal	Anus
3–5	Phallic	Penis/vagina
5–puberty	Latent	Period of inactivity
Puberty onwards	Genital	Adult sexual acitivty

Freud argued that childrearing styles and relationships with parents (especially mothers) in early years were of crucial importance to later development. Over-permissiveness or overstrict control could lead to development that is 'arrested' (stopped short) and thus affect the whole of later life.

Because he found that his patients could not easily recall the thoughts and the wishes they had experienced during this crucial period, Freud argued that there were three levels of consciousness. The first, or conscious, level was what was currently in a person's mind; the second, or preconscious, level could easily be recalled when needed; but the third, or unconscious, level was not open to recall. It acted as a repository for 'repressed' thoughts. A classical example of repression was the Oedipus complex in boys, the Electra complex in girls. All children, Freud argued, sexually desired the parent of the opposite sex, which placed the child in competition with the parent of the same sex. This dilemma could only be resolved by repressing (i.e. hiding from conscious awareness) this socially unacceptable urge deep in the unconscious mind and identifying with the parent of the same sex. Unravelling this process and locating where it had become distorted was the primary function of psychoanalytical therapy.

In his later work Freud put forward the idea that the mind was composed of three systems, the id – the instinctual and entirely unconscious *eros* (love) and *thanatos* (death) drives, the superego – corresponding roughly to the conscience (the prohibitions imposed by parents), and the ego (the rational mediating component between the id, the superego and conscious reality). Freud believed it is possible to enable patients to tap their unconscious minds by means of techniques such as free association and the interpretation of dreams. By bringing unresolved wishes and desires from early childhood to the fore, he sought to strengthen the egos of his patients.

Freud's followers and contemporary Freudian theorists such as Kris, Hartmann and Erikson have moved away from Freud's emphasis on the sexual drive and have instead emphasized the function of the ego in the growth and development of children and adults. The emphasis of Erikson (1963) in particular is on the way in which the individual ego is moulded by social forces to adjust personality development throughout life and produce socially acceptable behaviour. Whereas Freud was preoccupied with the psycho*sexual*, Erikson has shifted the focus to the psycho*social*.

Psychodynamics in general and ego psychology in particular have a clear message for the problem of child abuse, which is that any form of ill-treatment in the early stages of development is likely to create long-term emotional problems that can only be resolved by the development of insight through therapy and counselling. Failure to put right the damage thus caused is likely to affect all later relationships, including those with children, and so increase the chances of creating a cycle of emotional and other forms of abuse. Much of the work of Kempe in the United States and the NSPCC in the United Kingdom is based on this kind of theorizing.

However, mainstream psychoanalytic thought has not been particularly helpful with regard to child sexual abuse, largely because of the Freudian view of early sexual development, with its implication that children are prone to fantasy in this respect. One of the most notable critics of such ideas, whose work is focused on child abuse, is Alice Miller. Consistent with the original belief that Freud expounded in 1896, she argues that society is adultist and that sexual and other forms of abuse of children are widespread. Further, that disbelieving the alleged victims and assuming their revelations to be wishful fantasies actually damages their psychological health. Miller's influential idea of the inner child is described in chapter 28.

Behaviourism and learning theory
According to a behaviourist perspective, the only aspects of human behaviour that we can know about and study are those which can be readily observed. The child comes into the world as a *tabula rasa* (clean slate) with very few inborn or reflex responses. Virtually all subsequent behaviour is learned, primarily through the reward or punishment of its consequences. An American psychologist called Skinner (1953) demonstrated his principle of operant conditioning in experiments with pigeons and rats. Basically, any piece of behaviour that is reinforced by a reward or by withdrawal of an unpleasant stimulus is likely to be repeated, whereas behaviour that goes unrewarded gradually dies out. In the case of humans, rewards can include things like attention and affection or getting out of doing something they do not like. Interestingly behaviourists urge that punishment is usually fairly ineffective in the learning process. According to Skinner, 'In the long run, punishment, unlike reinforcement, works to the disadvantage of both the punished organism and the punishing agency. The aversive stimuli which are needed generate emotions, including predispositions to escape or retaliate, and disabling anxieties' (Skinner, 1972).

The behaviourist approach is sometimes likened to a black-box model of behaviour. The stimulus from the environment goes into the box, an observable response comes out and whether or not it is repeated depends on reinforcement. Old-style behaviourists are simply not concerned with what goes on inside the box, i.e. thinking.

Social learning theorists on the other hand accept the principles of behaviourism, but are prepared to attach some importance to what takes place within the box, and to accept that we learn by observing others (modelling) (Bandura, 1965) as well as by direct experience, and also that internal reasoning or cognitive processes play a part (Michenbaum, 1977).

From this perspective child abuse is seen to result from poor learning experiences and inadequate controlling techniques. Parents who themselves were treated harshly as children may well not have learned how to control their children in socially acceptable ways and resort to punitive/abusive methods. Parents who were overindulged as children might fail to set limits and resort to violence when matters get totally out of hand.

Learning theorists have used their ideas to create a range of therapeutic interventions known collectively as behaviour modification techniques. In the child abuse field particular emphasis has been placed on replacing unacceptable parenting techniques with those that are socially more acceptable. The Mcauleys have developed different ways of working with families where children are considered to be at risk (McCauley, 1977). They give considerable attention to the events leading up to abusive incidents and subsequent actions. They then specify age-relevant techniques of coping with these types of situations in non-violent ways, such as the use of 'time-out' (ignoring the children when they behave badly) and focus on rewards (such as praise and attention for good behaviour) rather than punishments. Behaviour modification techniques have also been used with actual and potential abusers to help them develop methods of self-control (see Reavley and Gilbert, 1978 and chapter 15 in this book).

Family dysfunction theory

Family dysfunction theory and the method of therapeutic intervention stemming from it, family therapy, are of relatively recent origin. They derive mainly from the work of psychiatrists and social workers in the mental health field. For a long time these workers had seen that family dynamics played a part in the illnesses of their patients and clients, and family assessment formed an important part of their work. The next step, however, was actually to use the family as a medium of therapy or change. Most family therapists in the 1960s were of a psychodynamic persuasion and their focus remained on working with the family to help the emotional needs of the individual. The therapist took on a fairly passive role, listening and occasionally clarifying situations. Communication patterns were a particular focus of concern, as it was felt that the existence of poor or contradictory messages between family members was a major cause of dysfunction.

An alternative approach within family therapy emerged from the work of Minuchin (1974) who employed systems theory (derived from the study of the working of complex interacting machines) as an aid to understanding and intervening in families. He theorized that the family was made up of parent–parent, parent–child and child–child subsystems and that it was important to maintain clear distinctions between them. Families could become 'enmeshed' – in a state where there was no clear structural pattern and roles (e.g. 'mother', 'child', 'father') broke down. Or they could become 'disengaged' – where the interaction between the subsystems had broken down. Both states are considered to be dysfunctional (damaging and causing problems) and the therapist's task is to work towards achieving a better balance (called homeostasis). Consideration is also given to the interaction of the family with wider systems (e.g. school, social services) and the same principles are applied. To achieve a healthy state, the family needs to avoid being totally closed to the outside. On the other hand it needs a degree of separateness as well. Minuchin's approach to family work was far more directive than that of psychodynamic family therapists.

Family dysfunction theories have been applied to the fields of physical and sexual abuse both to try and explain the processes by which such abuses occur and to treat them. For example, there is the notion of 'scapegoating', whereby all the family's problems become identified in one family member and this leads to physical or emotional abuse of that one person. Family dysfunction theorists would argue that the scapegoat has become necessary for the survival of the family unit, and so any efforts to make the family safe for the child must involve work with the whole family. The Rochdale unit of the NSPCC (see Dale *et al.*, 1986) has developed a range of family-based techniques in cases where children have been seriously abused. (See also chapter 22.)

With regard to sexual abuse, the work of Arnon Bentovim and his colleagues at the Great Ormond Street Children's Hospital has been most influential (Mrazek and Bentovim, 1981). Typically families where sexual abuse takes place are regarded as cut off from relationships with the outside world and the normal boundaries between parents and children are seen to have been breached. For example, it is argued that where sexual relationships between the parents are unsatisfactory, the father may turn his attention to one of his adolescent daughters who may gain status within the family and begin to take over the mother role. In this way the whole family dynamic becomes distorted and skewed from the norm. Therapeutic intervention is based on work with the whole family to try and unravel poor communication patterns and entangled relationships, which are seen as major causes of the abuse.

Sociological perspective
The sociological perspective on child abuse has until recently tended to have more prominence in the United States than in the United Kingdom and comes in three major variants: the ecological, the cultural and the social structural.

Ecological theories, such as that of Garbarino and Gilliam (1980), stress that children need to live in healthy environments if they are to grow up healthy and well-adjusted. On the basis of some evidence that there are links between rates of reported abuse and characteristics of social deprivation such as a high proportion of low-income families, a high proportion of single- (usually female) headed households and a high incidence of mobility, Gabarino and Gilliam argue that socially impoverished environments are likely to worsen and even stimulate any psychological stresses that are already present in families. Child abuse, according to this approach, results from poor parenting skills combined with social stress, most notably lack of family and community supports. The answer to the problem, following this line of thinking, is to avoid grouping families at risk in a single neighbourhood, and to provide sufficient services which are sensitive to the needs of local communities.

The social cultural theories are illustrated by those of Gelles and his associates (Gelles and Cornell, 1985). These theorists argue that the incidence of abuse is related to cultural support for the use of physical punishment on children. They conducted a survey of over 1000 families in various parts of the United States and found that about 70% had employed some form of corporal punishment. What Gelles termed 'abusive violence' (i.e. punching children, hitting them with objects and using offensive weapons against them) was much more widespread than national reports of the incidence of child physical abuse would suggest. Their conclusion was that the family is one of the most dangerous places to live in, not only for children, but also for women and the elderly, because it offers opportunities for levels of private violence which, if known about, would not be publicly tolerated. Following this line of argument, the way to tackle physical abuse is for us to take a wider societal approach to dealing with violence as a whole. As it stands, violence, while officially disapproved of, is in fact being passively condoned by the lack of a determined effort to eliminate it. We must change the way we as a society think about violence – and we must be prepared to *do* something about it!

The social structural approach is strongly represented by Gil (1970). In his research of officially recorded abuse in the United States in the late 1960s he found that the children on Child Protection Registers overwhelmingly came from the lower socio-economic classes. Gil argued that if society itself sets the preconditions for child abuse by condoning structural inequalities (i.e. by allowing many families to exist in extreme poverty and social deprivation) then it too must share the blame when a child is abused and such abuse should not be seen to be the result of individual pathology. This line of argument is the focus of chapter 8, and has also been strongly advocated by Parton (1985).

The social structural view implies that child abuse is an issue which should not be left to professional workers alone. It is of important political concern. At a practical level, however, it implies that where abuse takes place, greater attention should be paid to trying to redress the inequalities leading to impoverishment and poor living conditions, rather than focusing on changing the behaviour of individuals and families by psychological or psychotherapeutically based intervention.

The feminist perspective

There are many different theoretical positions associated with feminist thought, for example liberal, radical and socialist. However, for the purpose of analysing its contribution to the field of child abuse, focus will be on a broad-based radical approach which assumes that our society is patriarchal (i.e. dominated by men and male interests), and that prevailing beliefs about all aspects of social organization – indeed the dominant 'social construction of reality' (see chapter 1 – are framed from the male point of view. This kind of feminist analysis is particularly pertinent to the issue of child sexual abuse where perpetrators are predominantly male and more girls are abused than boys. Indeed, it is unlikely that such abuse would have become publicly recognized without the action and interest of feminists. The opening up of centres to provide a more sensitive service for women who had been raped led to the realization that many of these women had experienced sexual abuse as children. Indeed, their disturbing revelations confirmed views about male dominance in all aspects of life. Quite simply, feminists argued that sexual abuse of children was an extreme example of institutionalized male power or patriarchy.

The work of Rush (1981) is probably the best known of this type of analysis, although more recently MacLeod and Saraga (1987) and Nelson (1987) have made major contributions. Rush's view is that little is done in society to tackle issues like child sexual abuse and child pornography because they are not taken seriously enough by those in power, i.e. men. She sees society as being soft on child molesters and all too ready to find explanations for sexual exploitation of children other than the glaringly obvious one, the abuse of male adult power. 'We must face and accept the fact that it is men, not women, who actually seduce, rape, castrate, feminize and infantilize our young, and it is time for them, rather than for women, to be held responsible for destructive, exploitative sexual behaviour' (Rush, 1981, p. 195). Her view is that male assumptions about their rights to exercise sexual power and privilege over women lie at the heart of the problem.

The feminist perspective has not been so prominent in the general field of child physical abuse where women are relatively more likely to be abusers. However, it has been argued that abuse may partially result from the expectations placed by society on women to be carers. From this point of view the notion of motherhood is nothing more than a male construct of what the female role should be, whereas in reality caring for children, particularly in an impoverished environment, is a stressful task.

Research by Ong (1985) based on observations of an NSPCC Family Centre, highlights these issues. She argues that the mothers she interviewed would have been better helped if there had been less emphasis on natural mothering qualities and more attention paid to their accounts of their own experiences of motherhood.

The feminist perspective has important practical contributions to make in the field of child abuse on two fronts. At the individual case level, investigation and treatment (particularly with regard to sexual abuse) need to be far more gender sensitive, and women need to be empowered to play a more influential role in this work. At a broader societal level much more needs to be done to raise awareness of male domination and to devise strategies to change the status quo. Radical feminists would argue that nothing short of the overthrow of the patriarchy will achieve this. This in itself would, it is argued, reduce the incidence of all forms of child abuse. Less revolutionary strategies would include influencing men to view their sexuality in a less machismo way and thus lowering the chances of sexual abuse of children taking place, and involving men more in the care of their own children. This could limit the amount of physical and emotional abuse in two ways. Mothers would be less likely to abuse because the pressure placed on them by being sole carers would be removed. Fathers, by being more involved in their children's care, would become more realistic and sensitive to their needs and also less likely to abuse. Needless to say this would involve a major rethink about the normal roles of men and women in our society. In chapter 35 Jenny Kitzinger writes about feminist self-help.

Children's rights

In recent years there has been much discussion about the rights of children. While a good deal of this body of thought has been concerned with the wider political status of children, nevertheless it has clear implications for child abuse. If the general standing of children were raised and they were viewed more as independent beings in their own right and less as the property of their parents, then it is likely that they would have more redress in cases of child abuse and ultimately its incidence would lessen.

Freeman (1983) identifies two polar positions in the debate on children's rights, the 'liberators' and the 'protectors'. Liberator theorists (e.g. Holt (1974) and Farson (1978)) argue that children should be treated the same as adults in every way. Age is seen as irrelevant, the principle of self-determination as central – children should have the same rights as adults to vote, to privacy, to conduct financial dealings, to live away from home, to sexual freedom and to freedom from physical punishment. That they do not have these rights is seen as symptomatic of the paternalistic organization of our society, and the function of paternalism is seen as nothing more than an attempt by adults to keep all power vested in themselves, largely for selfish motives. This point of view seems to ignore the positives of parenting, such as protection of the child while psychologically and physically immature, and the practicalities of carrying out ideals, such as giving young children the right to live with whom they choose.

Extreme protectionists, on the other hand, limit their notions of children's rights solely to situations where children are thought to be at risk. This is in line with classical liberal thinking as proposed by Mill (1910). From this perspective individuals are free to do what they wish as long as they do not break the law or impinge on others' freedoms in any way. In Victorian times, when this theory was devised, children were very much seen to be the property of their parents. Gradually this situation has changed and currently we are moving towards a philosophy that sees parents as trustees to their children, i.e. they should hold rights over them only as long as they act in their best interests. These ideas are developed in chapter 14.

Freeman has attempted to clarify the debate by suggesting that there are four categories of children's rights. The first he terms 'welfare rights', which are equated with basic human rights such as those of having adequate nutrition, education and recreation. A second category is the right to protection. A third category is that of social justice, whereby the rights of children as citizens are emphasized. Finally, there is the category of rights against parents which might be applied solely to adolescents. 'Protectors' emphasize the former two categories, 'liberators' the latter two. Freeman develops some of these arguments further in chapter 13.

Such philosophical debates form the backdrop to society's response to childcare and child abuse. Indeed, uncertainty about the rights of children in relation to those of parents is a hallmark of our child abuse system. On the one hand, social workers are vilified for not paying sufficient attention to a child's welfare (and thus rights), as in the case of Jasmine Beckford (London Borough of Brent, 1985), and on the other, they are accused of being grossly insensitive to the rights of parents, as in the Cleveland affair. Those in favour of a non-adultist policy of emphasizing the rights of children and young persons would argue that changes in attitude on this broad front will play a major role in preventing child abuse occurring in the first place. The Cleveland Inquiry Report firmly supports a children's rights stance in its recommendations: 'There is a danger that in looking to the welfare of children believed to be the victims of sexual abuse the children themselves may be overlooked. *The child is a person and not an object of concern*' (DHSS, 1988, p. 245).

Conclusion
This review of theories relating to child abuse has taken into account a wide range of perspectives. In order to make sense of their contribution to our understanding of child abuse it is necessary to bear in mind the following factors. First, the levels of analysis of the different theories are widely divergent. The ethological, psychological and family dysfunction theories seek to explain child abuse within the individual or his or her family dynamics, whereas the sociological/political analyses look to the structures and ideologies of the wider society as important causative factors. This does not mean that they are not compatible with each other or have to be seen in 'either/or' terms. However, there is likely to be some dispute as to which perspective should carry the most weight.

A second, and related, point is that some theories are more directly applicable to specific cases of abuse than others. By and large, the biological/psychological perspectives are attractive to those who deal with child abuse at the ground level because they point to practical, achievable courses of action, i.e. direct therapeutic interventions. The broader sociological and political theories, while offering explanations, raise complex societal issues which have political implications over time, but have less immediate appeal to practitioners.

Thirdly, some theories have more relevance for some forms of abuse than others. For instance, the social structural approach emphasizing the effect of inequality and poverty has most relevance for physical abuse and neglect, in that the vast majority of officially recorded abuse takes place in conditions of poverty and social deprivation. However, as far as is known, sexual abuse is spread much more evenly across the classes and so social structural theories cannot be as applicable in this case. Similarly, sociological perspectives seem to offer much to our understanding of more moderate abuse/neglect, whereas biological/psychological perspectives seem to offer more understanding of how serious physical abuse and gross neglect might occur.

Fourthly, it is clear that some of the theories are ideologically in conflict. The most obvious example of this is the clash between feminist theory and the biological/psychological theories. The fundamental difference between the two is whether maternal/caring functions are 'natural' or societally imposed characteristics (the nature/nurture controversy). In particular feminists are critical of Bowlby's attachment theory: (a) because of its insistence on the instinctual nature of motherhood and (b) because of the restrictive implications of his view that even short periods of separation of a child from his or her attachment figure could have long-lasting damaging effects. More recently feminist writers have been highly critical of the mainstream family therapy approach to child sexual abuse which sees incest as a form of family dysfunction (MacLeod and Saraga, 1987; Nelson, 1987; Dominelli, 1986). They argue that this removes the focus from the (usually) male perpetrator who has abused his power over a child. They are highly critical of the story that the mother passively colludes in the situation by not offering sufficient protection to the child, and also of the readiness of family therapists to reconstitute the family after the event.

Having pointed to some differences between the theories concerning child abuse and some incompatibilities that are evident, it should be stressed that all add something to our understanding of the causes of child abuse and potential solutions to it. Given the range of situations which are now included under the official term of child abuse it is important to have a relatively open mind to a range of explanations in order to ensure effective and constructive intervention.

3 HOW PREVALENT IS IT?

Steve Taylor

*Lecturer in Medical Sociology, King's College, London and the
London School of Economics*

Ever since child abuse emerged as a distinct 'social problem' in the 1960s there have been demands from the media, practitioners, policy-makers and politicians for some kind of authoritative statement of the 'true' scope of the problem. However, it is important to remember that even where, in response to such pressures, child abuse is expressed in a numerical form, the reliability and validity of the figures cannot be taken for granted. Statistics should be subjected to the same kind of scepticism and critical scrutiny as any other form of evidence.

In this chapter I shall examine first, how researchers have attempted to 'measure' the extent of child abuse and examples of their findings. Secondly, I shall look at the kinds of problems involved in undertaking this work and why criticisms are voiced about the assumptions on which it is based. Finally, I shall advance some tentative conclusions and consider how much confidence we might have in the, apparently authoritative, statements that now appear in the media and elsewhere asserting that $x\%$ of children have suffered from this or that type of abuse.

Reported cases

One way in which researchers have attempted to measure the scope of child abuse is to generalize from samples of 'known' cases. In England and Wales, the most systematic and comprehensive attempts to do this have come from the research unit of the National Society for the Prevention of Cruelty to Children (NSPCC). On the basis of recommendations made by the inquiry into the death of Maria Colwell in 1974, cases of child abuse and suspected child abuse are now entered on Area Child Protection Committee Child Protection Registers (formerly Area Review Committee Child Abuse Registers). In some areas management of child abuse, including maintenance of the Register, has been delegated to the NSPCC. These areas, taken as a whole, cover about 9% of the child population of England and Wales. By careful examination of all cases of child abuse on their Registers each year, and then extrapolating to the population of England and Wales as a whole, the NSPCC is able to produce a general estimate of the level of child abuse for that year. The results of these studies for the years 1984–6 are summarized in Table 1.

The NSPCC data suggest that over 15,000 children were abused in England and Wales in 1986, a rate of 2.29 per 1000 children. The most commonly uncovered forms of abuse were physical injury (1.01 per 1000) and sexual abuse (0.57 per 1000). While any type of abuse can happen to a child at any age, specific types of abuse tend to be more common at particular age ranges. In 1986 the average age of children on the NSPCC Registers was 7 years; sexually abused children tended to be oldest (average age 10 years and 2 months), those who failed to thrive the youngest (1 year and 9 months average), with the physically abused around the mean (average 6 years

Table 1 *Number of registered children by type of abuse 1984–6**

	1984		1985		1986	
	No.	%	No.	%	No.	%
Physically injured	707	78.2	906	72.5	937	55.9
fatal	3	0.3	6	0.5	6	0.4
serious	56	6.2	93	7.4	81	4.8
moderate	648	71.7	807	64.6	850	50.7
Failure to thrive	34	3.8	28	2.2	46	2.7
Sexual abuse	98	10.8	222	17.8	527	31.5
Neglect	50	5.5	71	5.7	124	7.4
Emotional abuse	18	2.0	22	1.8	41	2.5
Total abused	907		1249		1675	
Physically injured rate per 1000 under 15		0.73		0.96		1.01
Sexual abuse rate per 1000 under 17		—		0.27		0.57
Accidental injuries	1		1		1	
'At risk' cases	208		336		461	
Total registered	1116		1586		2137	
Rate per 1000		1.16		1.67		2.29
Estimated No. of children physically abused in England and Wales	7038		9114		9590	
Estimated No. of children sexually abused in England and Wales	—		2932		6330	

* *Adapted from Creighton (1985, 1986).*

and 9 months). Boys tended to be more represented under the physical abuse and failure to thrive categories and girls were more represented under neglect and sexual abuse (Creighton, 1987).

The NSPCC records show a slow but steady increase in the incidence of reported cases in the late 1970s and early 1980s, followed by a much more dramatic increase in recent years. The 2137 reported cases in late 1986 represented an increase of 34% on 1985 figures which, in turn, were a 43% increase on 1984 (Table 2). While these figures may represent an increase in child abuse it seems more likely that they reflect increased reporting due to greater public and professional awareness.

Data on reported cases are not simply used to try to assess the scope of the problem; they are also used, perhaps more importantly, to try to establish why it comes about. It is believed that careful study of samples of reported cases can be used to try to identify the 'type' of child most at risk and those sections of the adult population most likely to abuse children. This work suggests that child abuse is not distributed randomly, but is concentrated amongst certain groups in society. For

Table 2 *Number of children registered by year**

	1977	1978	1979	1980	1981	1982	1983	1984	1985	1986
Total abused	723	749	711	815	898	783	—	904	1249	1675
Total registered	1000	1072	1077	1116	1189	1078	—	1116	1586	2137
Rate per 1000 under 15	0.62	0.67	0.68	0.72	0.84	1.06	—	1.16	1.67	2.29

* *Adapted from Creighton (1985, 1986).*

example, reported cases tend to be more common amongst the lower socio-economic classes and the parents of abused children tend to be characterized by their early parenthood, large numbers of children, marital instability and social mobility. The statistics also show a positive relationship between child abuse and crime and unemployment (Creighton, 1984). This kind of information is of more than academic interest. It is used to guide professionals towards identifying the children most at risk from future abuse (Kempe and Kempe, 1978). It is believed that systematic research into the factors 'really' associated with child abuse can help professionals anticipate risk by providing them with a more 'scientific' basis for their prediction. For example, one professional handbook tells social workers that:

> Young, isolated, immature parents are vulnerable [i.e. to abusing their children] particularly those who have experienced deprivation (either active or passive) in their own childhoods. Marital strife, early, abnormal or unwanted pregnancies, anxiety, depression or drug dependency can compound the risks of parents abusing their children. The environmental factors which cause stress should not be underestimated – financial difficulties, often associated with unemployment, inadequate housing, social and family isolation. (Taylor, 1988)

Using registered cases has the advantage of providing a readily available source of data on child abuse which has been professionally identified and subdivided into a range of types of abuse and neglect. It allows for cases to be followed up and the systematic identification of trends over time. However, this method has many critics. It is claimed that studies based on samples of reported cases grossly underestimate the *level* of child abuse because so many cases simply do not come to official attention.

There are many reasons why an act of child abuse may not be officially recorded. For example, the child may not recognize what is happening as abuse, or may be too frightened or too young to tell anyone. Alternatively, the child may tell but not be believed, or the family may manage to conceal the abuse from the authorities. Even when alerted, various professionals may not recognize abuse. They may be convinced by the family's claims of innocence or simply feel that they do not have enough evidence to register a case. The various stages that may intervene between an act against a child and its official registration are outlined in Table 3.

Even if reported cases do underestimate the level of child abuse (something few experts deny), the statistics of reported cases can still be useful for identifying the factors commonly associated with abuse, if those reported cases are an unbiased sample of cases as a whole, i.e. if non-reporting is due to chance. However, there is some evidence to suggest that reported cases provide samples that are *systematically* biased and are, therefore, of limited value for projecting guidelines over child abuse in general. First, some *forms* of abuse, such as physical injury or neglect, are more likely to come to public attention than those, such as sexual or emotional abuse, which are much more difficult to identify and prove (cf. Finkelhor and Hotaling, 1984). Second, families that have more frequent contact with health and welfare

Table 3 *From abuse to reported abuse*

---

1 Child abuse: known to perpetrator and (probably) victim

may be

↓

2 Known to others in family or community or not

may be

↓

3 Reported to professionals or suspected by professionals in course of routine work (e.g. casualty officer) or not

may be

↓

4 Investigated or not

may be

↓

5 Recognized and recorded as child abuse or suspected abuse or not

---

services or the police are much more likely to be identified and labelled as 'abusers', particularly if their personal characteristics and societal circumstances 'fit' those on the professionals' checklists (Taylor, 1988). Third, the data may be influenced by local registration policies. Some areas require definite evidence of abuse (or risk) before putting a child's name on the Register, while other areas seem to register almost every case they investigate as a matter of routine. Clearly, these differing policies, coupled with the general problems of decision-making in childcare cases, are going to influence the numbers of cases reported in different areas. Suspicions that data from reported cases may be seriously deficient both in numbers and quality have led researchers towards other methods of trying to establish the scope of the problem.

Survey data

The aim of studies based on self-completion surveys or face-to-face interviews is to cut through the stages between abuse and registration (Table 3) and bring the researcher into direct contact with abusers and/or abused individuals. This method – already established in criminology – involves contacting large numbers of the public to try to find out how many of them have either inflicted, or received, abusive experiences.

In a study of infliction of physical violence, Straus *et al.* (1981) conducted a survey on a sample of American families with one or more children between the ages of three and 17 living at home. From this survey, the authors estimated that 14 out of every 100 American children were being subjected to physical abuse each year. This figure was far higher than the 1% suggested by a wide-ranging study of reported cases in the United States (Krug and Davis, 1981). However, there are still concerns that studies attempting to identify potential perpetrators may underestimate the scope of the problem – especially in a 'taboo' area such as child sexual abuse – as many of those contacted may decline to admit their own (or others') abuse of children.

Studies of the experience of abuse are felt by some to produce more accurate information, as the targets of abuse may have less 'motive' to conceal the truth. With this method, samples of the adult population are contacted and asked whether or not they encountered abusive experiences in their own childhoods. In evaluating the extent to which this method may be an improvement on studies based on reported cases, it is important to bear in mind that target self-report studies generally only attempt to measure the *prevalence* of child abuse (i.e. what percentage claim it *ever* happened). Obviously, prevalence studies covering a person's entire childhood would normally be expected to produce much higher percentage figures than *incidence* studies, which only attempt to measure rates of child abuse in a fixed time. Comparison between data based on incidence and those based on prevalence is, therefore, extremely difficult.

Most of the victim studies on child abuse have been done in the United States and the majority are on sexual abuse which, it is felt, is the type of abuse least likely to come to public attention. While these studies have produced estimates of sexual abuse which are consistently higher than those based on reported cases, estimates have varied from 6 to 62% for females and 3 to 31% for males. In comparison, the most comprehensive sexual abuse victim survey in the United Kingdom produced estimates of 12% of females and 8% of males sexually abused (Baker and Duncan, 1986), while another survey – for the BBC *Childwatch* programme – by the same authors produced an overall estimated rate of 3%.

How are we to try to account for these wide variations? In an analysis of 12 of the major American studies of the prevalence of sexual abuse, Peters *et al.* (1986) examined why they produced such different findings and which approach is likely to give 'the most accurate estimate'. The answer could, of course, simply be that the individuals contacted in the various studies did have very different experiences of abuse in their own childhoods. However, Peters *et al.* suggest that the variations in the estimates of the rates have more to do with the different *definitions* of abuse used by the researchers and the different methods by which data were collected.

There is no generally agreed definition of sexual abuse amongst researchers. While some use a relatively narrow definition, others define sexual abuse in a much wider way to include, for example, indecent exposure and sexual propositions. While more general definitions have the advantage of providing data on a wider variety of experiences, there is also the danger of producing findings which are overgeneralized and lacking in precision. For example, in the definitions used by some studies, a respondent who had suffered repeated rape by someone charged with her care and protection, a respondent who had been indecently 'exposed to' once on her way home from school and a respondent who, at 14, had consented to have sex with her 19-year-old boyfriend would all be classified under the 'same' category and form part of the same percentage figure. Some researchers have attempted to refine a general definition by distinguishing between, for example, contact and non-contact abuse, but even then, a term such as contact abuse can cover a very wide range of different experiences.

Peters *et al.* found that studies employing a wide, or less restrictive, definition of abuse tended to produce higher rates of abuse, but they argued that this did not fully explain the differences, as different rates were returned by some studies which employed very similar definitions. They suggested that the way in which the data were collected – the methodology – also appeared to influence the findings. For example, random rather than selected samples, face-to-face interviews rather than self-administered questionnaires, and specific questions (e.g. Did anyone try to touch your genitals against your will?) rather than general ones (e.g. Were you ever sexually molested?) all appeared to produce higher rates of prevalence. On the assumption that concealment of sexual abuse is the major problem for researchers (and practitioners) to overcome, Peters et al. suggest that in the future researchers would be advised to use random samples, interviews and activity-specific questions, as these methods seem to 'draw out' higher rates of abuse.

In summary, survey studies, rather than relying on reported data, attempt to measure the extent of child abuse by locating abusers or victims amongst samples of the general population. While this has the advantage of cutting through some of the obstacles that may impede the registration of child abuse, many specific problems remain. First, because prevalence studies are retrospective, there is a whole series of problems arising from respondents' honesty and ability and willingness to recall things that happened many years ago. Also, studies based on retrospective recall obviously cannot provide estimates of current levels of abuse. Secondly, self-report studies of child abuse tend to have relatively low response rates and researchers do not know if those who do respond provide a numerically 'high', 'low' or 'random' sample of victims. Thirdly, it appears that the researcher's views as to what does (or does not) constitute child abuse and the ways in which research is constructed and administered have important biasing effects on what is 'discovered'. While prevalence studies strongly suggest that the proportion of the adult population who have had some form of sexually abusive experience is far higher than is commonly supposed, the problems of undertaking this research mean that it is difficult for anyone to say with certainty that the rate of child sexual abuse (or any other form of abuse) is, or was, $x\%$ (La Fontaine, 1988). However, researchers like Peters et al. are optimistic that more 'accurate' estimates will be made in the future. They see variations in projected rates of prevalence as the result of technical problems to be solved by careful research which will reveal the 'correct' definition of child abuse and the proper methods for discovering its scope. This view assumes that there are within societies, or social groups, true rates of child abuse which are being picked up to a greater or lesser degree by various research strategies (Table 4).

Table 4 *Calculation of 'true' rate of child abuse*

(a) Reported cases of child abuse
+
(b) Hidden or undetected cases
=
(c) True rate of child abuse

If we consider the equation presented in Table 4 the main problem for research can be seen to be discovering as many cases as possible from category (b), because this will bring researchers closer to a correct 'answer', category (c).

So far we have been looking at attempts to estimate levels of child abuse from the point of view of those engaged in this work. However, it is important to note that there are many social scientists who would not see the problem as merely a technical one. They would question the very idea of trying to discover the true rate of child abuse and the theoretical assumptions underlying such a quest. The next section examines the basis of this critique and some of its implications.

Child abuse as a social construct

The various attempts to measure the scope of child abuse are based on a positivist approach to social science. Positivism holds that science, and therefore good social science, proceeds by careful observation and description of factual phenomena, or things, and the relations between them. Only then may hypotheses and theories be constructed which can be tested by reference to the relevant facts. According to positivists, scientific explanation is characterized by its focus on factual things, i.e. what can be directly observed, and its attempt to exclude value and moral judgements.

There has been widespread criticism of positivism in social science, particularly from sociologists. Critics argue that not only has positivism a mistaken view of science (Keat and Urry, 1975; Taylor, 1982), but that, in any case, there are crucial differences between attempts to study the natural and the social world (Bauman, 1978). Unlike objects in the physical world, human beings, including scientists, attach meanings to actions and these meanings are the products of distinct and varying value and conceptual structures. These value structures mediate between what is in the world and how it is perceived by members of a social group at a given time (Berger and Luckmann, 1967). Critics argue that it is therefore impossible to achieve direct and relatively neutral observation of the social world, and that both the subject-matter of the social sciences (i.e. human action and interaction) and the relationship of an observer to that subject-matter are far more complex and problematic than positivists realize. These observations have a number of important implications for positivist attempts to establish the incidence and prevalence of child abuse.

First, positivists assume there are a number of 'facts about child abuse', including the scope of the problem, waiting to be discovered by appropriate research techniques. But critics would ask what exactly are these facts. The answer might be that they are, for example, beating, neglecting or sexually exploiting children. However, no behaviour is *necessarily* child abuse. Children have been savagely beaten, neglected and sexually exploited for centuries without people even feeling that it was wrong, let alone categorizing such behaviour as abuse. Child abuse is thus a product of social definition. Some sets of facts come to be labelled as cases of child abuse because they go beyond the limits of what is now considered to be acceptable conduct towards a child. These standards change over time and also vary, not only between cultures, but also between different members of the same culture. Child abuse is thus a social construction whose meaning arises from the value structure of a social group and the ways in which these values are interpreted and negotiated in real situations. From this point of view the positivist search for a true rate of child abuse implies either that child abuse can exist in some way independently of human thought about it (which is a logical absurdity) or that there is a consensus of values about the problem (which simply does not exist in the real world). (See also chapter 4.)

Secondly, neither the professionals nor the researchers who try to discover cases or rates of child abuse are merely 'standing back' and observing and recording what is going on. Rather, by defining child abuse in certain ways, by asking some questions and not others, they are *imposing* values on the fact-gathering process. In fact, there are some critics who argue that survey and formal interview data tell us far more about the values of the researchers than those of the subjects of the research.

Thirdly, in the process of 'fact gathering', one cannot assume a necessary correspondence and consistency of meaning between the researcher's questions and the participant's answers. Surveys and structured interviews attempt to compress a potentially limitless range of experiences into a limited number of preselected categories. This can give rise to all sorts of problems. For example, the questions may simply not reflect the respondent's experiences, or two or more respondents may answer that they have been subjected to a particular type of abuse (e.g. beating) but have actually experienced it in very different ways.

In this section I have looked at some powerful arguments against positivism in general and positivist attempts to measure child abuse in particular. At the core of this critique is that the positivist attempt to separate 'facts' from 'values' is untenable. In the next section I shall attempt some general evaluation of statistical data on child abuse in the light of these observations.

Evaluating child abuse

The problems involved in attempting to establish levels of child abuse, combined with the critical analysis of some of the assumptions on which these attempts are founded, should certainly make us initially sceptical of *any* statistical data on child abuse. However, this does not mean that all existing material should be rejected out of hand, nor does it deny the possibility of reducing obvious sources of error in the future. But we do need to recognize the problems inherent in the measuring approach and bear in mind that 'measurement' in the social sciences is not the precise instrument that prevails in the natural sciences (Willer and Willer, 1973; Pawson, 1988).

Studies based on reported cases, such as those by the NSPCC, are useful in the practical sense that a rapidly increasing number of identified cases of child abuse (Table 2) has obvious and important policy and resource implications. However, we should be cautious when told – as many practitioners are told on training courses, conferences and in child abuse manuals – that 'research proves' child abuse to be positively related to, for example, low social class, high number of children in the family, crime, unemployment and social problems. In practice, child abuse is seldom identified merely from the physical condition and behaviour of the child. Evidence of 'risk factors' from the parents' background and the social and economic environment (or the lack of it) can make it more (or less) likely that any given case is 'seen' and recorded as child abuse. The subsequent discovery and 'rediscovery' of this 'evidence' by researchers may operate as a self-fulfilling prophecy (Figure 1 overleaf). This argument does not, of course, reject the possibility that some 'factors' may indeed be linked to child abuse. But it does suggest caution before accepting their relevance and potential predictive power, and emphasizes the need to learn a great deal more about how cases come to be identified and recorded as child abuse (cf. Dingwall *et al.*, 1983; Taylor, 1988).

Proponents of survey and formal interview methods of 'measuring' child abuse often claim that their approach gives much more 'realistic' estimates of the true rates. However, social constructionist criticisms throw into doubt the very idea of a true rate, suggesting instead that child abuse exists throughout to the extent that we predefine it. It is, therefore, not a question of asking whether this or that estimate is 'true' or not, but rather, when confronted by a percentage figure, of finding out what *particular* truth the study is trying to discover and how much confidence we should have in its results.

There are two key questions which we can ask to help us evaluate the various percentage figures given in different studies of prevalence and incidence. First, we should find out what definition of child abuse was being used in the study. Generally, the wider the definition, the greater will be the percentage figure. In facing the varying rates given by different studies, or different approaches, it must be remembered that there is no means of fairly comparing rates compiled in terms of different definitions of child abuse. For example, the cases registered by the child protection agencies tend to involve severe abuse within the child's own domestic environment. In contrast, survey studies, as we have seen, tend to use much wider

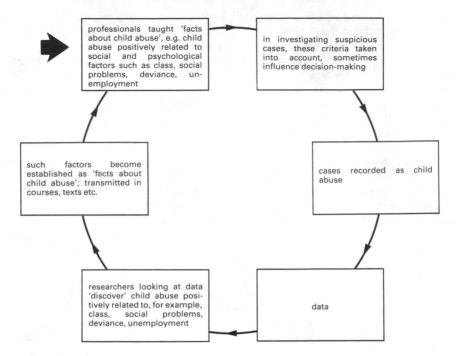

Figure 1. 'Facts about child abuse' may be cyclically 'rediscovered'

definitions of abuse. Thus, when confronted by a figure of 1% from a study of reported cases and a figure of, say, 10% from a survey study, we cannot assume that the child protection agencies are only picking up 10% of cases. Many acts picked up in the survey study would either fall outside the remit of the child protection agencies or, on investigation, not be registered.

Second, we must ask if the statistics obtained in a research study are likely to tell us what it may sound as if they tell us. Here, we must try to find out the methods used in the research because many researchers grossly misuse the survey method. Survey data only have a chance of being reliable when there is likely to be common understanding of a question between researcher and respondents. For example, if, as a researcher, I ask my respondents to tell me their age, occupation and educational qualifications, I can assume a common understanding of the question. As Pawson (1988) observes, 'such questions are "factual" because they refer to some *external* standard or practice or institution which is recognised in the public domain'. However, if I asked questions such as 'Has anyone ever shown you pornography?' or 'Did that upset you?', I cannot then assume that my respondents will share a common view of what is meant by 'pornography', nor can I assume that they will mean the same thing when they tell me that something did, or did not, 'upset' them. In short, the more I ask questions that can be open to a variety of interpretations the less sure I am about the consistency and reliability of my results.

The qualifications outlined above mean that we can have more, but still limited, confidence in the results of surveys that ask questions about behaviour rather than peoples' varying interpretations of events, and which use categories, such as 'sexual intercourse' or 'punched', where a relatively high common level of understanding can be assumed. By way of illustration, let us apply these methodological and theoretical 'tests' to the largest child abuse survey undertaken in the United Kingdom, the Mori poll on sexual abuse (Baker and Duncan, 1986). This was a study of a representative quota sample of 1029 adults interviewed between 6 and 10 September 1984. A child was defined as sexually abused when 'another person who is sexually mature, involves the child in any activity which the other person expects to lead to their own sexual arousal. This might involve intercourse, touching, exposure of sexual organs, showing pornographic material or talking about things in an erotic way.'

It is clear from this that the authors use a wide definition which would thus include a number of incidents which would not come to the attention of social services. What is particularly interesting here is that Baker and Duncan's estimated prevalence figure of 10% was widely quoted in the context of the Cleveland Inquiry. The most widely publicized aspect of controversy in Cleveland was concerned with whether or not a group of children had suffered from anal sexual abuse. Although Baker and Duncan's study had little to do with this specific problem, and in fact did not even include a question on anal abuse, the consistent quoting of the 10% figure in relation to the Cleveland cases suggested to some people that the doctors had only uncovered the tip of the iceberg of rape and buggery. This is a clear example of data being sensationalized and quoted inappropriately and, as the 'moral' panic about child abuse and the demand for 'proper figures' grows, this is happening more frequently.

The second consideration is what value we can attach to Baker and Duncan's data and, given the methodological test outlined previously, the answer must be not very much. Look again at the definition of sexual abuse given above. It is a minefield of ambiguity, including terms such as 'sexually mature', 'sexual arousal', 'touching', 'pornographic material' and 'talking about things in an erotic way'. In fact, it is almost a textbook example of how *not* to write a survey question. This does not mean that a 10% figure is necessarily wrong, for that would presuppose some correct rate, but it does mean that the sample is almost certain to include a variety of conflicting and ambiguous responses that undermine its value in scientific terms. Unfortunately, the same point can be made of the vast majority of survey studies of child abuse.

Summary

In this chapter we have considered research which has attempted to estimate the scope of child abuse through analysis of reported cases and survey methods. We have looked at specific problems encountered by each approach and at a general critique of the positivist assumptions underlying the search for true rates of child abuse.

At present, the greatest problem is not that we have difficulty in estimating levels of child abuse, but rather that so few people are aware of these problems and read far too much into the available data. It has been suggested here that, while some useful estimations of the problem are possible in principle, it must be recognized that what is being 'measured' is a theoretical concept of child abuse, necessarily constructed from moral and value judgements. The more we understand about how the behaviour we categorize as child abuse is defined, recognized and experienced, the more these theoretical concepts can be developed and improved. The more researchers become aware of the limitations of the survey method and improve their practice within these limitations, the more confidence we can have in the statistical data presented to us.

4 TAKING THE CHILD ABUSE DEBATE APART

Wendy Stainton Rogers

Lecturer in Health and Social Welfare, The Open University

Rex Stainton Rogers

Lecturer in Psychology, University of Reading

The traditional story of child welfare reform, the one we probably recall from our school days, focused on the reformer – a figure like Dr Barnardo or Mary Carpenter – whose challenge to deeply held beliefs and practices stemmed from a crusading dedication and an absolute conviction that what they were doing was right. What was often left unsaid at school was that such crusaders, precisely through their sense of moral vocation, sometimes pursued their goals so resolutely that they failed to consider the wider implications and 'knock-on' risks of what they were doing (Heywood, 1978; Manton, 1976; Wagner, 1982; Wymer, 1954).

As the events of Cleveland have shown (DHSS, 1988), we have neither outgrown such problems nor left them behind us. The troubles that have beset single-minded action programmes on child abuse also seem to stem from their very single-mindedness. However, in one way we are 'luckier' than Victorian society. Most of us, not just ecologists, are by now only too aware of the problems that have resulted from an 'act in haste repent at leisure' treatment of our own planet. We are coming to recognize the need to take a much wider, more 'risk-conscious' view about environmental policies. This feeling for ecology, a kind of 'greening' of our thinking, is beginning to influence ideas about social problems too.

In this chapter we will argue for, and report some research into, a multifaceted approach to child abuse. It is, we believe, a recipe for disaster for professionals ever to become so enmeshed in a particular theory or approach (however fashionable or alluring) that it becomes 'taken for granted'. We believe that single-minded models of the 'problem', its 'detection' and its 'solution' help to *create* the pressure under which child abuse professionals work. These encourage an atmosphere of 'crisis management' and 'split-second' decision-making that generates misjudgements and mistakes. To avoid getting 'locked into' this loop (which, by the way, these same professionals can recognize as precipitating child abuse when it happens in families!) requires an approach which allows people to stand back, to consider alternatives, to perceive 'the whole picture'. It also demands a preparedness to analyse and assess one's own actions and to see them not as one-off behaviours but as inputs which change whole ecologies in the social world.

For those of us who have had the luxury of being able to sit back and look at the current debate on child abuse from some sort of distance, it is patently clear that analyses of the issues are frequently shaped by *conflicting* models of and values about the social world – often ones so fundamentally different as to be likely to pass each other by like ships in the night. For example, the very notion of child abuse has quite contrasted meanings to those who approach it from:
– the 'social hygiene' standpoint of traditional social work;
– the 'feminist' perspective much evident in incest, rape and refuge work;

– the viewpoint of 'children's rights'.

By the same token, the appropriate responses in terms of social policy look far from the same to:

– those who see child abuse as a 'social problem';
– those who see it an issue about power and the exploitation of the powerless;
– those who see it as part of a far wider issue about the rights and entitlements of children in general and how these link in to other rights.

These are not the only perspectives on child abuse being voiced in the current debate, but they are ones which emerged with particular clarity in research we recently conducted.

How we conducted our research

We gave people sets of 80 statements about child abuse and asked them to sort these from 'strongest disagreement' to 'strongest agreement' into a grid, as shown in Figure 1.

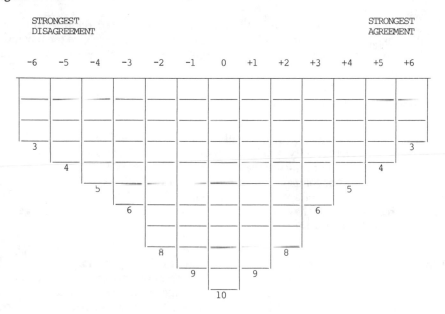

Figure 1. Q-sort response form

Using computer technology, we then looked for common patterns in the ways the statements were sorted out. Q method, as this procedure is called (see Brown (1980) for a full description) enables researchers to identify different 'accounts' or 'discourses' – whole viewpoints or ways of looking at a particular topic. Rather like a botanist interested in the diversity of plants that grow in a particular locality, the Q researcher aims to be a 'collector' (finding examples of accounts) rather than an 'enumerator' (counting up 'who thinks what').

For our study of accounts concerning child abuse we used two sets of 80 statements. One set (meanings) was focused on the concept of child abuse itself (e.g. 'There is nothing abusive about punishing young offenders'). The other set (social policy) covered different aspects of what we should do about child abuse (e.g.

'Everyone should be obliged, by law, to report child abuse if they suspect it'). Both sets of 80 items are included at the end of this chapter for reference (Appendices 1 and 2). We derived our statements from a variety of sources, which included interviews, statements in the press and on television, and academic books and journals. These two Q sets were sorted by a mixed pool of 56 people, some with a professional involvement in child abuse, some without. Rather like a well-chosen discussion group, the participants in this kind of study are selected not at random, but for their likely ability to give voice to whatever perspectives are current in society. They included people who reported themselves to be abuse victims and survivors, and others who labelled themselves as abusers.

Research using Q methodology allows differences in the accounts to be looked at in several ways. Firstly, the major points in each can be summarized to provide a kind of bird's-eye picture. Secondly, the accounts can be compared in terms of the contrast between reactions to particular statements. Thirdly, we can look at how people expressed themselves in terms of the comments they made about the statements they had sorted.

Let us examine first three of the accounts we uncovered relating to understandings of child abuse – although we found several more, these give the flavour of just how differently the people who took part in the study made sense of what 'child abuse' *is*.

Understandings of child abuse

Account 1
We live in a society which fundamentally fails to protect and properly care for the young and in which cruelty, exploitation and neglect of children is widespread. Adults, particularly men, misuse their power over the young and innocent, causing them serious emotional damage which persists into adult life. *All* adult–child sexual relationships are forms of abuse, and children seldom lie about being abused. We need to recognize just how vulnerable children are and to acknowledge our responsibility to protect them.

Account 2
What we see as child abuse needs to be looked at critically, children are not only abused by adults but by other children and by factors like poverty. While it may be tempting to blame child abuse for a wide range of immediate and long-term problems, conclusive evidence is usually lacking. We need to be equally cautious about claims that highly predictive 'risk factors' can enable us to identify where abuse is likely to occur. Child abuse is a *social* phenomenon not a 'disease' and we should not approach it using a medical model. Similarly, emotive language about 'innocent victims' can blind us to the fact that older children have a sexuality and even young children are capable of 'telling stories' about their experiences. At the same time, we need to recognize that adult power over children is universal, and with it the threat of abuse. Children's rights and a children's voice are much needed but we cannot stop all child abuse without creating a 'big brother' society which would harm children's later rights as adults.

Account 3
By now we have accumulated a great deal of case-experience about child abuse. We know the kinds of children most at risk, the family patterns that accompany a greater chance of abuse and the characteristics of abusers. Abuse is very emotionally damaging – not least because the abused may well work out their problems either through various mental or psychological symptoms or by becoming abusers themselves. Understanding abusers is quite possible through a psychodynamic

model and this same model can account for why mothers may collude in the sexual abuse of their children. Abuse needs to be seen in terms of the child's reactions and children's accusations should be believed.

To get a sense of how the summary accounts were built up and to 'bring them to life', let us now look at three of the statements in terms of how they were sorted and the comments people made about them. For each account we identified a few people whose sortings gave the clearest 'picture' and then we took an average of where they sorted each statement to in the grid (Figure 1). Each could be positioned anywhere between −6 (strongest disagreement) and +6 (strongest agreement). The first example shows the different ways in which the accounts regard adult–child sexual relationships. Their averaged positions were:

	Account		
	1	*2*	*3*
2. *All* adult–child sexual relationships are forms of child sexual abuse.	+6	−6	+1

Examples of the kinds of comments made were:
'I feel that children never have the knowledge or power to be able to freely consent to sexual relationships with adults.' (Account 1)
'Definitely not – for example this depends on legal definition of a child – is the 14- year-old husband of a 13-year-old woman (legal in some U.S. States I believe) abusing her? It's a matter of electing to do something – coercion and power play may be an abuse but that's another matter.' (Account 2)
'*All relationships are to an extent sexual.*' (Account 3)

Next, look at the way in which the three accounts responded to the idea of mother– child 'bonding':

	Account		
	1	*2*	*3*
18. If the natural bonding between a mother and her newborn baby is prevented or interfered with, the mother will be more likely to abuse her child	0	−5	+5

Example comments are:
'That has been suggested, but unless it occurs in 100% of the cases how can we know?' (Account 1)
'This is total crap, "natural bonding" is a nonsense.' (Account 2)
'Have read some research on this and think it is so.' (Account 3)

Finally, here are the differing reactions to the statement:

	Account		
	1	*2*	*3*
25. All children suffer from abuse from adults in the sense that the threat is always there.	+2	+5	−2

'*Seems a trifle sweeping as a statement*'. (Account 1)
'*Of course. This is how the typical British boys' school maintained "discipline" and built that wonderful "character" without which "Miss Whip Third Floor Correctional Training" would be out of a job!*' (Account 2)
'*Meaning?*' (Account 3)

These are only examples of what each of these three accounts is saying and these three accounts are by no means all the ways of looking at child abuse we found in our study. No doubt there are others still that we missed altogether. But it should be enough to establish the point that this is an area of real controversy. Quite simply, there is no social consensus or even 'expert' consensus over the way child abuse is understood.

Divergent accounts on social policy

What we should do about child abuse is just as widely disputed. Again, we will look at just three of the accounts that were identified in the research and will start with the summaries. While there were some areas of agreement (for example, that our response to child abuse is nothing to be proud about), once more strongly contrasting accounts emerged.

Account A

To tackle child abuse we need a fundamental change in social attitudes and a broad rethink about our social policies towards children in general. Children's basic rights need to be met and they need more power over their own lives and bodies. This may mean reducing the power of families and in particular of men. Abuse is a critical social and political problem and requires a lot more resources in treatment and in reseach, where good theory is sadly lacking.

Account B

Child abuse is one of many problems and injustices affecting our society. Of course we need to meet the rights of children and to strive to prevent their abuse, but not at *any* cost in terms of other civil rights and liberties. It is also important to ensure that our response to abused children does not abuse them further. Rather than seeking extra resources to expand current programmes and practices, we need a charter of children's rights and a commitment to empowering the young, whether they are identified as abused or not. We need political changes to establish a clear statement of our societal obligations to the young.

Account C

Child abuse is a serious social problem which cannot be tackled overnight. What we need are long-term policies based on existing knowledge and experience but with greatly increased training and resources. The powers of social/childcare workers should be increased and obligations to report abuse should take priority over other considerations. Equally, work in this area needs careful monitoring and control. The ideal is to help children *and* families *and* abusers themselves. We should not politicize child abuse policy and it is no good engaging in the scapegoating of men in general when looking for solutions.

Not surprisingly, these contrasting stands over policy are reflected in marked differences in reactions to particular propositions over action. First of all, this is shown by reactions to a statement about feminism:

	Account		
	A	B	C
30. The oppression of children by men needs to be tackled by feminist social policies.	+6	−1	−6

Examples of the comments on this statement were:
'*Clearly – but it's no use just blaming men – there needs to be critical insight into male sexuality and power.*' (Account A)
'*Feminism is a theory about women's rights and empowerment – these may but equally may not coincide with the rights and empowerment of the young.*' (Account B)
'*No – I find the views of the feminists too biased and would rather have a consensus of opinions.*' (Account C)
Reactions to securing specific rights for children in law differed like this:

	Account		
	A	B	C
49. To reduce child abuse we need to define and establish, in law, a charter of children's rights.	+2	+5	−3

This drew the following sorts of comments:
'*Yes – as "parents rights" without a framework of children's rights means that the status quo will be maintained.*' *(Account A)*
' *"Child abuse" is the abuse of children's human rights and until these have a firm basis in law and in social consciousness better lives for all children cannot be realized.*' *(Account B)*
'*No. What about NAYPIC [National Association for Young People in Care]? They are already doing work in this area.*' *(Account C)*

Finally, there were strong contrasts concerning the powers of professionals:

	Account		
	A	B	C
53. To reduce child abuse, social and childcare workers need more power and not less.	0	−2	+5

Typical comments here were:
'*Depends on what powers and how used.*' *(Account A)*
'*No they don't need more power, children do!*' *(Account B)*
'*Agreed. Power to remove abused children and enter property.*' *(Account C)*

Conclusion: diverse accounts of and for child abuse and why they may be 'in the best interests of the child'

Each of these accounts undoubtedly seems 'real' to the people who put it forward but considered *together* they are all just different 'accounts' – each with a story to tell. The challenge with which child abuse (like any other controversial issue) faces us is the need both to take action (which demands that we have 'made up our mind' about what is 'real') *and* the need to remain open-minded! We need to stay open-minded both in order to be able to negotiate with others who may see the issue differently and so that we can keep a check on ourselves. Having alternative viewpoints spelt out, seeing how each can so obviously carry conviction, is an important antidote to the dangers of single-mindedness.

The three accounts of child abuse and the three of child abuse policy on which we have concentrated here are competing alternatives for our attention. They come from contrasted experiences, trainings and concerns and, ultimately, they put forward differing views of what an ideal world should be like for the young.

Overall, viewpoints 1/A and 3/C respectively seem to capture the 'new wave' and 'traditional' professional approaches to abuse. The 'new wave' account focuses upon sexual abuse and sees abuse as a result of a misuse of power, concerns where feminist analyses have been influential (see chapter 2). Both in the view taken of abuse and in policies promoted, this stance is highly critical of our treatment of children in a strongly sex-role-differentiated society in which men hold most of the power. The traditional approach, by contrast, tends to regard child abuse as the cruelties and neglects which result from the problems and stresses (such as poverty and immaturity) that sap the abilities of parents to provide the good caregiving we can otherwise expect. The action needed, on this analysis, is an increase in resources and powers for child welfare work.

The perspective which comes from Accounts 2/B tended to be voiced by people less at the immediate, sharp-end of childcare work. It argues that 'declaring war' on 'social problems' may not only be ineffective (as it has been, say, over 'drug abuse'), but even produce more problems than it solves (as happened, say, over prohibition in the United States). These analyses lead in turn to a position over social policy which seeks a radically new approach, one which sees the pursuit of the well-being of *all* children as the place to start, rather than reacting to specific abuses themselves. Hence its emphasis on the pursuit of children's rights.

To claim any one of these perspectives (or indeed any other) as 'correct' in any ultimate sense is an act of faith not of knowledge. As we have tried to argue at the beginning of this chapter, faith that is not reflected upon and which is not subject to criticism runs the risk of crossing the boundary between concern and crusade. If you share our view that children should *both* be listened to better *and* be better cared for, that family life needs *both* support *and* to change, that power can be used for *good* as well as for *ill* then you may also share our view that understandings are tools to be used. For the crafting of better childhoods we need a well-stocked workshop of ideas and the personnel with the know-how about when and how to use them.

Appendix 1

1. A difficult baby (e.g. one that sleeps poorly, cries a lot or has a lot of feeding problems) is more likely to be abused.

2. *All* adult–child sexual relationships are forms of child sexual abuse.

3. There are certain ways of mistreating children that must be seen as 'child abuse', no matter where they happened, to what child, or by whom they were perpetrated.

4. A lot of times child abuse is not deliberate cruelty, but something that happens when an adult loses control and 'cannot stop themself'.

5. Government policies which condemn children to grow up in poverty should be seen as a form of child abuse.

6. High unemployment in a society increases the level of child abuse.

7. The dividing line between acceptable punishment and abuse is pretty clear-cut.

8. Child abuse is, in part at least, a consequence of the fact that children are denied any political voice.

9. People who abuse children are often 'working out' their own childhood anger and distress.

10. The power of men over women and children is an important factor in child abuse.

11. Many people who become abusers do so as a consequence of the abuse they themselves suffered in childhood.

12. The reported cases of child abuse are just the tip of the iceberg of the cruelty, exploitation and neglect to which children in our society are subjected.

13. However much they love them, the parent does not exist who has not been cruel to his or her children at some time or another.

14. Sexual abuse is more common in cultures which are prudish and sexually repressive than in those which are more open about sexuality.

15. What is – and what is not – child abuse can only be defined in terms of the *effect* upon the child.

16. Many abusing parents are too young for parenthood – either literally or emotionally.

17. An effective definition of child abuse must draw upon notions of the child's basic human rights.

18. If the natural bonding between a mother and her newborn baby is prevented or interfered with, the mother will be more likely to abuse her child.

19. Children very seldom make false accusations about sexual abuse.

20. Only a 'sick' minority have sexual feelings towards children.

21. Child abusers are more likely than non-abusers to have unrealistic expectations of the child's ability or understanding.

22. Some abused children seem to get 'hooked' on the thrill of violence.

23. Child abuse will remain a major problem so long as children are viewed as the 'private property' of those who care for them.

24. The use of a cane or a strap in schools is a form of institutionalized child abuse.

25. All children suffer from abuse from adults in the sense that the threat of it is always there.

26. The common denominator of all forms of child abuse is that it makes children feel bad and worthless.

27. All oppressed groups are at risk of being treated as sexual objects by those in power – children are no exception to this rule.

28. For all our current concern about child abuse, there has never been a better time than the present to be a child.

29. There's a lot of clap-trap spoken about child abuse.

30. Over child abuse there is a certain level of risk we have to run if we are to live in a free society.

31. A truly moral definition of child abuse looks to the treatment and conditions of all the world's children.

32. Some forms of child abuse are the product of a biological drive to promote the 'survival of the fittest'.

33. Ultimately, the recognition of child abuse is a task for *medical* diagnosis.

34. I have a sneaking sympathy with those prisoners who 'take the law into their own hands' with convicted child abusers.

35. Homosexual men are more likely than heterosexual men to sexually abuse children.

36. Certain children, for reasons that we do not fully understand, seem to develop styles of behaviour that provoke abuse.

37. The reasons for the sexual abuse of children are very different from the reasons why people physically abuse or neglect them.

38. The emotional damage caused by child abuse is often far worse than any physical hurt or injury.

39. Abusing children is a psychiatric disorder which requires medical or psychological treatment.

40. The 'sexual liberation' of the 1960s seems to have given people the idea that 'anything goes' sexually – even abusing children.

41. Whatever name we may call the adult client of a 14-year-old prostitute, 'child abuser' is not the right one.

42. The failure adequately to sex educate the present generation of parents is a factor in the sexual abuse we see today.

43. Inside every child abuser is an angry, frightened, hurting 'child' crying out for help.

44. Forcing young people into potentially dangerous sports and exercises is a form of physical abuse.

45. I suspect that the sexual abuse of animals and the sexual abuse of young children have very similar explanations.

46. Children often suffer more through being taken away from their families than through the abuse itself.

47. Being medically examined for sexual abuse can be a positive, therapeutic experience for the child concerned.

48. Parents have a duty to protect their teenage sons and daughters from their own foolishness and lack of experience, and a right to use reasonable punishments so to do.

49. The present social climate over 'child abuse' is akin to a witchhunt in which large numbers of innocent people are bound to be wrongly accused, persecuted and punished.

50. Child abuse is not so much a matter of a few cruel or inadequate parents mistreating individual children, as it is a reflection of a more fundamental disorder in which we, as a society, fail the young.

51. Children are sexual beings, aware of the power of their sexuality over others.

52. Publicity about child abuse cases, particularly those with a sexual element, tends to stimulate and provoke more abuse.

53. Societies that 'live close to nature' may not enjoy some of the so-called 'benefits' of modern civilization, but neither do they have the problem of child abuse.

54. A consumer society that encourages little girls to buy make-up, uses pubescent girls to advertise jeans, and offers role models like 'Madonna' stimulates the sexual abuse of girl children.

55. There is nothing abusive about punishing young offenders.

56. The kinds of education programmes designed to sensitize little children to sexual abuse, instead of protecting them may simply destroy their childhood innocence.

57. Governments find it more convenient to 'blame the individual' for child abuse than to find the resources to tackle the root causes of the problem.

58. Sexual abuse is more insidious in its effects than simple physical cruelty, because there can be, for the child, pleasure mixed with the pain.

59. Fundamentally all forms of child abuse come down to the misuse of adult power over children.

60. Many forms of mental illness and disturbance in adult life, from anorexia to depression, have their roots in abusive experiences in childhood.

61. In all our soul-searching about 'child abuse' we must not forget that a great deal of the suffering that children experience is at the hands of *other children*.

62. Child sexual abuse would have a very different meaning in a society where it was considered natural and normal for adults and children to share sexual enjoyment.

63. It is perfectly possible to have a society in which children are never abused.

64. Child abuse is a symptom of a decline in moral values.

65. In child abuse, as for so many other social problems, alcohol abuse has a lot to answer for.

66. Try as I may, I find it impossible to understand why some people abuse children.

67. Exposure to pornographic maga-

zines and videos makes people more likely to sexually abuse children.

68. The term 'child abuse' should not be used as an euphemism for acts like rape, buggery, assault and murder.

69. Women who put their own needs and wishes before those of their families have a lot to answer for in terms of child abuse.

70. The reasons why step-parents abuse children are no different from the reasons why biological parents abuse.

71. We should always assume that the child is entirely blameless in cases of sexual abuse.

72. Those who offer 12- and 13-year-olds alcohol or cigarettes are abusing them.

73. However worthy the intentions of people like Esther Rantzen, it is wrong to turn child abuse into entertainment.

74. Mothers sometimes collude with the sexual abuse of their children, or conveniently 'turn a blind eye'.

75. I am deeply suspicious of the motives of some self-styled experts in child abuse.

76. All children are entitled to a proper share of our nation's wealth. To deprive them of this is to abuse them.

77. Fathers who have intimately cared for their children since babyhood – bathed them, fed them and changed them – are less likely to sexually abuse them than fathers who have had a more distant relationship.

78. Different cultures have different ways of managing children's behaviour. What may be abusive in one culture may be perfectly normal and acceptable behaviour in another.

79. The rich and influential can abuse their children with impunity – who ever heard of a judge or doctor having their children snatched away from them?

80. Making parents frightened of being physically close to their children is not a way of reducing the risk of sexual abuse, it *is* a form of abuse!

Appendix 2
1. We need to approach the problem of child abuse in as rational and scientific a way as possible.

2. More than anything, to reduce child abuse we need a fundamental change in social attitudes.

3. Everybody should be obliged, by law, to report child abuse if they suspect it.

4. Professionals working with child abuse should be 'positively vetted' to ensure that nobody with a 'skeleton in the cupboard' is allowed to work in this sensitive area.

5. We need to put more resources into research on the prevention of child abuse.

6. Taking an abused child 'into care' is better seen as stemming from inadequacies in our welfare safety net than in the families concerned.

7. We need to put more resources into the treatment and counselling of abused children.

8. The more difficult we make access to abortion, the more child abuse will result.

9. Where acts of child abuse are *criminal* acts like murder, rape and assault, they should be treated as such.

10. Unless we are prepared to live in a 'big brother' society, some children will inevitably have to die each year as the cost of our freedom.

11. Our country has an obligation to ensure that basic standards of care, fair treatment and reasonable life-opportunities are provided for all its children.

12. People like doctors, priests and lawyers must be prepared to share information about child abuse with other professionals, even if this means breaking rules about confidentiality.

13. We should be prepared to censor out from books, films, newspapers, radio and television any material which might stimulate potential child abusers.

14. Our policies about child abuse should not undermine the general principle that parents should decide what is best for their children.

15. We need to put more resources into the treatment and counselling of abusers.

16. Parentcraft should be a compulsory part of the schooling of every child, both girls *and* boys.

17. Parents wrongly accused of child abuse should be entitled to adequate compensation to enable them to rebuild their families and their lives.

18. Our present policies over child abuse have the effect of punishing the young for the failings of their families and society in general.

19. The courts are the right place to decide on issues to do with the future of abused children.

20. Abused children who wish to stay with their families should *not* be forced to be separated from them.

21. Child abuse could be reduced by paying an adequate state benefit to anyone doing the job of bringing up a child.

22. We should keep politics out of the battle against child abuse.

23. Trying to understand why abusers offend is more likely to help us reduce child abuse than is punishing them.

24. The responsibility for reducing child abuse lies more with families than it does with the state.

25. Children will continue to be abused in large numbers until the fundamental injustices in society are tackled.

26. A policy of 'every child a wanted child' would do a lot to reduce child abuse.

27. Child abuse should be reduced if mothers of young children were discouraged from working outside the home.

28. Policy over child abuse needs to accept that children are far tougher and more resilient than is generally recognized.

29. The medical diagnosis of abuse should never be based on the assessment of just one doctor.

30. The oppression of children by men needs to be tackled by feminist social policies.

31. For their own good as well as that of society, those convicted of serious sexual abuse should be surgically treated to prevent them ever being able to perpetrate such abuse again.

32. Social policy about child abuse needs to recognize the rights of young gays to be properly informed about homosexual identities and lifestyles.

33. To tackle child abuse we should give every child, as of right, access to a 'second family' to whom they can turn in times of trouble.

34. One way of reducing child abuse would be to make the payment of 'family allowance' conditional on the child

being periodically examined by a doctor or health visitor.

35. We need to put more resources into research on the causes of child abuse.

36. We could do a lot to reduce child abuse by reasserting the virtues of traditional family life.

37. Current practice over child abuse reflects more the concerns of social workers and other professionals to avoid public criticism than the desire to do what is best for children.

38. It is worse than useless to have initiatives like 'ChildLine' unless there are the resources to meet the expectations they raise.

39. Resources should be allocated to make psychological counselling and therapy freely available on the NHS to help those adults who were abused as children.

40. Current social policy over child abuse has neither a good theory, nor a body of good evidence to guide it.

41. Our social policy needs to define child abuse in terms of infringements of children's human rights.

42. To reduce child abuse we need to re-examine the expectation that families can be uprooted simply beause Dad's job requires it.

43. We should abolish some categories of 'child sexual abuse' by modifying certain of our laws (e.g. the 'age of consent').

44. If state benefits were effectively targeted on those families who really need help, we could significantly decrease the number of children abused.

45. All children should receive a compulsory school medical examination each year that is sufficiently thorough to detect sexual as well as physical abuse.

46. There are many more pressing problems facing the United Kingdom today than that of child abuse.

47. Children should be given every opportunity to learn that their bodies are their own property, and nobody has a right to touch them in ways they don't like.

48. To hope that a single policy can reduce all kinds of child abuse is as pointless as expecting a single 'magic bullet' to cure a boil, a broken leg and a 'breakdown'.

49. To reduce child abuse we need to define and establish, in law, a charter of children's rights.

50. A major key to improving the way we tackle child abuse is to ensure that everybody who works in this area is properly trained.

51. Child abuse would be better managed if we had a single agency in charge, rather than expecting professionals from different agencies (like police, health visitors and social workers) to work together.

52. Any changes we make in child abuse policy must build in proper safeguards against wrongful and even malicious accusations.

53. To reduce child abuse, social and childcare workers need more power and not less.

54. We should strive to re-educate parents from immigrant cultures who resort to alien forms of severe punishment and unacceptable levels of control of their children.

55. To help to prevent child abuse, nursery, creche and playgroup facilities should be much more freely available.

56. The BBC and IBA should use every opportunity to achieve a massive public campaign of education about child abuse.

57. It will never be possible to identify 'high risk families' with sufficient precision to prevent child abuse.

58. Our efforts to tackle child abuse would be more effective if we transferred resources from social services to specialist agencies like the NSPCC.

59. Adequate, appropriate sex education is an important contribution in the fight against child sexual abuse.

60. Our policies about child abuse need to strike the right balance between protecting children and preserving family privacy.

61. Public health campaigns (e.g. against smoking and drunken driving) show us the way to reduce child abuse and to make it even more socially unacceptable.

62. Increasing the likelihood of detection and the imposition of the severest punishment on conviction are the surest means to stamp out child abuse.

63. Local authorities should provide 'babysitters' for harassed families before a potential crisis, in much the same way they provide 'home helps' to enable the elderly and disabled to cope.

64. The best way to reduce child abuse is to increase children's power over their own lives.

65. Social workers would be able to do more about problems like child abuse if they were enabled by law to become a true profession like doctors and lawyers.

66. Parents who abuse their children have shown they are not fit to be parents. Their children should be adopted by people who will love and care for them properly.

67. We will not reduce child abuse in society until men are taught to love and care for children to the same extent as are women.

68. We should set up a register of child *abusers*, and implement a system that will keep track of them at all times.

69. To reduce child abuse, the abortion of female foetuses should be freely available to women from cultural groups which value sons rather than daughters.

70. There is little that can be achieved in the short term to reduce the amount of child abuse going on. The best new social policies can hope to do is to make a better job of detection and providing help after the event.

71. Psychiatry has an important contribution to make to our policies on child abuse.

72. We need to move away from a situation in which abused children face further experiences of yet more adults forcing them to do things they don't want to do.

73. Our policies over child abuse need to be developed in the context of a broad rethink about our social policies over children in general.

74. Professionals working in the area of child abuse should receive more training about racial and cultural differences in childrearing and systems of disciplining children.

75. We don't need a policy about child abuse, but rather a policy to tackle the problems of abuse towards all vulnerable groups including older people and the physically and mentally handicapped.

76. Resources should be found to

develop drugs to control people's tendencies to abuse children.

77. We will not reduce child abuse in society until we have reduced the power of men over women and children.

78. The law should be changed to ensure that the child's views and wishes (e.g. about medical examination) are listened to and acted upon throughout the investigation of child abuse, and in any subsequent decision-making.

79. Doing something about the over-prescription of tranquillizers would make a contribution to reducing child abuse.

80. Britain can be proud of its response to the problem of child abuse.

FURTHER READING
Our forthcoming book,
STAINTON ROGERS, R. and STAINTON ROGERS W. *Stories of Childhood: Shifting Agendas in Child Concern* Harvester Wheatsheaf, Hemel Hempstead, (1992) addresses a much broader agenda than does this chapter. In it we explore the ways in which 'child concern' has been historically constituted, and is culturally and socially located. We look at some of the ways this has influenced child welfare practice.

SECTION TWO

SOCIAL AND CULTURAL CONTEXTS

5 THE DEMANDS OF PARENTING*

Gillian Pugh and Erica De'Ath

The tasks and skills of parenting

Many of the tasks traditionally inherent in family life, such as teaching specific skills, preparing for a trade, and passing on cultural and social norms, are now shared with other groups, notably schools and many of the influences shared with other groups, notably the peer group. Despite this, the family still provides the main basis for bringing up succeeding generations of children, and it still falls to parents to help children develop into complete adults and take their place in the wider world outside the home. In outlining some of the conditions which offer parents and children emotional security, learning opportunities and a system of values which provides for a creative relationship with society at large, Joan Cooper (DHSS, 1974a) suggests that a family home may be thought of as functioning effectively when it:

- offers adequate shelter, space, food, income and the basic amenities which enable the adults to perform their marital, childrearing and citizenship roles without incurring so much stress that anxiety inhibits a confident and positive performance;
- secures the physical care, safety and healthy development of children either through its own resources or through the competent use of specialised help and services;
- acknowledges its task of socialising children, encouraging their personal development and abilities, guiding their behaviour and interests and informing their attitudes and values;
- offers the experience of warm, loving, intimate and consistently dependable relationships;
- assures the mother of support and understanding, particularly during the early childrearing period, and provides the child with a male/father/husband model which continues to remain important through adolescence;
- offers children (2–6 years) an experience of group life, so extending their social relationships, their awarenesss of others and intellectual development;
- responds to children's curiosity with affection and reasoned explanations, and respects children through all developmental stages as persons in their own right, so securing affection and respect for others within the family circle and wider social network;
- co-operates with school, values educational and learning opportunities and encourages exploration and a widening of experience;

* The material contained in this chapter is edited from 'Parenting in the 80s', in PUGH, G. AND DE'ATH, E. *The Needs of Parents*, Macmillan Education, Basingstoke (1985). © National Children's Bureau, 1984.

- supports adolescents physically and emotionally while they are achieving relative independence of the family, personal identity, sexual maturity, a work-role, relationships within society and the testing out of values and ideologies;
- provides a fall-back supportive system for the young marrieds during their child-bearing period. (DHSS, 1974a)

What do parents require if they are to perform their parenting tasks as well as possible? Work with parents suggests there are four main areas in which support and guidance may be needed.

The first is what Rutter (DHSS, 1974a) has called '**permitting circumstances**' or necessary life opportunities and facilities. The interaction that takes place between economic, social and educational deprivation is a complex one, but many parents find it extremely difficult to bring up their children when basic personal and family needs are not taken care of first. As the British Association of Social Workers said in its submission to the 1973 DHSS consultations:

> When a family is suffering multiple deprivation . . . then intervention aimed at only one of the factors at work is unlikely to be successful. It cannot offset the downward spiral. There is a much better chance of helping families to mend defective emotional relationships and to escape from social isolation if at the same time they can be cushioned against money problems. (DHSS, 1974b)

Margaret Harrison points out from her experience of 'Home-Start' that some parents may themselves need parenting before they can respond to the needs of their own children (Harrison, 1982). Parents who as children were brought up in care, or who experienced inadequate parenting, may have unrealistic expectations of an idyllic family life and it is 'an insensitive farce' to try to promote better verbal or physical contact with a child or the need for positive reinforcement before first working with some of the parents' personal and social problems.

Second, parents require **information and knowledge** about sources of help within the community; about welfare rights and benefits; about common childhood ailments and how to cope with accidents; and perhaps most important of all, about human health and development and particularly what to expect at the different stages of child development and what part parents might play. Although professionals working with families and the many child-care books on the shelves testify to the extent of current knowledge on the different stages of development, the DHSS consultations on preparation for parenthood in 1973, suggested that there was still a surprising amount of ignorance among parents of all social classes about what can be expected of children of different ages and what their real needs are (DHSS, 1974b). In a survey undertaken by the authors in association with *Mother* magazine, in answer to the question 'with which of the following would you most like help now that you are parents?' the majority of both mothers and fathers put 'stages of development' at the top of their list, with behavioural problems coming second. Unrealistic expectations of behaviour at each age and stage is frequently a major source of frustration, anger and disappointment and is often a key factor in cases of child abuse (Franklin, 1977; Gorell-Barnes, 1979).

A better understanding of children's development must include awareness of social and emotional factors, as well as physical and intellectual. In *The Needs of Children*, commissioned as a response to the DHSS discussions, Mia Pringle suggests that children have four basic emotional needs which have to be met if they are to grow from helpless infancy to mature adulthood: the need for love and security; for new experiences; for praise and recognition; and for responsibility. She argues that we do now know enough about children's all-round development to take action:

If even half of what we know were accepted with feeling and applied with understanding by all who have the care of children, then the revolution brought about in children's physical health in the past forty years might well be matched by a similar change in their psychological well-being. (Pringle, 1975)

Third, parents need certain **skills**, many of them acquired over a life-time. These will include a core of social skills which all adults need if they are to function adequately, for example:

- the ability to love and undertake relationships, to care, to support and nurture other people, and to be sensitive to their needs;
- flexibility of mind and thinking, the ability to respond and to adapt to changing needs and demands;
- consistency of attitudes and behaviour, a reliable and dependable behaviour that provides a stable and secure environment where responses can be anticipated and rules are clear;
- the ability to communicate, through active listening, giving appropriate non-verbal and verbal messages, reflecting on feelings and negotiating;
- the ability to make decisions and to accept responsibility for them;
- the ability to cope with stress and deal with conflict;
- the ability to apply the knowledge and information, for a theory on how to cope with temper tantrums is no use unless it can be put into action.

They will also include practical skills such as those required to provide a home, manage the family's finances, produce a balanced diet and combine work with family life.

Fourth, parents needs **understanding of themselves** as parents and as people, and of their values and of how these affect the way in which children are brought up. The emphasis on understanding and responding to children's needs has sometimes obscured the fact that parents have their own needs for personal development and fulfilment. These needs have to be understood too, and the almost inevitable conflicts of interest within a family group faced up to and resolved.

Factors affecting the way parents bring up their children

These tasks and skills have to be examined in the light of the many constraints and influences within families, for the ways in which parents bring up their children cannot be seen in a vacuum. What are these factors? Some are personal and family characteristics, whilst others reflect social and environmental constraints.

Assumptions about the effect of childhood experience on one's own ability to parent were central to the thinking behind the DHSS consultations in 1973, when Sir Keith Joseph suggested that disadvantage was transmitted from one generation of a family to the next, and argued that more preparation for parenthood might help to break this cycle of deprivation (DHSS, 1974a and 1974b). The consultations themselves and Rutter's subsequent review of the research (Rutter and Madge, 1976) showed that whilst there are likely to be *indirect* effects on parenting behaviour through influences on personality development, and the acquisition of social values and attitudes, there was little systematic information on connections between personal childhood experiences and methods of bringing up one's own children. Indeed, such links as could be found tended to illustrate the point that many parents deliberately wanted to avoid doing to their children what they had gone through when young themselves. The factor most consistently associated with happiness, stability and satisfaction in marriage was the quality of their own parents' marriage. There is however, a much stronger inter-generational link with abnormal parenting. A high proportion of parents who abuse their children have experienced serious neglect and abuse in their own childhood, and mothers who have been separated from their own parents during childhood have been found to have marital problems and difficulties in child rearing (Frommer and O'Shea, 1973). Rutter (1972) also makes the point that a child's ability to form good inter-personal relationships in adulthood may be based upon bonds that he forms in the first three years of his life.

The style of parenting will also vary according to whether mother or father is the chief care-giver. Although traditionally parenting has tended to be synonymous with mothering, with the father's role seen principally as supportive and fairly distant, men are now spending more time with their children. One of the chief influences has undoubtedly been the shifting balance between the worlds of home and work as women increasingly seek to combine a job outside the home with bringing up a family, and rising unemployment keeps many men at home during the day. There is no reason why women should continue to bear the principal responsibility for their children's upbringing. Even Spock, in the latest edition of *Baby and Child Care* (1979), introduces a new section on 'The father as parent' in which he states:

> There is no reason why fathers shouldn't be able to do these jobs [home and child care] as well as mothers, and contribute equally to the children's security and development . . . It will be a great day when fathers consider the care of their children to be as important to them as their jobs and careers.

Although it has become fashionable to talk about role reversal and shared parenting, the increasing number of research studies into fatherhood show that although fathers' involvement with their children has increased (Beail, 1982; McKee, 1982), the majority of fathers do still principally see themselves in terms of their work first and their families second, while even women who work full-time see their primary responsibility as being to their families. Whilst most men do regard marriage and babies as an inextricable part of their adult career patterns (McKee and O'Brien, 1982) the development of gender identity and expectations regarding traditional roles are still deeply ingrained.

The quality of the relationship between the parents and their supportiveness to each other as parents are particularly important. The reason for having children will also affect the way in which these children are brought up, particularly when it is related to this relationship. A child can be seen as a symbol of unity or disunity, conceived to demonstrate love, to provide a common interest, to 'complete' a marriage or to end a disagreement, to 'save' a marriage, to tie a husband down or keep a wife at home, or to increase distance in the partnership. Reasons given by parents for having children often focus on what they hope the baby will give them, rather than what they will provide for the child (Hoffman and Hoffman, 1973; La Rossa, 1977).

Parents will need to balance their own needs for personal fulfilment as adults with those of their children, a potential conflict which has not always been recognised and certainly not resolved amidst the child-centred values of contemporary society.

In recent years we have also begun to accept the notion that children influence and shape parents' behaviour right from the day of birth, and that even small babies have an inborn ability to interact with others. Parents are often surprised to find how different each child in the family is and how differently they feel towards them, and studies have shown that parents' responses differ according to whether the child is a boy or a girl, and where he or she comes in the family (Rutter and Mage, 1976; Beail and McGuire, 1982).

The parents' social class is another determinant, as is so well illustrated by the Newsons' longitudinal study of child-rearing in Nottingham. The involvement of fathers, for example, or attitudes towards breast- and bottle-feeding showed considerable differences between the social classes. Perhaps the most marked contrast was in different styles of disciplining seven-year-olds (Newson and Newson, 1976) where the higher social groups used highly verbal democratically-based means of control, while the unskilled group used highly authoritarian and mainly non-verbal means of control, using words to threaten and 'bamboozle' the child rather than help him understand. These two styles, they argue, were adapted to their social position: privileged children are equipped to use the system, the disadvantaged children expect and get nothing. 'The child in the lowest social bracket has everything stacked against him, including his parents' principles of child upbringing.'

Different ethnic and cultural backgrounds will be an important influence on how children are brought up. There are now about three million immigrants and immigrant-descended people in Britain, and whilst some have been assimilated, others have remained culturally distinct, with their children being brought up in two sometimes conflicting cultures. In the Asian community, for example, arranged marriages are still a strong part of the cultural and religious tradition and can present emotional, economic and social dilemmas for young girls born and educated in this country who do not want to marry young, and, in opposition to their parents, may want to pursue their education and a career.

Social and environmental factors are also crucial determinants of parenting styles. We have looked at the 'permitting circumstances' which are essential to good parenting and at the complex interaction between economic, social, educational and emotional deprivation. Whether one parent has a job; who is caring for the children if both parents are working, and the adequacy of that care; the housing conditions and financial position; whether family and friends are near enough for regular contact; the strength of community support; the extent of isolation – all these factors have a bearing on how parents manage. The Newsons' study of mothers of one-year-old children in Nottingham illustrated how basic differences in living conditions can affect the attitudes and methods of infant-care and child-rearing: 'Any woman who has an automatic washing machine will testify to the dramatic effect it has upon her ability to show equanimity when her toddler continues to wet nappy after nappy; the mother who has to wash everything by hand, in water she has heated on top of the kitchen stove, is likely to be far more emotionally involved in toilet-training' (Newson and Newson, 1963). While fewer mothers today have to heat water on the stove, many families without washing machines live on isolated housing estates with no access to launderette facilities. They are also likely to be living very close to neighbours and thin council house walls will affect both the general irritability of the mother and whether and for how long baby is left to cry.

It is evident that the number of variables involved within the relationship of even one parent and child militate against an exact definition of a 'good parent' and it is neither possible – nor desirable – to produce a blueprint. We could all make a list of qualities and our lists would all be different. We might include sensitivity, empathy, stamina, patience, tolerance, persistence, self-control and a sense of humour, and the various social skills already mentioned. One study which attempted to identify what qualities were present in optimally-functioning families concluded that there was no right way or one way of parenting. Rather, there was an inter-relationship of a number of variables: leadership was provided by a clear parental coalition, power was not exercised in an authoritarian way, children had opinions that were considered and negotiation was common. Communication was clear, differences were tolerated, there were high levels of personal autonomy and an acceptance of personal responsibility for each individual's own feelings, thoughts and actions. In their conclusion the authors state 'that the skills in relating and

communication which the optimal family demonstrated are teachable and learnable'
(Lewis *et al.*, 1976).

FURTHER READING

These themes are further developed in De'ATH, E. 'Families and Children' pp 30–54
in *Child Care Research, Policy and Practice*, BARBARA KAHAN (ed.) Hodder and
Stoughton, London; (1989)

6 SETTING BASIC STANDARDS*

Rachel Calam and Cristina Franchi

Fundamental to the process of decision making about maltreated children should be a basic assumption that children have certain essential needs and rights. In this chapter, we talk a little about a longitudinal research project on abused children that we have conducted, and, using the experience that we gathered during this time, together with our knowledge of child development, make recommendations for certain basic standards which should be central in considering the needs of the child.

The observations contained here are based on our experience working as research psychologists at a Family Centre which dealt exclusively with the families of children who had been physically or emotionally abused, neglected, or who were failing to thrive. We were invited into the Family Centre with the aim of providing additional information on the families to that which had already been obtained through the usual professional channels. Each of the children had been placed on the National Society for the Prevention of Cruelty to Children (NSPCC) Child Protection Register as cases or siblings of cases of non-accidental injury (NAI) or suspected NAI.

In all, we were able to collect data on eleven 3- and 4-year-old children, from nine families. Because of the comparatively long time base of our research, we were able to collect information on some families over a two-year period, picking up younger siblings as they entered the age-range of our study.

The objective of the Family Centre was to provide a warm atmosphere of re-parenting for all: for the mothers, in the hope of making up for the emotional poverty that many had suffered throughout their lives, and for the children, so that they might be able to develop in a loving atmosphere, in which emotional damage arising from their home environment might be ameliorated.

We made formal observations of the mothers and their children interacting at lunch-times, and made extensive observations of the children at play together. We also interviewed the mothers about home life. We were able to collect a great deal of information through less formal means, being in the position of 'fly on the wall' at the Family Centre during the mothers' conversations about their children and family life, and staff discussions of their hopes and fears.

In getting to know the families we were struck by many aspects of the children's lives which in our opinion might be expected to cause emotional, behavioural or developmental problems at some time. Protected to a large extent from physical harm, the children appeared to show behaviour that indicated that aspects of home

---

* The material contained in this chapter is excerpted from Calam, R. and Franchi, C., *Child Abuse and its Consequences: Observational Approaches* (1987), and appears by kind permission of Cambridge University Press.

life were continuing to exert a deleterious effect on their behaviour and development. Hence, physical protection alone was not sufficient.

Each morning the children ran from the taxi into the arms of the nursery staff, and fell into the daily routine of the Family Centre. They played indoors or out, depending on the weather, and superficially appeared to be well cushioned from the darker aspects of their lives. To visitors making a quick tour of the Family Centre, a peep into the playroom showed a happy group of busy children. Closer observation revealed that much of this was attributable to the resourcefulness of the nursery staff, who kept the children occupied at all times, often with the clear intention of avoiding fights. Systematic observation revealed yet more problems that individual children were attempting to cope with. Keith rode round on a bicycle, apparently happily occupied, but observation revealed that this was almost at the level of a compulsion, and associated with anxious monitoring of the environment. Alan was adept at sneaking up to staff without being noticed, so that he could monitor their behaviour. Carl often guarded his little brother to the exclusion of any form of play.

In observing the children at play, we noted some specific aspects of their behaviour that indicated possible problems. Most of the children spent a considerable percentage of their time in the nursery not playing; for several, the emotional need to be cuddled and held by staff took precedence over play activity. Other children shunned adults, or actively resisted attempts to show them interest or affection. Such emotional needs and behaviours may have precluded the ability to experiment and play, or the learning through contact with adults essential to development. The children rarely played games with rules; the seeds of this organised form of play are sown in the development of consistent and fair two-way exchanges between adults and children, and it appears that these abused children had limited experience of such interactions.

Fantasy play, so fundamental to the exploration of possibilities and alternative ways of seeing the world, was almost non-existent among these children. Again, this may well reflect the emotional limitations of the children's home lives and the lack of shared creative play between parent and child. In these subtle ways the emotional environment of the family had its effects on the child's behaviour and interactions, development, and potential for the future. The child's ability to interact with others in turn shapes his or her ability to learn from the world. The child who has come to put up barriers closes off possible areas of interaction and learning.

The children's interactions with their mothers were confined to lunch-times, when the majority of mothers showed very limited amounts of interaction with their children. The mothers generally relinquished care of their children to the nursery staff, despite efforts to the contrary, and showed little interest or involvement with their children.

Abusing families present with many different problems, and the children may express the effects of their experiences in disturbed and difficult behaviour. Many of the children we studied were showing aggressive, hostile and overtly deviant behaviour, while others were quiet, withdrawn, or prone to watchful behaviour. In the children we studied severity of injury was not the major determinant of the degree of disturbance that they showed; the family environment that they were continuing to experience was likely to play a far more significant part.

The way in which child abuse is managed depends upon the definitions in use, and it would appear that although current limited definitions of child abuse go a long way towards ensuring the physical safety of the child, these may blind professionals to a wider range of problems experienced by family members, and to continuing rejection and neglect of the child. For therapeutic purposes a broader definition of abuse would be more helpful, and this must be based on a set of expectations on the behalf of professionals that the child is in an environment in which certain needs are being met. It cannot be assumed that the provision of a safe daytime environment for the child and support for the mother is enough to ensure that the child will develop appropriately. We have demonstrated that observation of the child may yield a great deal of information which can be used therapeutically, particularly if the child is observed interacting with his or her parents.

Studies have concluded repeatedly that the environment in which the child is growing up is likely to have a greater effect than the injury itself, and attempts have been made to take a wider perspective on the kinds of family problems involved. The history of the area of child abuse, however, makes it probable that attempts will be made to conceptualise other forms of abuse in the same way that physical abuse has been, with parallel attempts to develop definitions that encapsulate its nature and allow intervention. The study of sexual abuse and help for families where this form of abuse has occurred – an area where at present rapid developments are taking place – is undergoing the same process. Emotional abuse is a yet more difficult, diffuse concept, and thus considerably more difficult to develop adequate definitions for; arguably, the task is too difficult, and practitioners need instead to find other ways of thinking about emotional abuse.

In attempting to come to terms with the emotional abuse of children we need to examine the experience of living together for the families of the children for whom we are concerned. Kellmer Pringle (1974) outlines four basic needs of children: (1) the need for love and security, (2) the need for new experiences, (3) the need for praise and recognition, and (4) the need for responsibility. Here, we set out seven very basic rights, some of which overlap with Kellmer Pringle's. Our aim in doing so is to point out essential rights of the child, and to set these in the context of problems experienced by the families we worked with. These rights are: to be fed, to be clean, to play, to be safe, to be secure, to be valued, and to be allowed to be a child.

1 The right to be fed

People working with young children need to be aware that an underweight unhealthy-looking child may be in danger. A child may be receiving an inadequate diet as a result of lack of money, parental ignorance of nutrition or through other feeding problems. A parent may be withholding food inappropriately as a punishment, or may expect a child to feed him or herself when he or she is unable to do so. Mealtimes may be a source of tension between parent and child.

2 The right to be clean

It requires constant effort to keep young children completely clean; whilst mothers vary greatly in their tolerance of grubbiness, certain basic standards need to be met. The child whose nappy is not changed for days is not receiving an adequate standard of care. A mother may see a dirty nappy as a sign of naughtiness, or may not want to be bothered changing the child. Professionals need to ensure that parents have the basic materials and resources to keep their children clean. A parent who sees a dirtied nappy as a deliberate act of provocation needs help.

3 The right to play

Play is the 'work' of the child. From the beginning, children need to be talked to, picked up and encouraged to explore their environment. Children cannot develop without stimulation, and at first, adult caretakers are their most important source of stimulation. It is not enough to give children toys and expect them to play with them. A child can develop without toys – indeed, playthings can be improvized from many household items – but a child cannot develop without social interaction. An example of this is Eddie, who did not know his own name because his mother never spoke to him. Professionals need a knowledge of the norms of child development so that they can recognise children who are not developing at an appropriate rate.

Certainly, there are differences between children, but most children develop within certain broad parameters: for example, one would expect a 3-year-old to be talking. A child who sits passively in a corner during a home visit by a professional, not making any sounds and not seeking any attention from his or her parents, should not necessarily be perceived as a 'good' or happy child. Children have the right to grow and develop appropriately, and this entails a degree of mess and noise.

4 The right to be safe
Children need to be kept safe in a physical sense, protected from dangers in the environment that they cannot yet understand. This involves, for example, parents making their home safe through the use of fireguards, putting dangerous objects, drugs or household chemicals out of the way, and teaching the child about risks, at an appropriate age and in an appropriate way. Katherine 'taught' Kevin 'not to mess with the fire' by holding him against it. This is inappropriate teaching which amounts to abuse. The same is true of burning a young child with matches to teach him or her not to play with them. Similarly, expecting a young child to remember a rule after only one telling is inadequate teaching.

A child should be safe from physical assault. Professionals need to be aware that the use of continual physical punishment can easily deteriorate into habitual physical abuse. They must respond clearly on this issue and be able to present workable alternatives to parents.

A child should also be safe from sexual assault. Most sexual abuse of children occurs within the family and until recently its incidence was grossly underestimated. Professional and concerned adults need to be alert to the possibility of sexual abuse. No clues that the child's or adult's behaviour may give should be ignored, and children must have the means to seek help (Elliott, 1985). A child who cannot speak about his or her experiences can be helped through the use of dolls and play therapy techniques. Glasgow (1987) provides useful information on practical responses to the suspicion of sexual abuse.

5 The right to be secure
A child should be safe from fear: fear of violence, sexual abuse, or other assaults from others in his or her social world. It must be remembered that where one parent is abusing a child, the other parent is failing to protect that child. A child who lives in fear cannot be free to explore the world without constraint, and thus is blocked in learning and development. An insecure child will be an anxious child and may show a range of disturbed behaviours. Some of these behaviours, for example hypervigilance, may have adaptive value at home, but the child's development is hindered as a result. A child may be locked into negative behaviour as a means of gaining attention. Often, parents do not provide clear guidelines for good and bad behaviour, or do not adhere to any consistent rules. The child will be confused as a result, and will be unable to respond appropriately. Professionals need to be active in taking the child's behaviour into account and to be aware of the possible sources of different forms of difficult or withdrawn behaviour. They must also be able to observe the child's response to adults, both parents and others, and whether the child's behaviour changes according to whether or not his or her parents are present.

In order to be secure the child must be free from emotional abuse. Rather than looking for elegant definitions of abuse, professionals need to be aware of the appropriateness or inappropriateness of things that parents say and do to their children, and to observe the child's response. Parents often make idle and confusing threats which may diminish the child's sense of security. If parents frequently tell their children they do not love them or that they will send them away, or lock them up for hours and ignore their distress, or frighten and tease them excessively, then those children will be insecure. They may not show physical signs of abuse, but damage will still occur. It is probable that some parents may themselves have experienced this kind of rearing, and in order to break the cycle of deprivation across generations (Rutter and Madge, 1976) they need help in understanding how their child develops, and encouragement in responding to his or her emotional needs.

To be secure, children need to know that their needs will be met, and that they will not be neglected. The baby left to cry in the cot or pram for hours without food or comfort will be less secure. Children need to know that someone will care for them not only in terms of routine feeding and changing but also when they are uncomfortable or lonely.

6 *The right to be valued and understood*

Children need to feel valued and of worth; they need to feel that they are loved, and that they are appreciated for themselves. A child needs encouragement and affection in order to grow. Children who only ever receive negative messages about themselves may show low self-esteem and come to expect or even invite failure and rejection. This may affect later relationships, and ultimately they may seek to have a child who will love and value them and make up for the past. This solution, may, however, become a problem when the baby cannot meet the needs of the parent.

Children need, too, to be understood when they attempt to express their needs and worries. Children will do this in different ways at different ages, through actions, as well as words. While parents need to be able to interpret the child's needs on a day-to-day basis, professionals in all areas, including the legal system need the ability to recognise and value what a child is trying to say.

7 *The right to be allowed to be a child*

A parent who has a child in order that he or she may be loved will be disappointed. Children are rewarding in their own ways, but they are also very hard work. The process of childrearing is like a continuous problem-solving exercise: each week seems to bring new issues to tackle. For the parent, meeting these challenges appropriately and successfully gives a tremendous sense of achievement. Where this cannot be attained, the parent may feel rejected or let down, and childrearing becomes a burden.

Immature parents who know little of child development are ill-equipped for the tasks ahead. They may interpret the child's behaviour inappropriately, thinking their baby is doing something 'to get at them', or that, as one mother said, her infant 'has the devil in her'. Parents may have unrealistic expectations of their child, and be unable to recognise age-appropriate behaviour for what it is. They may also feel that all was well until they had the child, and hence that any change for the worse is the child's fault, rather than recognising the changes that they need to make in order to accommodate the new family member. All this will militate against the child's need to develop as his or her individual personality dictates. Through the experience of being accepted and understood for what they are, children in turn learn to accept and understand others.

Parenting requires flexibility, energy and much work, and parents who are under stress may need extra support in order to carry through their role successfully. Professionals need good training in and knowledge of normal child development. Parents need this too. For parents who are particularly at risk, the provision of education and guidance during pregnancy and the early months of the child's life may be helpful. If it is difficult to screen 'at risk' individuals, perhaps this is an argument for providing the same basic resources for training of all new parents. In particular, the parents' expectations of their infant are worthy of exploration, and parents may need to be told, for example, how to toilet-train a child, and at what age this is appropriate. The provision of this kind of advice by professionals is particularly valuable where the parents are without other sources of support or information due, perhaps, to social isolation.

We cannot protect all children at risk of abuse 24 hours per day, but we can, by looking for ways to ensure that basic needs and rights are being met, go some way to building a safer, happier future for them.

7 FAMILY LIFESTYLES AND STRUCTURES

Pamela Abbott

Senior Lecturer, Department of Social and Political Studies,
Plymouth Polytechnic

This chapter is about families that live together as domestic groups, each of which may have relationships with a wider group of 'kin' – grandparents, parents, uncles, aunts, cousins and so on. In the chapter I intend to make the ordinary and mundane into something extraordinary and strange by asking what families are like in the United Kingdom today, what families are for, why we live in them and how the members of them relate to each other. We shall find that there is no agreement about any of this; sociologists and others who ask these questions about the family come up with different and conflicting answers. We shall also see that different members of a family may experience family relationships in quite different ways, and that our ideas of what families are like are often at variance with actual experiences of family life. Many of us continue to hold idealized views of 'the family' even if our own experiences are at odds with them (Figure 1 overleaf).

Different forms of family

We are all familiar with the concept of the family (see Allan, 1985). Most of us live in a family or *have* lived in one. However, our understanding of what is meant by 'a family' may differ. Recently I asked a group of students to say whom they considered to be members of their family. One student said that her family was made up of herself, her younger brother and her mother and father; another said her family included not only her parents and brothers but also her grandparents and uncles and aunts and their families; a third said that she saw her family as just herself and her mother; yet another said her family comprised herself, her mother and her stepfather. All these groups are frequently described as families, and yet their structures are different. In some cases all those regarded as members of the family live together as a group, while in others the members of the family live at a distance from each other.

Sociologists and social psychologists have identified a variety of family structures and ways in which individuals relate to a wider kin-group (see Robertson, 1986). The core members of a family are generally identified as a married couple and their dependent children – the 'nuclear' family. In some societies a man (or more rarely a woman) may be married to more than one partner at a time – polygamy. However, in the United Kingdom divorce (the legal termination of marriage) and remarriage are possible and indeed common, leading to a pattern sometimes called 'serial monogamy'. In the United Kingdom at this time most families with children are of the nuclear form (although the majority of *households* – people living together and sharing domestic arrangements – are *not* nuclear families); parents and their dependent children live together independently of the wider kinship group. There is an increasing number of one-parent families. These arise most often because of

Figure 1. A single-parent father sews a button on his daughter's dress before school

divorce or desertion by the other parent, but may also follow the death of one partner or a woman deliberately choosing to have a child without a partner. Most one-parent families are headed by females. However, the majority of divorced people remarry and form, with the children of one or both families, a 're-formed' or 're-structured' nuclear family. The children may in fact be members of two nuclear families, relating to both of their 'natural' parents and their 'new' spouses and possibly step-siblings.

The relationships between nuclear families and the wider kinship group also vary considerably. Some families can be described as 'extended' – that is, the family operates as a wide group of kin living with, or in close proximity to, the core nuclear family and sharing social and economic support. Even when the family is not 'extended' in this way, some families have closer ties with parents and siblings (brothers and sisters) than others. Most of us, even when we have grown up and formed our own families, continue to think of our parents and siblings as 'family', but the extent to which we continue to depend on each other varies considerably.

Families as socially constructed

Generally when we think of the family as a group of people living together we think of a married couple living with their dependent children – the nuclear family. The traditional view is that the husband/father goes out to work and the wife/mother stays at home to look after the children and the home. This type of family structure is perceived to be natural; even though not everyone lives like this, it is still used as the benchmark against which to compare those who do not. We all know about this type of family; children's reading schemes, television advertisements, politicians' speeches, all represent it as the norm and the ideal. Most of us grow up with the goal of marrying and having children – creating this kind of family. Any other kind of family organization is thought of as less desirable or even deviant – as not conforming with what is natural and right.

The functionalist view of the family

Functionalists tend to be optimists, arguing that the family is demonstrably functional both for society as a whole and for its individual members – demonstrably because this particular form has become current in a society which has successfully survived, and therefore it *must* be functional. Its social functions are seen to be the control of sexuality between men and women, the socialization (upbringing) of the young into becoming hard-working citizens (and accepting a particular *form* of work organization as natural) and the provision of a place where the need for (mostly) male workers to recuperate from the demands and frustrations of outside employment are met. Its functions for individuals are the meeting of emotional needs for warmth, security and care, and the provision of an economically and emotionally secure place in which women can rear their children. The family is seen as based on a sexual division of labour – women as carers and men as economic providers – with the mother and father working together complementarily to provide for the needs of all family members. It is recognized that in modern industrial society some functions previously provided by the family, such as education and religious instruction, have been taken over by the state, and it is accepted that the welfare state has come to assist the family in performing its functions. However, this is not thought to have diminished the important role that the family performs, nor the popularity of the family. It is pointed out that despite an increase in illegitimacy and divorce rates, the vast majority of people still get married, and that divorcees frequently remarry. The family, it is suggested, is as popular and as necessary as ever.

This functionalist view of the family is shared by some social scientists. Psychological theories of development, for example, often implicitly assume that children are being raised in this type of family. Theorists of the functionalist school argue that the family is a universal institution, to be found in all cultures, and a functional and necessary one. Our particular type of family (nuclear), they argue, is the one most closely suited to the particular type of society (industrial) in which people in the United Kingdom and the United States live. They suggest that the family as an institution has adapted as our societies have changed, and that the modern nuclear family, based on affection and choice of partner, is the most evolved form. The nuclear family is potentially mobile, both socially and geographically, thus meeting the needs of employers for workers who are prepared to move around the country and to accept promotion: this is facilitated by a non-employed wife who is able to maintain the home and to move with her husband.

The 'New Right' view of the family
Other sociologists and social psychologists hold a more pessimistic view, less sure that the family today is adequately carrying out its essential functions for society. High illegitimacy, divorce and juvenile delinquency rates are indications, from this perspective, that there is something fundamentally wrong with the family in the United Kingdom today, a failure both in social cohesion and in the proper discipline (socialization) of the young. Many contemporary social problems are seen, in this view, as the result of a breakdown in moral values and an unwillingness among individuals to take on responsibility for their own and their family's needs and well-being. These New Right theorists suggest that the current situation has come about at least in part because of too much state intervention. People have come to rely far too much on a 'nanny state'. The solution, it is proclaimed, is a return to Christian values and morality and an entrepreneurial spirit. Not only should parents take on more responsibility for their children, but they should also take back the responsibility for the care of their disabled, sick and elderly family members. This, it is argued, is 'only natural'. The warmth and love of one's family is preferable to impersonal care by strangers and paid professional workers.

Critiques of 'golden age' theories
However, the idyllic view of family life has been questioned by historians, sociologists and anthropologists. Historical and anthropological research suggests not only that there is a variety of family structures and relations between family members, but also that a variety of family forms co-exist at any one time. Anthropological research indicates that there is no 'natural' family that is found in all societies, but a variety of kinship structures and ways of dividing domestic labour between family members. Historical study of British parish records suggests that extended families – households containing kin apart from the parent–child nucleus – were not the norm in pre-industrial Britain, although it is possible that more people lived in close contact with near kin than is often thought to be the case today.

It seems likely that there was a plurality of family structures, then as now. In some communities in the United Kingdom, extended family structure *is* still common – among the Scottish 'Travelling Folk', for instance, or where a small business or a corner shop is being run by the whole family as a family business. This is particularly to be found in communities of Asian or Southern European derivation. While many young Asians are setting up on their own – forming nuclear families when they get married – kinship ties continue to be extremely important for them (see Westwood and Bachu, 1988). There are too still limited areas in the United Kingdom where children tend to live near their parents when they grow up and continue to have close contact with them and their other relatives, forming a modified extended family. Even when children live at a distance from their parents, close contact can sometimes still be retained (Bell, 1968). Janet Finch, however, in research on family obligations in the 1980s, has found that people vary considerably in the extent to which they feel they should give financial and social assistance to family members; there is no normative consensus on how much we should help relatives.

Furthermore, increased affluence on the one hand, and the benefits available from the state on the other, give people more choice about where they live and with whom they interact. In the past, poverty and misfortune often forced people to seek help from relatives. Indeed, the 'liable relative' clause of the Poor Law (not repealed until the 1948 welfare state legislation was enacted) meant that certain individuals were legally responsible for the financial maintenance of certain kin; children were responsible for parents, and vice versa, and grandparents were responsible for grandchildren. Increased affluence and welfare provision mean that today most people can choose whether or not they want to stay in close touch with kin, rather than effectively being forced to do so out of fear of future need.

The Marxist perspective
Marxists have argued that the modern family is structured to meet the needs of a capitalist economy in another sense. Men have paid employment and maintain a wife and children. This helps to meet the needs of a capitalist form of industrial organization, for a healthy workforce maintained and reproduced into the next generation of workers. However, this means that women and children are economically dependent on their husbands/fathers. Marxist feminists have argued that this gives men considerable economic and social power in the domestic sphere. Furthermore, they point out that not all married men earn a 'family wage' – that is, one sufficient to maintain themselves, a wife and their children. Women, in this situation, are often forced to take paid employment and thus have to take on a 'double shift' – caring for the home and their family as well as doing their paid work. Married women, it is argued, form a 'reserve army of labour' who can be encouraged into work in times of labour shortage and sent back to home and family when the need is over.

The feminist challenge
Feminists, examining relationships in the family, have challenged the view that it meets the needs of all its members equally and have argued that women and children are disadvantaged in families. They argue that power is not equally shared within families – that men are powerful and women and children relatively powerless economically and socially and in terms of physical strength. The family, they suggest, is often a violent place for women and children, not a 'haven from a heartless world'. Even where women and children are not abused, the family oppresses and exploits them. (Black feminists, however, have pointed out that this is not true of all Afro-Caribbean families; the West Indies has a history of married women working and maintaining their independence. Also, the family has been a source of resistance to racism for many black women.) Despite the picture of marriage as a partnership of equals and the argument that men are increasingly offering help in the domestic sphere, women are still generally economically dependent on men, and help with domestic labour is minimal. Women have the main burden of children and they often carry it in isolation. The realities of the experience are often very different from the idealized picture of women as gaining satisfaction from their maternal role, and women find that they frequently do *not* 'naturally' know how to care for their children. Women often feel trapped and frustrated by their roles as housewives and mothers, even if they love their children and husbands. This is intensified for women whose husbands work long hours or are absent from home for long periods – for example, when the husband is in the armed forces, is a long-distance lorry driver or is sent abroad by his employer. Single-parent mothers have an additional burden, as they have to cope with little or no

support. Anne Oakley (1982) quotes a letter from a mother which was published in the *Sunday Times*:

> When I read a study of baby battering I can't help thinking, 'there but for the grace of God go I'. . . . If all mothers who have ever shaken a screaming baby, or slapped it, or thrown it roughly into its cot, stood up to be counted, we would make a startling total. (p. 223)

Furthermore, there is no break for the mother; the daily routine goes on and on, the tasks have to be performed. As one of the respondents in Boulton's (1983) interview study said,

> There are times when I feel like saying, 'I will feed you twice as much today so tomorrow I can just have a break'. Before, I could say 'the fridge badly needs to be cleaned but I can leave it'. With children they need feeding when they need feeding. Their nappies have to be washed every day. It's as simple as that. When they cry, you can't say 'Well, I'll see you in an hour'. That is when it hits you. The fact that it's seven days a week, twenty-four hours a day, and they make the rules. (p. 69)

Research by Brown and Harris (1978) in London's Camberwell district suggests that working-class mothers with children under five who do not have close ties with relatives are the ones liable to suffer from clinical depression. An American feminist, Jessie Bernard (1982), has suggested on the basis of medical statistics that 'being a housewife makes women sick'. Yet frequently men and those not caring for children in the family find it difficult to understand why women are not satisfied with their roles as wives and mothers. In her study of general practitioners, Helen Roberts (1984) found a consensus view that women should be satisfied with domestic roles and that the general practitioners were perplexed by women who expressed dissatisfaction.

Feminists would not, of course, deny that it is not only for women that the reality of family living fails to match the beauty and clarity of the conventional stereotype of the family; this is true for men also. Men too enter family life with expectations which are doomed to disillusion, and research on violence suggests that the immediate occasion of a man's violent assault on his wife or children may well be an instance of such disappointed expectation – dinner not prepared, the wife's sexual fidelity made suspect in his eyes by her actions, or the child crying rather than welcoming him. The family is portrayed as a place of warmth and love which provides emotional and erotic satisfaction and also provides a place where these may be expressed by men. The reality of crying babies, naughty children, burdensome housework and the distraction of his partner's attention from him to the child may add to rather than diminish for a man the frustrations of life outside. Even children who have moved from residential institutions to longed-for foster/adoptive homes have on occasion reported bitterly that the family is not 'all that it is cracked up to be'.

Continuity and change in family life

While there is no evidence for a dramatic change in family structures, changes in family life *have* taken place – especially since the end of World War II. Divorce rates have increased rapidly, so that now one in three marriages is liable to end in divorce, and many of these divorces will involve children. However, in the past many marriages were ended by the death of one partner – probably as many proportionately as now end in divorce – and children were often left to be brought up by a single parent or, if the parent remarried, by a step-parent. The frequency with which this occurred is perhaps evidenced by the number of fairy stories and other traditional stories which feature either a single-parent family or a wicked step-parent. Relationships in families were also arguably very different. In pre-industrial Britain, marriage was an economic contract – it was very difficult for people to survive on their own (as of course it still is in many societies). Historians have argued that children were also seen in economic terms – that is, in terms of the contribution they could make to household income. High infant mortality rates meant some parents were not able to invest love in their babies in the sense or to the degree that is now seen as the norm. From an early age children were expected to work alongside adults, and children as young as seven were sent away to work as servants or to be apprenticed. Men were permitted by law to punish their children by physical means, as well as their wives and their servants. The common phrase 'rule of thumb' comes from one legal judgement that a man could beat his wife provided that the stick he used to do so was no thicker than his thumb. Indeed, it was seen as a man's duty to control his family. Historians have argued that the warmth and affection seen as characteristic of modern British families, and the notion of marriage as a partnership between equals, are recent inventions.

Marriage for most Britons is no longer just an economic contract, but may be seen as one based on love and choice, although arranged marriages are still common among some cultural groups living in the United Kingdom. Children are borne for emotional rather than economic reasons, and parents invest considerable love in their children. They also have expectations for their children, hopes for the future, and they may experience considerable disappointment if the children do not live up to these expectations. Indeed, many parents may derive great personal satisfaction from the successes of their children and feel frustration when they fail. In the modern world children have, to a large extent, come to be seen almost as personal attributes of individual parents, something on which the worth of the self can be judged, and they may be used for personal satisfaction as if they were possessions. While no longer seen as an economic asset, children can continue to be seen as the property of their parents.

Despite this, the state does intervene in family life both to protect children and to ensure that children are reared correctly, kept healthy and educated. The health visitor, the social worker, the school attendance officer and others all police the family – keep it under surveillance – to make certain that it cares appropriately for child members. This creates considerable tensions, both for families and for those that police them. Thus *the family* is seen as having needs and wants, rather than explicit recognition being given to the fact that families are made up of a number of individuals all of whom have their own needs and expectations, and that at times these may be in conflict, and decisions may need to be made about whose interests are to be prioritized.

Critiques of the family as the best place for children
The idea that the modern family is the best place for the socialization of children has not gone unchallenged, despite an essential agreement by professionals, politicians and the public that this is the case. In the 1960s a number of psychiatrists, the best-known of whom are probably Ronald Laing (1960) and David Cooper (1972), suggested that the strains of family life were not conducive to the development of stable personalities and argued that in extreme situations children could become mentally ill as a result of the way in which they were treated by their parents and other family members.

Of special importance here was the assumption that parents love their children and feel a need to confirm this view in their verbal utterances. On the contrary, Laing argued, the strains of family life and the fact that parental love turns out *not* to be natural and inevitable meant that parents' actions often failed to conform to what they said. Thus a parent may tell a child that he or she is loved while at the same time pushing the child away by his or her behaviour. These contradictory messages confuse the child and make it difficult for him or her to develop a stable understanding of the world and his or her place in it. David Cooper (1972) argued that the nuclear family is a fundamentally unhealthy place because of forced emotional closeness, a closeness which fosters internalized dependence and prevents children developing independence as they grow older. Similarly, the social anthropologist, Edmund Leach (1967) argued that the strains and tensions of family life were reasons why there were so many social problems in contemporary society; people had to take out their tensions and frustrations *outside* the family (in direct contrast to the functionalist view of the family's functions). The problems in family life arise from people's high expectations of it, the financial strains imposed by the high cost of children and the pressures placed on mothers to care for their children – especially when the husbands/fathers are absent altogether or away for long periods. All the tensions are heightened in 're-formed' families; the new parent (generally a father) may well find it difficult to relate to the children and have unrealistic expectations of their behaviour and the amount of affection they will display towards him.

Leach looked back at a 'golden age' of extended families and a more open social environment for children, free from the enclosed and intensely interpersonal pressures of the modern nuclear family. As we have seen, there is considerable evidence that such a golden age never in fact existed. Nonetheless, one possible alternative to nuclear family life would be some more communal way of organizing people's lives and responsibilities for children. Certainly the experience of the Israeli Kibbutzim suggests that children brought up in a more communal system and without the constant attention of parents can develop perfectly stable personalities as adults.

Conclusions
The family is considered to be an important institution in the United Kingdom today; indeed, in recent years both the Conservative and Labour parties have expressed concern to provide policies that meet the needs of families. Professionals generally argue that the family is a vital institution for the socialization of children and for meeting the emotional needs of adults. Families which do not conform to social expectation are seen as deviant – as a minority and a danger – and when things go wrong the blame is generally placed on individual family members rather than on the way in which families are structured and the burden of expectations placed on the members of them. We tend to have an idealized view of the family; we enter into family life with expectations that are frequently frustrated, and the family home, for some women and children, is the place where they are beaten and abused. (Children, of course, have even fewer resources and choices than other family members; they cannot choose to leave in the way that an adult member of the family can.) However, high divorce rates coupled with a high rate of remarriage suggest that adults are still looking for an ideal rather than rejecting the institutions of marriage and the family as such.

Furthermore, the family continues to be a key institution for children. Despite an increase in the number of one-parent families and of 're-formed' families, the majority of children are brought up in stereotypical two-parent families. In spite of all the problems and frustrations of modern family living, most parents do care for their children and most adults appear to gain considerable satisfaction from family life. What we must be careful to do, however, is not to assume that there is in any real sense 'the family' – a structure and set of relationships to which all families do or should conform. There is a variety of family structures – extended families, nuclear families, re-formed families, single-parent families – that all co-exist in the United Kingdom at this time, and a variety of ways in which family relationships are or could be organized. To suggest that only one form of family and one way of organizing family life is 'normal' is to suggest that all other forms are 'deviant'. Research by historians, anthropologists and sociologists challenges the view that certain family structures are inevitably more stable than others or superior for the socialization of children or for meeting the emotional needs of adults. Finally, it is important to challenge and question the view that families naturally love and care for their members, that family life is inevitably superior to other ways of living or that families equally meet the needs of all their members.

The publications of the Family Policy Studies Centre (231 Baker Street, London NW1 6XE) provide comprehensive, up-to-date information and commentaries on change in family structures and relationships and on social policy as applied to the family.

8 CHILD ABUSE IN A SOCIAL CONTEXT

Martin Loney

In popular debate when people talk about child abuse, they usually mean the physical or emotional damage done to a child by one or more adults. They normally assume a family setting, although often one which includes a step-parent or live-in lover. Up until recent concerns about 'ritual abuse' it has been this concept that informs the work of the social services, is what newspaper articles and television programmes are about and is generally what is portrayed by child welfare agencies in their fund-raising efforts. It is a powerful image and one which is capable of mobilizing considerable outrage. What can be more grotesque than a parent who deliberately harms or neglects his or her child?

This depiction conveys a strong but concealed ideological message. By directing attention to the abuse carried out by individuals, it is a message which simultaneously ignores the social factors that may bring about such abuse, and entirely conceals the very real abuse caused by social arrangements which are a result of government policies.

A number of consequences flow from this particular construction of child abuse. The depiction of child abuse as an outcome of the 'sick' behaviour of a small number of individuals and families implies the need for skilled professionals to help those at risk. When intervention fails to protect a child, the assumption is that this is because the professionals are not doing their jobs properly. By this means the problem of child abuse is constructed in a way which is ultimately reassuring. Not only is its prevalence limited by the fact that it is only 'problem families' who pose a risk, but by making the prevention of further abuse a 'professional task', the rest of us are 'let off the hook'. We can safely assume that given adequate professional training and competence, the incidence of child abuse can be substantially reduced if not altogether eliminated. More importantly, no attention needs to be given to the possibility that broader social changes might be required – changes, for example in the resourcing of health and social services, which could entail considerable controversy and result in substantial cost to powerful groups in society. Framed in the terms of the 'sick' behaviour of deviant individuals and families, and the competence of professional workers, the debate about child abuse is taken out of the realm of politics and placed in the hands of experts.

The stage is now set for the familiar situation where every 'failure to protect a child' leads to immediate public outcry for a public inquiry, in which the answers to the questions 'how' and 'why' may rapidly devolve into a social work witch hunt and a lawyer's gold-mine. Such inquiries are not only very expensive (particularly in the context of the inadequate resources usually available in the failed intervention), but also completely overlook the broader social context and the resourcing of health and social services.

A good example is the inquiry into the death of Kimberley Carlile. The lawyer in charge of the inquiry, Louis Blom-Cooper, responded to the charge that the inquiry had failed to look at the real issue of resources with the claim that the terms of reference precluded it from doing so: 'If there is a big issue about resources then central government has got to set up some committee to review it' (Philpot, 1988, p. 15). When he was questioned on the relationship between child abuse and poor economic and social conditions, he could offer little insight and seemed unaware of the extensive literature: 'I'm not sure that I'm qualified to say but I would have thought that, clearly, there was a correlation but I think there are many causes. It's like crime, you can't pin down any particular factor as being the cause of criminal activity' (*ibid.*, p. 15).

Having thus excluded the question of whether the problem is one of inadequate resources and wider social and economic factors from its competence, the inquiry was free to focus on the specific question: in this *particular* set of circumstances what went wrong? A question explicitly constructed in this way ensures that only *individualistic* responses can be considered. The scapegoat in this case, as in so many others, was a social worker on whom Blom-Cooper unhesitatingly passed the judgement that 'he should not in future perform any of the statutory functions in relation to child protection'.

The inquiry's conclusions allowed the media yet again to portray the problem, not as one of the poverty and bleakness of the domestic background from which Kimberley came, or indeed of the grossly overstretched resources of rate-capped Greenwich social services, which had seen its Child Protection Register (at that time called the Child Abuse Register) increase by 240% in three years (*Guardian*, 12 December 1987). Rather the problem was one of 'social work incompetence'. Clearly individual workers may on occasion be negligent or reveal standards of practice well below what should be expected. But what is important to note here is the way in which inquiries are so constituted: that it is these and related procedural issues which predominate, to the virtual exclusion of any concern for the wider canvas on which abuse takes place (DHSS, 1982, 1991).

Redefining child abuse

The American expert, David Gil, offers a definition of child abuse which, in contrast to the popular, individualistic image, allows for the development of a holistic approach rooted in a concern for the fullest development of a child's potential. It is an approach which enables us to develop a framework which incorporates both individual and societal factors, and highlights the short-sighted and politically self-serving focus of the contemporary British debate.

Gil argues that child abuse should be judged in terms of a child's potential. Whenever there is a gap between a child's actual circumstances and the circumstances that would assure his or her optimal development, then the child is being abused. Gil recognizes that this definition implies that abuse occurs in 'most existing institutional settings for the care and education of children, since these settings usually do not facilitate a full actualisation of the human potential of all children in their care' (Gil, 1979).

Gil identifies the importance of wider social policies in facilitating or denying children's development:

> As direct or indirect consequences of such policies, millions of children in our society [the United States] live in poverty and are inadequately nourished, clothed, housed or educated; their health is not assured because of substandard medical care; their neighbourhoods decay; meaningful occupational opportunities are not available to them; alienation is widespread among them.

He emphasizes the importance of tackling abuse on the broader social policy level rather than narrowly focusing on the individual and the family: 'The societal level is certainly the most severe. For what happens at this level determines not only how children fare on the institutional level, but also by way of complex interactions, how they fare in their own homes' (*ibid.*).

Using the approach suggested by Gil, it becomes clear that the focus on child abuse in the United Kingdom is very one-sided. It encourages the mobilization of public concern and the launching of major inquiries when children are killed or sexually abused by parents or by other members of the household, but it excludes from public scrutiny those children who die of poor diet, damp housing, in bed and breakfast accommodation and the tenement. It also excludes from the debate strong evidence that there is a massive difference in infant mortality rates between rich and poor, and disregards the higher incidence of disease amongst poor children, their lower educational attainment, their greater risk of incarceration and so forth.

Poor housing and homelessness

In 1986 Shelter's magazine, *Roof*, reported one case of homelessness which was to have fatal consequences for a child, yet which would certainly never feature in any inquiry set up by the present government:

> The coroner's jury returned a verdict of accidental death this summer on fourteen month old Debbie Beattie who plunged down several floors in the Mount Pleasant Hotel in London's Kings Cross. Last year open verdicts were recorded on the deaths of Shamin Karim and her children Nizemul and Shalaha, aged five and four, who died in a hotel fire in Marylebone. (Stearn, 1986, p. 11)

These are extreme consequences of government policies which have seen the number of homeless children rise to perhaps as many as a quarter of a million (*Guardian*, 18 December 1987), a trend likely to get worse as the number of mortgages foreclosed reach record levels in the 1990s.

Poverty

Homelessness is an extreme example of the kind of abuse which can be triggered by social policies or their absence. Many more children in the United Kingdom find their lives blighted by poverty which serves to exclude them from full participation in society. Many studies have documented the hardship and stress faced by poor families (Bayliss, 1987). The final report of the 10-year research programme into transmitted deprivation, commented:

> Hopelessness and despair are commonly noted among families on very low incomes, although many women, and it is usually the women who are being assessed, managed to 'keep cheerful'. In addition to feeling trapped in poverty many families feel a constant anxiety about money. The monetary consequences of poverty, which include disconnection of fuel supply and acute shortages of cash to buy food or clothe the children adequately, must create situations where children are not properly cared for in a material sense. And the psychological consequences of chronic anxiety and despair are hardly conducive to happy child rearing. (Brown and Madge, 1982, pp. 160–1)

It is therefore not surprising that cases of 'child abuse' tend to be drawn from the poorest and most deprived families. In an analysis of referrals to Strathclyde social services during 1984–5 it was found that in 76% of child abuse cases and 77% of child neglect cases the family were on supplementary benefit (now income support). Seventy per cent of all children received into care in Strathclyde were from families where the head of the household was unemployed (Platt, 1987, pp. 39, 51).

Given the overwhelming nature of the evidence about the harm done by child poverty, and the extent of public concern over child abuse and neglect, we might expect poverty to be a major social priority. But the statistical evidence indicates that there is a continuing and marked growth in the incidence of child poverty. The number of children under 16 dependent on supplementary benefit rose from 456,000 in 1965 to 1,950,000 in 1984. In 1986 one in six children lived in a family dependent on supplementary benefit (Piachaud, 1986, p. 2). Townsend (1988) and other researchers have shown just how meagre is the lifestyle a family on supplementary benefit (income support) can afford. Yet while most people's income in the United Kingdom has risen, in real terms, by some 40% since 1965, supplementary benefit levels have increased by only 14%.

Poor health
The children of the poor will find their lives blighted disproportionately by ill-health. A British Medical Association Report, *Deprivation and Ill-health* (1987), draws attention to the range of adverse consequences of poverty faced by these children:

> The effects of deprivation on the physical and mental health of children and on development are a particular concern, because in addition to immediate harmful effects there may be long term irreversible consequences affecting the individual in adult life and even the next generation. For example, poverty in childhood followed by greater affluence may be associated with increased risk of heart disease. Frequent respiratory tract illness in childhood is associated with poor living conditions and may be related to chronic respiratory disease later in life.

Faced with the evidence of the harm done by child poverty and its rapid growth, what have government policies tried to do? The answer, which concerns many social theorists, is that current government policies seem to be likely further to impoverish poor children and add to their number. Economic growth has gone hand in hand with a steady deterioration in the situation of the poor and a growing gap between their lifestyles and those of the mainstream of society. This is readily illustrated by examining the broader movements of income in the United Kingdom. Between 1979 and 1986 the income of the bottom 10% of workers rose, in real terms, by 3.7%, while that of the top 10% rose by 22.3%. In cash terms the contrast is even sharper, amounting to some £4 per week at the bottom of the scale and £50 per week at the top. This gap, far from being addressed by tax changes, is further exaggerated when the impact of income tax and national insurance contributions is taken into account. For a married couple with two children on half average earnings, tax and national insurance contributions *increased* by 163% between 1978–9 and 1987–8. For a couple on 10 times average earnings they *decreased* by 21%. Not only have market forces worked to increase the gap between rich and poor, but so too have government policies (Walker and Walker, 1987).

Poverty contributes markedly to the United Kingdom's high rates of infant deaths, which are some one and a half times as high in social classes 4 and 5 as in social classes 1 and 2. The figures for ethnic minorities show an even more marked disparity. This inequality contributes to the United Kingdom's poor record internationally, with an overall infant death rate nearly twice that of the Scandinavian countries (Himmelweit, 1988). Thus, we should be clear that at the extreme, even in an advanced industrialized country, poverty continues to kill just as surely and certainly more widely than any sadistic family members.

The international dimension
The problem of child poverty in the United Kingdom is considerable but it pales into insignificance when we examine the plight of children in much of the Third

World. In many Third World countries income differences are even more marked than they are in the United Kingdom, whilst in absolute terms poverty may mean quite literally the absence of food. Child labour has been recognized as a continuing problem in the United Kingdom, with the worst abuses taking place where children in poor families are desperate for any income (Low Pay Unit, 1985). In many Third World countries poor children work as a matter of survival, often in Dickensian conditions and on occasion being sold into effective slavery by parents otherwise unable to provide for them, or driven into the growing sexual services industry. These forms of exploitation represent some of the least acceptable consequences of the imperial relationship between the First and Third Worlds (Minority Rights Group, 1982).

A growing number of writers in the social policy area have begun to argue for the need to broaden our concern away from just a national focus towards an international focus. Townsend, for instance, has argued that:

> The mass poverty and extreme inequality of the Third World has to be related to the increasing extent of poverty being recreated or deepened in the First World. The internationalisation of finance, manufacture and commerce, particularly the relocation of industrial employment overseas, and the increasing influence of international agencies like the International Monetary Fund and the EEC is weakening the capacity of even rich nation states to stray from conventionally approved social policies. (Townsend, 1985, p. 34)

How much longer can we allow ourselves to feel smug by giving donations to 'Live Aid', when the clothes we wear and the videos we watch are 'cheap' because they were assembled by children in the Third World for starvation wages? How much longer can we feel angry towards 'child abusers' when we ourselves belong to a group of people only too willing to exploit children for profit?

Children's rights?

The 1959 United Nations Declaration of the Rights of the Child seeks to establish a set of principles which should be reflected in the provision made for the world's children. These include access to health and social services, education, freedom from discrimination, protection against neglect, cruelty and exploitation and the provision of a nurturing environment, 'an atmosphere of affection and of moral and material security' (United Nations, 1977, pp. 333–9). Clearly, humankind needs to take some fairly massive steps forward to realize these principles.

One difficulty which needs to be tackled is that there is often little agreement about what children's rights amount to in practice. To many, the idea that children can be beaten for rule-breaking in school is a barbaric legacy of less-enlightened times. For others, such punitive powers are essential for good discipline.

What is a child's right – to a 'proper upbringing' or to be free from physical coercion? Schools which are ill-equipped, staffed by demoralized teachers, housed in decaying buildings are unlikely to afford the most stimulating environment for the young. Do children have a 'right' to a good education? And if so, whose responsibility is it to provide it – the state (by way of public spending on education) or parents?

One issue which continually surfaces in the discussion about children's rights is their relative powerlessness. It is indeed a feature of contemporary society that while great efforts are made to promote children's welfare they rarely involve the participation of children themselves. Children's voices and views are simply not assumed to be centrally relevant. This is well illustrated in the debate which at the time of writing (September 1988) has been taking place around Kenneth Baker's Educational Reform Bill, in which there is a move to extend 'choice' in the educational field. It has quickly become clear that the choice which is being referred to is not that of children but of their parents. Parents not children are to decide whether schools should opt out of the state system; the proposed new National Curriculum in fact significantly reduces the range of choice exercised by children within the school system, through the central designation of the content of the great majority of the school day. At the same time the growing emphasis on testing school children as early as age seven, whatever its merits may be in enabling a more effective ranking of schools, could scarcely be seen from a child's point of view as anything more than the imposition of yet another competitive hurdle, without any reference to the child's feelings in the matter. Indeed the exclusion of the child's voice from the whole debate speaks volumes about the way in which contemporary British society sees the role of the child.

However, this neglect of the child is not unique to British society. The director of a new transnational project on childhood recently observed that even for social scientists the child remains largely hidden:

> I was responsible for two projects concerning family and divorce in Europe, and one of the insights which I got in this capacity was . . . even these highly distinguished family sociologists . . . did not show a real and noteworthy interest in childhood. Of course, much talking was done about children. . . . To the best of my knowledge there is no theoretical and methodological tradition which we can profit from, there is no conceptual apparatus which has come even close to international agreement. Childhood has no conceptual autonomy, not even, alas, in single countries. (Qvortrup, 1987, pp. 17, 18)

A service in crisis?
One consequence of the growth of concern about child abuse has been a mobilization of more resources, but these have proved inadequate even to respond to the very limited definitions of child abuse which inform public policy.

While growing poverty and homelessness have placed additional burdens on social service departments, these departments have experienced increasing difficulties in recruiting and retaining staff, notably in deprived inner city areas but also in areas such as Cleveland which have been the subject of adverse publicity. Social workers already fully stretched and mindful of the risks of any mistakes have refused to take on further cases, and increasing numbers of children on the Child Protection Register have remained unallocated. In Haringey, in January 1988, for instance, 92 of the 297 children on the Child Protection Register had no allocated social worker. The borough, the sixth most deprived local authority area in the country, nonetheless faced the need to make cuts in expenditure of more than 20% to meet central government targets (Harris, 1988). The voluntary sector too, has been under increasing bombardment. 'ChildLine', launched in October 1986, has been taking in 1988 some 700 calls a day, but the switchboard logs a further 7000 attempted calls. In the United States growing concern about child abuse has similarly overwhelmed service providers. In New York callers reporting suspected abuse to the Central Register may be placed on hold for 10–15 minutes with some 50% of callers estimated to ring off before a worker answers. In general, workers have typically not yet seen 22% of all reported children 40 days after an initial report (Loney, 1987).

This lack of resources inevitably magnifies the possibility of mistakes, and encourages the professionals involved to work defensively, taking children into care where – given adequate resources – they might not have needed to. It is 'safer' when support services are in short supply to do this rather than to seek alternative courses of action which may expose the worker to subsequent criticism if they prove inadequate. Doran and Young (1987) succinctly identify the central issue:

What the public has to decide is whether it is willing to pay for the civil liberties of children. Is its concern matched by resources to implement it? Talk of the technical problems of correct diagnosis or the treatment of the abused child masks the fact that the problem is more of the quantity of cases than the quality of care. Both the sifting of cases and the treatment of children are well developed, but they are labour intensive and expensive. And, if the resources are forthcoming, the public will have to accept that the increased rights of children will, inevitably, impinge on the rights of the family . . . but here again, adequate resources would make it possible to minimise such inevitable conflict between children's rights and the rights of adults.

A balance of rights

The issue of resources is not, of course, the only one which is raised in determining the correct balance between the rights of the family to privacy and non-interference and the obligations of the wider society to assume responsibility to protect children. The tension generated in considering this balance is perhaps illustrated by stating the extreme positions: on the one hand are those who regard family privacy as sacrosanct, for reasons which range from assumptions about 'parents' rights' to civil liberties arguments about the intrusive power of the modern state. The extreme counterview, informed by perspectives which range from an 'adults know best' viewpoint to radical feminist concerns about the power games of fathers, stresses the need to monitor and control the potential for violence and abuse which exists in the privacy of the family setting.

There can be no easily agreed middle way between positions so fundamentally opposed. This divide, sometimes called the 'liberal democratic dilemma' is one with no simple or easy answers. However, the issue of resources is crucial for both sensitive and effective intervention, as identified by Doran and Young (1987). When intervention is not only mediated by contradictory philosophical arguments, but carried out by professionals who are under-resourced, inadequately trained, pilloried by the press and without any adequate delineation of relative areas of responsibilty or expertise, then the possibility of either inadequate protection or overzealous interference is immeasurably enhanced.

Abuse *within* the care system

This issue is equally central to the argument about the efficacy of care after any intervention has taken place. We cannot assume that the care of the state is necessarily superior to that of a neglectful or abusive parent. The Kincora scandal in Northern Ireland, which revealed that children in care are being sexually abused by some of those entrusted with their care, was remarkable not simply for that fact, but for the form of the local authority's investigation, and the ultimate lack of punitive action against many of those responsible. It is worth noting that in 1991 the Beck case indicated a greater willingness to respond.

Elsewhere local authorities have been taken to court for selling off valuable children's homes, seemingly showing more concern for the corporate balance-sheet than for the traumatic effect on children suddenly uprooted. Teenage boys in the care of Solihull Council obtained a High Court judgement in their favour when the council sought to close Richmond House. In that case the judge ruled that the council should consider the welfare of each individual child expected to be in the home by the proposed closing date (*Community Care*, 17 November 1983).

The desire to reduce the costs of care has increased the attraction of fostering, yet many foster placements break down and local authority supervision is often inadequate. An inquiry into the death of Shirley Woodcock, taken into care by Hammersmith social services department, described the department's policy as 'fostering at all costs', and noted that a key factor in the quality of care provided was the absence of sufficient staff and resources (*Community Care*, 20 January 1983). Lack of continuity in care is a common complaint and one research study found that no less than one in 10 of the children taken into care would have to move to 10 or more foster parents or children's homes (*Guardian*, 29 September 1982).

Increasingly, the voices of those in care and of those who have been raised in care have also entered the debate. Questions which they have raised about the stigmatization of care, the absence of the effective development of those skills necessary for independent living and the failure to place the interests of the child at the centre of the care agenda demand a response (Berridge and Cleaver, 1987). Is being 'taken into care' an abuse in itself?

In a society in which children are relatively powerless it is certainly not the intention of this chapter to argue against an obligation to protect them. However, difficulties arise not only because of the uncertain quality of how we respond. The problem of *when* to respond is relevant. It is by no means always clear that a child has experienced abuse, or alternatively who is responsible. The moral panic generated by child abuse, the understandable caution of professionals afraid to take risks that might render their career in ruins, and the crusading zeal of social work and medical practitioners, may all tilt the balance towards taking action too soon or on insufficient evidence.

A number of lessons emerge from Cleveland, many of which are the focus of other chapters in this book. The point I wish to emphasize here is that whilst society has a clear duty to protect children from sexual and physical abuse, it has an equally clear duty to seek to ensure that no child is separated from his or her parents without good reason and that great care is taken to ensure that parents are not wrongly separated from their children. It certainly requires no great feat of imagination to understand the anguish that arises when parents are not only wrongly accused of abuse but subsequently also have their children removed from them.

Where care proceedings are brought, the test which the court applies is not the criminal one of 'beyond reasonable doubt' but the civil one of 'the balance of probabilities'. This may inevitably lead to children being separated from their parents where the standard of proof is less than adequate. The work of Parents Against Injustice (PAIN) has done much to focus public concern on this issue. The interpretation placed by the courts on injuries to children can be critical for the outcome of the cases, yet recent research on brittle bone disease, for example, has indicated that in a number of cases where children were separated from their parents there was a perfectly plausible medical explanation for the injuries the children had sustained, which should not have cast any doubt on the competence of the parents. In some cases this evidence has not been accepted by the courts and in other cases it has emerged too late for those parents whose children have been removed from them permanently (Sharron, 1987).

Conclusions

The argument in this chapter has been for a wider focus on child abuse and for a recognition of the broader social context within which it occurs. We need to understand that although not all abuse is a consequence of poverty and its related hardships, poverty is a factor which may trigger abuse and in itself denies children and their families the opportunities which society should afford to all our children. We need further to recognize that our understanding of the role of children in contemporary society is both inadequate and insufficiently examined. The importance of listening to children in abuse cases has been well documented, even if legislation still does not fully recognize this. We need to listen to children, however, not simply over this but over a whole range of areas in which we should seek to empower them, to enable them to become self-conscious participants in making their own history and remaking our society. Finally, we need to take on board the fact that any realistic programme to tackle child abuse and neglect will demand considerable social and economic changes and that even the achievement of the modest objectives set by current policy-makers will remain elusive so long as social service departments, particularly in deprived areas, are so grossly under-resourced.

FURTHER READING
The classic in this field is NIGEL PARTON'S *The Politics of Child Abuse*, Macmillan, London, (1985) which still offers the best argued case for widening our definition of child abuse. Parton himself now admits he did not fully address issues of gender and sexual abuse in that book. These are examined more thoroughly in his more recent contributions to *Taking Child Abuse Seriously: Contemporary Issues in Child Protection Theory and Practice* (The Violence Against Children Study Group, Unwin Hyman, London) 1989. A number of recent books address issues of childhood exploitation. Some of the better ones are:
MOORHEAD, C. *Betrayal: Child Exploitation in Today's World*, Barrie and Jenkins, London (1989); TOWNSEND, P. *The Smallest Pawns in the Game*, Granada, London (1980); and VITTACHI, A. *Stolen Childhood: In Search of the Rights of the Child*, Polity Press, Cambridge (1989)

9 CHILDREARING IN A MULTICULTURAL SOCIETY

Wendy Stainton Rogers

Lecturer in Health and Social Welfare, The Open University

Chapter 1 about the social construction of childhood argues that what it is like to be 'a child' depends a very great deal upon when, where and how your childhood is spent. Childhood was very different in Britain 100 years ago, and differed then (as now) according to family status in society (Smelser, 1982). Growing up in the warm climate of the West Indies, in a home that backs onto a communal yard full of other parents and children is literally 'a world away' from growing up in a high-rise flat in cold and rainy Birmingham (Barrow, 1982). A childhood spent in a Muslim household will differ from growing up within a Jewish or Catholic family.

All this may seem so obvious as to be hardly worth stating, save for one very important observation. Despite the very obviousness of the diversity of childhoods, we live and work in a society which tends to assume that there is just one kind of childhood that is 'normal and ordinary'. As Pamela Abbott describes in chapter 7, this idealized image is of a childhood spent in a traditional, two-parent, nuclear family where the husband–father is the breadwinner, and the wife–mother keeps the home and cares for the children. The assumption that this is what is 'normal' is built into contemporary British law and social policy; it is the image presented in advertisements, children's comics, school books and toys. But it does not reflect the diversity of childhoods and childrearing practices in our society; rather it reflects the consensual values, experiences and assumptions of the people who have the most influence on the mass media, politics, social organization, economic and other resources in our society.

These image-makers and settlers of norms have included the academic thinkers and researchers who wrote the basic textbooks about childrearing. For example, Kellmer Pringle (1974) listed six styles of childrearing that meet children's needs:

- full-time parenting throughout childhood;
- full-time parenting for under-fives;
- shared parenting;
- child in daycare, parents both work;
- single-handed parenthood by choice;
- alternative styles of group living.

While Kellmer Pringle's list does at least recognize that care within the traditional nuclear family is not the only 'good' way of bringing up children, her thinking still adheres to the conventions of white, middle-class British culture, assuming a male–female, two-parent family as the 'norm' against which to judge other ways of rearing children.

Today this kind of blinkered approach is being increasingly challenged, particularly now that a few people from 'minority' groups (such as black people, lesbians, people with decidedly working-class roots) are slowly gaining a foothold in academic life. It is becoming recognized that there is a wide diversity of equally good but different ways of bringing up children. This shift has been nicely summed up by Robert and Rhona Rapaport: 'Families in Britain today are in a transition from coping in a society in which there was a single overriding norm of what family life should be like to a society in which a plurality of norms are recognised as legitimate and, indeed, desirable' (Rapaport and Rapaport, 1982, p. 476).

In this chapter I try to give a broad view of the diversities of childrearing. Although many factors (such as religion, social class and ideology) influence the way children are reared, there is not room here to do justice to them all, and so I have concentrated upon those that arise out of differences in ethnic origins. I will explore a number of different aspects of cultural variability in childrearing, including the extra pressures that arise if you grow up as a member of a 'minority' in a society where those in power have very different values and expectations from those of your culture. It needs to be remembered that my own background is that of a white, middle-class woman. Inevitably my account will be limited because of this, but I have done my best to use as sources of information the work of people from ethnic minority backgrounds.

This is a very large area, and even though I have concentrated upon the general pattern of alternatives in the United Kingdom (which, for example, is rather different from the United States), it is impossible to cover all the many cultural differences and the subtleties in a short chapter. I have therefore made some suggestions about further reading at the end of the chapter, which offer much more detailed information.

Different family structures

Most children in the United Kingdom are brought up within a family – although, as we will see, what this means in practice is very fluid. The traditional 'Victorian' model of childrearing within the nuclear family is one of strict division by gender (Smelser, 1982). The father is the 'breadwinner', with little if any responsibility for the day-to-day care of the children, particularly when they are very young, although he may be involved in their sporting or leisure pursuits. As the head of the household, he is, however, the final authority figure, expected to hand out discipline when there has been any serious misbehaviour. The mother, on the other hand, is expected to carry out all the basic physical care of the children, which includes looking after minor injuries and illnesses as well as feeding them and keeping them clean. She monitors their behaviour, and it is she who is expected to instil the appropriate values, and appropriate behaviour according to their gender, position in the family and social status in the community. She is, at the same time, expected to meet their needs for emotional warmth and affection.

This kind of traditional division of labour is to be found in a wide variety of cultural groups. For example, it is the basic model for South Asian families that immigrated to the United Kingdom from India, Pakistan and Bangladesh in the 1950s and 1960s (Ballard, 1982; Morrish, 1971); and for both Turkish and Greek Cypriot families that came to live here (although in smaller numbers) at the same sort of time (Oakley, 1982).

However, these imported cultural patterns differ from the 'Victorian' British model in two important ways. First, such families tend to be much more strictly patrilineal (where property and authority are based in the male line, and pass from father to son). A household consists of a man, his sons and grandsons, together with their wives and unmarried daughters, and the children. Only sons remain family members for life; daughters leave on marriage and join another household. The division is not so much between husband and wife, as between men and women. Households tend to be large and consist of several generations, and even within the home men and women tend to live separate lives. Women generally stay at home, only allowed outside if carefully protected (e.g. by the conventions of *purdah*) and chaperoned.

The second contrast is in the greater importance of what we can loosely translate as 'honour' (*izzat, philotimo*), which applies to the family as a whole, but most particularly to its male head. Any behaviour which goes against accepted cultural rules, by any member of the family, brings shame and dishonour to the family and is an immediate threat to the man's esteem and respect in the community. He will lose face if he is seen to be unable to exert his authority and ensure his family members conform to the norms of good conduct.

These two aspects of family organization create conditions in which the care and rearing of small children is shared by the female relatives who live together in the household. As children become older, their care becomes increasingly divided by gender, with girls remaining with the women of the household, to be taught their future domestic duties and kept in the safety of the home; and boys increasingly introduced to the world of men, and educated both by their relatives and outside the home. Outside interference in childrearing and the management of adolescents will be resisted, because this would expose private family troubles to the community, and thus bring dishonour. If there are problems (such as a parent using overharsh physical punishments) then it is up to other family members to intervene.

In a real sense, then, childrearing in this kind of culture is a communal concern, with the tasks and responsibilities of daily and domestic care shared among the women of the household, and the overall moral standard-setting and control resting with the male head. This kind of shared, communal care among kin can also be found in some traditional communities in the United Kingdom, such as the Scottish Travelling Folk (Whyte (1979) provides a very readable account). It has also been imported into the United Kingdom by communities based on matrilineal family structures, where inheritance is through the mother and the female line; and those based on polygamous marriage, where a man may have several wives. Both systems are still common throughout West Africa (Stapleton, 1978).

Another major 'minority' group in the United Kingdom has its cultural origins in the West Indies. West Indian family structures are diverse, in part because of the great variety of lifestyles to be found in the various islands that make up the area (including Jamaica, Trinidad, Guyana, Barbados and St Kitts). Barrow (1982) has identified three main family styles operating in these communities:

- *'Christian marriage'* based upon the traditional 'Victorian' model of a nuclear family;
- *living together* without formal marriage, in relationships that may be fairly transient or permanent, with children which may or may not be the father's offspring;
- *mother-households* in which the mother or grandmother is the sole, stable head of the family.

In the West Indies, 'Christian marriage' tends to happen (if at all) later in life, when a couple have acquired adequate resources and steady employment to enable them to buy a house and afford a lavish wedding. Living together is more usual when people are younger and poorer, and although the man will tend to undertake the role of breadwinner, his commitment is sometimes less. Some couples stay together for life, other people live with a series of different partners over their lifetimes. In mother-households resources tend to be limited, and the care of small children is shared between sisters and with grandmothers, cousins and aunts so that the women can earn an income and tend crops. Henriques (1953) estimated that in Jamaica, about half of the households are mother-households. Driver (1982) attributes this style of family life to a history of slavery, and to the effects of high male unemployment.

Thus West Indian children may experience care within a household that consists largely of women, and be raised by their grandmother and aunts as much as by their mother. Alternatively, they may live with their mother permanently, but have a series of stepfathers. Or they may grow up within a traditional nuclear family.

Changing families

With immigration into the United Kingdom, these family systems have had to accommodate to new circumstances. For example, it is more difficult to live together as a large household within the kinds of houses typically available in this country. Some Asian families have joined several houses together, but increasingly new generations of parents are setting up nuclear family homes in smaller houses. Although they do try to live as close as possible to the rest of the wider family, women in these families lose easy access to a close network of kinswomen, yet may still be expected to stay at home (Ballard, 1982). West Indian women who grew up in mother-households may no longer have a close network of kinswomen with whom to share childcare. If they have children and want to work outside the home, they have to rely on poorly paid (and often overstretched) childminders (Barrow, 1982). Parents from Africa, unable to leave their children to be cared for within their extended family while they study, may place them with foster parents for several years in the expectation that the children will be returned as soon as they are qualified – expectations that have not always been met (Biggs, 1978).

At the same time the traditional nuclear family lifestyle has itself been changing, as Pamela Abbott notes in chapter 7, with the increase in the divorce rate placing many children in single-parent or reconstituted families, and with a majority of mothers now working outside the home, particularly once their children go to school.

Together these trends have contributed to the current *pluralistic system* in which there co-exists a large variety of different approaches to childrearing, with some inevitable tensions between them. It is also a *dynamic system* within which new generations adjust to changing social conditions and pressures.

Childrearing outside the family

One of the changes that has occurred is that there are now more alternatives available to childrearing within the family, such as refuges for women subjected to violence by their partners. Some women are by choice setting up women-only households in which to bring up their children away from what they regard as the patriarchal domination of men. Although the 1960s was the time when communes were most popular, there continue to exist a small number of extended 'alternative' households, usually run by groups of middle-class people in rural areas. These may be based on friendship or upon a religious order (Abrams and McCulloch, 1976; Wilson, 1982).

But we also need to remember that some quarter of a million children in the United Kingdom sit down each morning to an institutional breakfast, and spend most of their time living outside a family. Together with those in foster care, these children are being reared by people other than their parents, who undertake the task as paid employment (see chapter 10 for a fuller description). Over half of those children living in institutions do so in boarding-schools (most of which are private). The rest live in a variety of residential establishments, usually run by local authorities.

It is important not to confuse these forms of institutional and foster care, directed and controlled by the state or run as educational regimes, with the kinds of indigenous shared care to be found in other cultures. As Ware (cited in Stapleton, 1978) describes of West African children: 'that a child lives with his grandparent, an uncle or even distant cousin in no way implies that a family is breaking up. Unity is in fact maintained by dispersion. The basic family unit is a series of interlocking meshes rather that the isolated cell of western middle class norms' (from Stapleton, 1979, p. 28).

For the West African or the Travelling Folk, what is officially called 'fostering' in the United Kingdom is frequently just a variant of extended family care. And what a white, middle-class person would call 'boarding-school education' would be regarded by them as inhuman, institutional care at the hands of strangers.

Secondary socialization

While most children are likely to receive their first and most important socializing influences within their families, all children in the United Kingdom also experience socialization via outside influences. These include the impact of schooling (both formal teaching and the influence of the other children); of the mass media (particularly, today, television and videos); for some, religious instruction; and for others, things like membership of 'Brownies' or CND. The wider community in which children grow up may also have a dramatic impact (see, for example, chapter 12 about children growing up in Northern Ireland), and for all children it will be important.

Collectively these are called 'secondary agents of socialization' (the family being regarded as the primary agent). 'Socialization' is the word used to describe the way that individuals become members of society – acquiring their social roles according to their gender, social position and so on. It is the process by which we gain our taken-for-granted ideas, values and expectations, and become competent at the skills and tasks expected of us as members of our communities and social groups.

Embedded in the notion of socialization is a recognition that it is an active and directed process – that children do not simply 'grow up', but are actively *brought* up. The adults in any society seek to determine – quite deliberately much of the time – what kind of person a child will become. They try to instil particular values, to teach the child what kinds of behaviour are appropriate, to pass on the rules of conduct individuals in that society are expected to follow.

The functions of childrearing

LeVine (1980) suggests that whatever the many differences between alternative systems of childrearing, there are three goals that are common: to ensure that the child survives; to enable the child to become independent; and to transmit cultural values.

The differences lie in the balance between these. Basic survival may appear the most fundamental, but in extreme conditions it may be that individual children sometimes have to be allowed to die so that others in the family can survive (see Scheper-Hughes, 1987). Independence too varies in the degree to which it is valued. Whereas it is seen as highly desirable in western culture, alongside individual freedom (Rokeach, 1968), in many other cultures group loyalty and inter-dependence are much more important.

It is probably the passing on of cultural values that is the most universal goal. What vary, of course, are the values themselves. For instance, in many cultures respect for elders is of fundamental importance. Children must learn to treat adults – indeed, everybody older than themselves, including older brothers and sisters – with great politeness and respect. Kaye (1962), for example, describes childrearing in Ghana in these terms:

> It is generally considered a sign of disrespect for a child to address an adult, except to reply to a question. Children are expected to lower their voices politely when replying to adults' questions. In the presence of visitors, children are required to sit quietly without saying anything, or leave the room. (p. 166)

Together with such ideas are different expectations about children's and adults' obligations to each other. In contemporary western society obligation tends to be seen as a one-way process (parents have strong obligations to their children, but children have few obligations to their parents). In other cultures obligations tend to be more widespread (to other kin) and mutual (children have duties to their parents, and to the extended family). These include the showing of courtesy and respect, and contributing to family life and well-being – by doing housework, caring for others, working in the family business or trade.

While in all cultures there is a recognition that young children are inevitably dependent, cultures differ vastly in the age at which children are expected to assume adult responsibilities. As an example, in Greek Cypriot families the whole family ministers, effectively 'on demand', to the needs of babies and toddlers. But as they move into the third and fourth years the indulgence declines, and children are expected to run errands and undertake other small tasks. As they approach puberty they come to be regarded as junior adults, given their say in family discussions, and having alloted responsibilities. However, they remain not fully adult until they marry, being until then economically and psychologically dependent on their parents (Oakley, 1982).

Thus, in all cultures childhood is treated as an apprenticeship for adulthood. In western cultures the adulthood for which the child is being prepared is one of self-reliance and reaching one's individual potential, and hence the stress is upon education and personal choice. In many other cultures childrearing is directed to an adulthood of mutual interdependence within an extended family; it therefore focuses more on learning how to become a productive member of the community, knowing your 'place' and developing loyalty to the group.

Different ways of managing behaviour

There are three main ways that adults seek to manage children's behaviour. First, they can use rewards to encourage good behaviour, and punishments and threats to control misbehaviour. Second, they can use systems of emotional control, relying on motivations like guilt and shame to ensure that children conform to accepted rules of conduct. Children learn that 'this is the way such things are done', facing disapproval, loss of face or loss of self-respect if they break the rules. Third, adults seek to manipulate the child's behaviour by explaining the consequences of wrongdoing, reasoning with the child and negotiating acceptable standards.

Although most systems of childrearing incorporate all three, there are variations in which techniques are most usual, and in the ages and situations considered appropriate for each. For example, John and Elizabeth Newson (1976, 1978) found that although the vast majority of parents smacked their small children when they were naughty, middle-class parents tended to smack their children less (particularly as they got older) and reason with them more. In contrast, severe physical punishments have been common in the public schools of the rich, and at the time of writing, corporal punishment (e.g. caning) is still practised in schools outside the state sector (see chapter 14).

Similarly, some cultures, such as those originating in West Africa, have tended to adopt a harsh, disciplinarian approach, which they regard as a sign of caring and committed parenthood. Ellis (1978) illustrates this by the answers given by Ga adolescents she interviewed. When asked what they *liked* about their parents, they said things like 'my father punishes me to be good' and 'she insults me . . . when I am bad'. When they were asked how they would bring up their own children they said they would be even stricter than their parents: 'If a person is trained strictly then that person becomes a good person' (Ellis, 1978, p. 48).

Other cultures focus more on emotional control. This is more typical, for example, in those originating from India and Pakistan, where the communal sense of *izzat* (honour) provides a powerful mechanism to control misbehaviour. Children learn from an early age to feel a sense of shame and humiliation if they betray the family's honour. Not just the adults around them, but the children of their own age will reproach them and regard them as disgraced if they break the rules.

Bringing up children in a multicultural society

Newspaper articles and television programmes often refer to the 'problems of ethnic minorities' as if being in a minority, or even being from a non-indigenous culture, are circumstances that place people at an inevitable disadvantage. Of course this is not true. So long as the 'minority' to which you belong is in a powerful position – such as the British in India in the last century – then maintaining your cultural values and adjusting to new conditions will be relatively easy. The problems faced by people from minority groups in the United Kingdom are at least as much a product of their relative powerlessness as they are to do with being in a minority, as and of itself, or even having to make cultural adaptations to new circumstances.

Bringing up children as a member of a disadvantaged minority group, there are several kinds of problems that have to be faced: the fear that your children will become enculturated away from the values and standards you hold dear; confusions, misunderstandings and mistrust because of your different values and assumptions; ways in which existing customs and traditions are difficult to adapt to new circumstances; a lack of positive role models for your children; the effects of racism or prejudice towards you and your children.

Particularly in cultures based upon strong traditions, parents fear that their children will become 'infected' by the beliefs and values of the dominant culture. For example, in communities where women are expected to be virgins on marriage, the concern will be that daughters will adopt the mores of pre-marital sex promoted within western culture. Sons who would normally be expected to take their place in the family business may be lured away by the promise of personal wealth and fulfilment. Who will care for us when we are old, if our children fail to maintain the close kinship ties that have existed in our family for generations? So parents may become much stricter and more inflexible than they would be otherwise, or they may do all they can to insulate themselves and their children from the wider community, at the same time cutting themselves off from community help and support.

The kinds of confusions that can arise generally have to do with actions or decisions having different meanings for people with different cultural backgrounds. An example noted already is the way that West African parents see fostering as a normal and ordinary thing to do, which does not imply any lack of caring for their children. They are therefore incredulous when they return to reclaim their children, to find a foster mother unwilling to hand them over. Further confusion arises because the two sides fail to understand each other's attitudes to having children. In western society 'you should not have children until you can care for them yourself' – you should put off childbearing until you have finished your studies. In African cultures to be childless is a tragedy, and couples want to guarantee they can have children soon after marriage. Being a student is no reason to wait.

Similarly a number of examples of difficult adjustment to new circumstances have been already described. Jocelyn Barrow vividly describes childhood in the Caribbean:

> In the Caribbean children spend most of their time playing outside the house with mud, sand, water and climbing trees and playing with animals. Even the grinding poverty of the area provides these young children with an advantage: since parents are too poor to buy toys children are forced to use the odds and ends found in the 'backyard' resulting in a lot of creative and imaginative play. This play provides them with intellectually stimulating experiences. The play with sand and water or mud develops their manipulative skills and physical co-ordination in readiness for school. In keeping with the oral tradition of the West Indies – part of our African heritage – there are always two or three older women talking to the young children, telling them stories, teaching them and answering their questions. (Barrow, 1982, p. 225)

Barrow notes that this pattern of care does not transpose easily to Leeds and Brixton, where West Indian children may be being looked after for much of the day in cold and damp rooms, cut off by climate and lack of outside play space from other children and adults. Frequently they must be left by their parents with unregistered childminders who do not have the resources to provide sand trays, water troughs, toys or books, and where the economic and social pressures also prevent the childminder from having much time to play with the children or tell them stories.

At the beginning of this chapter I described how childrearing diversity is made 'invisible', by advertisers and the makers of television soap operas portraying just one kind of upbringing as normal and ordinary. Similarly, people from ethnic and other minorities have been represented as marginal rather than 'ordinary folks', much less people with power, influence or qualities of leadership. Slowly things are changing, though some commentators see what is happening as little more than tokenism. But it was not until the 1987 general election that black children and young people could see a black woman in parliament. Children from minority groups are deprived of powerful, positive images with which they can identify. So motivating them, or helping them to feel good about themselves, is all the more difficult.

Finally, belonging to a minority group often means being subjected to prejudice and harassment. Not only does this place additional stresses on adult carers (such as isolating them from their friends and community), it means that they must teach children how to cope with living in a society in which they may be victimized. They may need to be extra protective of their children, restricting their opportunities in order to keep them safe at home.

Conclusion

Despite these extra difficulties, the vast majority of families facing them are able to bring up their children with great flexibility, accommodating to new circumstances while retaining their dearly held cultural traditions. And while young people from minority cultural groups may (like other young people) rebel against their parents, most 'return to the fold' in young adulthood, and proudly preserve their culture, albeit also adapting to social changes and gaining familiarity with the wider culture in which they live.

Ballard (1982) notes that what tends to happen, even in teenage years, is that young people become extremely capable at acting appropriately in different settings – switching their modes of behaviour according to the context in which they find themselves. Weinreich (1979) has conducted a number of studies of the way young people from ethnic minority cultures develop fluent senses of themselves. They face conflicts in their search for identity, but generally they do ultimately find strategies for feeling good about themselves. The more we, as a society, are prepared to respect and value the diversity of ways of being and ways of doing things in a multicultural society, the easier they will find this task, and the more successful they will be.

FURTHER READING

For a broad overview of the diversity of family lifestyles and systems of childrearing, a good place to start is the book *Families in Britain*, edited by R. N. RAPAPORT, M. P. FOGARTY AND R. RAPAPORT (1982). This contains the chapters by Smelser, Ballard, Driver, Barrow and Oakley cited in this chapter (see references for full details), together with others on topics like single-parent families, families in poverty and families and divorce, and a good review article by PHYLLIS AND PETER WILLMOTT, 'Children and family diversity'.

A good source of information about socialization is *The Integration of a Child into a Social World* edited by M. P. M. RICHARDS (1974). Particularly useful is the historical review of changes in childrearing: 'Cultural aspects of childrearing in the English-speaking world' by JOHN AND ELIZABETH NEWSON.

For an introduction to the topic of cultural diversity, *Minority Families in Britain* edited by V. SAIFULLAH KAHN (1979), offers a wide-ranging series of articles, although some can be tough reading at times! Somewhat older, but with a great deal of background information about West Indian, Indian and Pakistani culture, including details about their religions, is provided by *The Background of Immigrant Children* by IVOR MORRISH (1971). A more detailed description of the impact of immigration on West Indian families is provided in *West Indian Families in Britain* edited by J. ELLIS (1978). Good, recent reviews are provided by AHAMAD, B. (1989) 'Child Care and Ethnic Minorities' pp 152–168 in *Child Care Research, Policy and Practice*, Hodder and Stoughton, London, and the Commission For Racial Equality (1981) *Caring for Under-fives in a Multi-racial Society*. Both offer good examinations of the issues raised for children from ethnic minorities, and the kinds of services they require.

Finally, *The Yellow on the Broom* by BETSY WHYTE (1978) is simply a 'good read'. It is a personal account of the author's childhood as a traveller woman in Scotland. It offers an insight into life as a member of an indigenous 'minority' group in the United Kingdom, and a first-hand description of what it is like to be forced by social progress to undergo cultural change.

10 CARING FOR OTHER PEOPLE'S CHILDREN

Adrian Ward

Senior Lecturer in Social Work, University of Reading

In this chapter we will be examining what happens when children are looked after by people other than their own parents: what it feels like to be the carer as well as how the child may feel, and what sort of special difficulties may arise and why. This is an important area of study because we know that many cases of child abuse and neglect involve people other than the child's natural parents. Neustatter (1986) quotes National Society for the Prevention of Cruelty to Children (NSPCC) research in which it was found that 'father-substitutes were implicated in 61 per cent of physical injury cases and 88 per cent of sexual abuse cases where the children were living with them'. These statistics should be viewed with some caution, however (see Giles-Sims and Finkelhor, 1984). There have been some particularly shocking cases involving step-parents in recent years, for example the cases of Heidi Koseda and Jasmine Beckford (see London Borough of Brent, 1985), and other cases in which children have been abused by foster parents, residential workers, teachers, childminders and others. We need to try to understand why this happens.

One useful starting-point is to reflect that we all know what it is like to be cared for by someone else. Every child has some experience of being cared for by someone other than his or her own parents, whether on a daily basis at school, with a childminder or baby-sitter, or (for some) with foster parents, adoptive parents or step-parents. Most people will also remember from their childhood at least one night spent away from home in a hospital or other institution. Equally, most adults have some experience of caring for someone else's child, even if only briefly – whether through minding a neighbour's children for an afternoon, other short-term caring of grandchildren or other children of relatives, or in the course of their work, in teaching, nursing, police work or many other professions.

Whether you have had this experience as a child or as an adult, you will know that it is not always an easy experience. Rules, habits and mutual understandings which can usually be taken for granted between children and their own parents do not always transfer easily to other situations. Things can quickly become fraught when a problem or conflict arises, and feelings may run very high, including feelings of panic and resentment on both sides. Of course, in the great majority of these situations, the problems soon pass or resolve themselves: if the arrangements were temporary anyway, then relief comes soon, and where the arrangements are of a longer-term or regularly repeated nature, ground rules are established, and from there trust and even love will develop, and the difficulties subside. In some circumstances, however, the difficulties remain serious and may even lead ultimately to situations in which child abuse or neglect occurs. It is these circumstances which we need to understand, although it should be emphasized that our focus here will be on the difficulties inherent in parenting others' children rather than on specific examples of child abuse. We will examine the subject in two stages, looking first at some general aspects of caring for other people's children, and secondly at some specific difficulties which may arise in particular settings, drawing examples from step-parenting and residential care.

'Parenting' means not only the physical care of the child, of course, although it is often through this physical caring that many of the other aspects of parenting are expressed, such as concern for the child's emotional well-being and development, and passing on the norms and values of the parents' culture. Parenting also involves the building and rebuilding over time of a loving relationship, set within the context of a wider family and social background. Parents and children are all familiar with this shared and developing history, and they remind each other of it constantly, both at a conscious and unconscious level: it is this factor, among others, which helps the child to establish a sense of personal identity.

Different types of carers
The different settings in which children and young people are cared for involve varying degrees of parenting, depending on such factors as the length of time spent with the child, the purpose of the setting and the role of the carer(s) in relation to the natural parents as well as to the child. A continuum of involvement (see Table 1) can be visualized.

Table 1 *Continuum of involvement for parenting by carers*

Full-time parenting	Residential care	Day care	Sessional/ occasional care
Natural parents	Boarding-school	Day nursery	Playgroup
Step-parents	Children's home	Childminder	Intermediate
Foster parents	Assessment centre	School	treatment centre
	Detention centre	Nanny	Youth club
	Hospital		Day clinic
	Prison		Leisure and recreation facilities
			Baby-sitter

At one end of the continuum, full-time parenting by the natural parents involves 24-hour responsibility, seven days a week (even if the parent is not with the child all that time) and a long-term commitment to the future of a particular child. Some have described this level of commitment as 'irrational' whereas others have pointed to the genetic investment that biological parents have in the success of their offspring. Step-parenting and foster parenting involve similar full-time responsibility, but may or may not involve a long-term commitment to the child's future, or at least, not to the same extent. Indeed, many foster parents foster children for relatively short periods without the expectation of eventual adoption, and plans for their long-term future may be the responsibility of a social worker on behalf of a local authority which has assumed 'parental rights'.

Residential care for children and young people can serve many different functions, including education, punishment and treatment as well as care (see Table 1). Residential care is characterized by a pattern of group rather than family living in which the carers share out total responsibility through shift-work and the specialization of roles. For example, in boarding-schools there are subject-teachers, a school nurse or matron, cooks and cleaners, as well as particular teachers with a pastoral caring role as house-parents. The length of time over which commitment to the child extends depends on the duration of involvement (hospitals for example often only necessitate short stays) and is located at an institutional rather than an individual level. Moving further along the continuum, those working with children on a daily or sessional basis are usually in a position of sharing care with parents who still assume their full parenting responsibilities. The degree of involvement with children may be extensive but for a limited period, as in the care given by childminders or nursery workers, or it may be associated with a specialist function such as education or recreational activities, and any long-term commitment to the child is likely to be extremely limited. This description is far from comprehensive, but serves to highlight some of the differences and commonalities between the roles that different sorts of carers play in relation to children and to the extent to which 'parenting' is involved.

As is made clear in chapter 5, parenting is by no means a straightforward task. It involves balancing many conflicting needs and demands, including the parents' own needs. For most parents the stresses of parenting are outweighed by the rewards and joys of seeing their child grow and develop towards independence. But a question arises as to whether these stresses are greater when the child is not one's own or the rewards and joys any less? What are the factors which make the difference between parenting one's own child and someone else's?

Lack of a shared history
When you take on parenting someone else's child, the shared and developing history that is the basis of confidence-building and mutual trust is lacking. In fact there may be factors which actively inhibit the development of trust: the child may have experienced the breakdown of trust in the past and may be very wary of starting again with someone else, or may perhaps retain a loyal commitment to the parent with whom he or she no longer lives which prevents emotional investment in any new parental figure.

Childcare workers, including foster parents, find ways of helping children both to retain a strong sense of their earlier history and to begin to invest emotionally in their new life, through the use of life story books and other techniques (Fahlberg, 1979; Ryan and Walker, 1985).

Grief and loss
There is an important theme of loss and grief which runs throughout any consideration of looking after other people's children. For some children this loss may refer to an actual bereavement, and for some to desertion by a parent through divorce, while even some of those being cared for on a temporary or part-time basis may experience the separation from their parents as highly traumatic. For a vivid portrayal of the reactions of young children to temporary separation, see *John* and other films in the series 'Young Children in Brief Separation' by James and Joyce Robertson. Additionally, a few children have been so acutely deprived of interest and affection right from their infancy that they seem to be in a permanent state of mourning (or of denial) – grieving not so much for others as for themselves. Looking after a child such as this will be an exceedingly difficult task.

When a child loses a parent, it may also lose that part of itself which was invested in the parent, and may thus lose the ability or will to form a new attachment. Where it is the child who has had to leave a difficult family situation to go into foster care, both the child and the foster parents may have to cope with ambivalent feelings about the natural parents and siblings whom the child has temporarily 'lost'. Those taking on the care of someone else's child may in addition find their own sense of loss reawakened.

The experience of loss is known to be a source of considerable stress and potential distress for most people (Marris, 1974), and is likely to have a strong influence on the thoughts and feelings both of the child and of the new carers. We should not forget that the parent whose child goes into foster care may also suffer powerful feelings of loss. See the videotape *It's Like a Bereavement* (BAAF), which features interviews with parents whose children are in long-term foster care. What will be most important will be the extent to which the loss has been recognized and mourned: the child who cannot accept the fact that a much-loved parent has died, or that the family situation had broken down irretrievably, is likely to be quite unable to accept the reality of a new carer. Such a child may do all that he or she can in order to prove that the new parent is not good enough, or not worthy of recognition or respect. It is important to enable children to face the reality of loss and to experience the full process of mourning, if they are to develop more appropriate relationships with new parental figures.

These issues will not arise in every situation to the same degree, and in many cases plenty of positive 'gains' can be identified both for the child and for the new carer which will easily outweigh the losses.

Thinking we know best

Many of us have a tendency to feel that other people's children have not been brought up properly – that we would have done it differently and made a better job of it. On the other hand some of us are overconscious of our limitations and fearful of failing completely in the parenting role.

These feelings, eloquently described in a useful article by Anthony (1958), may not matter very much until they are put to the test. It is one thing to have such feelings about a friend's children who visit for the afternoon, but quite another to have them about the child to whom one is step-parent, foster parent or childminder. The temptation is to try to improve or alter the child, without negotiating fully and openly with the child's natural parents about the child's needs, habits and behaviour, and working out together how to handle any difficulties.

Sexual feelings

Between most children and their parents there are natural taboos and 'incest barriers' governing the expression and satisfaction of sexual needs. These inbuilt rules do not necessarily apply when we are caring for other people's children. As Anthony (1958) expresses it: 'The child's attractive appearance may wake so much response in the worker that he may either emotionally seduce the child or, reactively, treat him with special harshness.' The confusion and ambivalence arising within the care worker may compound the difficulty of an already demanding task and taken to extremes this complicated set of feelings may result in the sexual abuse of the child.

Examples

In order to illustrate the range of issues which may arise for those looking after other people's children, we shall now consider brief examples from two settings. Step-parenting and the residential care of children have been chosen since they incorporate many of the key issues.

Step-parenting

People may choose to take on the task of step-parenting for a variety of reasons, but there is always some degree of choice – even if they do not always fully realize what they are taking on. Most researchers who have studied step-families suggest that people enter into these arrangements with 'loving hopefulness and enthusiasm' (Robinson, 1980), although for some people, the reality which follows is quite different from their expectations. In fact the evidence from a national study of children in step-families suggests that while most step-families function well enough, when things do go wrong they may go badly wrong (Ferri, 1984) and this view is supported elsewhere. In an article in the *Guardian* (Toynbee, 1985), an adult's memories of step-childhood are quoted thus: 'Neither of my parents beat us, but they did nothing to hide their antagonism or resentment, and we came to wish we had never been born' (p. 10). On the other hand, an American study makes it clear that the common notion that step-parents are more likely to abuse their children than are natural parents is not conclusively supported by research evidence (Giles-Sims and Finkelhor, 1984).

Another common notion with which step-parents have to contend is the image of the 'wicked stepmother' as portrayed in many fairy tales and other childhood stories. Many actual stepmothers have described how difficult it was for them to overcome the stigma associated with this childhood image. The impact of this and many other myths on the task of step-parenting in the real world is fascinatingly described by Brenda Maddox (1975).

With these introductory comments in mind, we will now consider the issues facing one step-family and speculate on some of the possible feelings and dilemmas of the individuals involved.

Jenny (aged 29) was divorced three years ago, following her husband Bill's desertion. She has recently married Mark (26), who has not been married before and has no children of his own. Jenny's two children from the first marriage, Paula (11) and Ben (7), continue to live with Jenny and Mark in the same three-bedroomed council house in which they have lived for the past 10 years. When her first marriage broke up, Jenny became very depressed, and found that she actually received a lot of support from Bill's parents who live nearby, but who had originally been very critical of her for marrying so young, and who now felt that she had brought all her troubles upon herself.

Jenny still feels some unresolved grief for her first husband, and thinks that in some way she failed Bill, even though it was he who walked out on the family. Jenny has high hopes for her new marriage, although it has all happened in something of a rush, and she feels she has not had enough time alone with Mark to really get to know him. She sometimes finds that the children get in the way of her developing relationship with Mark, but she also feels some concern that they do not appear to accept him fully. Jenny is uncertain over the sharing of parental roles between Mark and herself, for example Mark seems to want to control the children in a much stricter way than she has ever felt necessary.

Mark finds that he has taken on a far more complicated situation than he had anticipated. His main motivation for getting married was his love for Jenny, but he now finds that he has very little time with her alone, as she is always preoccupied with the children. Mark is very inexperienced in looking after children, and was an only child himself. He feels he does not really know Paula and Ben and is uncertain as to how far he is entitled to discipline them or the extent to which he can be close and intimate with them. He is particularly troubled by the sexual feelings he has for Paula, who is developing physically and bears an increasingly strong resemblance to Jenny. He finds Ben contradictory – sometimes friendly and playful, but at other times provocative and hostile. If anything, Ben resembles his father more than his mother, which further feeds Mark's ambivalent feelings about him.

The two children have mixed feelings about the situation. On the one hand, wariness and even resentment of Mark, coupled with ambivalent memories of their own father and a new uncertainty over their relationship to Jenny. On the other hand, they have feelings of closeness and loyalty to Jenny and a strong clinging to each other.

The issues which have arisen in this family include the following:

- conflicts of loyalty which each person is experiencing;
- unresolved feelings of loss and grief;
- confusion and lack of clarity about parental roles;
- mismatching between expectations and realities;
- further complications which may develop out of each person's attempts to deal with the difficulties which they face.

It is important to recognize, however, that each family's situation is unique. The various factors described here will therefore arise in varying degrees and combinations – and in some circumstances they may scarcely arise at all, or they may be relatively easily dealt with.

Residential care
Many of the issues which arise in step-parenting can also be found in residential care. For our purposes here, we will use the example of children's homes to illustrate the issues which arise for those looking after other people's children in the residential setting – although even within the scope of the term 'children's home' may be included several different types of unit, such as assessment centres, 'family-group homes' etc. (see Berridge, 1985, p. 14). Despite the increasing professionalization of residential childcare, and the fact that the children's homes continue to perform 'a variety of valuable functions for the child care system' (*ibid.*, p. 128), for many of the staff this form of employment is still a low-status, low-pay profession with a lack of adequate support and training, and with many young and inexperienced workers.

The Wagner Report (National Institute for Social Work, 1988) on residential care comments that residential services (across all client groups): 'depend on a vast army of low paid, untrained people; the vast majority of whom are women, many working part-time' (p. 71). The lack of training and support is crucial, and increases the likelihood of the workers feeling isolated and insecure. For example, Dunham (1978), writing on staff stress in this work, comments that a source of insecurity is: 'lack of psychological knowledge, a feeling that one is out of one's depth with a particular child or the (unit) as a whole'.

The children in residential care (like many of those in fostering and adoption situations) may have already suffered major losses in their lives and endured various traumas. In addition, many of these children will have been abused at home (whether emotionally, physically or sexually), and may compulsively attempt to re-create abusive interactions with their new carers in order to test out how far they can be trusted.

There is clearly a risk that individual workers will lose the capacity to reflect and respond appropriately to the child's needs and will be drawn into retaliation. Indeed, some residential workers find themselves in a situation which mirrors that of 'abusive parents', in that they are: 'chronically over-stressed and under-supported, have incompatible demands made on them, and are alienated and relatively powerless to control their fate' (Durkin, 1985).

At an institutional level the staff group as a whole may react by developing over-rigid, routinized or grossly insensitive care practices. In some settings, the abuse may take the form of a violent 'subculture' which develops between some of the children with the collusion of a subgroup of staff – a good description of this phenomenon may be found in David Wills's (1971) account of the approved school which was later transformed into the Cotswold Community. At an even more serious level, the abuse may even take the form of organized ill-treatment of the sort recently uncovered (or partly uncovered) at the Kincora Boys' Home in Northern Ireland (see Committee of Inquiry into Children's Homes and Hostels, 1986).

These examples of ill-treatment and abuse, however, are thankfully not typical of residential care, and they clearly represent a very extreme version of the difficulties which can arise. Residential care can and does offer very positive parenting to many children.

If residential workers are to provide good enough parenting for the children in their care, they need to be clear about what they are doing and what the expectations on them are, and they need to have proper support through any difficulties. In this respect, the needs of residential workers are just the same as those of step-parents, childminders and anyone else looking after other people's children.

Conclusion

The question was posed earlier in this chapter as to whether the stresses of parenting are greater when the child is not one's own, and whether the rewards and joys are less. We have considered some of the factors which are likely to make it more difficult to parent someone else's child, and two examples of the ways in which these and other factors may combine in any given situation. This evidence does suggest that it is potentially more demanding, more confusing and less rewarding to parent other people's children than your own, but also that, given the right conditions, many of these difficulties can be overcome.

We should remember that many of the people in each of the settings mentioned in this chapter make a great success of looking after other people's children. It has not been our intention here to suggest that looking after other people's children always leads to terrible difficulties. Rather we have tried to show that it is a complicated task, in which people may well have to face extra stress factors and potential conflicts in addition to those which parents have to contend with, and often with less confidence and support.

FURTHER READING

A good overview of the issues is provided by *Child Care: Concerns and Conflicts*, Hodder and Stoughton (1989). Edited by SONIA MORGAN and PETER RIGHTON, it has chapters on permanence, transracial placements, fostering and a whole section on practice issues in residential care.

11 THE ABUSE OF DISABLED CHILDREN AND YOUNG PEOPLE

Geoffrey Watson

A few years ago I discovered – beyond doubt – that a disabled child who was well known to me had been sexually abused. It came as a shock. My own view of social reality had been that handicapped children were sacrosanct, not to be touched. Other children, perhaps, but not the disabled. Yet as I carried out research into the subject I found that such children were not in fact protected by taboo. They proved to be no less objects of desire for a potential sexual abuser than other children. And they were more likely to be physically abused, though in both cases firm evidence has not always been easy to find.

In this chapter my aim is to describe some of the disabilities from which children suffer and the way in which such children are in special danger of being abused. I shall close by suggesting how we may try to help.

What are they called?

In chapter 1 Rex Stainton Rogers describes how we make a social construction of childhood. In the past we used the words 'idiot' and 'moron' in regard to certain people, and we built up a social construction that they were to be feared, or that they were useless and only to be left in a heap in the corner. Those reformers who came to believe that such children could lead a worthwhile life in their own right, had first to change these labels. They spoke of 'mental handicap' and 'retardation'. Today these names have themselves gained a negative meaning, and new ones are preferred. 'Handicap' is giving way to 'disability' or 'learning difficulty'. The children are the same, and they are the subject of this study. For convenience, we can classify the main headings into five groups:

1 Physical disabilities

These include the effects of accidental injury and also blindness and deafness. They may be present at birth as in spina bifida, where a fault in the spine leads to a paralysis in the limbs (of varying severity according to its position), or cerebral palsy, where the trouble lies in damage within the brain. If the motor centres of the brain are affected, then arms or legs may be useless or 'shaky', or the child may be unable to speak. Note that they may otherwise have normal or superior mental ability. Cerebral palsy can also occur after birth, perhaps as a result of abuse. Thus shaking a baby can cause a 'whiplash' effect and brain damage.

2 Behavioural or emotional problems

Some children, who may be of high intelligence, are so severely disturbed that they act in ways which may be harmful to themselves or to others. The cause may lie in some early neglect or maltreatment, although often it is difficult to determine the precise problem.

3 *Learning difficulties*
The cause may be unknown, or may be associated with social conditions. It may be due to brain damage, or to a specific genetic imbalance, such as Down's syndrome. Neglect and malnutrition can lead to a permanent deficit in growth and intelligence, 'failure to thrive' or a condition which is sometimes called abuse dwarfism.

4 *Specific problems*
These include epilepsy, speech defect and autism. The latter can lead to strange, disturbing behaviour, including self-injury or a cutting off from the world, so that the child appears to have little intelligence. Yet at times such children are capable of remarkable creative work.

5 *Stigmatization*
I knew a girl who appeared to be normal in every way, except that she was fat. She specialized in being a hockey goalkeeper. Yet when I got 'beneath the skin', as it were, I found a desperately unhappy child whose life was patterned by gibes, remarks and expectations relating to her fatness. To be called names is the beginning of abuse. Any child who is different can suffer in this way. To be the 'wrong size' (small or extra large), to have a prominent birthmark, to be an albino, to be the only black child in a white class; in all these cases there may be a stigma. Some groups have religious or magical beliefs about the stigma; it may be thought to be a mark of the devil, so that the child becomes an outcast.

The severity of the disability
Any disability may be mild or severe, but either sort can lead to abuse. There is a saying that while severe disablement causes sorrow, a mild one causes disappointment. In the latter case children may appear to be normal, and yet be unable to reach the standards of their peers; their parents think that they could do better.

Learning difficulties are classified as mild, moderate, severe or profound. The Warnock Report (DES, 1978) suggests that in the United Kingdom one-sixth of all children have special educational needs. Some of these needs arise from specific learning difficulties such as problems with reading. Some are severe, but most of them are mild.

Children with profound learning difficulties may have a lack of understanding and ability to reason, or may be unable to move, speak or communicate. They may engage in head-banging, pica (eating inappropriate objects), or coprophagy (eating dung or filth); they may be violent, rebellious or untrustworthy; they may expose their body improperly or engage in public masturbation (for more information see Hogg and Sebba, 1986).

Why disabled children are at risk
Like myself, you may not expect disabled children to be abused. However, in my research I have come across six main reasons why they can be at risk.

1 *Cultural factors*
Some societies search for what is 'normal', or perhaps for some ideal of beauty and perfection. In doing so they reject deviants. Indeed, as Brian Corby explains in chapter 2, they may 'cull' them by allowing them to die, so that they can bring up those who are not deviant. Rex Stainton Rogers points out in chapter 1 that a society may 'construe' different ages at which a child becomes a person, so that it becomes legitimate to kill those who are not yet considered to be persons. The religious beliefs of parents may cause them to regard handicapped children as unclean or material for sacrifice. The children are feared or hated; they are abused.

Parents feel they have an investment in their children and want them to turn out well. The child will not learn? Let it be punished. Perhaps the disability results from sin on the part of the child. Worse still, it may result from the sin of the parent. Let it be exorcised by suffering. Does the whole family suffer from various troubles? Then there must be a cause, a scapegoat. And the scapegoat is the disabled child – with more punishment as the answer.

2 Abuse-provoking characteristics

Some children have characteristics which 'provoke' abuse (see Rusch et al., 1986). Fear, aggression, destructiveness, whining, hyperactivity or withdrawal are such qualities. Emotionally disturbed youngsters may provoke both physical and sexual abuse. Premature children are small and may have a high-pitched crying, which some mothers cannot stand. Any 'abnormal' children may be at risk of child abuse, especially because the usual bonding between the children and their mothers may be delayed or lacking.

Unattractive children in themselves may draw physical abuse (and handi-capped children are often unattractive). They may show tantrums, incontinence, violence, noise, poor feeding and sleeping patterns and unpredictability.

3 Extra stresses on caregivers in the family setting

Families with handicapped children can have immense frustrations, brought on by problems such as lack of sleep, an endless demand on their time, or the caring for permanent incontinence. They may suffer social isolation and cannot see an end to the care. And the child may appear to be totally unresponsive. It is not surprising that carers may develop antagonistic reactions to the child and a negative perception of the child's behavioural difficulties. Where there are other children it becomes difficult to decide on priorities for the allocation of resources. Parents may find that they never have a break. Conditions become ripe for physical abuse, which may consist of a genuine attempt to control the child by punishment, or which may be uncontrolled violence due to frustration.

Some families rise to the challenge of a handicapped child and give protection and even over-protection to their child. (Indeed, it may be a non-handicapped brother or sister who gets a raw deal in the family!) They may make full use of support groups and schools.

However, many families under stress tend not to use the services which are available and the behaviour of the handicapped child may worsen. Conflict develops within the family, such as bullying by the brothers or sisters, while from peers there may be rejection, sexual exploitation and stigmatization. Between the parents marital stress may develop, especially if their role in dealing with the child is not clear-cut. In a family which is already stressed, minor illness or other mishaps can trigger abuse.

The more a child is helpless, the more opportunities arise for exploitation such as sexual abuse. The child who cannot communicate normally is less able to complain. And if disabled children do confide about abuse, they are less likely to be believed.

4 Institutional abuse

If the child is given day or residential care, the problems can be three-fold: 'professional' child abuse; neglect; and denial of rights.

'Professional' child abuse comes from an unexpected quarter – the medical and other professionals. Gostin (1987), in an article entitled 'Ammonia up the nose, compressed air in the face: abuse or therapy?', questions some of the methods used to 'treat' disabled children. The methods may range from straight punishment (spanking) to isolation. A sudden shock, such as a loud noise, may be used to change behaviour, although some children (e.g. Down's children) may have a cardiac weakness. The problem is that such techniques are given full theoretical justification with a name such as 'behaviour modification'. The 'Pin-Down' scandal showed that behaviour modification can be used to justify effective solitary confinement. In the past deaf children have had their thumbs tied together in the playground so that they could not sign to each other with their hands, and so learn to lip-read.

Neglect consists of the failure to meet needs, to provide suitable conditions for the social and intellectual development of the child, or to arrange for the child to leave the institution if improvement has occurred. It can easily occur in institutions where there are many problems, including poorly paid staff with low status trying to care for too many children and young people. There is often a lack of resources. Staff may not be trained (one study found that 30% of staff in some UK institutions were without training). Hence the staff try to take short-cuts. Hewitt (1987), writing about the United Kingdom, quotes the case of mentally handicapped girls who were lined up naked and hosed down like cattle.

Maureen Oswin has described the lack of stimulation which is given to some inmates of institutions (see Oswin, 1984). Dennis (1973) worked in the United States with two similar groups, one in an institution and one outside. He found that the abilities of the first group had become very poor indeed as compared with the second, suggesting that lack of stimulation is itself abuse and leads to further handicap.

Denial of rights involves the deprivation of letters or visits, or of consultation with outside agencies, or lack of privacy for intimate needs.

5 Lack of treatment or opportunity to learn

If the social construction of carers (whether parents or not) is that handicapped children do not have a life of their own and cannot learn, then truly they will not learn. The child becomes a heap in the corner. Such neglect is itself a form of abuse. Some parents delegate their care by placing the child in an institution. The abuse still occurs if there is a lack of diagnosis or treatment in the new setting, or if the child feels rejected and is never visited.

Imagine that you are a cerebrally palsied child who can hear and think, but cannot speak or move. Then imagine that you are left alone without help or stimulation of any kind. That, indeed, is abuse.

6 The dilemmas of handicap

A great problem arises when physical growth outstrips mental development. The child becomes strong, but is motivated by an immature mind and can be difficult to control. In particular the sexual development at adolescence requires great delicacy on the part of the carer. If a teenager requires intimate care and attention, then the opportunity for abuse is increased.

In the case of the young person with cerebral palsy, the situation is reversed: the mental development may be normal, but parts of the body do not function. Intimate care may again be necessary. Meanwhile, to ignore developing sexuality is in itself a form of abuse. Yet a problem can arise for carers who endeavour to assist the young people in their sexual expression – the risk is two-faced, a risk of sexual abuse, or of being accused of it. Hence the dilemma.

Blind children are at risk because, if attacked, they may not be able to identify their attackers. But that said, attackers have sometimes been caught out when a child has identified a garment by touch. Deaf children, too, may be vulnerable as they often have difficulty in communicating, or in finding someone in whom to confide. Emotionally disturbed children can act sexually and hence offer opportunities for abuse. Any helper has a double bind: how to show affection and make contact with sensorily impaired children (by touching, for example), while at the same time avoiding charges of abuse. This problem is one for all teachers, but especially for teachers of handicapped children. The same tightrope has to be walked by anyone who teaches them sex education. Such dilemmas lead us into our final section, when we shall consider whether we have any answers.

How can we help?

In chapters 1 and 2 Rex Stainton Rogers and Brian Corby both describe how some people wish to protect children, while others give themselves the aim of empowering or liberating them. The conflict between these two modes of thought is perhaps all the more crucial where there is a handicap. To protect is a simple (though not an easy) concept. But many people go further; they seek to enable disabled people to live as fully as they possibly can. The aim is to help them to help (and protect) themselves. The means are perhaps three-fold: communication, openness and education.

1 *Communication*

This is the key word for anyone who seeks to detect abuse, or wishes to teach, counsel or help our children with special needs. Even though a child may be able to understand and use normal speech, any communication may need to be backed by clear presentation with concrete images, such as pictures, models or dolls.

In most cases, the child *can* communicate, but the worker needs to discover how each one does so, in spite of defects in organs such as those of speech, sight, hearing or limbs. It is much better to talk directly to the child than to use an interpreter. A child with speech problems may have learned other techniques such as operating a computer or a keyboard with one finger, a toe or a handband pointer. A child with severe learning difficulties may use sign language (e.g. Makaton). A blind child can hear and talk, but needs models, sound, touch or bodily demonstration. A deaf child may use lip-reading or a sign language. Kiernan (1985) gives a list of methods.

We have to be ready to attend to disabled children. As with other children, they can be believed. But caution must be used with disturbed children, who may live in a fantasy world.

2 *Openness*

We have noted the problems of care and sex education. How can we avoid the dangers of being charged with abuse? And how indeed can we detect real abuse when it occurs? One answer is openness. A network of people needs to be drawn in, with a central core of child, teacher, parent, surrounded by friends and self-help groups and then including social and community workers and administrators. Draw everyone into plans for sex education, for example. Let others be present when you work with the children. Let everyone know what is going on.

Further, it should be possible for each child in an institution to have a 'friend', from outside the institution, to whom he or she can turn and who keeps an eye on his or her general welfare. Such a person is sometimes called a 'citizen advocate' (e.g. see Wolfensberger and Zauha, 1973).

3 *Education*

People can be taught. Parents can be taught to cope. Brothers and sisters can be taught to support the disabled member of the family. Disabled children can be taught. Severely autistic children may bang their heads or do themselves serious injury (which can usually be distinguished from abuse by others). Something has to be done, but the child need not be abused. There are effective ways of teaching such children. A first step is to ask why the child behaves in this self-destructive manner. (Is it fear? Is it lack of stimulation?) Then a suitable programme can be constructed.

Children can be educated in social and sexual behaviour. In the Netherlands keeping children ignorant of sex is regarded as a form of abuse and officially listed as such. Handicapped children have feelings like anyone else, and have a right to know what is happening to them. Further, sex education can help to guard and guide them in their development. Nearly all handicapped children can understand and be taught the concepts of sexuality, provided that suitable teaching methods are used (see Watson, 1984; Craft, 1987).

Children with learning difficulties do not 'pick up' sexual information as other children do, often by jokes or innuendo. They may not understand the diagrams and jargon which is used in sex education. Any teaching must in any case be 'generalized' to new situations. Hence 'concrete' methods should be used, e.g. real condoms demonstrated rather than shown in pictures.

Role-play can familiarize children with real situations and is especially useful for teaching social skills. Positively, children learn to make relationships; negatively, they learn how to say 'no'. They can be taught that they have the control of their own bodies. Michelle Elliott, in chapter 36, describes how children can be protected from abuse. She has adapted her methods to children with learning difficulties. An important aspect is the concept of 'good' and 'bad' touching.

Among the general population it is not known how many children suffer sexual abuse and remain unharmed or recover spontaneously. However, in some cases the emotional upset is so great that the child – though originally 'normal' – becomes numbered among 'the handicapped'. Other initially disabled children may suffer similar trauma. Sinason (1988) has shown how a skilled therapist may be able to approach the child and help to heal the damage. She has bridged the gap between the child's world and the world of reality, even in cases where the child has been thought to have profound difficulties and to be unable to communicate.

A disabled child is a person like anyone else. All that is asked is just a little extra help.

FURTHER READING

ANN BRECHIN and JOHN SWAIN provide a good overview of the needs of young people with learning difficulties, and ways of meeting them in their chapter 'Professional/client relationships: creating a "working alliance" with people with learning difficulties' in *Child Care: Concerns and Conflicts*, MORGAN, S. AND RIGHTON, P. (eds.) Hodder and Stoughton, London (1989).

12 SOCIETY AS CHILD ABUSER: NORTHERN IRELAND

Ed Cairns

Lecturer, Psychology Department and Centre for the Study of Conflict, University of Ulster

Introduction

According to LeVine (1980), parents in all societies share a common set of goals *vis-à-vis* their role as parents. These are firstly to ensure the physical survival of their children, secondly to enable their children eventually to become independent, and finally to pass on to their children those cultural values and attributes that they themselves hold most dear. However, an important rider to this principle is 'that the particular ecological and environmental context will often determine which of these goals will most influence parental thinking and practice' (Scheper-Hughes, 1987).

This chapter presents a case study of a society in which, it could be argued, the third of the universal goals of parenthood noted above has become predominant. In other words it seems that in Northern Ireland, at least, some parents may be stressing the importance of cultivating particular cultural values, even when, it could be argued, this may be threatening the actual physical survival of some if not all of their children. This is because in Northern Ireland, for some people, the common good is more important than the rights of an individual child. The result is, as this chapter demonstrates, that children have not only become direct victims of the political conflict in several ways – physically, psychologically and economically – but have also become the indirect victims of an ideological struggle to establish just which version of the common good should prevail in Northern Ireland in the future.

Victims of violence

Physical victims

Political violence has been rife in Northern Ireland for some 20 years. During this time children have become the victims of societal violence in many different ways. Perhaps the most obvious is that children have been physically victimized. Details of this are sketchy, however, as no official record is kept of the age of victims of physical violence. Despite this it has been estimated that some 150–200 children under the age of 14 years have been killed or injured to date (Cairns, 1987).

Of course, this is only a small proportion of the total number of victims of the troubles, which now runs into several thousands of dead with much larger numbers of injured. Nevertheless the small number of child victims has attracted proportionately more publicity than have the adult victims. The media are particularly attracted to stories about children in Northern Ireland, especially those that are a little out of the ordinary, for example, the story of the little girl who can claim to be the youngest victim of the violence, injured by a bullet even before she was born. Both sides in the conflict have not hesitated to use child victims for publicity purposes. Thus, despite the fact that relatively few children have been killed or injured in the violence, a booklet produced by a unionist politician to condemn the violence of the IRA has on its cover the almost life-size photograph of the face of a small child – the nose and eyes blackened and bruised, the face pockmarked, no doubt by flying shrapnel from a bomb. Similarly, when those who oppose the tactics of the forces of law and order wished to take action against the use of rubber bullets as riot-control weapons in Northern Ireland, they chose the death of a child as a test case in an attempt to persuade the European Commission on Human Rights that the British government was in breach of the European Convention on Human Rights by using such weapons.

What such people obviously realize is that the death of a child as a result of the political conflict appears to have a special impact upon the people of Northern Ireland. While people may have become inured to the death of adults, this is not so where the killing of children is concerned. It is, therefore, almost certainly no coincidence that two of the main peace movements that have developed in Northern Ireland during the last 20 years received their initial stimulus as the result of the death of children. The first of these was a movement known as 'Witness for Peace' which was started by a clergyman whose son was killed in Belfast on a day on which 11 people were killed by a series of explosions which rocked the city. The second was the internationally acclaimed movement known as 'The Peace People'. The incident which helped to found this organization was one in which three children, including a four-week-old baby, were killed by a car which was out of control due to the fact that the security forces, who had been pursuing the car, had earlier shot and wounded the driver. Sadly only a shadowy trace of both these movements remains today.

Psychological victims

Possibly because they are small in number, or because of ethical considerations, little research has been conducted involving children who are the victims of physical violence in Northern Ireland. Instead, what has interested social scientists most is the possibility that vast numbers of children may have become psychological victims of the ongoing political violence. Here some children have indeed suffered horribly. Many have been left fatherless, some even witnessing the actual assassination of their father or waving goodbye to him as he and his car were blown apart. Others have seen their fathers, brothers, uncles dragged off to jail in the middle of the night, not to return for many years. In the period 1969–73 many thousands of children were forced to flee with their families to the safety of religious ghettoes as waves of intimidation and counter-intimidation swept the major housing estates of Belfast (Darby, 1986).

However, the majority of children have experienced stress due to the violence in much more subtle ways. What research suggests is that while a small proportion of these children have succumbed to this stress (Fraser, 1974), perhaps developing symptoms such as fears about going out of the home, fainting fits on hearing cars backfiring or other loud noises, sleeping problems and the like, most children have apparently coped well. This resilience on the part of children in Northern Ireland (and indeed in other 'war-torn' parts of the world; see Bryce and Armenian, 1986) is, as yet, not well understood. However, several hypotheses have been advanced by way of explanation. Perhaps the most popular is simply that children, especially those who have grown up with the violence, have become used to an environment in which armed soldiers and policemen are a part of everyday life. Evidence to back up this suggestion comes from a study in which it was shown that the proportion of children being referred to a child psychiatric clinic in Belfast because of the 'troubles' has dropped markedly since the early 1970s when the violence first began.

Another hypothesis being used to explain the relatively low level of child psychiatric casualties, is that denial is one of the major coping mechanisms being used by the residents of Northern Ireland (Cairns, 1987). Research has shown that children, even in the quietest parts of Northern Ireland not directly affected by the violence, are still well aware of Northern Ireland's media image as a violent society. However, talking to children from the most violent areas about the violence or, for example, studying the essays they write, it is not unusual to find that children will mention the political violence but often only as an afterthought following mention perhaps of the green fields, the friendly people and other positive attributes (see Davey, 1987, for a similar reaction among Berlin children to the wall). Further, this reference to the violence is often accompanied by some phrase such as 'of course it is not as bad as people think' or 'there has been a lot of trouble but it is mostly in another part of town'. Perhaps the years to come will show that the greatest psychological damage inflicted on the children of Northern Ireland (and other similar areas throughout the world) is that they have been socialized to find violence acceptable and human life cheap (Chikane, 1986).

Economic victims
Northern Ireland is one of the least well-off regions, not only of the United Kingdom but of Europe. The statistics speak for themselves. More people are unemployed (almost 19% in 1986 compared to 11% in England). No doubt as a result of this the average weekly household income (£180.75 in 1985) is the lowest in the United Kingdom, where the average in 1985 was £216.23. This is made worse by the fact that households in Northern Ireland tend to be somewhat larger than in the rest of the country (3.05 versus 2.6 people). All of this means that more children in Northern Ireland live in families dependent upon supplementary benefit (income support) and a higher proportion of the population is in receipt of family income supplement (family credit).

This economic gloom is not, of course, solely the result of the violence. But there is no doubt that the violence has contributed greatly to lack of investment by new companies and even to the closing down of some existing businesses. Further, it is interesting to note that in successive years when a government survey has asked the people of Northern Ireland 'What is the most important problem facing Northern Ireland today?' the greater proportion of respondents mentioned unemployment first and then the troubles.

Taking sides
However, what people outside Northern Ireland, and indeed some people inside Northern Ireland, may not realize is that children there are being victimized daily in all sorts of other more subtle ways. One of the most ubiquitous of these is the enormous pressure that children come under to take sides. The conflict in Northern Ireland is above all a numbers game. At the moment the majority of the population (about 60% or more) wish, it can be argued because they are at least nominally Protestant, to remain part of the United Kingdom. The minority, at least nominally Catholic, wish to see Northern Ireland joined with the Republic of Ireland. This means that in effect each general election is a referendum about the constitution of Northern Ireland. In these circumstances it has even been argued that the number of children a couple decide to have is essentially a political decision. Certainly, from time to time it is claimed that one side is trying to 'outbreed' the other. And while there is no hard evidence to back up this claim it is a fact that Northern Ireland has the highest birth rate of any region in the United Kingdom – almost 18 children per 1000 population compared to around 13 in each of England, Wales and Scotland.

The paramilitaries
Of course, in such a situation it is not enough simply to produce more children than the other side. It is also vital that the next generation maintains its cultural

allegiances. The crudest ways of attempting to ensure this are adopted by the paramilitary organizations on both sides of the community through their 'youth wings'. Here children and young people are indoctrinated into the ways of the movement and given training in order that they may become useful adult members (Figure 1). Indeed, at times it has been claimed that the paramilitaries actually use children and young people to varying degrees in their military campaigns. At one time this became something of a propaganda issue with newspaper reports and government spokesmen claiming that children were being used, for example, to create diversions or indeed to shield gunmen (Figure 2). Backing up this speculation that the so-called 'godfathers of terrorism' make use of children and young people are the statistics, which reveal that some under-16-year-olds have indeed been charged with various 'political' offences ranging from murder to possession of firearms (Cairns, 1987).

The schools
However, this form of victimization involves only a relative minority of young people in Northern Ireland – mainly those who live in the working-class ghettoes inhabited almost exclusively by the supporters of one or other of the warring factions. Almost certainly many more children, if not the vast majority of children in Northern Ireland, are exposed to much more subtle psychological pressure to take sides. One source of such pressure is the divided educational system which Northern Ireland has. In effect over 90% of children in Northern Ireland attend schools which are segregated by religion (ironically only the 'special' schools for the handicapped or mentally retarded escape this particular pressure). The most obvious impact this has is that for virtually all of their childhood children from the two communities rarely if ever meet. Proving that what they are taught in their separate schools in any way prolongs or heightens the conflict is much more difficult. However, many people are deeply suspicious of the divided school systems and feel that if nothing else they do nothing to heal the wounds in Northern Irish society. Further, those who run the two school systems, particularly the Catholic authorities, often protest vehemently against the existence of their schools being thought of as in any way maintaining the political conflict. At the same time both sets of authorities bitterly resist any attempts to change the status quo.

The family
One argument which the school authorities have so far failed to use in their defence, but which is almost certainly valid, is the suggestion that children have already been subjected to sectarian indoctrination before their school life even begins. In other words there is a strong possibility that the greatest pressures of all to take sides come from the child's own family. Certainly researchers in other societies have noticed that the family is one of the main channels for the transmission of cultural attitudes and values. For example, Burman (1986) points out that to understand the mechanisms of control in South Africa one should examine the most basic units of society and in particular understand that the 'phenomena of repression or exclusion have their instruments and their logic at the effective level of the family'. Exactly how parents in Northern Ireland achieve this has not yet come under close scrutiny. However, it has been said, for example, that in Northern Ireland history is something which people 'learn at their mother's knee'. Further, it has also been suggested that parents in Northern Ireland may be taking steps to influence their children's cultural attitudes even before the children are born (Cairns, 1987).

People outside Northern Ireland are often fascinated to know how it is possible to tell the difference between a Catholic and a Protestant without actually asking directly. One of the major cues is in fact a person's first name and this only works because both groups use relatively unique sets of first names for their children.

Figure 1.

Obviously parents must, at some level, realize this and thus be aware that they are, in effect, sending their children out into the world virtually labelled as Protestant or Catholic. It could be argued, therefore, that the very act of naming children in this way says something about the parent's views about the importance of ensuring the foundation for the establishment of a firm cultural identity in the next generation. Similarly it could be argued that parent's continuing support for the denominational school system is also a reflection of the importance of transmitting cultural attitudes and values to their children.

Behind this desire to keep young Catholics and Protestants apart during their

Figure 2.

most formative years there almost certainly lurks another, rarely articulated motive. Interestingly this motive only becomes apparent when it fails to achieve its goal and Catholic boy falls in love with Protestant girl or vice versa. The resulting 'mixed-marriage' (as it is known) or even threat of a mixed-marriage, often reveals Northern Irish parents at their worst. Whole families, on both sides of the community, are thrown into crisis. Veiled threats often based on old superstitions are issued ('You know this will kill your mother, son'), clergymen are asked to intervene, disinheritance looms large. If the young couple ignore all this and marry, parents, both sets, often refuse to attend the wedding, local clergymen may refuse to officiate. Perhaps not surprisingly, such marriages are relatively rare in Northern Ireland. Parents often claim that they are against such marriages because the young couple will find it difficult to lead a normal life in a divided community like Northern Ireland. However, social scientists would also argue that mixed-marriages are so strongly resisted because they signal the ultimate in failure to pass on group loyalties not only to one's children but perhaps more importantly to one's grandchildren.

Children for peace

Not only are children caught up in the struggles of those who wish to make war in Northern Ireland, they are also caught up in the struggles of those who wish to make peace. What all this amounts to is that there exist substantial numbers of adults who feel that the way to reconcile the two communities in Northern Ireland is by first beginning with the children. Ironically, what this means in reality is that there are adults who want the children of Northern Ireland to do what adults appear unwilling to do themselves.

The concrete manifestations of this desire take several forms, the best-known being the Integrated School Movement. As a result of the work over the last 10 years, of groups composed mainly of parents, there are now some seven schools attended by both Protestant and Catholic children in roughly equal proportions. While at present these schools only cater for a very small proportion of the total school-age population, they do appear to represent a growing trend (Dunn, 1986). Those who believe in bringing children together in this way would no doubt see the ideal as being a Northern Ireland in which all children attended the same schools regardless of their religious background. However, realizing that for many different reasons this is not likely in the foreseeable future, people have adopted what they probably consider to be the next-best option – short but intensive contact for children from the two communities in the form of integrated holidays. These holidays involve taking groups of Catholic and Protestant children to places outside Northern Ireland (such as the United States or the Netherlands), for periods from two to four weeks in the summer, or, less expensively, running holidays and summer schemes within Northern Ireland. More recently a third form of peace-making has evolved, again aimed at children but this time allowing them to remain in their segregated schools while encouraging them to learn more about each other and to meet on occasion. This scheme, glorying in the title of EMU (Education for Mutual Understanding) is receiving substantial government backing.

However, it should not be thought that these well-meaning ideas are received by the majority of people in Northern Ireland with equanimity. Complaints have come from both sides, especially about the creation of integrated schools. The Protestants complain that the existing 'state' schools (i.e. the *de facto* Protestant schools) are open to all and therefore specially created integrated schools are not needed, while the Catholics contend that a proper Catholic education can only be provided in a proper Catholic school. However, some of the worst invective has been reserved for the EMU programme which, according to a pamphlet written by an ultra-protestant clergyman is 'an assault launched against the Protestant children . . . in order to brain-wash them into accepting ecumenical concepts'.

Conclusions

To people who live outside Northern Ireland, or have never visited it and whose only knowledge of the place has come from news bulletins it undoubtedly must appear a strange and alien land. However, the fact that, as noted above, children in Northern Ireland come under considerable pressure from the society in which they live must not be regarded as solely a Northern Irish phenomenon.

Exactly the same thing happens in every society and in some societies the pressure put on children has not simply been psychological (Suarez-Orozco, 1987). Particularly where cultural identity is important, issues such as conformity to parental wishes, multicultural education and intergroup marriages will never be far from the surface of community life. It is important, however, not to impute malicious intent to the adults of Northern Ireland in their attitudes and behaviour towards children. Above all they would argue that everything they do is 'for the sake of the children' if not for the sake of their children's children.

FURTHER READING
Possibly the classic in this field is NANCY SCHEPER-HUGHES' edited volume *Child Survival: Anthropological Perspectives on the Treatment and Maltreatment of Children* D. Reidel, Dortrecht (1987).

SECTION THREE

THE LEGAL CONTEXT

13 THE CHILDREN ACT 1989 – BETTER PROTECTION FOR CHILDREN?

Jeremy Roche

Senior Lecturer in Law, Polytechnic of East London

Wendy Stainton Rogers

Senior Lecturer, Department of Health and Social Welfare, Open University

Introduction

This chapter looks at the way in which the Children Act 1989 will affect child protection work, in the context of the Act's overall philosophy and objectives. The Act does not apply to Scotland (which has a different system of law) or to Northern Ireland, although both are currently reviewing their child care law (July 1991). However, much of the Act's philosophy is equally applicable to these parts of the United Kingdom. The Act seeks to promote 'good practice' by giving effect to certain principles and concepts, which are further strengthened by the *Regulations and Guidance* published by the Department of Health (1991). Before examining the provisions relating to child protection work, it is important to place the Act in context and to have an understanding of its purpose. (More information can be obtained via the Open University Course **P558 The Children Act 1989: Putting it into Practice.**)

Background to the Children Act 1989

For almost 20 years the issue of state intervention into family life has been in the public eye. From the tragedy of Maria Colwell in 1973 until the series of highly publicized child deaths in the mid-1980s, the social work profession was criticized for failing to protect children from parental mistreatment. When, in the spring of 1987, the Cleveland affair burst onto the public stage it was crusading doctors and over-zealous social workers who were condemned for over-reacting in their desire to protect children. This raised issues of the accountability of social work power, the professional authority and power of the medical profession and the consequent vulnerability of parents and children: family life was seen to be under threat. Since then, events in Rochdale and Orkney have only served to increase public anxiety. At the same time, the publicity surrounding these later cases failed to acknowledge the real possibility of abuse and, arguably, has resulted in the professionals' ability to protect children being undermined. The 1980s also witnessed reviews of the law relating to children by the Law Commission and the Department of Health and Social Security.

The agenda for change was therefore a complex one, comprising anxieties over family privacy, the accountability of professional power and the situation of the child: it was unified only by the recognition that 'something had to be done'. The Children Act 1989 is intended to resolve some of these problems and to make the law relating to children simpler and easier to use, more consistent and more suited to the needs of children. In addition, the Act seeks to achieve something more fundamental – to bring about radical changes in how we perceive, and consequently in what we do about, children and families who are facing difficulties.

The philosophy of the Children Act 1989

Section 1 of the Act contains three key principles, which are intended to guide the court in its decision making. First, the Act restates that the welfare of the child is to be the 'paramount' consideration when the court determines any question with respect to the child's upbringing or property (s1(1)). Section 1(2) states that the court shall have regard to the general principle that any delay in making decisions about the child's upbringing 'is likely to prejudice the welfare of the child'. In order to give effect to this principle, the Act provides for preliminary hearings to draw up a timetable and to give directions in certain proceedings: court control is seen as one way in which 'drift' of the child (e.g. into long-term care) will be avoided. Another illustration of the aim of reducing delay is the possibility of early challenge to the new emergency protection orders. These orders may be challenged after just 72 hours if the parents were not present at the original hearing. The third principle is the 'presumption of no order'. The court will now have to be satisfied that it is better to make an order than not to do so: in some circumstances this will require that more information about future plans for the child is provided.

In addition to these three key principles, Section 1 of the Act contains the 'welfare checklist': a list of the factors that the court is under a duty to consider in proceedings for a care or supervision order. The first item on this checklist is the 'ascertainable wishes and feelings of the child concerned' considered in the light of his or her age and understanding. Other items include the child's 'physical, emotional and educational needs', the likely effect of any change in the child's circumstances, and the child's 'age, sex, background and any characteristics . . . which the court considers relevant'. The checklist is designed to achieve a clearer focus on the child's interests and a greater consistency in decision making. It will be an important guide for those working with children and those who prepare reports for the court hearing family proceedings.

The Act also introduces radical changes in the court system hearing 'family proceedings' and greater flexibility in its decision-making powers. Not only does the court (whether a magistrates' court, county court or High court) have a more inquisitorial role, with increased powers to control its own proceedings and to require information, but, as a consequence of this new role, it has more options available when deciding whether to make an order and which order to make. For example, in care proceedings the court might decide not to make a care order, and instead make an order enabling the child to live with relatives.

Children's rights

In 1985, a milestone in legal history was reached in the House of Lords decision in the Gillick case. Lord Scarman said:

> Parental rights are derived from parental duty and exist so long as they are needed for the protection of the person and the property of the child . . . parental right yields to the child's right to make his own decisions when he reaches a sufficient understanding and intelligence to be capable of making up of his own mind on the matter requiring decision.
>
> (*Gillick v. West Norfolk and Wisbech Area Health Authority [1986] AC112*)

Throughout the Act there is considerable emphasis on listening to children and taking their wishes into account, consulting them when decisions have to be made and providing them with access to effective complaints procedures, which must contain an independent element. There are a number of provisions in the Act that give children the right to make decisions for themselves. An example is that the Act gives them the right to refuse to submit to a court-ordered examination. Finally, the new concept of 'parental responsibility' allows for those relationships that are important to the child to be legally recognized, facilitating the continued involvement of parents and the wider family in caring for children and participating in making decisions about them. The concept of parental responsibility also symbolically expresses the Act's commitment to working *with* parents in order to promote the child's welfare – parents do not lose responsibility for their children even when they are in local authority care. They share responsibility with the local authority. There are numerous provisions in the Act that give detail to this commitment to partnership, for example the duty on local authorities to provide services for children who are 'in need', and the new concept of 'providing accommodation' for children, which leaves parents with full parental responsibility.

Child protection

The Act makes it very clear that *compulsory* measures of intervention can take place only when a court makes an order on the basis of a perceived risk of *'significant harm'* to the child. All other interventions can take place only on the basis of partnership between the social services and the family. The provision of proper support for children in need is seen as the means of avoiding situations in which coercive measures of intervention may have to be considered. Planning and co-operation are advocated as being doubly beneficial to children, in that their lives should be less disrupted and the agencies of child protection should be better able to manage the situations that arise 'avoiding the fire-brigade' work that characterizes some current child protection practice.

Threshold criteria

The 'threshold criteria' are laid down in Section 31(2):

A court may only make a care order or supervision order if it is satisfied –
(a) that the child concerned is suffering, or is likely to suffer, significant harm; and
(b) that the harm, or likelihood of harm, is attributable to –
   (i) the care given to the child, or likely to be given to him if the order were not made, not being what it would be reasonable to expect a parent to give to him; or
   (ii) the child's being beyond parental control.

The Lord Chancellor explained their significance to the Joseph Jackson Memorial Lecture:

Those conditions are the minimum circumstances which the Government considers should always be found to exist before it can ever be justified for a court even to begin to contemplate whether the State should be enabled to intervene compulsorily in family life.

((1989) 139 NLJ 505, 506)

The fact that the court is satisfied that the child 'is suffering significant harm' does not mean that a care or supervision order will automatically be made – the Section 1 principles come into play and the court will have to consider whether making an order would be better for the child than making no order at all. There will be a number of consequences resulting from this, including the court needing more information and being drawn into some of the decision-making dilemmas that have, hitherto, primarily affected social services departments.

In order to fulfil the threshold criteria it is clear that the harm must be significant, but what does this mean? The Act provides definitions of harm, but does not provide a definition of significant harm. The *Regulations and Guidance* state that:

> Minor shortcomings in health care or minor deficits in physical, psychological or social development should not require compulsory intervention unless cumulatively they are having, or likely to have, serious and lasting effects upon the child.
>
> *(DH, 1990, vol. 1, para 3.21)*

While this is, and will remain, a question of professional judgement, the Act makes it clear that it is not possible to argue for compulsory powers of intervention solely on the basis that this would promote the welfare of the child. It is also important to note that there are two limbs in the threshold criteria: the significant harm test, and the requirement that this harm is attributable to the parenting of the child or the child's being beyond parental control.

Orders available
The Act introduces three new orders: the child assessment order (CAO), the emergency protection order (EPO) and the recovery order (RO), as well as redrawing the basis on which the court can make care and supervision orders. While the EPO replaces the much criticised place of safety order, and is different from it in a number of key respects (see below), the CAO and RO are new.

Child assessment order
Only a local authority or authorized person (the NSPCC) can apply to the court for a CAO. The purpose of the order is to enable those carrying out an investigation to resolve, one way or the other, any anxieties that they have about the child and family.

The CAO is fundamentally about assessment, not immediate protection. It should be seen as a way of strengthening the powers of the local authority to assess the well-being of a child and carry out an investigation. If the court does make a CAO, it will last for a maximum of seven days, the child will only be taken away from home for the purpose of the assessment and the parents will retain full parental responsibility for their child. Any person who is in a position to produce a child must do so, and comply with the terms of the order.

Emergency protection orders
The EPO, while a replacement for the discredited place of safety order, is very different from that order. There are two aspects to the EPO. First, it offers local authorities and the NSPCC a means to pursue an investigation that is being frustrated because they are being denied access to the child. Second, any person can apply for an EPO in order to protect the child from significant harm. In these circumstances the person must convince the court that he or she has reasonable grounds for believing that the child is suffering significant harm, or likely to do so, unless removed (e.g. from the parent's home) or retained (e.g. in hospital).

If, on an application for a CAO, the court is satisfied that there are grounds for making an EPO and that it ought to make such an order, it can do so. This is designed to cover the situation in which the court, on hearing evidence on an application for a CAO, decides that the situation is more serious than had originally been thought, or where new evidence is presented which indicates that there may be an emergency, e.g. in the report of the *guardian ad litem*.

While an EPO lasts for a maximum of eight days, with the possibility of an extension for up to a maximum of a further seven days, it can be challenged after 72 hours. As with CAO, the court can order that the child be medically examined, subject to the mature minor's right to refuse to submit to such an examination. There is a presumption of reasonable contact between child and parent whilst the order is in force, and, if a parent is aggrieved with the contact arrangements, the matter is decided by the court, not the local authority. Finally, there is a duty to return the child home as soon as it is safe to do so, even though the EPO is still in force.

The intention behind these provisions is to minimize the disruption and trauma experienced by children by ensuring that they maintain contact with their parents and others, that their feelings about medical examination are properly recognized and that they are returned home as soon as possible. This reinforces the message of the Act that working with, rather than excluding, parents is a good practice, and that even in situations of perceived emergency, good child-centred practice requires that the existing relationships that the child has with adults and other children are respected. This includes instances where the police have taken the child into their protection. In this case the police are required not only to inform the local authority but to tell the child what they are doing, what their plans are for him or her and to discover the child's wishes and feelings.

Recovery orders

This new order was introduced to enable the recovery of a child who is in care, in police protection or the subject of an EPO. If the child has been taken away from the 'responsible person' or is missing, the order operates as a direction to produce the child or to disclose the child's whereabouts. It also authorizes a constable to enter and search premises for the child and to use reasonable force if necessary.

Care and supervision orders

The centrepiece of the provisions relating to care and supervision orders is the threshold criteria discussed above. When introducing the Second Reading of the Children Bill in the House of Lords, the Lord Chancellor said:

> Here we seek to strike a balance between the need to protect children from harm in emergencies and the need to allow aggrieved parents to challenge action taken in respect of their children – the need for which was graphically illustrated by what happened in Cleveland . . . as a matter of principle it is important for the law in a free society expressly to protect the integrity and independence of families, save where there is at least likelihood of significant harm to the child from within the family.
>
> *(Hansard, House of Lords, 6 December 1988)*

The balance has been struck in such a way as to permit effective and substantial intervention in order to protect children. The Act makes it clear that a care or supervision order can be made if the court is satisfied that the child is suffering harm *or* is likely to do so in future.

However, intervention does not have to take this coercive form. Support for families in which children are in need is seen as just as vital a part of local authority functions, and one which may operate so as to prevent a situation from deteriorating. When a care order is made, the provisions relating to contact are designed to encourage a continued relationship between child and parents, thereby avoiding 'drift' into long-term care. Further, the local authority is under a duty to promote contact between children and their parents and relatives, unless this is not reasonably practicable or consistent with the children's welfare. While the child is in care, parental responsibility is shared between the parents and the local authority, but the latter can determine the extent to which parents may meet their responsibility for the child. When it is likely that the child will return to the family, this model is unproblematic. However, when the situation is more serious, with less chance of rehabilitation, working in partnership may present its own difficulties.

The court also has the power to make a supervision order, but only if the threshold criteria have been fulfilled. If the court does make a supervision order, as opposed to a care order, there are two new powers available. First, it can make at the same time, for example, a residence order which will result in the child who is subject of the supervision order living with the person named in the residence order. Second, the court can include directions in the supervision order requiring the child and the 'responsible person' to act in a particular way. One advantage of these powers is that they allow the court to exercise more control over the return of a child home. This will be of particular importance given the severe limitations placed by the Act on local authorities' use of the wardship jurisdiction.

Conclusion

Above all, the Act is based on the idea that children's needs come first. The problem is that there will always be adults who are important to the child, with whom it is necessary to work if the child's needs are to be met. This partnership must be built on concern for the child, placing the child at the centre of the proceedings and taking the child's perspective seriously. For some professionals this will mean new ways of working and a change in attitudes, especially where their conviction of what is best for the child conflicts with the wishes of the children and adults concerned. For the courts it will involve a more active and inquiring approach, coupled with a greater openness in decision making. As a result of these changes, children should have more say in far-reaching decisions about their own lives and futures, no matter how 'out of tune' or awkward this might sound. Ultimately, to echo the words of Butler-Sloss (DHSS, 1988), the child should be treated as 'a person and not [simply] as an object of concern'.

FURTHER READING

A very clear and concise account of the Act, particularly useful for social workers and others in the child welfare field, is provided by ALLEN, N., *Making Sense of the Children Act 1989: A Guide for the Social and Welfare Services*, Longman, Harrow (1990).

BAINHAM, A., *Children. The New Law*, Family Law/Jordan, Bristol (1990) is a very good review of the Act with excellent critical commentary. It contains a copy of the Act. The DEPARTMENT OF HEALTH's, *The Care of Children: Principles and Practice in Regulations and Guidance*, HMSO, London (1990) is essential reading for anybody working in this field. It covers the implications of the Act for all concerned with child care and child welfare.

An excellent guide to, and discussion of, the impact of the Act, particularly useful for welfare professionals is EEKELAAR, J. AND DINGWALL, R., *Reform of Child Care Law: A Practical Guide to the Children Act 1989*, Routledge, London (1990).

MASSON, J., *The Children Act 1989: Text and Commentary*, Sweet & Maxwell, London (1990), provides a key text for anyone wanting to know about the Act in depth. It comprises a copy of the Act and detailed annotation. Finally, WHITE, R., CARR, P. AND LOWE, N., *A Guide to the Children Act 1989*, Butterworth, London (1990) is particularly useful for lawyers and experienced welfare professionals. It too contains a copy of the Act.

14 CHILDREN'S RIGHTS AND THE WELFARE OF THE CHILD

Jeremy Roche

Senior Lecturer in Law, North East London Polytechnic

Any discussion of children's rights and the welfare of the child has to recognize the tension that exists between those who argue for legislation to protect children better from the adult world, and those who see the best protection for children being in recognizing children as independent beings and treating them as adults, i.e. not discriminating against them, whenever possible. This tension is discussed by Brian Corby in chapter 2. For present purposes I am assuming that there will be some children who, because of their very young age or through handicap (see chapter 11), will be in need of special protection and will not be able to speak for themselves. However, I argue that the older the child becomes, and the less physically dependent, the greater the importance of treating the child as one would any other person.

In dealing with children the legal system in England and Wales (see chapter 13) is based on the central idea of the 'welfare of the child' – this is the 'paramount consideration' in any court proceedings involving the care and upbringing of a child. In practice it is the court which decides what in fact this means. Historically it has done so in quite different ways. In the nineteenth century the child's welfare was seen as inseparable from the father's right to 'own' the child (save in exceptional cases where this assumption would put the child's life or morals in danger). The courts were motivated less by arguments about the child's welfare and more by the assumed importance of the father's rights.

Today a father's rights are seen, in the United Kingdom at least, as fairly unimportant within debates about the child's welfare. The welfare of the child is not only the guiding principle, but is also openly (and often repeatedly) stated as such by professionals working with children, such as social workers and police officers. This is not simply a change in language. Since the early nineteenth century a great deal of legislation has been written into the statute book, designed either to protect children or to promote their welfare (e.g. laws about child labour, education etc.). But while we can therefore see our society today taking seriously 'the welfare of the child', this does not solve the problem of what this term means or refers to. The Law Commission, in a pamphlet about children affected by divorce (1986), said of the welfare rule:

> The main criticism of the rule is unpredictability and, as a consequence, uncertainty. In determining these issues the courts have to rely on value judgements and although each individual case is assessed on its own merits the court may be tempted to adopt rules of thumb . . . such rules of thumb may be arbitrary, controversial or out of date.

This uncertainty has been made worse by the range of situations facing the courts.

The 'openness' of the concept allows those involved professionally with children to act on their own perceptions of what is in 'the child's best interests'. Once we recognize that the child's welfare has no fixed meaning – that it is socially problematic – we see that the welfare of the child turns from a catch-phrase which sounds good to a potentially powerful mechanism by which some people can impose their views about what is right for children on the rest of society. As such this is part of a wider argument about authority and power in society: who decides and how?

One important issue is that the condition of the child is seen through the status and actions of his or her parents. The child is 'at risk' precisely because of the quality of parenting he or she is receiving. Whether the parents drink excessively, have been heroin addicts, have had other children die in mysterious circumstances, are of unorthodox sexuality, all these are seen to be relevant and possible grounds for intervention. The child is the central concern, yet is almost eclipsed by the figure of the mother and her social worth. The child used to be seen as the 'property' of the father. Now he or she has become a 'product', usually of the mother, and an object of professional judgement. Possibly one of the most hopeful signs that have emerged from the Cleveland Inquiry is the acknowledgement that above all else a child is a person and has rights of his or her own and the specific attempts by the Children Act 1989 to put that principle into practice (see Chapter 15).

Child welfare – poverty and inequality

Some of the writing on children's rights and the welfare of the child either only talks about the procedural defects and injustices in our childcare system or treats the issue as an abstract discussion. Both ignore the social reality of what poverty means for children and families in the United Kingdom today. This can result in an individualist explanation of child abuse. Yet Gil (1975) argues that the most severe form of child abuse is precisely at the societal level. By this he means that inadequate diet, housing, education and health care can cause far greater physical and psychological damage to children and their families than abuse expressed in other ways. According to the Child Poverty Action Group (1987) in the United Kingdom in 1983 31 per cent of all children – almost 4,000,000 children – were living in or on the margins of poverty (see chapter 8 for a fuller development of this argument).

The United Kingdom has a poor record on such 'collective abuse' when compared with other European countries. For example, according to a survey published in the *Observer* (10 April 1988; see Moss, 1988) Portugal, with a third of the income of the United Kingdom, is much further ahead in developing childcare services. The only country in Europe which fared as badly as the United Kingdom in the survey was the Republic of Ireland.

Impoverished and disadvantaged families are more likely to be subject to the supervision of welfare professionals concerned about the upbringing of the children of the family. They may have, by virtue of their social location and experience, a certain set of expectations and attitudes regarding public authority. Public power and the legal system is not something they use but something that is used against them. Such families may lack the verbal skills necessary to challenge the definitions and anxieties of the caring professions and yet have problems which they need help with. As the British Association of Social Workers recognized in its evidence to the Cleveland Inquiry, when the health and social services and police are acting together 'it poses a risk to the family and the family's rights, and their rights to natural justice' (DHSS, 1988, para 13.21).

Intervention is justified by claiming to be acting for the welfare of the child. But to talk about the welfare of the child is not enough. It has to be asked what this means in practice for families. It has been argued that greater use should be made of the power that social services departments have under childcare legislation to make cash payments to support families with children so that the children can be looked after by their families. This power is there but very unevenly used. Why? What ideas about poverty, neglect and the deserving poor influence decisions about whether such important help will be given? Further, what is often going on is an argument over adult power, with adults or professionals claiming on behalf of the child or in the name of the child a superior decision-making authority. The welfare of the child can so easily become a slogan behind which adults argue their own perception of the 'good' of the child. We need to see the welfare of the child as including the child's identified expression of his or her own needs.

Who decides?

There will be circumstances where adults who are not the parents will intervene in order to promote or safeguard the welfare of the child. The child may be too physically or emotionally vulnerable or the circumstances exceptional so that direct intervention into the parent–child relationship is seen as necessary. It is in this sphere that the question of family rights has been most strongly debated. The overzealous removal of children suspected of being victims of sexual abuse in Cleveland highlighted the issue of professional power and family rights. At a less dramatic level, everyday decisions which affect the lives of parents and children are made routinely by welfare professionals.

Individual social workers have an important degree of discretion which informs not only whether they perceive a problem in the first place but also how they should respond. This discretion I would argue is not a question of arbitrary, random whim on the part of the individual professional concerned. Rather it is an effect of the professional training and culture within which the worker concerned operates.

The world-view of social work is said to be insufficiently aware of the value of alternative culturally different lifestyles. Given that all too often child neglect goes hand in hand with poverty, the presence of a caring and loving relationship between parent and child is at risk of being obscured. Culture and class often separate professional from client. This distance affects how the professional sees the situation and how he or she is seen by the client. This distance is exacerbated by the existence of poverty. In this context to talk of family rights, or parents' or children's rights, is increasingly problematic.

Upbringing

The theory is that as long as the family brings up the child in a healthy environment it will not be subject to interference by outsiders. The problem with this is that it does not tell us who decides whether the family is efficient and healthy, and it suggests that in the absence of public intervention the family is 'free' space. Both these issues surfaced in the Gillick case (*Gillick* v. *West Norfolk and Wisbech Area Health Authority*, 1985). Mrs Victoria Gillick wrote to the Area Health Authority regarding a DHSS circular about the giving of contraceptive advice and treatment, seeking an assurance that 'in no circumstances whatsoever will any of my daughters be given contraceptive or abortion treatment whilst they are under sixteen'. In so doing she claimed she was merely acting on her parental right to make decisions to best promote the well-being of her children. It was her version of what constituted a healthy parent–child relationship which was being urged on the courts and thus on public agencies. The courts were being asked to endorse this relationship of 'parent-power'. The *Times* in its editorial entitled 'Gillick's Law' (18 October 1985) stated:

The main contention on one side is that the law ought to be arranged so as to lend support to those parents who are conscientiously doing their duty to care for the health and morals of their children in their upbringing, and . . . to lead them to a proper understanding and right use of the sexual drive, as the parents themselves understand these things.

In the House of Lords' rejection of Victoria Gillick's argument, Lord Scarman confirmed a recent trend in the law, stating that parental rights are derived from parental duty and these exist only so long as they are needed for the protection of the child. For Lord Scarman the key question was not whether the child was 16 but whether this child was of a sufficient maturity and understanding such that she was able in her own right to make her own decision.

This 'child autonomy' argument was not the only basis on which the decision was arrived at. Lord Fraser based his decision in part on trusting doctors to exercise their discretion responsibly. While agreeing with Lord Scarman, he stated that doctors would be justified in giving such advice and treatment without the knowledge of the parents if satisfied that the child understood the advice, that she could not be persuaded to tell her parents and that she was likely to continue or start having sexual intercourse with or without contraceptive advice and treatment.

Nonetheless, the decision was a landmark for children's rights. It followed an earlier Court of Appeal decision in favour of Mrs Gillick that had had the effect of denying the availability of important services to children whether dispensed by doctors or others, e.g. social workers, nurses, youth workers, counsellors. In reversing this decision the Lords made social resources once again available to young people who considered themselves in need of such services.

Although there is debate about the impact and potential of the Gillick decision, it is clear that some children at least have benefited in that their self-defined needs are not being ignored or denied. They have access to the needed information and the right to decide what best promotes their welfare. This has the potential of disturbing power relations within the family. It was her daughters (and not her sons) that Mrs Gillick was anxious should not have contraceptive advice and treatment without her knowledge and consent. Family members are not free from social assumptions about their respective roles and needs. This decision gave to the daughter the right to define her own health needs without recourse to either the courts or increased family conflict.

The physical punishment of children

Much of that which is done for children's benefit connects with ideas held by adults about what it is to be a child (see chapter 1). At times the child's welfare requires the immediate imposition of discipline, e.g. to stop a child from burning him- or herself. But all too often punishment consists of the parent declaring to a tearful child that the smack he or she is about to give is 'going to hurt me more than it will hurt you'. Alice Miller (1987a) argues that talk about methods of childrearing is really talk about power relations and should be recognized as such. Nowhere is this more evident than in the sphere of corporal punishment.

It was not until this century that in the penal system the routine flogging of male children was abolished: well after it had been for adult males. The reason for this was that the punishment was assumed to help children learn to be 'good'.

In the United Kingdom the physical chastisement of children is still permitted in the privacy of the home, but in Sweden and Finland parents are forbidden by law to use physical punishment on their children. A survey conducted by the Children's Legal Centre found that 11% of Conservative members of parliament and 69% of Labour members were against parental corporal punishment although there was much disagreement on the question of using the law to prohibit such behaviour (*Childright*, April, 1988).

The issue of physical punishment in this country has focused on the school. By 1983 the United Kingdom was the only European country to retain beatings as part of school discipline. This had already given rise to a clash with the idea of parental rights and the teacher acting *in loco parentis*. In 1982, in the Cosans case (*Campbell and Cosans* v. *United Kingdom*), the European Court on Human Rights found the U.K. government guilty of breach of the European Convention on Human Rights by failing to respect the parents' objections to corporal punishment. It was, however, seen to be the parents' rights and the child's right to education which had been infringed, rather than the child's right not to be beaten.

In 1984 Janice Jarman, the mother of children taken into care on the grounds of school non-attendance was successfully prosecuted for their non-attendance, which was due to her opposition to the continued infliction of corporal punishment. Yet in 1978, admittedly in a different context, the European Court on Human Rights had held that the judicial birching of a 15-year-old boy was a violation of Article 3 of the Convention which states that 'No one shall be subjected to torture or to inhuman or degrading treatment or punishment.' In this case the Court argued:

> The very nature of judicial corporal punishment is that it involves one human being inflicting physical violence on another human being . . . his punishment . . . constituted an assault on precisely that which it is one of the main purposes of Article 3 to protect, namely a person's dignity and physical integrity.

As a result of the two cases in which it was found to be in breach of the Convention (see *Childright*, September 1986), the U.K. government proposed a change in domestic law which would give to the parents the right to decide that their children should not be physically punished at school. However, following an amendment moved in the House of Lords, corporal punishment was abolished outright in state schools. Since then the European Commission has ruled that the caning of a 16-year-old girl, Karen Warwick, constituted 'degrading punishment' contrary to Article 3 of the Convention. This is the first clear decision from Europe that the schoolchild has a right not to be beaten (see *Childright*, November/December 1987). The U.K. government has still to respond to the Commission's ruling, by declaring that all such beatings are unlawful, even in some privately run schools, where it is still currently permitted (see Newell (1989)). It is interesting to note that despite the European Commission's ruling, Karen Warwick's family's civil action against the education authority was dismissed even though the caning she received had broken blood vessels in her hand such that she could not use it for four days and the marks were still visible two months later. The judge said: 'I cannot say that by modern standards this was improper, inappropriate or disproportionate.'

What is clear is that even though the use of the European Commission and Court is expensive and slow, these institutions can have a positive impact on domestic law. The Warwick case holds out the promise of an end to the British practice of beating schoolchildren, through its recognition of the child's right to dignity and physical integrity. Increasing the status of the child is no longer a sufficient reason for discriminating against him or her. Mere age of itself is no longer sufficient reason for ignoring the child's viewpoint, for denying its validity or for silencing a child through violence (see *Childright*, July/August 1987).

Confidentiality

The concern for taking the question of child sexual abuse seriously may result in the agencies and professionals involved failing to see that it is crucial that children feel able to speak in confidence to others. Part of the appeal of 'Childline' lies precisely in its confidentiality and anonymity. The child retains control over the timing and outcome of seeking comfort and advice. The child is not robbed of power by beginning to speak about the things that really concern and upset him or her. There is always the danger in matters concerning the abuse of a child that his or her basic rights will be ignored and that this will be justified in the name of promoting the welfare of that child.

The Cleveland Inquiry Report recommends that 'professionals should always listen carefully to what the child has to say and take seriously what is said' (DHSS, 1988, para 12.65). However, it also draws attention to the fact that promises which cannot be kept should not be made to a child; in particular professionals 'in the light of possible court proceedings should not promise a child that what is said in confidence can be kept in confidence'. There is another problem – that of children, though physically able to speak, not having the confidence to do so. The denial of 'safe' places in which to begin to tell their stories may have the effect of condemning children to remain where they are. The Report acknowledged in its discussion of the question of confidentiality that there was a conflict between professional ethics and the public interest in the detection of child abuse. It saw 'no easy answer to this problem'. It noted the following submission from the Children's Legal Centre:

> We are very concerned that the desire for 'inter-agency cooperation' and 'multi-disciplinary team approaches' to child abuse can conflict with children's desire, need and right to speak in confidence to others about things that concern them. . . . The Children's Legal Centre believes that children's right to and need for confidential advice and counselling has been ignored by many if not all the agencies involved. (DHSS, 1988, para 12.68)

The denial of a confidential and trusting relationship with the child, the denial of the child's right to be heard on the question of the invasion and examination of his or her body contribute to the degradation and domination of children by adults, and may not only compound the original abuse but confirm the feelings of powerlessness suffered, rendering the child more vulnerable to future abuse. This applies whether we are talking about Cleveland or the parental 'right' to chastise their children physically.

The child as a witness
Historically the presumption was that while adults understand the nature of an oath, children under the age of 14 were not able to do so, but on questioning by the judge to determine this matter the child might be allowed to give evidence. This has now changed, with a child assumed to be competent to give evidence unless shown otherwise. However, despite important reforms in the Criminal Justice Act 1991 and the Children Act 1989, there is a continuing controversy over the question of children's evidence in civil and criminal proceedings, in part because the child may be the only witness (as the victim) to extremely serious offences. The 1991 Criminal Justice Act will, from October 1992 enable a child's evidence in chief (but not cross-examination) to be provided to the court by way of a videotape, so long as the interview has been conducted according to a Memorandum of Good Practice. It is worth noting that the Cleveland report – and more recently, the inquiry following the failure of proceedings in the Orkney cases (under Scottish Law) concern has been expressed about the techniques used in investigative interviews. The public debate continues but at least it is fed not by traditional ideas about the child's propensity to lie but by more concrete concerns over e.g. the use of leading questions in interviews and their impact, the undermining of the position of the defendant in criminal proceedings, and the mechanics of effective cross-examination of the child witness.

In care

The controversy surrounding interventions into family life is fuelled by the very real concern over the conditions in which children 'in care' are provided for. Not only are some children moved many miles from home, they are also moved very frequently. In addition, there have been a number of well-known scandals concerning the abuse and sexual exploitation of children in care. In the Kincora affair in Northern Ireland (see Committee of Inquiry into Children's Homes and Hostels, 1986) and the more recent cases in Staffordshire (ie the 'Pin-Down' Regime) and Leicestershire, the powerlessness of the children and their inability to complain effectively has raised serious questions, not just about the effectiveness of formal complaints procedures but also about the attitude of the system and its staff to those who are 'in their care'. Hopefully in England and Wales at least, the Children Act's provisions for a mandatory complaints procedure including an independent element will help to overcome some of these problems.

Under present childcare law, the local authority has to take into account the wishes of children: this includes a decision to close a children's home. For many teenagers in care a small-scale children's home is the most secure and positive environment they can hope for. The use of the law tends, however, to be limited. As long as the local authority complies with its duty to consult and formally takes into consideration the welfare and needs of the children, it can still decide that closure is the most appropriate course of action. At a time of financial crisis in local authority spending, the running down of residential provision, which is more expensive than even special fostering schemes, can appear very attractive. The National Association for Young People in Care (NAYPIC) recently successfully prevented the closure of a community home in Bridgend by helping the residents present their case to the social services committee. In the absence of any other voice, local authority social services committees have necessarily to act on the uncontradicted advice of the social workers concerned. When another voice, particularly a well-organized voice, is heard, this may have more impact than immediate recourse to the limited powers of the courts. The law currently imposes a duty to listen to and take account of the wishes of the children in decisions about where they will be looked after. Organization of children themselves and a change in attitudes whereby what children say about their lives is taken seriously will more clearly promote the rights of children in care. The Children Act 1989 provides the framework, but this by itself is not sufficient to promote the rights of such children.

Conclusion

In this melting-pot of debates around children's rights, the rights of parents and families, and professional anxiety about children's welfare there exists no ideal, correct practice. One way forward may be to put greater stress on dealing with children in a way which will build up their confidence and give them a sense of having some power and control over their lives. There will be situations of emergency; these are exceptional and the discussion of how to respond in these cases should not blind us to the way in which we often deny children's rights and that they could, if more confident and knowledgeable, be their own best protectors.

A genuine commitment to children's rights, whilst acknowledging all the difficulties of using this term, would as a minimum include a commitment to supporting the development of children's organizations, to listening to what children collectively and individually have to say about things concerning and affecting them, and to treating them with respect. Support given should be relevant and practical and such that it allows children to decide for themselves wherever this is possible. The Children's Legal Centre argued in *Childright* (January 1988):

Until children are recognised as individual people with rights of their own, including developing rights to self-determination and equal rights to protection from all kinds of assault, they will continue to be dominated, degraded and abused, and frequently will feel powerless to complain or stop the abuse.

A commitment to this principle does not involve closing our eyes to the need to protect, to the difficulty the child may experience in initially being listened to perhaps for the first time. The issue is not simple, but we compound the problems by routinely excluding the child. The child's voice and autonomy will have disturbing effects. The child may see things quite differently from adults. Perhaps both can learn. In the words of Rabindranath Tagore:

Children have their play on the seashore of worlds. They know not how to swim, they know not how to cast nets. Pearl fishers dive for pearls, merchants sail in their ships, while children gather pebbles and scatter them again. (*Gitanjali*, 1986)

FURTHER READING

A good exposition of the specific arguments against corporal punishment is given in PETER NEWELL's *Children are People Too: The Case Against Physical Punishment*, Bedford Square Press, London (1989). FRANKLIN, B. *The Rights of Children*, Blackwell, Oxford (1986) provides a number of helpful chapters, including a good one on 'The Rights of Children in Care' by GERRY LAVERY and 'Children's Rights: A Scottish Perspective' by RUTH ADLER and ALAN DEARING. MICHAEL FREEMAN's *The Rights and Wrongs of Children* Frances Pinter, London (1983) is still the classic in the field. JOHN SPENCER and RHONA FLIN's book, *The Evidence of Children: The Law and the Psychology* (1990) is a scholarly but readable account of the vast body of work in this area, and essential reading for anybody involved in investigative interviewing or criminal prosecutions concerning sexual assaults towards children. Finally, a thoroughly 'good read' which is wide-sweeping in its coverage is *Changing Childhood* edited by MARTIN HOYLES Writers and Readers Publishing Cooperative, London (1979).

15 THE ABUSER – PUNISHMENT OR TREATMENT

Nicholas Tilley

Principal Lecturer in Sociology, Trent Polytechnic

Introduction

When a case of child abuse has been recognized, there are a number of possible outcomes for the abuser. The choice is not simply punishment *or* treatment. The two can be combined, although in some cases neither may be appropriate. There is a range of actual responses to different types of abuse and various categories of abuser, but there is no universal panacea and individual cases must be assessed in terms of their own merits.

Punishment but not treatment

If a person is to be punished there must be some law which renders their actions criminal and there must be due process through which it is established beyond reasonable doubt that they have committed the crime (Benn and Peters, 1959; Quinton, 1954). What workers in some agencies dealing with child abuse might consider to be unsatisfactory childcare practice is not necessarily criminal. Emotional abuse, poor general parenting and non-extreme forms of neglect do not ordinarily provide an adequate basis for prosecution. In the case of sexual abuse in particular, but also of non-accidental injury, it can be very difficult to obtain evidence which would be sufficient to secure the conviction of the abuser, and children are sometimes reluctant to sustain their allegations in the face of the consequences for themselves and their families. Under the Criminal Justice Acts 1988 and 1991, the unsworn evidence of a child need no longer be corroborated in order to secure a conviction and evidence can be given either by live video-link or by video recording of an earlier interview. However, if prosecution is not possible then neither is punishment a realistic response to an abuser.

Punishment is not considered to be just if the abuser could not have acted otherwise. We punish on the assumption that offenders are capable of taking responsibility for their actions – of knowing and controlling what they do. It is certainly conceivable that for some abusers this may not be the case. We respect the individual as a person capable of moral choices when we inflict punishment for rule-breaking. In accordance with this, 'retributivists' would argue that abusers 'deserve' punishment in proportion to the nature and severity of their abuse. However, according to the utilitarian view, in contrast, inflicting pain or unpleasantness on others is wrong and punishment can only be justified to the extent that some greater good will result. For example, it may be that punishment will reform the offender or deter others from abusing; also, for the period of incarceration potential victims will be protected from abuse. However, it must be said that the track record of punishment in improving behaviour, and having 'utility' on that basis, is not good.

In cases of child abuse, punishment not only hurts the abuser but often his or her dependents as well. Financial or other support for family members may be removed with the incarceration of the breadwinner, which might change the balance of the 'greater good' in a utilitarian argument. Children who have been abused often carry a great burden of guilt for having split up the family and causing distress to other family members. Furthermore, the abuser often suffers in excess of the court's sentence because of the reactions of fellow prisoners. Many spend their entire sentences in isolation for their own protection.

On the other hand, punishment may have some less obvious benefits. Firstly, the burden of guilt on the abused child may actually be lightened if the community's judgement on the guilt of the abuser is publicly and formally demonstrated in court. It may help the child to acknowledge that he or she was not to blame for what happened and that it was the abuser's fault. Secondly, as Emile Durkheim pointed out, the punishment of offenders has an important role in reinforcing the basic values of the community (Durkheim, 1933). It expresses a collective judgement that children have a right to adequate care and freedom from abuse. Thirdly, once someone has been convicted of an assault or sexual assault on a child, this may make it much easier to protect that child, and yet keep them together with the rest of their family. If offenders are to be prosecuted and hence punished, it is inevitable that law enforcement agencies will be involved. Every area in the United Kingdom will have its own procedural guidelines for professionals set down by the local Area Child Protection Committee. This does not necessarily curtail routine police involvement in every alleged case of abuse or imply that the police will automatically pursue prosecution when they are involved.

Treatment but not punishment

In the Netherlands the criminal justice system in general is less punitive than in the United Kingdom and offenders are more likely to be treated than punished. Consistent with this philosophy, all forms of child maltreatment, or 'mishandling' as it is termed, are dealt with by a well-publicized network of Confidential Doctor Bureaux, run by experienced paediatricians with a staff of social workers and administrators.

> If the bureau staff suspect that there is some 'mishandling' they will arrange for the child to come to the bureau with a friendly adult. The doctor will talk to the child about what has been happening at home, listen to his or her story, and then make contact wih the parents. If the problem is serious the parents will be asked to come to the office as soon as possible and the child may well be kept away from home until they arrive. The bureau staff have no obligation to inform the police, but they might let them know what is happening. Liaison with the police is friendly and regular. Some police stations actually have social workers on their staff specifically to handle child abuse cases. The police defer to the Confidential Doctor about possible investigations. Prosecutions are seen as a last resort. (Jay and Doganis, 1987, p. 174)

The Confidential Doctors do not treat the abusers or families themselves but will help to organize a treatment programme involving self-help groups, local voluntary organizations and various types of therapist. The threat of legal action can and sometimes is used as a lever in the last resort. In this way the co-operation of the vast majority of abusers is achieved, families are more readily kept together and reporting, including self-referral, is encouraged (Findlay, 1987–8).

Offering 'treatment' presumes that the abuser's behaviour is in some way abnormal or pathological and therefore that there is 'something individual, or wrong' with the with the family situation of the individual, who abuses the child. The discovery of non-accidental injury goes back to radiologists and doctors in the United States who described the 'battered baby syndrome' as a medical condition (Pfohl, 1977) and the medical model of disease and treatment has had a pervasive effect on the other disciplines and professions which have a key role to play in the identification and management of child abuse cases. The aim of treatment is to enable individuals to assume 'normal' or non-pathological and socially acceptable ways of behaving towards children.

The treatment of abusers and offenders can take many different forms which are underpinned by different theoretical models (see chapter 2). Intervention can be focused at one of three different levels – the individual, the family or the community or environmental level – or it may involve some combination of all three. The choice of treatment plan will depend on various factors concerning the nature of the abuser as well as the type of the abuse (for example, physical abuse or neglect as opposed to sexual abuse), whether or not the abuser is currently a member of the child's household, and significantly, the availability of resources locally.

A precondition for treatment is that the abuser must recognize the need for it and accept that what he or she has done cannot be tolerated. Some will embrace this readily, others resist. Kempe and Kempe (1978) estimated that about 10% of abusers are untreatable and remain dangerous to their children for various reasons to do with their psychiatric condition or their refusal to acknowledge that behaviour must be changed. More recent estimates give a more pessimistic view based on the efficiency of treatment and put the proportion of untreatable families at between 20 and 87% for physical abuse or neglect and between 16 and 38% for sexual abuse (Jones, 1987). However, it is very difficult to define the 'untreatable abuser'. New methods of treatment are being devised all the time, and hence the previously untreatable may become treatable. Some may be treatable in principle but with results too slow for the child's interim suffering to be tolerable. We cannot know what success an untried programme might have had in any case. Any figures for untreatability should be approached with great caution.

Punishment and treatment

Punishment need not preclude treatment for the individual abuser but, with the notable exception of special prisons such as Grendon, very little in the way of treatment is usually provided during custodial sentences in this country. Indeed, it can be argued that associating treatment with punishment can infringe the rights of prisoners, where responses to rule infringement are shaped not by the nature of the offence but by the nature of the offender, whose integrity as a moral agent is ignored. Some paedophiles, for example, whilst accepting the state's right to punish them for breaking the law as it stands, would not accept that there is anything morally wrong in what they do and would argue instead for a change in the law.

Those under probation orders of various kinds, some of which require residence in a probation hostel, can and do receive treatment through the criminal justice system. In parts of the United States suspended sentences and probation orders are used in a flexible way with treatment as a condition of avoiding custodial sentences and as a precondition of being reunited with the family. (See chapter 33 for a description of this kind of scheme in the UK.) In the United Kingdom the threat of prosecution and punishment of the abuser may be used to persuade families to co-operate in treatment programmes. A blend of punishment and treatment may be considered just when the abuser is thought to be only partly responsible for his or her behaviour, such as where family circumstances and living conditions have put considerable stress on individual parents and increase the likelihood of abuse.

Where there is insufficient evidence for prosecution or conviction (and hence punishment) in a child abuse case, there may still be adequate grounds for other types of legal sanctions. Thus, it may be possible for the police to take the child into police protection or for the local authority to apply for an emergency protection order. These actions may be experienced as punishment by the parents even if not officially sanctioned as such. Certainly some of the parents involved in the Cleveland sex abuse crisis interpreted removal of their children from home as presumption of guilt with the onus on them to prove their innocence. And many children experience being removed from their families as a type of punishment for the act of disclosing that abuse was happening.

Neither punishment nor treatment
Where abuse is denied and there is insufficient evidence for conviction and where parents or other alleged abusers refuse to participate in treatment programmes or are otherwise deemed untreatable, neither punishment nor treatment is logically possible. In such circumstances a purely child protectionist strategy has to be taken.

Table 1 *Outcomes for abusers by type and degree of abuse (1977–82 combined)**

| Outcomes for abusers | types/degrees of abuse | | | | TOTAL |
| | Injuries due to physical abuse | | | Sexual abuse | |
	Fatal	Serious	Moderate		
Registered cases prosecuted (%)	69.4	21.3	8.1	52.5	7.6 $N=496$
Of these, outcomes (%) were:					
Convicted	40.0	59.8	51.0	49.0	52.2
Conditional discharge	0	1.8	9.8	1.9	6.7
Absolute discharge	0	0	1.6	0	1.0
Acquittal	8	1.8	2.6	1.9	2.6
Pending	52.0	36.6	35.0	47.2	37.5

From Creighton (annual).

What happens to abusers?
Table 1 indicates the pattern of decision-making in relation to identified abusers in England and Wales as shown in the National Society for the Prevention of Cruelty to Children (NSPCC) records which cover about 10% of the population. It can be seen from the number of court proceedings as a percentage of registered cases that the more serious the injury, the more likely that there will be a prosecution (69.4% of cases involving fatal injuries compared with only 8.1% of cases with moderate injuries). Sexual abuse cases also have a high rate of prosecution (52.5%). We can conclude from this that treatment (often combined with threat of legal action in the form of an official warning from the police) is the commonest response to non-fatal and non-sexual abuse. This may be said to reflect the way in which the family is seen as a private sphere in relation to violence, within which the police have historically been reluctant to involve themselves.

Other sources tell us that natural fathers are four times as likely to be prosecuted as natural mothers; that when charged, mothers are less likely to be convicted; and that if convicted, mothers are more likely to be given a conditional discharge. This pattern may reflect differences in the severity of the abuse or differing reactions to abusers of different sexes or both.

Treatment options

As already stated, intervention by treatment can be focused at one of three levels – the individual, the family, or the community or environmental level – or it may involve some combinations of all three.

Individual level

There is a range of possible treatment options for the individual abuser or offender which are based on different theoretical approaches. A number of the better-known options are outlined below:

1 *Behavioural approaches* The distinguishing characteristic of treatments based on behaviourist principles is their focus on changing behaviour regardless of its possible causes or of the attitudes and insight of the individual concerned. Behavioural analysis of abusive incidents may be used to work out, for example, how a person's response to a child's behaviour escalates into violence, and in subsequent attempts to re-educate that person in new ways of responding to potential flashpoints. This can be achieved through 'modelling' (the therapist acting as a role model) or through direct teaching of more effective ways of managing difficult behaviour, such as alternatives to physical punishment and the use of rewards to increase the likelihood of desirable behaviours. The same principles can be used in programmes of social skills training to enhance the wider social and parenting skills that so many abusive parents are lacking.

Other behaviourist techniques, such as systematic desensitization, may be used to alter an individual's response to stressful and anxiety-provoking situations. For example, persistent, high-pitched crying in a young baby may provoke extreme tension and anxiety in a parent which sets the scene for explosive violence. It is possible to train someone to relax and reduce tension through progressive muscle relaxation and deep breathing. The tension-provoking stimulus (in this case a recording of a crying child) can be introduced gradually and at low volume during relaxation sessions until the individual is able to cope with exposure to the real thing without becoming overwrought (Hutchings, 1980).

Aversion therapy has been used in the treatment of sex offenders. This can take the form of giving drugs to make the abuser sick, or administering electric shocks every time he or she is presented with an inappropriate erotic stimulus such as a picture of a naked child. In time the image and reaction become associated (conditioned) so that the mere sight of a naked child is enough to make the abuser feel sick or fearful. Although it may be quite effective in the short term, this type of conditioning does not always generalize sufficiently to related situations (for example, a child with clothes on might arouse attraction without an adverse reaction) and the effect gradually wears off, so it is unlikely to prevent re-abuse in the longer term without further treatment.

2 *Individual psychotherapy* Psychotherapeutic approaches tend to view abusive behaviour as symptomatic of underlying personality or relationship problems. The main aim of psychotherapy is to help individuals to understand their previous experiences (particularly, within the psychoanalytic tradition, the formative experiences of early childhood) and allow them to express their true feelings. Through this process they can gain insight into their current personal problems including abusive behaviour (see chapter 30).

3 *Group therapy* Peer group pressure can be a very effective way of changing

individual attitudes and behaviour and of offering support and encouragement during the process of change. Some groups (such as Parents Anonymous described in chapter 34) are run on self-help principles and all participants will themselves have experienced the anguish of having their childrearing abilities questioned and feeling inadequate, helpless and hopeless as parents. Other therapeutic groups for abusers are extremely intensive and run by skilled professional therapists who may use the power of the group process to force individual abusers to face the reality of their offences and the damage that they have caused to the children concerned. An example of the latter would be the type of therapeutic groups run in prisons such as Grendon.

Family level
Approaches based on variants of the family dysfunction model see abuse as symptomatic of the wider problems of relationships within the family system. The aim of family therapy is to break into these complex and destructive patterns of family dynamics, to improve effective communication between family members and to restore relationships to a positive footing in which roles and responsibilities are clear and the boundaries between generations are fixed (see chapter 32).

Within a family systems approach to treatment it is often desirable to single out subsystems, such as the interaction of a child with one parent or the marital relationship, for separate attention. This could take the form of individual or joint counselling sessions or it could involve a more practical, behavioural approach in which specific aspects of behaviour are identified and tasks are set for the family to work on between sessions. Task-centred work usually involves drawing up an agreement or contract between therapists and family members that sets out the responsibilities of both parties, the targets and timescales for improvement and what will happen if the contract is not adhered to (see chapter 22).

Community/environmental level
If social and economic disadvantage produce stressful living conditions which contribute to physical abuse and neglect then the abuser may be considered less than fully culpable for his actions. One way of decreasing the likelihood of future abuse would thus be through attempting to improve living conditions and reduce stress. Social interventions as treatment for the abuser could take the form of better housing, financial benefits, day care for the children, improving social support networks, for example by involvement in community groups, etc.

In the case of sexual abuse, the connection with poverty and social disadvantage is less apparent, but at present statistics suggest that the vast majority of abusers are male. Treatment at a social level involves consideration of the ways in which girls and boys are socialized into sex-stereotyped roles and of changing the attitudes of adult males generally towards women as objects of sexual attraction, dominance and exploitation.

Multilevel treatment
Comprehensive treatment programmes such as those offered by the Department of Psychological Medicine, Great Ormond Street Children's Hospital or the Child Sexual Abuse Treatment Program in Santa Clara, California, are based on the principle that 'there is no one therapeutic modality or fixed treatment plan which can meet the overall needs of the family' (Bentovim, 1980). The therapeutic package may include any or all of the above elements and a particular feature of the American scheme is the important role attributed to self-help therapy and support groups run by formerly abusing families known as Parents United (Giaretto, 1981).

In the absence of specialist schemes, a therapeutic package may be put together by a social worker or NSPCC worker drawing on the facilities and resources available in their local area. Unfortunately, these are often seriously limited and treatment options for abusers and their families may fall far short of the ideal.

Effectiveness of treatment

For various reasons it is very difficult to measure the effectiveness of treatment or punishment. Definitions of success, the period of follow-up, the choice of who is given the punishment or treatment, problems in knowing whether or not there has been re-abuse all render measurement difficult, and studies using different measures cannot be compared directly.

In one overview of the evaluation of a large number of treatment programmes in the United States (Cohn and Daro, 1987) it was concluded that 'successful intervention with maltreating families requires a comprehensive package of services which address both the interpersonal and concrete needs of all family members' (p. 437). The programmes that were most successful, particularly in the case of physical abuse and neglect, were those that included psychotherapy and parent education elements and in which professionally run services were augmented by the peer group pressure and support provided by self-help groups. Nevertheless, the overall conclusion was pessimistic since, despite the efforts of the most intensive and imaginative treatment programmes, success rates were not high and a substantial core of families had multiple, intractable problems and their children remained at risk. Between 30 and 47% of children were actually re-abused while treatment was in progress. It seems that sexual abuse may be more amenable to treatment, since Jones (1987) estimated that re-abuse occurred in only 16% of cases. Nevertheless, the notorious unreliability of evaluation studies must always be remembered.

Conclusions

Whatever general statements can be made about the effectiveness of various kinds of treatment or punishment, they cannot sensibly be used to determine the response to particular cases in which decisions have to be made. The Cleveland Inquiry Report (DHSS, 1988) stresses the dangers of mechanical responses to child abuse. As part of the response to child abuse, criminal prosecution and punishment offer protection of children during incarceration, the symbolic assertion of the wrongness of abuse, respect for the abuser as a human agent, and the victim's assurance that he or she has been wronged. Treatment acknowledges the fact that many abusers are not entirely autonomous choice-makers and, if successful, provides for the longer-term safety for children. It may even be facilitated through the exercise of legal powers, including criminal prosecution. It is not possible in advance to prescribe what is appropriate in all instances. Instead it is necessary for practitioners to make careful assessments of individual cases.

FURTHER READING

HORTON, A. L., JOHNSON, B. L., ROUNDY, L. M. and WILLIAMS, B. (eds.) *The Incest Perpertrator: A Family Member No one Wants to Treat*, Sage publications Inc, London (1990)

SECTION FOUR

RECOGNIZING AND RESPONDING TO SUSPECTED ABUSE

16 EXTRACT FROM *THE BONE PEOPLE**

Keri Hulme

[The novel is set in New Zealand and tells of Joe, a Maori, and his fostered mute son, Simon. Joe had been bringing up this little boy alone since his wife, Hana, died some time before. Kerewin is a recent friend of Joe and Simon. Simon, Joe's foster son, visits Kerewin who lives in a tower, and she finds him passed out on the floor.]

Kerewin stares.
You wouldn't believe it. You couldn't.
You come in, feeling clean and straightened out and high on holiness, and what awaits?
One drunken kid, lying hunched and untidy all over the floor. Snoring like a bluebottle.
Two bottles overturned, and alcohol rife through the air.

O hell, look at the window!

She shakes her head in disbelief.
Two hours and he does this much damage?
Man alive, a six year old debauchee. . . .
Her heart mourns the window (but I can buy another one).
She walks across to the cupboard, avoiding the puddles (O tatami, you weren't got for this . . . to be good and golden for bare feet not to be . . . I *hope* that's drink . . . still, if the worst comes to the worst, I can always turn it over . . .) and digs him in the ribs with the toe of her foot.
No response. Not so much as a blink or an offkey snore. He dreams on oblivious, sound in his stupor.

It would be kind to let him sleep it off. I'm not kind.

So she picks him up, her heart kicking with a kind of misgiving at his lightness, and climbs the spiral to the shower, and turns the water on at needlespray and coldest. For a minute he lies under the blast, limp as a skin in her hold.
Then he jerks, and screams.
Highly startled, she drops him. She has never heard him scream before.

'He screamed, my God could he scream. He's a fluent screamer. . . .'

It's a fierce high agonising to the ears sound.

---

* The material contained in this chapter is excerpted from Hulme, K. *The Bone People*, Hodder & Stoughton, New Zealand (1985).

The child goes on screaming. He starts to fight the cubicle walls, the floor, the water, in a blind panic to get anywhere out.

She watches, pulled back clear of his flailing arms.

He's not seeing where he is. He's terrified.

Then, understanding part of his terror, she reaches in and turns the spray off.

The boy crouches in the inch of water, shuddering and retching and sobbing. He is sickly white, and he hasn't opened his eyes yet.

'Simon.'

It stills him a little. More shivering and gasping, but the screaming panic is done. So she repeats his name again and again, kneeling down by the shower stall.

Conversationally she says.

'Did you think that was the sea or something? The same water where you almost drowned? I'm sorry, it was a foolish thing for me to do . . . I didn't think deeply, you see. I just said to myself, the urchin's riddled out of his mind. So many sheets in the wind there's none left to steer the ship with. So get him sober fast. And how to do that? O easy . . . like in the song, you know it?'

Singing softly,

'What shall we do with a drunken sailor, ear-lie in the morning?
Put him the scuppers with a hosepipe on him. . . .'

'Only, there's just a shower here. No scuppers, no hosepipe . . . but it wasn't the wisest thing in the world to do, I admit that now.'

He is nearly quiet, only the occasional whimper, though his breathing rushes yet.

She sighs,

'Actually it was a bloody stupid thing to do, eh?'

Godgodgodgodgod, thinks Simon.

It is a beat in his head in time with the drips. With the steady splat of water running on to the cold steel floor under his hands.

In time with the aching pulses in his thighs and back and chest and legs.

But listen: snap. Cigarillo case. It *is* Kerewin.

Scrape of match, and a flare of flame.

The water is nearly all out of his ears.

There's a rattle as she puts the matchbox away.

'So hokay? You know where you are now? Third floor the Tower, all over the shower . . . or are you still a bit under the weather?'

He puts out his hand, groping blindly, and Kerewin takes it, holds it gently.

'Sorry about that, Haimona. I sure as hell didn't mean to frighten you . . . wake you up in a rough fashion, yes. I was nasty, I meant to do that. But not to scare you, really.'

He shakes her hand, goes to shift upright, and his other hand slips under him and he skids forward on the shining steel floor nearly chinning himself before Kerewin's grip pulls him up short.

'Sweet hell, boy, easy.'

She leans in and lifts him to his feet, steadying him out the door.

Rat-tail hair and soaked clothes, a sodden sorry sight.

'Struth fella, talk about a joygerm . . . but I don't suppose you feel like smiling.'

She has conned that the tears are still running off his face mixed with water. He can feel it, the way she's looking.

'I think you'd better have a proper shower,' says Kerewin gentlevoice. 'Then you'd better go to bed for a while . . . I forgot about that bloody flu you're smote with. Help us undone with your clothes, e Sim.'

It is because I am tired, he weeps helplessly. I can't stop. I can't say. I *can't*.

We've had it, he thinks. It's finished and it's all my fault.

He is shaking again.

He can't remember when he last felt this sick.

He makes no protest, gives no resistance. He even helps undo buttons and slide off clothes.

And Kerewin didn't say a word.

Except when he was naked, she took one of his hands, and turned him round carefully, supporting him so as not to make his head spin more, and then she tipped his face up towards her, and stared into his drowned eyes, as though she were seeking a meaning to it there.

'Why didn't you say *anything*?' There was pain in her voice, 'Why did you keep quiet?' but he shook his head.

And that was all she said.

. . .

Day into Nightmare.

What the *hell* do I do *now*?

O, I know what I'm supposed to do. Ring up Child Welfare and report the bloody mess he's in.

'Excuse me, I know a small child who's getting bashed . . . it looks like he's been thrashed with a whip (but I hope to God not).'

I can just hear it.

'You've known him *how* many weeks and you never suspected he was getting so badly treated?'
'Uh, well, he's very good at hiding his pain.'

I can just hear it.

She is furious with herself, not only because she must have hurt him.

Joe, you good kind patient sweetnatured gentlefingered everloving BASTARD.

But I knew all along, herr Gott. Something always felt wrong.

No, I didn't.

I had suspicions when he was here with his face battered.

But he never said it was Joe, and Joe didn't admit it was him.

I've seen him slapped.

Hell, everyone slaps kids.

I really didn't know. I really didn't. Just the nagging feeling that something was wrong between them, right from the first.

Christ, no wonder he always sleeps in that twisted fashion.

Joe.

(No more chess.)
(No more gay and grogging nights.)
(No more joking ritual of meals.)

(No more sweet and drifting conversation.)
(No more heart-sharing.)
(The end of the dream of friend.)

Joe Bitterheart Gillayley, what on earth possessed you to beat up Simon?

I mean, *Simon*.
That's Haimona, cherished and cuddled and kissed.
That's Haimona, quickwitted laughingeyed and bright all ways.
That's Haimona, all three feet nothing and too few pounds of him.

So okay, he can be a fair little shit at times, but you know why he is.
God in hell, even *I* know why he is.
It's the sick twisted secrecy of it.
I'll bet he threatened the child with murder if he revealed his wounding.
And the urchin flinched the first morning I knew him.

(And where did you learn that luverly block? Conditioned reflex, ma'am.)

And by the look of the scars on him, it's all been going on for a long long time.
Man, I wouldn't bash a dog in the fashion you've hurt your son.
I'd shoot it, if the beast was incorrigible or a killer, but never lacerate it like *that*.
Aue, Joe.
From the nape of his neck to his thighs, and all over the calves of his legs, he is cut and wealed. There are places on his shoulder blades where the . . . whatever you used, you shit . . . has bitten through to the underlying bone. There are sort of blood blisters that reach round his ribs on to his chest.
And an area nearly the size of my hand, that's a large part of the child's back damn it, that's infected. It's raw and swollen and leaking infected lymph.
That was the first sign I had that something was wrong. Despite his soaked clothes, his T-shirt stuck to his skin.
He didn't make a sound. All his crying was over.
And he wouldn't meet my eyes.
Somehow Joe, e hoa, dear friend, you've managed to make *him* ashamed of what *you*'ve done.
Neat job.

. . .

She wiped up the puddles from the matting – the tatami is tightly woven and more or less waterproof – and scrubbed away the stain the creme de cacao had made.
She gathered the shards of bottle, and tapped her nail against the cracked window.
She went and rang a Christchurch number and ordered a new pane of glass. They yelped with surprised joy, Yes Miz Holmes, consider your pane on the way. . . .
. . . Pane? A massive bowl-like curve, specially made, specially transported, and specially installed. Costly, rather. But the crack was unsightly, a blow to the eyes, although the pane would still keep out wind and rain.
She sat down with a cup of coffee at the ready, and made a fire for company.

Simon is upstairs, sleeping I hope.

(Washed and dried with extreme care: ointment, anointment, much good may they do him. Covered with padding and gauze, all the places where the cuts are open or bonedeep. A dessertspoonful of milk of magnesia to stop his retching.

'Happens when you drink that much,' she lied to him cheerfully, while praying in a cold way that he hadn't been hit too hard in the stomach. The child had managed a sickly grin.

And a cup of warm milk to help remove the taste of the spoonfuls of painkiller and sleeping potion he had obediently swallowed.)

Dammit, I could have fed him ground glass and he'd have passively opened his mouth and sucked it in . . . may the painkiller work. I can't stand the way he kept on shaking, then wincing.

She sipped the coffee thoughtfully.

Joe will be at the Duke. God knows when he'll get away from there, but he'll probably turn up here soon after. Heaven keep me from kicking the bugger to death when he finally arrives. So, gentle soul, you still have a few hours to decide what to do next.
And what can I do?

I can do nothing.

Make Simon keep quiet about this discovery. How?
Say nothing to Joe – at the moment, I'd have to bite my tongue through.
Tell nobody – let it continue, let the child endure it by himself.

No way.
I could tell Joe, but not tell anyone else.

Who else to tell anyway? The fuzz? The welfare? That means the experts get to wade in, but how does the section in the Crimes Act go? Something about assault on a child, carries a sentence maximum five years, child removed from environment detrimental to physical or mental health and wellbeing . . . sheeit and apricocks, that's no answer.

But just telling Joe wouldn't do any good . . . I'd have to look out for the child, and that means getting heavy. Getting involved.
She shivered.
It always happened.
You find a home and you lose it. Find a friend, grow a friendship, and something intervenes to twist it, kill it.
So what the hell can I do?

17 LABELLING CHILDREN AS ABUSED OR NEGLECTED

Robert Dingwall

Research Fellow, Wolfson College and Centre for Socio-Legal Studies, University of Oxford

In chapter 1 Rex Stainton Rogers introduced the idea that childhood is a social construction. While there might be certain unchangeable facts of human dependency, each society develops its own means of providing for the care of children and for the perpetuation of its way of life. These institutions reflect the values, attitudes and beliefs of adults about what will best fit a child for the world they live in or are trying to create. The other side of this, of course, is that problems in childcare are defined by reference to the same values, attitudes and beliefs. They are just as much social constructions as the positive ideals which adults might try to promote. This fundamental sociological truth was first stated more than 50 years ago:

> The term *social problem* indicates not merely an observed phenomenon but the state of mind of the observer as well. Value judgements define certain conditions of human life and certain kinds of behavior as social problems: there can be no social problem without a value judgement. (Waller, 1936, p. 922; original emphasis)

This insight is of great practical importance for the study of child abuse in two ways. On the one hand, it directs us to examine the values of what a sociologist would call the 'moral entrepreneurs', the people who attempt to 'sell' a particular definition of abuse to the rest of us in our society. What do they really mean by that definition? Just as importantly, what does it tell us about their positive ideals? What kind of society do they want us all to live in? What model of a proper family or a normal childhood would they like us to adopt?

On the other hand, it underlines the need to see child abuse as something that is produced by the decisions of people who are in contact with children. It is essential to be clear what this means, because people who are unfamiliar with such ideas sometimes think that it implies an indifference to the plight of maltreated children or that it is some sort of criticism of the caring professions. What is being argued is that, in nature, all that exist are patterns of behaviour between adults and children. Violence within these has no more moral significance than the action of the cuckoo chick which ejects its competitor fledglings from their shared nest. But when we place the behaviour of adults towards children in a social context, it becomes available for labelling in a way which imposes a moral evaluation. Until quite recently, for example, it was considered both lawful and morally legitimate for schoolteachers to beat children, within certain broad limits (see chapter 14). Indeed, this was often alleged to be positively beneficial to the child on the receiving end, to be done for his or, more rarely, her own good. Most observers of such an event would not define it as an act of abuse, unless the sanction appeared to be out of proportion to the act of wrongdoing, or the child was in some way handicapped or the teacher appeared to be deriving some gratification from the act.

The point is that for some treatment of a child to be described as abusive or neglectful, an observer must recognize it, formulate it and label it. If that definition is to have more than trivial implications, it must be assigned by somebody who has the socially recognized authority to impose the label. This is the core of the argument for studying the decision-making of health, education, social work and legal agencies in contact with children. Indeed, it is as important as studying 'abusing families' themselves, since their identification as candidates for inclusion in a research project usually turns out to depend upon some prior labelling decision by an agency or group of agencies (see chapter 3).

If we do not understand how a decision has been made, we may confuse factors associated with the decision-making process and those associated with the behaviour we call abusive. To what extent does the alleged concentration of child abuse and neglect among certain social groups reflect the fact that some groups are more likely to be subjected to the surveillance of health visitors and social workers, rather than genuine differences in the nature of adult–child relationships?

The protection of children
These concerns lay at the back of a study of agency decision-making in child abuse and neglect which was carried out by two colleagues and myself in three English counties between 1977 and 1983 (Dingwall et al., 1983). Many previous writers and some of our informants held the view, which is still common, that child abuse and neglect are obvious to the trained professional eye. As C. H. Kempe, the founder of child abuse studies, and his colleagues wrote, back in 1962, 'To the informed physician the bones tell a story the child is too young or too frightened to tell' (Kempe et al., 1962).

To reach this conclusion, its authors adopt what legal writers would call a 'principle of strict liability'. This is illustrated in a quotation from an interview my colleagues and I carried out with one of the leading U.K. medical consultants of the time:

> R.D.: No, I was thinking that, you know, it's a very difficult task surely for a house officer in a busy accident set-up like the Victoria, you know, he has very limited social background information on a child.
>
> Cons.: I don't. I haven't found this nor did Henry Kempe. The so-called grey areas as far as we're concerned don't exist. And what we would say to the in . . ., you've probably read the instructions that the Area Review Committee issued, the form, haven't you, you know that if a child under two years of age is injured, seriously injured, then it shouldn't have happened. You know, if it gets seriously injured in a road traffic accident, it shouldn't bloody well have happened because it should be in the back of the car sitting in its little old seat with its whatnots on, you know, I mean I regard that as gross neglect, don't you?

The principle of strict liability implies that *any* substantial injury to a small child is sufficient to justify an allegation of parental neglectfulness, represented by some act of omission or lack of care, if not of actual maltreatment. For the reasons set out in the introduction to this chapter, however, my colleagues and I were doubtful about this version of how decisions were made or, indeed, whether they could ever be made in quite this way.

Accident departments and child health clinics
We identified two particular settings where we thought these views could be tested. Doctors working in accident departments and child health clinics see quite large numbers of children but have relatively little information about their social

circumstances. If a strict liability approach were used or child abuse and neglect were easy to diagnose on physical signs alone, then we would expect to find a substantial number of cases being identified in these settings with relatively little difficulty. In fact, we found relatively few.

Children represent between one-quarter and one-third of all patients seen in accident departments. About 80% of them have injuries which could be defined as non-accidental in a strict liability sense. We found that, in practice, each one was assessed in the light of such information as the staff could obtain about the child's social background and their observations of the demeanour of an accompanying parent. This information was then used to determine whether or not to accept any explanation of the condition the child 'presented' when seen at the hospital and, hence, to label the injuries as accidental or not.

Similarly, doctors working in child health clinics used such social background information as they had available to help determine whether children who were underweight or developmentally delayed were exhibiting signs of maltreatment or of normal variation in the human population. Again, the principle of strict liability would oblige them to consider all these children as suffering from inadequate parenting unless and until a full clinical investigation revealed some underlying natural disorder.

In both settings, we remarked upon the important potential contribution to be made by nurses and ancillary staff. They generally had a much more detailed knowledge of the social geography of the local community, which alerted them to details that the doctors did not recognize as significant. This enabled them to identify children as coming from families of regular patients or from neighbour-hoods where abuse or neglect were thought to be particularly prevalent. They also tended to have more sophisticated skills in assessing parental demeanour.

The potential contribution of these staff was undervalued in the major teaching hospital we studied, which maintained a rigid hierarchy between the house officers and the supporting staff, but was well recognized in the provincial units, where the paediatric consultants encouraged experienced nurses to bypass or override the junior doctors if necessary. This is not to say that the nurses were better or worse than the house staff at identifying abuse, but rather that their experience and knowledge made a larger number of children available for the application of that label.

Our overall conclusion, though, was that, if a strict liability approach based on clinical evidence was actually enforced, both accident departments and child health clinics would overflow with identifications of child abuse. Something like this appears to have happened in Cleveland and precipitated the chaos which led to the subsequent inquiry (DHSS, 1988). But since this is so obviously an exceptional state of affairs, a different analysis is needed to understand what is going on. Before introducing this, however, some consideration should be given to the possibility of a strict liability approach based on social evidence.

Social evaluation
This can be more clearly seen in the work of health visitors and social workers who are specialists in the collection and assessment of social information. They base their judgements of children's treatment on ideas of what normal family life is like. These ideas change according to the nature of the area in which they are being applied. In other words, they are relative to the professionals' understanding of how children in that community are generally treated. The professionals' ideas have two dimensions, which we described as the material and the interpersonal environments of the child.

The *material environment* includes the physical conditions of a home (the state of the property and its furnishings) and the physical condition of the occupants (the state of their clothing and general self-care). Although this sort of information is quite obvious to any visitor to the home and can be assessed without any specialized knowledge, its significance is often discounted precisely because of this. Part of the mystique of professional work lies in the rejecting of 'naïve' ordinary-person criteria in favour of those which are only available to someone with an appropriate training. Social workers appear to be somewhat more prone to this than health visitors, and it is a part of the barrier which makes relations between the two occupations more difficult.

Workers visiting people in their homes begin to evaluate families as soon as they pick up an address on a referral. This is part of their knowledge of the social geography of the community and enables them to set a standard for judging the family.

> When we get out to [the military base] the first family we go to see are the Chaucers. H.V. doesn't expect her to be in because there is a note on the midwife's discharge form that she was planning to go north to visit a dying parent. She was breast-feeding, which H.V. says is peculiar for the [service]. There is a lot of pressure against it from both families and their friends. She remarks on the fact that the garden has been done. This again is unusual and she regards it as a mark up. (Extract from original field notes)

The location and, to some extent the structural condition of a home are not seen as matters over which people like council tenants or service families have much choice. What they actually do with the property, however, is within their control and, as such, can be used as evidence of their 'good character'. Are they respectable people making the best of unpromising circumstances or disreputable people dragging the place down? In the same way, clothing may be poor or second-hand – but is it clean and well-patched? Money may be short – but is it being spent on food or electricity bills or on selfish adult pleasures? In our research, we noted that changes in material standards were treated as evidence of improvement or decline in the overall competence and moral character of parents. As such they formed part of the basis for determining whether parents' accounts of their child's condition were or were not likely to be believed.

The *interpersonal environment* concerned the conduct of parents towards each other, their children and the community. Such behaviour was seen as being even more within the control of the individuals concerned and thus a still more reliable guide to their moral character. For example, both health visitors and social workers used the way that couples had planned their families, if at all, as an indication of their general responsibility for controlling their lives, their relationships and the future of their children. Failure to limit the number of children or to space them apart could be treated as evidence of parental thoughtlessness, selfishness or incompetence.

Little significance was attached to whether or not parents were married or to whether children were the legitimate offspring of the adults caring for them. However, these relationships were assessed by comparing them with standards which were effectively those of an idealized traditional family. If there was evidence of other failures, for instance through wife-beating, prostitution, petty crime, unemployment, alcoholism or drug addiction, parents could be considered as morally blemished. From this it might be inferred that they were also more likely to be capable of maltreating their children.

But as with physical signs, if strict liability were applied on this basis, then very large numbers of children might be labelled as abused or, particularly, as neglected, in the sense that their care was defined as less satisfactory than the ideals in which those observing them had been trained. The interesting question, then, may not be why so many children are taken into care or placed on Child Protection Registers but why so few of the apparent candidates for this are chosen.

What we had found was that evidence, both physical and social was necessary for the labelling of a case of abuse, but that these forms of evidence were not in themselves sufficient. It should be stressed that neither form of evidence was seen as coming before or being more important than the other. Social evidence influenced the interpretation of physical signs: physical signs could prompt a questioning of social circumstances. But some other element was needed to explain how most possible candidates were eliminated.

The rule of optimism

This led us to consider the possibility of some form of situation liability. In contrast to the principle of strict liability, this says that a conclusion about the responsibility for a child's condition can only be reached after an extensive inquiry into the precise circumstances of the events alleged. Taking the instance given by the informant quoted earlier, for example, the *intentions* of the parents taking their child out without a seat-belt would become relevant: was the accident an unforeseeable event that a reasonable parent could not have anticipated? But if the health and social services had to carry out such a detailed investigation into every case that came to their attention, this would impose an impossible workload. The answer must lie in some routine practice which more or less automatically eliminates most possible reasons for concern.

We called this practice the 'rule of optimism'. This can be stated formally as the principle that, in a situation of uncertainty, child protection workers should favour the interpretation of signs and symptoms which least stigmatizes parents. If you like, parents should be viewed as 'innocent until proven guilty'. This rule provides two general techniques for discounting most sources of concern.

The first of these is a justification which we called 'cultural relativism'. A justification is a 'get-out clause' which can be used to reduce the importance of less-than-desirable behaviour by pointing to alternative standards which may allow the behaviour to be judged as 'good enough'. In our study this was used to justify the beating of West Indian children, by seeing such treatment as the reflection of a traditional use of physical punishment in that community. Similarly, the under-nourishment of Asian infants was treated as less serious than similar underfeeding in other families, by arguing that it was the result of the transplantation of customary dietary beliefs to an alien setting. With children from ethnic minorities, there is, of course, a difficult balance to be struck between simple racism and attempting to guarantee a minimum standard of protection to every child within the jurisdiction of British child protection services. However, the same process can also be observed in relation to the majority community. Similar justifications might be applied to particular housing estates or kinship groups. In the northern area we studied, lower standards were applied to almost the whole population as a way of responding to the gross physical and social deprivation of the community.

The second technique is an excuse which we called 'natural love'. An excuse is a means of discounting otherwise unacceptable behaviour because the people involved are, for some reason, incapable of acting responsibly. 'Natural love' describes the way in which workers think of the relationship between parents and children as something which is a fact of nature, unlike the social and changeable affections of adults for each other.

However, the other side of this assumption is that, if the love of parents for their children is part of their human nature, those who fail to show this love must be, in some sense, not human. Such an allegation is so monstrous that it can only be sustained by the most compelling evidence. If there is any sign of emotional warmth, however little, parental conduct can be excused. Some of the saddest cases in our study, for instance, involved the children of mentally handicapped parents. These parents clearly had considerable affection for their children, but were incapable of providing for their care, to the extent of causing great physical and mental suffering.

There seem to be two situations in which these discounting devices fail. One is that of 'parental incorrigibility' where parents refuse to co-operate with the professional workers involved. Their moral character is fatally damaged by 'standing on their rights' and denying the place for a voluntary, helping relationship between child protection workers and the public. A family with nothing to hide would have no reason to reject inspection, would they? For example, the mentally handicapped parents just referred to would often be given a huge investment of professional and non-professional staff time and effort to support their childrearing. Only when this help was rejected and the parents demanded to be left alone 'like other families' were children compulsorily removed.

The rule of optimism also breaks down where there is a 'failure of containment'. This describes the situation where a family's circumstances become public knowledge outside a core group of professionals. As their control of information about the situation weakens, the group of professionals may choose compulsory intervention for defensive reasons, in the knowledge that others may judge the family more harshly by ordinary standards than they have done themselves.

The idea of the rule of optimism became popular through its use by witnesses to the inquiry into the death of Jasmine Beckford and in the subsequent Report (London Borough of Brent, 1985). In the course of that discussion, it came to be treated as a psychological property of child protection workers. Effectively, it became a catch-phrase to describe the professional naïveté of which social workers are so often accused. This is a dangerous misunderstanding. The rule of optimism is a response to both an organizational and a psychological problem. Child protection services face formidable difficulties in screening out relevant information from the flood of incoming data (Dingwall, 1986), a problem which is also experienced by individuals in any other 'overload' situations (Sheldon, 1987). The rule of optimism is one of the ways people and organizations defend themselves in situations where they are being expected to make complex decisions on the basis of insufficient information and limited resources.

Although we did not discuss this in our original study, the rule of optimism would also account for the reluctance to accept that children in residential care, for whatever reason, could be maltreated. Although their caregivers have no 'natural' bond of affection with the children, their good character is assumed by the process of recruitment. If a service cannot trust its own resources, who can it trust? How much uncertainty can anyone be expected to handle?

By such means, child protection services judged which parents might be capable of maltreating their children. In the process, they seemed to weed out not only middle- and upper-class families, but also most traditional working-class families, members of ethnic and religious minorities and mentally incompetent parents. This left the 'rough' working-class, particularly single women who lived with a succession of boyfriends, as the most vulnerable to allegations of abuse or neglect.

In the years since we completed this study, a new form of abuse has become prominent – sexual abuse. We did ask about this quite systematically but uncovered too few cases to justify an extended discussion. In 1977–82 it was already recognized as a large potential problem, but child protection services despaired of being able to persuade children to come forward or adults to inform; and of them being able to produce evidence that would satisfy a court if compulsory measures were necessary.

Nevertheless, we did collect some evidence which suggested that the rule of optimism operated in a similar way. One incident was particularly memorable. A colleague and I interviewed the consultant in charge of the accident service at a provincial district general hospital. We asked him specifically about the investigation of vulval injuries in small girls. He replied that they had a number each year, but these were usually caused by some form of impaling accident. We observed that other departments in our study had taken a more critical attitude to such accounts and the interview moved on. About two weeks later, we were interviewing in a social services area office in the catchment of that hospital. We asked the area officer about referrals for sexual abuse. He remarked on this question. They had not had any for years but the accident department had sent them two in the last fortnight!

Why optimism?

The prevalence of the rule of optimism requires some explanation. Some critics, like Louis Blom-Cooper, have seen it as evidence of a widespread dereliction of duty in child protection services. Indeed, he has gone so far as to call for the complete dismantling of the current agency system and for the creation of a new, integrated agency for dealing with all questions of child health and welfare. While this idea has other merits, it would not escape the pressure which dictates the use of this optimistic approach in health and welfare services. It would not be a simple matter to invert the rule of optimism into a 'rule of pessimism'.

If child protection work is ineffective, it is not because of a disrespect for the legal duties of the agencies involved. It is because child protection must be reconciled with other important social values, most particularly those of the freedom and autonomy of families. The surveillance of families by an occupation like health visiting, for example, is only possible because of the tacit bargain that parents will not be harshly judged, that it is an occasion for them to demonstrate their respectability rather than to have it minutely inspected. If it were not for this bargain, child protection work could not be conducted largely on a voluntary basis. Social workers, health visitors and others are not law-enforcement agents, a kind of family police.

A rule of pessimism would undoubtedly require much more use of compulsory powers and greater confrontation between child protection workers and the public. It is certainly possible to conceive of a society where this might happen but it would be very different from the one in which we now live. This was graphically demonstrated in Cleveland where the social services department took at face value Blom-Cooper's demands, in the Beckford Report, for a more pessimistic approach. Their attempt to treat all referrals as suspect until proven otherwise exploded in a barrage of political and media outrage at this threat to the ideals of family life. As this episode demonstrates, without wider social reconstruction, a unified child protection agency would be no less bound to operate within the same philosophy of optimism as its much-criticized and much-misunderstood predecessors.

Every society generates its own pattern and rate of child maltreatment by the values which it adopts to judge, support and monitor childrearing. In any discussion of the appropriate response, it is essential to distinguish clearly between the scientific questions of the explanation of particular patterns of adult–child interaction and the possible collective and individual responses, and the moral questions about which forms of behaviour should be considered unacceptable and the extent to which they can be policed without undermining other cherished values. Much of the confusion in our response to child maltreatment results from the failure to make this distinction clearly.

18 RECOGNIZING ABUSE

Anne Bannister

Team Leader, NSPCC and Greater Manchester Child Sexual Abuse Unit

Most healthy children collect bruises from time to time, in falling for instance or in fights with other children. Such bruises are most likely to be on knees and shins or arms and elbows. A child who has fallen on its face may have a bruised forehead and nose or a cut lip.

There are, however, certain signs which we might term 'indicators of abuse'. Experience has shown that some injuries are hardly ever caused non-accidentally. There are also warning signs which may indicate sexual or emotional abuse or chronic neglect.

Physical indicators of abuse

Children who are seriously injured or killed often have a long history of frequent bruises or other injuries reflecting a long-standing pattern or spiral of abuse. Child abuse is seldom a 'one-off' incident. Teachers or neighbours may notice a child who always seems to have some bruises or injuries, especially if the injuries get progressively worse. A careful teacher or nursery officer, by making a regular note of the child's appearance, may be able to detect a 'pattern'. Perhaps the injuries always appear on Mondays or Tuesdays, after the weekend? By sharing this information with others, stress factors in the home can sometimes be pinpointed and maybe removed.

Some types of bruising are particularly characteristic of non-accidental injury.

- Handslap marks may be visible on cheeks or buttocks.
- Twin bruises on either side of mouth or cheeks can be caused by pinching or grabbing, sometimes to make a child eat or to stop a child from speaking.
- Bruising on both sides of the ear is often caused by grabbing a child as it runs away. It is very painful to be held by the ear, as well as humiliating, and this is a commonly presented injury.
- Babies who are handled roughly or held down in a violent way will have grip marks on arms or trunk. One of the most serious injuries to a child is done by shaking. This can cause haemorrhage to the brain as it bangs inside the skull. Only an expert could detect this (on X-ray) but the gripping bruises on arms or trunk would be a warning signal.
- Black eyes are most commonly caused by an object such as a fist coming into contact with the eye socket. A heavy bang on the nose, however, can cause bruising to spread around the eye and a doctor will usually be able to tell the difference.
- Bruising to breasts, buttocks, lower abdomen, thighs and genital or rectal areas could be an indicator of sexual abuse, but sometimes bruises can be confined to grip marks where a child has been held so that sexual abuse can take place.

Other types of injuries such as burns, scalds, fractures and poisoning may sometimes be caused non-accidentally. Of course children do have accidents. They may fall off slides or out of windows and break bones; they may pull pans of boiling water over themselves; they may mistake tablets for sweets or drink bleach from under the sink. Leaving aside the issue of the extent to which parents are culpable for failing to provide a safe environment or exercise sufficient vigilance, it is clear from experience that some types of injury are less likely to have been accidental than others and should always arouse suspicion. For example, it is possible for a child to be accidentally burnt by a cigarette – if the child runs into the end of it whilst it is being held firmly. But a casual brush against the end of a cigarette will not usually cause more than a slight mark.

- A round, red burn on tender, non-protruding parts like the mouth, inside arms and on the genitals, will almost certainly have been deliberately inflicted.
- Some types of scalds, known as 'dipping scalds' are always cause for concern. An experienced person will notice skin splashes caused when a child accidentally knocks over a hot cup of tea. In contrast a child who has been deliberately 'dipped' in a hot bath will not have splash marks.
- Bite marks are always cause for concern, there is usually a bruise and teethmarks can be seen. The size of the marks is the important factor here. Two- to four-year-olds sometimes bite other children but naturally the resulting marks will be small.
- Evidence of old or repeated fractures can be detected by a doctor or radiographer as can the sort of spiral fracture caused by twisting a child's limb.
- A torn frenulum (the skin inside the upper lip) in babies can be caused by a parent forcing a bottle into a child's mouth when the baby is reluctant to feed.
- Any injuries to the genitals or rectal area could indicate sexual abuse, as could bleeding from these areas. A skilled doctor will be able to note if there is abnormal dilation of these openings or if there is unusual reddening, but most medical signs like these would have to be accompanied by information from the child since there could be other explanations.

A child who is neglected may show obvious signs – be underweight, dirty, smelly, always hungry – but there is a great need for caution here. There is a difference between a child who is often dirty and one who is never clean. A child who wets the bed can sometimes smell if there has been no time or hot water for a bath. Whether a child is underweight is difficult for a non-medical person to decide since there are many factors to take into account, but health visitors and school doctors will notice if a child is well below average in height and weight and may be failing to thrive. Height-for-weight charts are typically kept for all children, so that this can be monitored. It is especially significant if the child puts on weight during a short period away from home (in hospital or foster care for instance).

Behavioural signs
Children who are physically neglected or abused also often have behavioural problems. A teacher may notice a child who is too compliant or who seeks constant attention. Another common sign is 'frozen watchfulness'. This is the child who watches adults acutely in order to adapt his or her own behaviour to try and avoid abuse. This can occur with children being abused physically, sexually or emotionally. A child who is constantly told that he or she is stupid may smile frequently in the hope that this will compensate. On the other hand a child who is always 'put down' may react by being constantly angry and aggressive. A child who is too strictly controlled at home frequently will assert his or her own strict controls over friends or other adults. It is important to remember that many behavioural signs are natural

defensive reactions to an unnatural or abusive relationship or a difficult situation. A child who is constantly aggressive or always a victim is hardly a happy child who is enjoying life.

Behavioural signs and symptoms may often be the only outward indicators of sexual abuse since physical signs are not always present or may be difficult to observe in the normal course of events. Some of these signs reflect general disturbance and can occur when a child is suffering in some other way; perhaps because of separation from a parent or through the birth of a new baby. We list below the most common signs but stress that they must be looked at together with any information from the child and in the light of family circumstances. Just as it is not usually possible to decide whether sexual abuse has occurred on medical evidence alone, so it is not possible to decide on the grounds of behaviour alone. It is possible though to use the behaviour as a starting-point for investigating the situation.

- Pseudo-mature or sexually explicit behaviour. The eight-year-old girl who acts as though she were about 18 in a sexually provocative way, the four-year-old child who grabs the genitals of adults, the 14-year-old boy who seems to have missed out on childhood and is disturbingly 'knowing' may behave in these ways as a result of abuse.
- Continual open masturbation or aggressive sex play with peers. Many children masturbate occasionally or in private, for curiosity or comfort, but when it is constant and in public it is a cause for concern. Even more worrying is the child who attacks another at school or nursery, for instance, and simulates intercourse. This kind of behaviour must be distinguished from normal sexual curiosity between peers, which is seldom aggressive.
- Overly compliant behaviour or 'watchful' attitude. This has already been mentioned with regard to physical and emotional abuse. Of course sometimes sexual abuse is combined with physical abuse and the whole is used as a punishment. The child feels she has been sexually abused because she was naughty and this makes her feel guilty. Even when the sexual abuse is not overtly violent or aggressive the child is often given some 'verbal explanation' by the abuser, which places blame on the child. For example 'you are so pretty' or 'you are evil and no one but me will love you'. Obviously this is emotional abuse too and it may be this that causes more damage to children than the sexual acts.
- Acting out aggressive behaviour, severe tantrums. This is just a child expressing anger, sometimes not against the person he or she is most angry with. It can often be too frightening for the child to be angry with the abuser so another carer receives the aggression. Note that tantrums may be normal in a two-year-old, not so usual in a five-year-old.
- An air of detachment or 'don't care' attitude (particularly in a younger child; in adolescents it may not be cause for concern). Some children detach themselves from reality as a defence mechanism when reality is too hard to bear.
- The child appears happy only when in school – or conversely is kept from school by a parent. This sign also applies to other kinds of abuse.
- The child has few friends in school and does not participate in school activities. This could be because a powerful abusive parent is deliberately isolating the child.
- The child does not trust anyone. Of course too trusting behaviour might also be suspicious but a child who has never learned to trust must engender suspicion.
- 'Tummy pains' with no medical explanation. (A child may say 'it hurts down there'.)
- It is quite common for children who have been sexually abused to have eating problems. It is fairly usual, of course, for a small child to use food as a weapon

167

against parents, to be 'faddy' or refuse to eat a meal. Children also eat for comfort sometimes just as adults do. Some abused girls have special problems with body image though and may develop anorexia (self-inflicted starvation) or become very obese.

- A child who is frightened, especially of being abused during the night, may have problems with sleeping, bed-wetting and nightmares. Again sleep patterns are sometimes hard to establish in a young child and bed-wetting is common in any stressful situation. Many children go through a stage of nightmares, but an older child having nightmares or difficulty in sleeping or a 'dry' child who starts bed-wetting continually may arouse suspicion.

- There have been studies to show that children who run away from home are often running away from physical or sexual abuse. If a child constantly 'runs away' the real reason for this should be sought from the child. A frightened, embarrassed child may not give the reason at first. Children often deny that they are being abused but they seldom invent stories of sexual abuse. Instead of literally 'running away' some children inflict wounds on themselves or attempt suicide. Recently people have realized that these are serious attempts to get out of an abusive situation or are expressions of anger or self-disgust. They are not simply 'attention-seeking devices' as it used to be thought.

- Some sexually abused children can become clinically depressed. Nowadays doctors are recognizing these signs in children. Teachers and other carers may notice a child who is very withdrawn or who is regressing to the behaviour of a much younger child. This behaviour often shows also in children who have been abused in other ways.

- Sgroi (1982) reminds us that the presence of sexually transmitted disease must be cause for concern as must a pregnancy where the father is 'unknown'. There are explanations other than sexual abuse but in the past adults have been only too happy to accept explanations which meant they did not have to face an unacceptable reality. This ties in with chapter 17 in which Robert Dingwall refers to the 'rule of optimism', that is the expectation that child abuse will *not* occur.

Risk factors

In chapter 3, on the prevalence of abuse and the use of statistics, Steve Taylor highlights the dangers of uncritical acceptance of any data on child abuse. In particular he points to the self-fulfilling prophecy when a professional looks for certain conditions in a family where abuse has occurred and then records these conditions as 'risk factors' in an abusing family. This must always be a danger and it is extremely likely that not only are insignificant factors being recorded but also significant ones are being missed.

It is not helpful, however, to 'throw out the baby with the bath water' and to ignore completely what is known about the relationship between family circumstances and child abuse. By looking at factors which may increase the risk of abuse we might be able to identify high-risk families and prevent abuse by changing their circumstances. It is always difficult to assess the impact of preventative measures since we cannot be sure whether abuse has been prevented because of our intervention or whether it would not have happened anyway. We all know of families where 'risk factors' seem to be high but children are well cared for and not abused. This might be because our statistics are quite wrong or because there is an unknown factor, like a supportive neighbour for instance, that is acting as a 'safety-valve'.

In any event it is worth looking at the risk factors suggested by Kempe and Kempe (1978) and others in the course of many years experience of working with child abuse.

Parents' personality

Some parents may still be feeling angry because of their own abuse or because they have witnessed violence in the home. Sometimes this anger erupts violently and inappropriately against their own children. Some parents too have felt rejected or isolated in their own childhoods and may have no ongoing support in the present. This too can lead to physical or emotional abuse of their own children or even neglect. Most sexual abusers have been physically, sexually or emotionally abused. This is not to say, of course, that those who have been so abused are likely to become abusers. If that were so most sexual abusers would be female since (as far as we know) twice as many girls are abused as boys. In fact over 90% of sexual abusers are male.

Marital and family relationships

Sometimes it is obvious that there is a power imbalance in the family. Perhaps the man is controlling and his wife is unusually compliant and child-like. Often the parents are two very immature people, each dependent on the other, neither being capable of providing support. Their interaction with the child may be unrealistic, they may expect the child to provide love and appreciation to increase their own self-esteem. These inappropriate family relationships can produce physical and emotional abuse or neglect. The relationships may also be present when sexual abuse has occurred but it is much more likely that the relationships are a result of sexual abuse rather than the cause. Most sexual abusers begin offending in adolescence, that is before they have children of their own.

Vulnerability of the child

It may be that some children are especially vulnerable to being physically abused. If the mother has had a difficult pregnancy or birth she may find it harder to relate to the child; premature birth or low birth weight can also lead to frustrations and anxieties which may be displaced onto the baby. Nowadays better care is taken in hospitals to ensure that babies are not separated from their mothers for long periods, but in the past this separation has sometimes led to problems of lack of 'bonding' between mother and child. It must not be forgotten that 'maternal overload' can be the final factor in a chain of events leading to child abuse. Just one child too many, too soon, could be a precipitating factor. Disappointment about the sex of a child is usually overcome by most parents very swiftly after the baby's birth but a few parents will remain profoundly distressed and, combined with other factors, abuse or neglect could be a consequence.

Social deprivation

Many families live in social circumstances which provide constant stress and aggravation. There may be unemployment, poor housing and financial problems but their children are not abused. They may be well integrated within the community, have a network of extended family and friends and they may make good use of facilities such as family centres, day nurseries, schools and leisure activities.

The families at risk are those whose social circumstances are poor and who are also unable, perhaps because of their personality problems, to integrate into the community. They present as isolated, maybe resentful and aggressive to authority, perhaps secretive and self-contained. They may have been offered support and rejected it. Sometimes a chaotic family with no support will be unable to get their children to schools and nurseries, especially if finance is limited, and it is in these circumstances that abuse may occur.

Precipitating incident

Finally, there will always be a precipitating incident that marks the beginning of abuse. It may be a stressful time of day (meal-times, bedtimes) or in the middle of the night when a child refuses to sleep. It is tempting to consider only the precipitating incident and to decide that the abuse was a 'one-off', unlikely to be repeated, especially if the abusing parent is remorseful.

There are patterns of abuse, though, and unless there is a complete reversal of some of the factors that led towards the abuse it will be repeated on any future stressful occasion. This pattern may become an escalating spiral of abuse leading to serious injury or death.

Factors in sexual abuse

Research into child sexual abuse has not really been established long enough to draw many conclusions about risk factors. Finkelhor (1984), a leading researcher in the field, points to statistics that show that sexually abused children report the presence of a stepfather in the family more often than a natural father or no father at all. This is irrespective of who the abuser was. Children who have lived for a period without their mother or who have a poor relationship with their mother are also more vulnerable. Children with few friends appear to be at risk but this may have been deliberately contrived by the abuser. Whatever the cause, it means that the child has no one in whom to confide, no one to believe, support or reassure him or her. This means that it is easier for the abuse to be kept secret. It also means that the child is more likely to show serious emotional damage in the future. Gelinas (1983), in a study on the negative effects of incest, found that a child who was able to tell someone and who was believed, supported and told that he or she was not to blame, was unlikely to suffer the more serious long-term effects of sexual abuse.

Child abuse can cause damage far beyond the obvious bruise or broken arm. Children will always cry for help and adults must train themselves to hear. To listen to the children and to share that information must then be our aim if child abuse is to be discovered and prevented.

FURTHER READING

BROWNE, K., DAVIES, C. and STRATTON, P. (eds.) *Early Prediction and Prevention of Child Abuse* Wiley (1988)

A useful collection of articles which focus on the issues and dilemmas surrounding the prediction, identification and prevention of child abuse.

19 THE INVESTIGATION OF SUSPECTED CHILD ABUSE

Paul Griffiths

Director of Services, ISPCC, Dublin

The investigation of allegations of child abuse needs to be conducted in a systematic manner, since few cases are clear-cut and there is often considerable confusion. Whatever kind of abuse is being investigated, the process is frequently met by resistance and hostility on the part of parents and denial by the child. Many referred children and their parents have never enjoyed acceptance or support and may have long histories of antagonism towards authority figures. In the past they may have warded off most successfully anyone who wished to pry into their lives; they may threaten or even use violence. In addition it is important to bear in mind the way in which the information obtained may be used at a later stage (e.g. for evidence in criminal proceedings).

Nonetheless, however great the need to accomplish an effective assessment of what has happened and what other factors may be involved, it is crucial to recognize that the needs of the child and other children within the family are paramount. The child's wishes, where possible, should be respected and acted upon.

The Cleveland Inquiry Report (DHSS, 1988) advised that 'One should go at the child's pace, that interviews should be limited to one or at the most two sessions and if the child is not ready or willing to talk at that stage, so be it.' The requirement to ensure safety and freedom from abuse for the child therefore has to be weighed against the child's fundamental right to be involved in determining his or her own future.

General principles of investigation

Once suspected abuse has been reported, timing needs to be considered. Injured or severely neglected children will obviously need urgent medical attention; young children must not be left alone in the house; children must not be subjected to more violence, threats or neglect. The younger the child, generally speaking, the more urgency should be given to following up the report. Usually, an initial contact will be made on the same day as the referral, unless there is good reason not to do so.

The person who made the original referral, if known, should be interviewed first, before proceeding with other parts of the investigation, so long as this does not endanger the child. Most referrals are made by people in the immediate neighbourhood of the family concerned: neighbours, relatives or professionals such as health visitors or teachers who see members of the family on a regular basis. Often only limited information is proffered initially, and so one of the first tasks is to get as much detail as possible from this initial source. Although those who report suspected abuse have a right to anonymity, professional workers have a duty to co-operate according to locally agreed procedures for the management of child abuse cases.

The next stage is usually to interview the child and the parents, although it is not always clear whether the child should be seen first, or the parents, and whether they should be interviewed separately or together. The advantages of seeing the parents together include being able to go through the process of investigation, take a full social history, assess the nature of the marital and parental relationships and find out whether they tend to take a similar or conflicting view of events. Most importantly, do the parents accept responsibility for the abuse or deny it? If the child is present at the interview, this means that there is an opportunity to assess the way that the parents and child relate to one another, including any communication problems. The child's actual abilities, growth and behaviour can be compared with the parents' knowledge about the child and their expectations.

Whatever the particular approach, the principle of honesty is essential from the outset. All the family should know what interviews have been conducted. The family should also be assured of confidentiality as far as possible, although care needs to be taken not to collude with long-standing family secrets, and it may sometimes be necessary to challenge unwillingness to discuss openly areas that are central to the investigation. The nature and content of the investigation process and the reports being produced should be explained clearly to the family, including the purpose of visits, the duties and responsibilities of the agency to protect children, and their responsibility to follow up all allegations of child abuse and neglect. Where a medical examination is to be included in the investigation, this too should be carefully explained. Adequate time should be allowed so that parents and children can ask questions and clarify their position.

Consultation with others

It is obviously essential to consult with other professionals who may have past or current information about the family. This can include developmental records provided by the health visitor, information about school attendance and behaviour from teachers, educational welfare officers and/or educational psychologists, and any background of drug/alcohol abuse or criminal record from the police or probation service. One of the most useful improvements that can be made to investigation is for the professionals concerned to develop and use comprehensive and accurate systems of information pooling.

Interviewing parents

At the time of referral, given the anxiety and stress engendered by the crisis, there is a tendency for the investigating worker to be drawn into a series of extended therapeutic interviews with family members. In my view this is counter-productive, as the purpose of the investigation becomes confused with therapy. In any case, short but frequent contacts enable the worker to keep the family informed as to what is happening and demonstrate concern without leaving all feeling undermined. In addition they allow workers to observe family behaviour at various times and in a variety of situations. Initially, frequent short contacts give family members an opportunity to begin to build a relationship with the worker and the agency and to develop trust of other concerned professionals. This improves the quantity and quality of available information for presentation at the case conference, and future planning objectives are more likely to be achieved with the full co-operation of family members.

Nonetheless, assessment interviews do provide opportunities to help parents make sense of what has happened and to show them support and other practical help. The main task must be, of course, to elicit information upon which the future risk to the child's safety can be assessed. But it is not possible to conceive of a child in isolation from his or her parents, and good child protection avoids alienation of parents wherever possible.

Problems arise when a parent seeks to form an alliance with the worker either against the child, or against his or her partner, by trying to place the blame upon them. Alternatively, the abusing parent may appear to accept all the blame and guilt for the situation. Techniques that avoid such traps need to be developed. While it is appropriate for abusers to take responsibility for mistreating their children, workers should avoid being expected to arbitrate. Workers also need to cope with attempts to sabotage the assessment process and to 'fog' the issues – 'You don't know what it's like, you've never had children have you?' Denial is commonly present as a defence – in some cases, the causes or perpetrator of suspected abuse may never be known.

Practical considerations include timing, choice of location and structure of the interview. Sensitivity is needed to decide at what point in the day the parents are most likely to be responsive and co-operative (e.g. avoiding interviews at meal-times, at the end of school days and at children's bedtimes, which can be stressful periods for all families. Similarly sensitivity is required to chose the best place for the interview – would home, office, hospital or police station be the most appropriate? Sufficient time needs to be allocated to complete the initial investigation, and it is often easier to control the interview and there are usually fewer distractions when interviews are conducted out of the home. On the other hand interviews at home enable assessment of the living conditions and home circumstances. Home visits may also be necessary when a family is not able to travel. It is a matter of assessing all the circumstances, and weighing up advantages against disadvantages.

Where the child and/or parents feel unable to co-operate with the investigation, the agency's position has to be stated firmly. One technique to 'unstick' a locked position is to suggest that the parents' explanations for the abuse are examined fully with the other key investigating workers (e.g. police, paediatrician), however incredible the account given may appear. Procedures for managing allegations of child abuse are designed both to exonerate parents as well as to establish that some parents have been mistreating their children. Being incorrectly suspected of abuse is a frightening, demeaning and potentially destructive position for parents to be in. Where suspected abuse is discovered to be unfounded, counselling should be offered to parents to help them to recover from the distress of the investigation and its aftermath.

However, in the event of strong evidence in the face of denial, direct confrontation with the parents should be avoided. Confrontation may precipitate violence, withdrawal or flight. Basic ground rules for the interviews are to avoid official jargon, give clear reasons why the parents are unable to get what *they* feel is right and to avoid unrealistic promises. It should then be possible with all but the most irrational of parents to diffuse potential violence. Sometimes it is advisable for two workers to carry out the investigation, particularly if it is already known that family members have behaved violently in the past.

Most parents respond to a sensitive and empathetic investigative approach. To make this possible requires close supervision and support so that workers can avoid being overwhelmed with the multifarious problems the family present. In affording the parents space to examine the current position, they usually begin to recognize that helping agencies genuinely do wish to diffuse the emotional 'white heat' of the crisis, and are willing to embark on an action plan to recovery. One technique which I have found helpful during the process of investigation is to invite the parents to discuss the normal behaviour of the child or children. If the allegations have any foundation, invariably the worker will be accosted by a catalogue of problems, struggles and issues rather than the child(ren) being seen in any pleasurable sense. Childrearing will be regarded as a constant uphill battle. The worker should constantly process the information offered, and give feedback to the parents objectively. To become just a 'sponge' – recipient to a tidal wave of negative information – is confusing to the parents and disabling of the worker.

With allegations of physical abuse or neglect both parents are usually interviewed together initially. It may be appropriate to involve the child at the same time – depending of course on the child's age, vulnerability and need for protection. Come what may the child should be consulted and kept informed.

Allegations of sexual abuse

In cases of alleged sexual abuse the investigative process may need to be different, particularly where there has been only a vague or incomplete description by the child, there is no unequivocal medical evidence, the alleged abuser denies the abuse and the non-abusing parent refuses to believe the child. The Cleveland Report (DHSS, 1988) stressed that in such cases it is essential to proceed at the child's pace and that it may be necessary to conduct a series of interviews. Investigations should be expected to take place over a longer timescale than those for physical abuse.

The child should be able to have a 'trusted person' or ally present throughout the interviews. This may be the non-abusing parent or a teacher, or the person to whom the child first reported the abuse. Often children simply want the abuse to stop and when they come to realize the far-reaching consequences of their allegations they may withdraw them and retreat into their own secret worlds. 'All I wanted was for my monster daddy to go away and for the nice daddy to be there all the time!'

So it is important to recognize what risks the child has to face, to empathize with conflicts he or she faces and to be honest at all times with 'what the deal is'. This is much more likely to gain the trust of the child and consequently to gain his or her co-operation.

Interviewing children

A number of techniques have been developed for interviewing children about abuse (see, for example, Lawrance, 1988) based on the overriding principle that the child should be taken seriously and believed; respecting the uniqueness and privacy of the child; proceeding at the child's pace. This approach may compete with the other pressing demands (e.g. having to complete an investigation quickly with a view to criminal or civil proceedings), but however slow or painful the process may be, it is in the child's long-term interest to be able to discover what (if anything) has happened and plan how the child will best be protected in the future.

Interviews may be conducted for a number of purposes. These include interviews solely concerned with establishing what happened and planning for the child; and interviews conducted in order to provide evidence for civil (e.g. care) or criminal proceedings (e.g. prosecution of the abuser). From October 1992 in England and Wales it will be possible for a child's main evidence about a violent or sexual assault to be provided to a court by way of a pre-recorded videotape of an interview, so long as the interview is conducted according to a Memorandum of Good Practice (HMSO, 1992). Consequently different approaches will need to be taken to interviews conducted for different purposes. For example, while in planning interviews, the use of specially constructed 'genitaled' dolls may be appropriate, their use in evidential interviews will need to be severely restricted – and generally it will be better not to use them at all.

There needs to be a clear structure to the interview and when the anatomically correct dolls are first introduced this must be done in such a way that their presence seems 'natural'. Only later should they be undressed and then only if necessary (e.g. so that names for body parts can be established). The dolls may be named to clarify any allegations. Possible abuse may be re-enacted and recapped in an atmosphere of reassuring and believing the child.

The use of video interviews and live supervision of the interviewer from behind a one-way mirror is increasingly being seen as helpful to the process. Children should have the technology being employed and the reasons for its use explained to them. If children are reluctant, say, to be videoed, then their wishes must be respected. In practice, most children will settle quickly. Often a one-way screen is also used so that the interviewer has the assistance of colleagues behind the screen who can suggest (via ear microphones) different avenues of approach. Observers outside the interview often pick up aspects of behaviour which the interviewer may not see, and so they can help to direct the interview along avenues that those in closest contact may have missed. Children also like to see parts of the recorded interview, and this can often help to restore their self-esteem. Police investigators have commented that by playing the pre-recorded video of the child disclosing abuse to the alleged perpetrator, there is an increase of likelihood of confession, which reduces the possibility of the child having to give evidence in court.

Children, particularly those who have been abused over a lengthy period and who have had to hide their feelings, usually express considerable relief that the cause for their pain is at last understood and established – 'It's as though I've been carrying a big stone with me all my life, and it's been taken off me.' Validation and reassurance are no substitute for long-term therapy, but ground rules of valuing and believing should be established right from the initial interview. However painful, this should be a positive and therapeutic experience.

The process of developing rapport with the child who has been damaged by abuse needs to proceed slowly and gently. The investigator has to take into account that the child may still be being abused, but because of fear the child may continue to deny that anything is happening. General questions about home, school, likes and dislikes should be used to open up the interview. The routine of life at home can be revealing – details about what happens at getting-up time, bedtime, who prepares meals, runs errands and so on. Only once this everyday information has been established should the interviewer progress to less safe territory – sleeping habits, dreams, fantasies and fears. From here it may be possible to ask direct questions like 'Has anybody done anything rude to you?' or 'Has somebody hurt you?' Open-ended questions avoid later allegations in court that the child was led to answering in a way which would please the interviewer. Skilled interviewers working within this model use hypothetical 'what if' questions to help the child explain what has happened. Some interviewers use puppets and toy telephones to ask questions in a less threatening manner.

Medical examination

Generally speaking all children suspected of being physically or sexually abused or neglected should be medically examined. The permission of parents (or other carers) needs to be obtained (even if the child is subject to a place of safety order) and the child too should have the examination and its purpose thoroughly explained and his or her consent established. A child should never be medically examined against his or her will. Apart from possibly providing corroborative evidence of a forensic nature to confirm the account given by the child, it also has the benefit of giving the child and parents information about whether or not there is permanent or reparable damage. Almost always it is possible to reassure them that any physical harm will heal, and that any infection can be rapidly and effectively treated. Children should be given the choice of either a female or a male doctor if possible. They are entitled to be examined by a doctor who has been properly trained to carry out such examinations; where sexual abuse is alleged this should be a paediatrician and/or police surgeon.

In cases of alleged sexual abuse, gentle examination of genitalia in addition to other parts of the body is undertaken to look for soreness, unexplained lesions, untreated infections and sexually transmitted diseases. Trace evidence such as blood and skin samples and semen may be collected if abuse is recent. At all times the child's modesty and right to privacy should be respected.

As the Cleveland Report (DHSS, 1988) recommended, on no account should children be subjected to repeated medical examinations solely for evidential purposes. Bona fide medical rooms in hospitals, surgeries or Rape Crisis Suites, specifically for such examinations are strongly preferred to police stations which can, despite good intentions, reinforce the child's sense of guilt and badness.

Medical evidence is, of course, just one piece of the jigsaw – the successful investigation of any aspect of abuse relies upon multidisciplinary skills brought together, shared and from which plans for management of all members of the family are made.

FURTHER READING

WATTAM, C., HUGHES, J. and BLAGG, H. (eds.) *Child Sexual Abuse: Listening, Hearing and Validating the Experiences of Children*, Longman Group Ltd, Harlow. (1989) The Violence Against Children Study Group *Taking Child Abuse Seriously*, Unwin Hyman Ltd, London. (1990) This publication includes a useful discussion of the political context of child abuse and issues such as gender and ethnicity. DHSS *Protecting Children: a guide for social workers undertaking a comprehensive assessment*, HMSO, London (1987)

20 SUPPORTING PARENTS SUSPECTED OF ABUSE

Jo Tunnard

Director, Family Rights Group

Introduction

The Family Rights Group (FRG) is a small charity, primarily serving England and Wales. It was established in 1974 and is funded by the DHSS and charitable trusts. Its work is based on the primary assumption that children suspected of being abused are best helped through the establishment of a partnership between their families and the professionals, with parents involved in and enabled to participate during the investigation and subsequent planning for the protection of their children.

As society's concern about child abuse widens, an increasing number of families are becoming enmeshed in the state's system of intervention. Although these families do include some parents who inflict serious harm to their children, they also include an ever-increasing number of parents whose child has been found with a bruise, whose child's behaviour seems unusual, whose child has commented on something that occurred at home, whose child has been injured while in the care of other people. This point is not made to belittle the hardships that many children undergo, nor to belittle the cruel behaviour of some parents. It is made, rather, to serve as a reminder that the public inquiries into tragic, and thankfully relatively few cases where children have been killed have resulted in management procedures that now leave little discretion to individual workers not to invoke child protection procedures where someone somewhere has noted anxiety about a child's situation.

The vast majority of children on whom child protection procedures are invoked (an estimated 80%) do not become the subject of legal proceedings and are not removed from their parents. They remain at home because it is considered that their parents will be able to protect them from injury or neglect. For most of those relatively few children who are removed from home, the plan of the professionals is to reunite them with their parents.

In this chapter we give a brief description of the work of the FRG with families of children involved in child protection procedures or in state care. We then comment on seven key issues that crop up in our work. We have selected them because they raise important questions about the help that is offered by statutory and other agencies to family members, including parents suspected of abuse. The issues are as follows:

- *Improving ways of providing emergency protection*, to minimize the risk of trauma to children and to enhance the possibility of working in partnership with families from the start
- *Involving parents in decision-making*, by giving them information, using written agreements and enabling parents to participate in case conferences and other meetings

- *Encouraging the involvement of parents' representatives*, to help clarify the views of each of the parties and mediate between them
- *Making better use of the extended family*, to use to the full their strengths and their sense of responsibility towards their young relatives
- *Improving what happens after separation*, by offering families choices about where children will live, and making clear arrangements for access
- *Dealing with sexual abuse cases* in a way that precludes a non-abusing parent from taking a defensive position and that encourages professional support for mothers as protectors of their children
- *Supporting the development of local support groups*, to enable family members to give each other moral support in times of stress, and to point the way to improvements in legal and professional practice.

The work of the Family Rights Group

Our work in FRG is concerned with the reasons why and the manner in which children are admitted to public care or become involved in child protection procedures; with the way families are treated once children have been separated from their parents; and with the help that is offered to families whose children remain at home or are returned to them. The Group acts in the interests of children by seeking to avoid the unnecessary separation of children from their families and by seeking to ensure that those children who are not able to live at home maintain good and regular contact with their families in a way that is beneficial to the children. The Group runs an advice service; uses the information gained from the advice work to organize training courses on childcare law and good practice; and responds to central and local government policy documents and initiatives on childcare and family services.

The advice service is for members of the public who write or telephone with queries about their child or young relative in local authority care or involved in child protection procedures. We also advise professional workers, especially social workers, solicitors, health visitors, general practitioners, elected members and members of parliament about legal issues or how best they can advise and help individual families. Our solicitor and social worker advise approximately 700 families each year from about three-quarters of the local authorities in England and Wales.

Common queries in our work are about child protection procedures, access to and from children in care, housing, foster and residential placements, cash payments to and from the local authority, involvement in planning meetings, written agreements, clarification and challenge about decisions made about adoption, preparation and follow-up work when children return home, and the use of the extended family to help and protect children. Our involvement is sometimes limited to a single response to the letter or call but in many cases leads to discussion and correspondence with local authority departments; joint meetings with social workers to try and improve communication, discuss disagreements and agree future work; attendance at review meetings and case conferences; and representation in care and related proceedings.

The people that we advise are but a small fraction of families involved with social services and they are, inevitably, people who are unhappy with some part of the service on offer. However, their worries and their satisfactions are strikingly similar to those of the families of the 2000 children whose circumstances have recently been subject of research studies, and are reported in the DHSS summary *Social Work Decisions in Child Care* (DHSS, 1985). Of the major issues that arise in our work with families and professionals, the following are crucial for those who are striving to provide a high-quality service for children and their relatives.

Better ways of providing emergency protection

There must be scope to consider what steps are necessary for each individual child, but the overriding principle should be to secure the child's protection in a way that causes the child least trauma. In making this decision the local authority will wish to weigh in the balance the damage that might be caused by the precipitate and possibly unjustified separation of the child and the family and the need to prevent further possible harm to the child. In addition, the local authority must consider the extent to which co-operation with the family might be jeopardized by taking the dramatic step of applying for a place of safety order.

On the basis of advising family members and professional workers, we would urge that more alternatives are explored in providing emergency protection for children. The emergency protection order is not the only means of protection and should, in our view, be used only as a last resort. A voluntary agreement should always be explored first, especially when children are already in a safe place. In other cases the sudden removal by strangers to an unknown place and with unknown carers is generally distressing and breaks the continuity that is vitally important for children.

Several options should be considered before an emergency protection order is applied for. Children could be placed with other members of their family or could be provided with accommodation if their parents consent. Parents and children could be admitted to hospital temporarily or could be offered temporary accommodation together. If the suspicion or allegation is of male sexual abuse, the male adults in the household could be encouraged to leave the family home voluntarily on a temporary basis. If this is not agreed to, it may be possible to obtain an injunction excluding them from the household via the wardship jurisdiction.

The need to involve parents in decision-making

Although many local authorities are making determined efforts to improve their practice, many families are still told very little about departmental systems and policies that might have a dramatic effect on their future as a family, and even now some continue to get no information in writing. When families are given nothing in writing they are prevented from understanding the world that they and their children have entered. They are also prevented from mulling over the information in their own home, or with a friend or adviser. Even if the social worker does take time to explain things orally it is unreasonable to expect that families will hear and understand information given when they are feeling distressed, confused and perhaps resentful of the social worker. As a result, families can be left with mistaken ideas about what they can and cannot do once their children are in public care, or involved in child protection procedures.

It is important that parents and older children receive written information about the general service offered by the social services department, about the local authority considering their case, and about the named person to whom they should refer worries or complaints. Under the Children Act this is a duty.

Parents also feel more involved and supported when agencies are prepared to negotiate written agreements with them. Such agreements enable parents, children themselves, foster carers and social workers to be much clearer about the problems that have led to social services involvement, the goals to be achieved, the tasks to be performed by each party, the method of regular review of the agreement, the contingency plans that might be needed, and the system of appeal against decisions that are not agreed with.

Parents should be invited to meet with professional workers in child protection conferences, statutory reviews and other meetings. Until recently the normal practice in child abuse cases has been for parents to be excluded from both initial and review conferences. In some cases parents have been allowed in only right at the end, to be told what has been recommended and/or decided by the conference. But under the Children Act 1989 and associated guidance, it is clear that parents should be enabled to participate in the main proceedings.

First, parents know a great deal about themselves and their children and can often speak better than professionals on their behalf. Second, parents can correct wrong information or give extra information or explanations about events. Third, their participation gives case conference attenders the opportunity, often for the first time, to meet the people about whom they are making recommendations and decisions. Fourth, families can appreciate the professionals' concerns better if they are able to hear them directly. Fifth, decisions will be more informed and able to be reached without the need to adjourn for further discussions with the family. Sixth, the plan has more chance of being successfully implemented. For key workers cannot work *on people*, they can only work *with them* and, as we know from our personal lives, we are all more committed to those decisions that we have been involved in, even where we might disagree with them.

Encouraging the involvement of advocates and parents' representatives
Any client of any service should be able to question or challenge decisions made and to enlist the assistance of someone else to help them to do that. Families, like other people, choose with care whom they wish to involve, be it a close friend, family member, professional worker or specialist agency, and their right to involve the person of their choice should be respected. Professional workers should never take the view that people who disagree with them do not have the interests of the children at heart – there can be more than one view about what is best for a child. There needs to be negotiation about the steps to take and a third party can often play a very important role in clarifying the views of the people directly involved and in mediating between them.

It is part of our current programme at FRG to work to establish family advocacy units to provide families with an advocacy service that is local, and so accessible to them; that is independent of the local authority; and that is committed, in the words of Tony Newton, Health Minister, in 1984, to redressing 'the balance between the power of local authorities and the rights of natural families'.

Making better use of the extended family
Professionals need to appreciate better that children's wider families are usually deeply concerned for their well-being, and may have much to offer both in the short and long term. The resource of the extended family is too valuable to be ignored. Relatives can provide information, maintain relationships with the children, support and encourage the parents, and provide a temporary or long-term home for the child. In some cases professionals will not work with the extended family because they see a danger of collusion. In one recent case social workers refused to meet with the extended family at all unless they accepted without reservation that the child had been abused by her father. This family were desperately keen to do all they could for the child.

We would suggest that such a response is misguided. Relatives are usually prepared – in the child's interests – to suspend their own disbelief and accept directions from social services in order to do what they can to maintain links and provide continuity and support for their young relatives. Enabling them to do that requires professionals being prepared to involve relatives at an early stage, to do so with careful planning, and to approach them as concerned first and foremost about the child's welfare.

Recent research findings (by Jane Rowe *et al.*, see DHSS, 1985) show that children do better when fostered by relatives rather than non-relatives; that continuing contact with grandparents is beneficial for children living with non-relatives and with little or no contact with their parents; and that the positive view of the role of grandparents taken by the researchers was supported by the social workers responsible for the children in the study.

Improving what happens after separation
Where children are placed with strangers, it is important that carers and parents are introduced beforehand, and that carers are selected for their willingness and their ability to include parents in the care of the children. Preparatory meetings provide for a direct exchange of information between families; they enable children to have greater confidence in foster parents because their parents have already had links with them; and they will reveal, exceptionally, any profound differences which might make the placement unworkable, and give social services the opportunity to reconsider it.

Children should meet prospective carers before the placement starts. If they cannot be accompanied on an introductory visit by someone whom they know and with whom they feel secure, then the new carers should visit the children in surroundings that are comfortable and familiar to the children.

Sustaining links between families in the early days is very important in paving the way for a good relationship between children and parents in the future and for co-operation between families and professionals. Time and care should be taken to prepare people for visits. In our experience parents are devastated on contact visits when their children ask them questions such as when will they be going home and why the parents will not stay with them at the end of the visit. Such upset can lead an unprepared parent to respond by promising that the child will be home soon, or the parent will be back the next day.

Where contact needs to be supervised (for example if it is feared that parents may intimidate their child), social workers should consider involving other relatives or foster parents, as their supervision may be less obtrusive.

When deciding on a placement, it is crucial to consider how best to maintain links not only with parents but also with brothers and sisters, grandparents and other relatives. School, neighbourhood and friends may also be of great importance; children should face no more changes than are absolutely necessary for their well-being. The Children Act 1989 stresses the need to find placements for children that will encourage and enhance their religious, cultural or ethnic backgrounds.

Sexual abuse
We are conscious of the particular problems raised by sexual abuse cases: sexual abuse is serious abuse of trust which often presents particularly difficult evidential problems which must be handled with great sensitivity in order to ensure that the process of investigation and the methods of protection of children do not cause more harm than they prevent. The problems are exacerbated by the refusal of our society to acknowledge the extent of sexual abuse. There is also the problem of just how well-kept a secret child sexual abuse can be on the part of the abuser and the abused child. This successful secrecy can prevent the parents, or the mother, from knowing or feeling able to believe what has been happening. Such disbelief is not peculiar to natural families: social services departments sometimes find it very difficult to believe that child sexual abuse might have occurred in a foster family or in a residential establishment.

In most situations it is important for social workers to approach parents with an open mind. If they do not, parents may take a defensive position which will diminish the possibility of future work together and will deprive the social worker of an opportunity to gather full information about the family. At FRG we think it would be fruitful if the social worker's first interview is generally with the child's mother. This will provide an opportunity for the social worker to explain what a medical or other professional or other person has said, to harness the mother's concern for her child, and to offer her time to reflect on the possibility that her child might have been sexually abused.

Current attitudes towards sexual abuse seem to suggest that women are responsible, in part at least, for their partner's sexual abuse. This view has made social workers wary of supporting mothers as protectors of their children. Many women do not know that their children are being abused. Where they do suspect it, many will need help and encouragement to set aside their loyalty to, and dependence on, their partner. In blaming the mother and failing to acknowledge her needs, professional practice has tended to unite the two parents against social services.

We believe that parents and children have much to gain from mothers being provided, from the very beginning, with a social worker of their own who has the skill and is given the time to work closely and supportively with the mother to help her consider a possibility which will be deeply shocking and threatening to her. Without a great deal of genuine sympathetic support in the early stages mothers may feel that they have little choice but to back their male partner.

More work is needed to keep children with their mothers, and also to explore and use strengths within the extended family. We acknowledge the risks involved in children being at home but we all know that there are risks in separating children from their families. A new family may not provide any more security for the child, and children are sometimes sexually abused while in care.

Local support groups
The family members who seek our advice are of different ages, and from different cultures and backgrounds. Their children are involved in child protection procedures or in state care for different reasons. They come from different parts of the United Kingdom. But one thing is strikingly similar – they feel overwhelmed by a sense of guilt, bewilderment, frustration and isolation. Having your child under public scrutiny or in care is not something you talk about on street corners and few parents of children in care are offered the opportunity to meet others.

Local support groups can and do provide a much-needed opportunity to meet others in a similar situation, to find a sympathetic ear, hope in the face of adversity, consolation when a case is lost and children are placed in care or for adoption. At present there are 24 groups operating in England and Northern Ireland.

While the common function of the groups is that members give each other moral support in times of stress, most of the groups do other things besides. They accompany parents to meetings with professional workers, to help parents put across their views and understand what is being said. They are invited to speak at training sessions for foster carers and social workers. Some are consulted by local authorities when they produce draft policy statements about childcare matters, such as complaints procedures, and the payments that parents can be required to make towards the cost of their child being in care.

One group helped a couple take their case to the European Court on the grounds that the British government had violated their right to family life because they were denied access to their child and had no legal remedy against that decision. Their successful case in Europe, and that of four other families heard at the same time, will help improve the law on access in the near future. The same group, Parents' Aid Harlow, have published a booklet of questions and answers for families of children in care (Parents' Aid Harlow, 1991). Its fifth edition has been revised and updated in the light of the Children Act 1989. Some local authorities buy it in bulk and give it out to each family of children in their care. Finally, another group have made a video about their children, who have been adopted against their wishes.

There is also a newly established Grandparents' Federation for grandparents of children in state care. They have a mailing list of 150 grandparents and have organized several meetings and produced their first newsletter. The common link of the grandparents is the desolation they feel when they discover that their offers to care for their young relatives are rejected by the local authority, when they find that they have no effective remedy against such decisions, and when they learn, as happens so often, that they are not allowed to continue meeting their young relatives once a decision has been made to place them in a new family.

These grandparents are determined to influence changes in legislation and in policy so that the strength of the extended family is recognized and used. Their determination is fuelled not only by the recent research findings about the benefits of care by relatives, but by their knowledge from that research that the placement of children in care with their relatives is on the decline in England and Wales.

FRG maintains an up-to-date list of local support groups for families with children in care and will be happy to refer people to their nearest group or to the Grandparents' Federation.

Conclusion

Society's concern about child abuse raises important questions both about the way children are protected from harm and the protection of families from unnecessary and unhelpful state intervention. We know that within the system there are many social workers and other professionals who are committed to enabling families to promote the well-being of their children. We know, too, that parents and other relatives almost always want to do their best for children and that the aim of state intervention should be to work in partnership with those adults. The British research studies referred to earlier in this chapter considered the circumstances of 2000 children in care in England and Wales, including cases of actual or suspected child abuse. The Introduction to the DHSS summary of those studies (DHSS, 1985) highlights the way forward for improved services for children and their families.

> Serious failures in the delivery of services to parents of children in care have been noted by American researchers in recent years and also found in these British studies. Lack of practical resources and the harsh realities of how little social workers can do in the face of financial hardship, bad housing and environmental degradation are, inevitably, recurring themes. But, more usefully, these research studies shed light on areas in which improvements in practice do not depend on practical resources or on other agencies. The need to consult, inform and work *with* parents; the value of enlisting the help of the wider family whenever possible; the importance of recognising and understanding parents' response to separation; all these are suggestions which have immediate potential for improving practice.

Useful addresses

Family Rights Group, The Print House, 18 Ashwin Street, London E8 3DL. Tel: 071–923–2628; Helpline 071–249–0008

21 INTERAGENCY WORK IN CHILD PROTECTION

Christine Hallett

Reader in Social Policy, University of Stirling

Avril Osborne

Social Work Services Inspectorate, Scottish Office

It is now widely accepted in policy and in practice that an effective response to child abuse requires a co-ordinated multidisciplinary approach. Yet a series of highly publicized child abuse inquiries in the 70s and 80s has revealed the repeated failures of professionals to co-operate with each other, to pass on information, to plan jointly and to work effectively together. The latest most comprehensive version of *Working Together* guidance (Department of Health, 1991) requires the establishment of machinery for interagency co-operation including Area Child Protection Committees and a child protection register in each locality, together with arrangements for multidisciplinary child protection conferences. Each area is also required to produce a procedural handbook outlining its arrangements and the roles of the key agencies.

The legal framework
The lead agencies in child protection are the social services departments in England and Wales, social work departments as they are known in Scotland, and the social services departments within the health and social services boards in Northern Ireland. All have a statutory duty to protect children and to provide services to help keep children within their own families. The Children Act 1989 (England & Wales) emphasises the need for social services departments to work in partnership with parents and to avoid court-based intervention wherever possible. In some cases of family difficulty, parents may request that their child be provided with accommodation by the local authority (usually in a foster or residential home). Only when there is evidence that a child has suffered or is likely to suffer significant harm, can the local authority contemplate legal intervention to take the child into care (see Chapter 13 for an explanation of threshold criteria for care and supervision orders). However, being 'in care' does not mean that the parents lose parental responsibility, nor that the child will necessarily be removed from the family, nor that the child may not be returned. In 1989, for example, only 24 per cent of the 41,000 children whose names were on the child protection registers in England were in care, and of these a considerable number were living at home. In emergencies, other legal powers can be used (emergency protection order) to remove the child from immediate danger and place him or her in a safe environment, usually a foster home, but sometimes a hospital when treatment is necessary, or a children's centre. Consideration is then given to ensuring the child's continued safety and welfare.

Scottish legislation differs from that in England, Wales and Northern Ireland, but the preventive approach is similar, and is backed by statutory powers. Where compulsory measures of care are needed, a children's hearing, comprised of trained, but lay members of the public, sits to hear the case, with a Reporter to ensure that the proper procedures are observed. Social work departments may apply for authority to remove a child to a place of safety. The Reporter must then investigate the circumstances and may return the child, or alternatively bring the child and parents before a hearing of the panel within seven days. Proceedings are non-judicial, and where parents contest the grounds of referral of the Reporter, the matter is referred to the Sheriff's Court for judicial proof to be established or otherwise. In Scotland, the children's hearing has power, if the grounds of referral are accepted at the hearing or proved in the Sherriff's Court, to make a supervision requirement. This lasts for up to one year, and the panel can make an order such that the child resides with the parents, or in the care of the local authority. This situation is then reviewed at least annually by the panel who can extend supervision requirements as necessary. Parental rights remain with the parents.

Within both forms of childcare legislation, social services departments must hold periodic reviews of their plans for the children in care, their well-being and progress, and must take the views and wishes of children into account. The law in Northern Ireland is more closely patterned on English law, with similar powers on the part of the police and health and social services (in Ireland a joint body) to investigate and remove children to a place of safety. In Northern Ireland a juvenile court system operates, and children may be made subject to legal controls until their 18th birthday.

The roles of different agencies in child protection

The roles of the various agencies involved (summarized in Table 1) vary according to their professional responsibilities and to the stage of the case. Some, notably the police, are more heavily involved at the investigation stage, others in assessment of the child and the family situation and yet others in intervention after abuse has been identified to help the child, family and sometimes the abuser.

The role of social workers in child protection

Social services/social work departments are the lead agency in child protection and they should be notified of all suspected cases of child abuse. The key steps that any social worker in the United Kingdom will take on receiving a referral that a child is at risk of abuse, or has been abused, are:

* investigation of the situation, particularly the physical and emotional state of the child, seeking the co-operation of the parents, and with the primary aim of protecting the child;
* liaison with senior members of the department;
* consultation with police and health colleagues;
* liaison with other key agencies – such as the NSPCC or RSSPCC, the probation service, the child's school – in order to gain as much information as possible on which to base a decision;
* assessment of the position of all other children in the family or household.

An increasingly common feature of child abuse investigations (particularly for sexual abuse) is a joint investigation by social workers and the police in order to spare families, children in particular, a succession of different interviews and examinations for different purposes. Whilst throughout the investigations the social worker will, ideally, involve the family and children as much as possible, it can be difficult to maintain a supportive ethos in such tense and difficult situations, particularly when a decision has to be taken to obtain an emergency protection order to remove the child from home.

An investigation thus moves through a series of stages from the point of referral onwards and includes the receipt and recording of a referral, immediate allocation for investigation, consultation with other professionals and decision-making as to the child's need for immediate protection involving the court or children's hearing system as necessary. Within a short period, usually a matter of days, the social services department will also call a full interdisciplinary child protection case conference to discuss the case. (This is explained later.)

The role of the police in child protection

The police have a general responsibility for the protection of life, and the prevention and investigation of crime. There is a need here to draw the distinction between their roles and responsibilities for criminal investigation and, separately under civil law, for child care proceedings. In both cases the police have a duty to protect children, but their roles will differ within the two systems. Within their *child protection* role, they will investigate and assess the need to protect a child at risk, normally in consultation with health and social services. In order to do this, they have full emergency powers, not available to other agencies, to remove and detain a child in police protection, without prior application to a court. Currently, a named police officer can be granted a warrant to enter households. They are then usually involved as part of the multidisciplinary team in making decisions (e.g. within child protection conferences) about the child's future welfare.

Secondly, police officers undertake their usual role in the *investigation and prosecution of a crime*. This involves gathering evidence about crimes committed against the child or children and, if these are discovered, the police may refer the case to the Crown Prosecution service for prosecution or, in Scotland, report the crime to the Procurator Fiscal, who then decides on prosecution.

It is important to remember, however, that increasingly the police will not see prosecution as their primary function and may, in consultation with other professionals, consider that it is not in the child's interests. Thus, even when a member of the public or of another agency contacts the police directly about suspected child abuse, interagency procedures ensure the involvement of the local social services department, either before or immediately after a preliminary investigation. A police officer, usually specially trained in child abuse investigation, establishes the nature of the allegation, often working jointly with social workers in deciding whether or not the child needs immediate protection. Only exceptionally will the police take independent action. The police, in seeking evidence for criminal prosecution, will take statements from the child (often working jointly with social workers), the parents or others suspected of abuse and any witnesses.

The role of health professionals in child protection

The role of health professionals in child protection varies considerably. One key role is in early identification. Some health professionals, such as general practitioners, health visitors, midwives and school nurses are well placed to identify children who may be being abused, as they come into contact with almost all children in the course of health surveillance or other activities. Their primary responsibility is to arrange any necessary immediate treatment and to refer such concerns to the social services department, often after consultation with colleagues or managers. Other health professionals such as accident and emergency staff, child psychiatrists, community child health doctors and paediatricians are in contact with a smaller proportion of the child population but also need to be alert to the possibility of child abuse and the need to refer their concerns for investigation.

Another vital role is the part played by paediatricians, and sometimes police surgeons and general practitioners, in examining children who may have been abused. The request for such examinations may come from social services departments and/or the police or general practitioners. A clear indication of clinical

Table 1 *Child abuse – investigation and protection*

	Role	Investigation responsibility	Protection responsibility
Local authority social worker	General promotion of welfare of children Has a *statutory* duty to investigate all reports or allegations of child abuse	Investigates all reports of a child believed to be at risk May apply for an emergency protection order or a child assessment order (England and Wales) or a place of safety order (Scotland and N.Ireland)	Participates in case conferences and reviews Usually key worker with child and family. Supervizes child in community or residential/ foster care
NSPCC staff	Identification and prevention of cruelty to children	May investigate when child believed to be at risk May apply for an emergency protection order or a child assessment order (England and Wales only)	Participates at case conferences May monitor post-registration situations and carry out longer-term assessments
Health visitor	Promotion of health, and support of parents	Monitors child's development Reports suspected abuse to social worker or police for investigation	Supports, advises and monitors post-registration situations

General practitioner	Maintenance of child health in community	Should refer any suspicion of child abuse to social services or police	Monitors post-registration situations
Paediatrician	Medical examination to identify clinical signs of child abuse and to provide treatment, if required, on referral from social services, the police, GP or accident and emergency department	Should refer any suspicion of child abuse to social services or police, and play a full part in the investigation	Monitors post-registration situations
Police	Protection of life and limb	Investigate possible child abuse	Do not usually routinely monitor post-registration, but attend case reviews, and will investigate again as necessary
	Prevention and investigation of crime	Emergency power to take child into police protection	
	Submission of cases for criminal proceedings	Investigate crime; charging and gathering evidence for prosecution	
School teacher, education welfare officer, psychologist	Monitoring of child's well-being within the educational setting	Should notify suspected cases of child abuse to social services	Monitor pre- and post-registration

signs of physical, sexual or emotional abuse is of great importance in the protection of children and in the prosecution of abusers. However, clinical findings always need to be considered in the context of the investigations of other agencies, notably social workers and the police.

At later stages of the child protection process child psychiatrists and psychologists and paediatricians may be involved in assessment of the child and the family or in providing ongoing treatment or therapy. Health visitors, school nurses and general practitioners may also provide support to children and families and play a part in monitoring the child's well-being, post investigation.

The role of the NSPCC in child protection
Uniquely, among voluntary bodies, the NSPCC (in Scotland the RSSPCC) employs social workers whose central concern is to prevent cruelty to children. Increasingly the Societies are creating, in co-operation with local authorities, child protection teams to provide specialist preventative, assessment and treatment services. NSPCC (*but not RSSPCC*) staff also have powers to investigate and bring care proceedings. More information about NSPCC child protection teams can be found in chapter 22.

The machinery of interagency co-operation

Area Child Protection Committees (formerly Area Review Committees)
Area Child Protection Committees provide a forum for initiating, monitoring and reviewing local child abuse policies. They have developed in a number of ways to reflect local situations but generally there is one associated with each local authority, serving all the health authorities (or parts of them) that are within its boundaries.

They are accountable to the agencies that make up their membership, which usually include senior officers representing:

- the social services, social work departments;
- the NSPCC or RSSPCC where appropriate;
- health authorities, including health service management, medical and psychiatric services, and nursing;
- family practitioner services, including general practitioners;
- education services including the education authority and teachers;
- police;
- probation service (England, Wales and N. Ireland);
- armed forces (where appropriate).

The aim is to have people with sufficient authority to speak and make decisions on their agency's behalf. The chair is usually drawn from the social services/social work department.

Specifically, the tasks of the ACPCs are to establish, maintain and review local interagency guidelines on procedures to be followed in individual cases; to review significant issues that arise from handling cases and from reports of inquiries; to review progress in prevention, treatment/intervention and interagency training and make recommendations to the responsible agencies and to conduct case reviews.

The local procedural handbooks developed by ACPCs in accordance with government guidelines provide the framework within which interagency work takes place and should be familiar to all staff likely to come across cases of child abuse.

The Child Protection Register
Registers of children who have been or are believed to have been abused have existed for more than 20 years and have been called NAI (non-accidental injury) registers, child abuse registers, and most recently, child protection registers. They

are maintained in each area on behalf of the Area Child Protection Committee and are usually administered by the social services/social work department. The child protection register is a register of children for whom there are currently unresolved child protection issues and for whom there is an interagency protection plan. Criteria of registration (normally following a child protection conference) have varied over time and from area to area. The categories recommended in the most recent government guidance are physical injury, sexual abuse, emotional abuse and neglect. The register is kept under strict guidelines of confidentiality and only named professionals in the agencies have a right of access to the information. Information is thus readily accessible at a central point and can be checked whenever a new referral is received. The objectives are speedy registration if required following investigation, but equally speedy de-registration if the professionals involved consider that the child concerned is no longer at risk of abuse and that formal interagency working is no longer necessary to protect the child. The child protection register also provides a source of information about the numbers and categories of cases of abuse meeting the registration criteria and a mechanism whereby the position of all children on the register can be reviewed at six-monthly intervals.

Child Protection Conferences

An important arena for interagency work is the child protection conference which is normally called quickly following initial investigation and any emergency action necessary to protect the child.

The child protection conference is usually convened and chaired by the social services department. The main investigative agencies, social services, the police and health are involved as well as schools, nursery staff, probation officers, the NSPCC/RSSPCC, local authority legal advisers and others depending on the circumstances of the case. In Scotland, the Reporter or Procurator Fiscal may be included. Increasingly and in accordance with government guidelines, parents and children (depending on their age) are also invited to take part.

The initial child protection conference provides the prime forum for the professionals and the family to share information and concerns, to assess the level of risk to the children and to make recommendations for action. Conference members pool and discuss a range of information about the child and family under investigation, often starting with the precipitating factors that led to the investigation. The outcomes of any medical examinations and other investigation are shared. The child's well-being and family situation described, and initial assessment of family functioning and the degree of risk to the children is made as far as possible.

The only decision to be made at the case conference is whether or not the child's name should be placed on the child protection register and, if so, to allocate a key worker, usually from the social services department to co-ordinate the case. The case conference also formulates advice to the agencies involved, for example, about assessment of the child and family and outlines a multidisciplinary plan for the protection of the child. Issues such as the necessity for legal action to protect the child may be discussed. While the child protection conference is not empowered to take decisions on such issues, which remain the prerogative of the separate agencies, it is rare for the recommendations of the conference to be overturned.

Increasingly, a core group of professionals most closely involved with the case will be designated by the conference to work together and meet on a regular basis. At periodic intervals, (usually every six months) the full conference is reconvened and the situation of the child and family is reviewed, a decision reached as to the continued need for registration of the child and future plans for interagency work agreed by the professionals and the family.

The position of parents
There is an inescapable link in child protection work between children, their parents, and the machinery of state. For the vast majority of the public, there is no conflict or tension between the rights of children and the rights of parents. In some child abuse cases, however, parental duties to care adequately for their children may well have been breached. (Although this need not be the case if the abuse is extra-familial.) When there has been a breach of parental duty, resulting in significant harm to a child, the state will, by law, consider the child's rights and interests as paramount, and will intervene as necessary to protect children (although see chapter 14 in which it is recognized that this concept is by no means straightforward). How, in these circumstances, should professionals engaged in child protection act towards parents during the investigation of possible child abuse, and in any subsequent care and criminal proceedings?

Central to current thinking is the notion of involvement of parents in decision-making – by informing them at every step of an investigation, telling them of suspicions or concerns, clarifying the outcomes of investigations and their rights to appeal against any decisions made. Not only should parents be informed about the progress of an investigation, but their opinions should be sought and information they wish to be conveyed should be passed on to the investigating team. Whilst the practice in this respect varies, current guidelines to professional agencies are that parents should attend part or all of any child protection conference or review held about their child, unless, in the view of the conference chair, their presence would preclude a full consideration of the child's interests. As case conferences have no judicial basis, parents have no legal right of appeal against a decision to place their child's name on the child protection register, but they should be informed of such decisions, and of the decisions of subsequent reviews. Since the majority of the children on child protection registers live at home the full involvement of their parents in promoting the child's well-being is essential. Parents need to understand the nature of the concerns about their children and to participate fully in making plans for their future protection.

Current issues in interagency work
Reference has already been made to the increasing importance attached to joint interviewing by police officers and social workers in order to reduce the number of times a child may need to tell their story. In suitable cases, a videotape of the interview may be recorded, which, under England and Wales legislation, may replace the child's main evidence in any criminal prosecution, so long as the interview is conducted according to the 'Memorandum of Good Practice for video recorded interviews with child witnesses in criminal proceedings' (Home Office, 1992). However, the child still has to be capable of being cross-examined in court, so that in many cases it would still not be possible to prosecute an alleged abuser based on the evidence of a young child. In all areas of the UK joint interviewing and video recording may now be used to contribute evidence for civil proceedings to protect the child and in such cases cross examination is not a requirement.

Compliance with child protection procedures
Although there is widespread agreement about the need for a multidisciplinary approach in child protection, the extent to which various professionals wish or can be compelled to comply with the local procedural guidelines can vary. Some, such as social workers, health visitors and the police, work within hierarchical structures where superior officers can act to promote compliance. Others, such as general practitioners, consultant paediatricians or head teachers, may work more independently with less opportunity for the exercise of bureaucratic control. For various

reasons, different professionals may be reluctant to invoke the procedures, for example through fear that the control of events may pass to others such as the police or social workers, through a reluctance to be seen as betraying the family or through concerns about confidentiality. Guidance to medical and nursing staff has emphasized that the interests of the child are paramount and that the ethics of professional confidence should not prevent the proper disclosure of information to other professionals.

Children's wishes

Respecting the wishes of children in interagency work in child protection has increased in importance in recent years. The Cleveland Inquiry Report (DHSS, 1988) stressed that the child is a person and not an object of concern and children's involvement in decisions about their future is an important principle underpinning the Children Act 1989. Professionals from all agencies involved in child protection need to listen carefully to children and explore their wishes concerning their future lives. An issue causing some concern is the large number of children now using national telephone helplines, who are disclosing a whole range of abuses, but who are unwilling to identify themselves. The implications for child protection services in terms of the numbers of abused children now believed to be in the population, and their reluctance to be exposed to investigation and possible removal from home, are wide. The difficult challenge in interagency work is to develop services which can respond to the needs and wishes of children and young people who may be being abused.

Interagency work

Interagency work in child protection presents something of a paradox. It is accepted as necessary and desirable; it is widely practised yet it is also characterized as difficult and problematic. Detailed procedural guidance has been produced at central and local levels which require and promote it. Nonetheless, even after 20 years of this area of work, difficulties such as poor communication, lack of role clarity and discrepant expectations can still prevail. Power struggles, status issues and conflicting responsibilties can interfere with the primary task of protecting children. No matter how well-prescribed procedures are and how sophisticated in allowing professionals the exercise of discretion in complex situations, ultimately the basis for working together is respect for other professionals, accurate knowledge about their roles and skills and a will to collaborate in the interests of children. These attributes vary widely from individual to individual and between professions. To foster them effectively partly rests outside the child protection system, in the qualifying and post-qualifying training for the respective professionals.

In working together there are formidable practical and logistical difficulties involved in co-ordinating disparate networks of individuals and in resourcing interagency work. These include severe pressures on professional time, shortages of skilled and experienced staff, competing work priorities, insufficient administrative support and outdated communication systems. (For a fuller discussion, see Hallett & Birchall, 1992.) Policy developments, such as the creation of internal markets in health care and local management in schools, may lead to less administrative uniformity and to a situation where prices are charged in circumstances in which co-operation has hitherto been uncosted at field level and exchanged freely.

Conclusions

The last 30 years have seen the issue of the abuse of children coming into professional and public focus in an unprecedented manner. As this chapter has demonstrated, a key response in public policy and professional practice has been to emphasize the need for interagency work and to set up procedures to facilitate it, in the identification, assessment and provision of help for abused children and their families. A similar effort also needs to be placed upon preventive strategies which can lead to changing the patterns of socialization and behaviour which lead adults and, in the field of child sexual abuse, principally men and youths, to abuse children. Meanwhile interagency work will continue to play a vital role in child protection.

FURTHER READING

DEPARTMENT OF HEALTH *Working Together on Interagency Co-operation for the Protection of Children from Abuse,* New edition, HMSO, London (1991)

HALLETT, C. & BIRCHALL, E. *Co-ordination and Child Protection: a review of the literature,* HMSO, London (1992)

HOME OFFICE in conjunction with DEPARTMENT OF HEALTH *A Memorandum of Good Practice: Video Recorded Interviews with Child Witnesses for Criminal Proceedings* (1992).

22 WHAT HAPPENS NEXT?

Peter Dale

Team Leader, NSPCC Child Protection Team

Outcomes of child protection conferences

Once an investigation into a case of suspected child abuse has begun, at an early stage a child protection conference will be convened. There are several possible conclusions to a child protection conference. First, the conference may conclude that abuse did *not* occur – that the injuries were accidental, and that no further action should be taken.

The second possible outcome is that the abuse may be definitely established, either because there is incontrovertible evidence, or by the parents confirming that abuse did happen. In such situations, at a minimum the child's name (and possibly those of brothers and sisters) will be placed on the Child Protection Register (see chapter 21) and a 'key worker' appointed. In addition, a decision will be taken by the social services as to whether the child (and siblings) needs immediate protection (e.g. by removing the child from the home), if this has not already been done. In the large majority of cases where minor injuries have occurred for the first time, it is likely that the outcome of the case conference will be to put the child's name on the Child Protection Register, but without any legal proceedings and with the child remaining at home within the family. This course of action is all the more probable when the parents show a generally positive relationship to their children and each other, and are reasonably co-operative with the professionals.

With clear-cut cases of more serious abuse, decisions will be made as to whether the children can remain at home, and the family be offered help, or whether the injury or the risk is so great that legal action must be taken to ensure protection of the children and to enable a full assessment to take place. At such times the police will also listen to opinions regarding the appropriateness of prosecution.

Many families in circumstances where there has been a single incident of abuse, often connected with unusual stress, respond extremely well to the help offered by the social services and other sources. This might include providing individual, family or group counselling to try to resolve the emotional problems of the parents (often remaining from their own unsatisfactory childhoods) which have begun to be taken out in frustration on their children. Equally important may be the provision of direct practical help – perhaps assistance in reducing financial or housing pressures, or the provision of a childminder to offer a needed break for the parents and additional stimulation for the child.

In cases where problems are more severe, the help provided by a Family Centre (see the extract from Holman (1988) in chapter 29) can often prove to be the key factor in enabling the family to resume or develop an acceptable level of functioning without the children having to go into care. With a successful response to such help, the crisis usually passes, parents feel confidence in professional services, and often can be encouraged to develop further sources of support through community self-help groups (such as OPUS, see chapter 34). So long as further abuse does not occur, after an appropriate time the child's name can be taken off the Child Protection Register as a mark of the family's progress. It is worth reminding ourselves that cases like these never reach the front pages of newspapers, but are in fact far more common than the mistakes that do make headlines.

In other cases, work done with the family in this way is not so successful. There are further incidents of abuse, and ultimately another case conference will be held and care proceedings may be commenced. It is very important in the course of such work that social workers do not become blinded by what Robert Dingwall (see chapter 17) has called the 'rule of optimism'. If abuse of children continues to occur despite a great deal of help being offered it is vital to reassess the question of the child's safety. Regular and effective supervision of social workers is crucial, as the perspectives of even experienced practitioners can become insidiously distorted by the emotional pressures which result from working with families where the safety of children is the main concern.

The majority of case conferences deal with relatively minor incidents of child abuse, or are convened as follow-up conferences to monitor progress, or to consider some new development in older cases. A small proportion deal with fresh cases of serious abuse, and it is in such cases, and cases of repeated abuse, that legal action is likely to be taken to protect the child and any other children in the family. In these situations the children will be removed from their parent(s) and placed in foster or residential care.

The third possible general outcome of a case conference, and in many ways the most unsatisfactory one for the family, child and professionals alike, is when the severity of an incident and levels of concern remain unresolved. This may include situations where explanations for an injury are unclear or discrepant, or where a case conference is attempting to assess risk to other children in the family following abuse (or suspected abuse).

One of the most difficult consequences of situations where concerns about child abuse have remained unresolved has been the tendency for the families to be left in angry, bitter and contentious relationships with the agencies concerned – the social workers, health visitors and doctors. Court cases may occur where professionals find themselves having to give evidence about their observations of parenting failures over a long period of time, where no *single* incident was sufficient for legal action to be taken. Parents often experience this as 'betrayal' by the professionals they thought had been on 'their side'. They may actively cut themselves off from further contact with agencies, sometimes to the detriment of their ability to care for their remaining children.

Bitter and antagonistic relationships between parents and professionals were one of the major characteristics of the events in Cleveland, described in the Butler-Sloss Report (DHSS, 1988). The Report illustrates how one social services department was faced by an enormous and sudden increase in the numbers of medically diagnosed cases of sexual abuse. At that time in Cleveland there was no co-ordination of services between agencies for investigating cases of suspected sexual abuse, and investigation came to involve a virtually automatic removal of the children from their families by the social services department with no constructive help, evaluation or support being offered.

The events in Cleveland occurred in the context of a significant and continuing increase in cases of suspected child abuse, and a level of public awareness which has been referred to as a 'moral panic'. The media assumed a high profile on abuse following a stream of public inquiries into child abuse deaths prior to the Cleveland Inquiry. Social workers in particular increasingly came to feel that they were being made scapegoats when children were simultaneously presented as being at risk from evil parents (and from the social workers who did not protect them), and at risk from interfering social workers removing them without cause from loving and blameless parents. However, while the Cleveland Inquiry confirmed the reality of child sexual abuse, it also highlighted the phenomenon of system abuse. System abuse involves a damaging experience to a child as a direct consequence of inadequate or inappropriate investigation procedures and practices. It may arise from the investigation itself, or from the subsequent means of 'protection'.

Care of children in care

Taking any child into care, particularly on an emergency basis and against the parents' wishes, is an unpleasant, unhappy and often harrowing experience. Social workers may have little choice between available foster homes, and occasionally may be unable to find *any* foster home with vacancies. Hospitals and children's homes sometimes have to be used inappropriately in emergencies, or the child moved quickly from an initial foster home when a more suitable place is found. In many areas the notion of the *choice* of an *appropriate* foster home for the particular needs of a child is a rare luxury. This contributes to a feeling of professional dissatisfaction that the child's emotional needs are not being met in care despite the physical protection provided; a feeling approaching bewilderment and abandonment for the child placed in surroundings that are not ideal (which perhaps involves a move to an unknown area some distance away from the family home, change of school, fitting in with a very different family or social culture etc.); and feelings of resentment on the part of the parents at their powerlessness to have any influence on the decisions being taken in respect of their child.

Foster parents provide a service to social services departments in general, and individual children in particular, which is invaluable and largely unrecognized and unrewarded. Fostering abused children, both on an emergency basis in the short term, and on a long-term substitute family basis for children who cannot return home, is a task which requires enormous depths of understanding, commitment and caring – and professional support. Many foster parents report that the element of consistent professional support from social workers is sadly, and often tragically, lacking. For hard-pressed social workers the aim of *protection* itself has too often tended to become the single goal. This has meant that after the initial burst of activity to protect the child following abuse and to obtain parental rights through a court, it is too frequently the case that little else is done in a structured way to plan for the child's future, or to support its new caregivers.

In the course of preparing a court report I learnt about two physically abused children who had been placed late at night with brand-new foster parents, approved for short-term fostering. The foster parents had been told that the boys would be there for 'three or four days'. Three *years* later both boys were still with the same foster parents who were totally bewildered by their inability to obtain from the social services department any consistent statement about their plans for the future of the children. At least this placement had not broken down, and despite the total lack of planning on the part of the social services department, the boys had not been subjected to the experience of multiple placements. Other children are not so lucky, and during their care 'careers' may experience a huge and disorientating number of placements. That this can occur despite the good intentions of protection is irony indeed for children who have been taken into care following abuse.

Berridge and Cleaver (1987) have researched the area of foster home breakdown, and their book tells a very depressing tale of disturbed children, inappropriately placed with inadequately prepared foster parents who receive little ongoing support. They found a rate of foster home breakdown as high as 40%.

Some children had upwards of 10 or 12 *different* placements during their time in care.

Assessment and decision-making

Unfortunately, despite a good deal of research, there is no 'checklist' which can reliably predict which parents will injure or re-injure their child. Each case of serious child abuse requires careful assessment, and what is needed is the wider development of services which can devote the time and specialist skills required to do this work in a careful way within a context which enables most parents to work co-operatively at this task.

Several National Society for the Prevention of Cruelty to Children (NSPCC) child protection teams have demonstrated in recent years the value and potential of developing a structured programme for assessment of families where serious child abuse has taken place. The core of such assessments lies in a *team* of workers acting together in a structured way with all family members (together and separately), over a period of several months. The task is explicitly stated as being to work towards a recommendation for the long-term future of the child. The assessment focuses on the personal histories of the family members and their relationships with each other, and includes direct individual therapeutic work with the abused child. A written agreement is used to clarify how the assessment will proceed.

Written agreements typically include points such as the following.

- The assessment will usually take between four and nine months to complete, and sessions will take place on a regular basis at the child protection team's premises. Parents, and other family members when requested, agree to attend all sessions on time.
- Parents and other appropriate family members (often grandparents) agree to co-operate in work which focuses on their current and past difficulties and relationships.
- Parents agree to working on tasks between sessions (this often involves written work, or keeping appointments with other professionals, e.g. attending a drug dependency clinic), and will co-operate with all other professionals involved.

Such a *structure* for assessments provides an opportunity for therapeutic change and *maturation* which many of the families have not previously experienced, sometimes despite long histories of involvement with a diverse variety of different agencies. Although in the initial stages parents often feel extremely angry or demoralized because of the removal of their children and the atmosphere of the court proceedings, the offer and availability of a structured and extensive assessment usually begins to be seen as providing a *context of hope* that some way can be found to tackle their difficulties. Often the independence of the NSPCC child protection teams is very valuable, particularly when antagonistic feelings have developed between the parents and the social services.

In the experience of child protection teams, where the parents are able to accept and work with the assessment, it is often possible for children to be returned to their families. The parents are helped gradually to withdraw from their previous defensive focus of 'fighting' outside agencies, and to use this energy instead for tackling their own personal and relationship difficulties. This positive change in attitude is a very significant feature of many assessments.

One consequence is often the development of a remarkable determination to work towards positive change. This involves an honest and painful evaluation of the incidents of the abuse, the impulses of the abuser and why a non-abusing parent, despite being aware of the risk, may have failed to *protect* the child. With such key issues being openly explored and understood, the focus can move to an examination of the particular emotional, marital and parenting problems which were troubling the parents before the abuse occurred. Progress in these areas, along with positive changes in the relationship between the parent(s) and child provide indications that return of the child to the parents may be a serious possibility. Rehabilitation in such cases is always on the basis of a further written agreement with the team, and therapy and supervision continue with the child and family, often for a period of up to two years.

Sometimes during the assessment work the parents will recognize that it would not be safe or appropriate for their child to return to their care, and *agree* that a permanent alternative family would be the best outcome for the child. During the work of a child protection team only a small proportion of children are normally placed for permanent separation *against* the wishes of their parents. It is important in child abuse work that 'success' is not measured only by the cases of abused children who can be safely reunited with their natural parents. 'Success' also involves cases where parents come to recognize that this would not be right (perhaps through acknowledging a previously concealed underlying emotional rejection of the child), and can then take an active part in planning for an adoption to which their consent will be given. This not only avoids a damaging period of legal uncertainty, but also enables the parents to experience a more therapeutic separation from their child, and in many cases to continue working on their difficulties with a view to being able to care appropriately for future children.

The main features of families where it is not possible for children to return home are the following. For full details see Dale *et al*. (1986);

- Young, immature parents still preoccupied with their own adolescent or early adult needs who have severely emotionally deprived personalities with established patterns of explosive anger.
- Unplanned pregnancies leading to unwanted babies, with *severe* parental relationship problems including violence.
- Serious injuries to a baby or young child which the parents are reluctant to be open about or to take responsibility for. The parents may continue to blame the baby or child for provoking the abuse.
- Parental attachment and commitment to the child remaining doubtful – demonstrated through inconsistent attendance at access sessions with the child, or disinterest and lack of awareness of the child during such sessions.
- Lack of progress in seeking or responding to help with long-standing personal or family difficulties – such as alcoholism, drug dependence or psychiatric conditions. This may contribute to a continuing negative pattern of impulsive, destructive or criminal behaviour.
- Parents not able to adjust seriously unrealistic expectations of their child's behavioural development, and continuing to get angry at what they perceive as the child's disobedience, lack of co-operation and often lack of love for them. This may also involve serious problems in attending consistently and appropriately to basic childcare.
- Persistent failure by the parents to co-operate with the assessment, e.g. in attending sessions, discussing relevant issues, carrying out tasks etc., despite being clearly aware of the consequences of this behaviour.

Permanency planning
Many social work teams suffer from inadequate resources and diminished professional confidence. In such situations the 'professional' response may be to focus on *protection* itself as the only achievable goal. Under these circumstances, once in care, children may not be the focus of clear action or planning to

determine their futures. Recognition of the damage created by such experiences has fuelled the movement in childcare over the last decade towards 'permanency planning'. Permanency planning holds that any child in care should be placed with a permanent substitute family if there is little prospect of a successful return to the natural parents within a short time of going into care.

Following Rowe's research (Rowe and Lambert, 1973), which noted the low percentage of children who return to their natural homes after being in care for six months, the figure of six months is often quoted as the 'cut-off ' point for decision-making about the child's future. In recent years many social services departments have vigorously pursued policies based on this information in respect of abused children, arguing that this is the only way to provide such children with stable and appropriate upbringings, and to avoid the damaging experiences of 'drift' in care, or repeated admissions to care possibly following further abuse.

Permanency planning has clearly been a vital move in the lives of many abused children where it was inconceivable that they could return to their own homes in safety, although there is a good deal of debate as to whether continuing contact with natural family members should be a more widespread practice in such situations (see chapter 20). Permanency planning policies have been criticized for failing to provide natural parents with sufficient and appropriate help and ongoing support to care successfully for their children themselves; and the accusation has been that the policy has been pursued too readily in less severe cases by social services departments which have lost the professional confidence to take the calculated risks which successful rehabilitation following child abuse requires.

The way forward
In the wake of a long sequence of fatal child abuse inquiry reports and the Cleveland Inquiry, multidisciplinary projects aiming for a more co-ordinated approach to investigations of suspected child abuse are being developed in many local authority areas. The experience of some early projects, for example one in Hastings in East Sussex, has highlighted the need for equal attention to be paid to the development and co-ordination of assessment and treatment services (Dale, 1988).

Work with child abuse of all forms in areas where effective co-ordinated *investigation* services are linked to comprehensive *assessment* and *treatment* programmes demonstrates that proper protection for children, together with effective help for families, can be achieved by adequately resourced social work teams working in close liaison and co-operation with other relevant professions.

SECTION FIVE

THE EFFECTS OF ABUSE

23 THE EFFECTS OF PHYSICAL ABUSE AND NEGLECT

Helen Kenward

Principal Social Worker monitoring child abuse, Northamptonshire County Council

Denise Hevey

Lecturer in Health and Social Welfare, The Open University

The physical abuse of children covers a wide range of actions from what some might term 'justifiable chastisement' such as slapping, spanking or caning to the sort of actions which most would agree constitute deliberate, sadistic cruelty against children. These include inflicting burns with cigarettes or by holding the child against the bars of an electric fire; dipping the feet or buttocks into scalding water; punching, kicking and biting; twisting limbs until bones break; or beating a child until he or she is rendered unconscious. In the middle of the spectrum are cases in which normal punishment has 'gone over the top' and left marks, or when parents have lashed out in anger and frustration which may have equally severe, albeit unintended, consequences such as when brain damage is caused by shaking a baby.

Neglect, on the other hand, is usually defined in terms of an absence of actions – a failure to provide or respond to the changing needs of a growing child. This could range from the inadequate but well-intentioned efforts of mentally challenged parents unable to cope with the complex demands of running a home and caring for an active toddler; through the detached disinterest of a clinically depressed parent who just 'lets things go' and ignores a child's cries; to the deliberate deprivation of food, warmth, protection and affection.

Jenny had been emotionally rejected by her own parents and had run away on several occasions. She was only 16 when she gave birth to Tessa, a small, frail-looking child. Jenny was determined that she didn't need anybody and refused all offers of help and advice. Tessa began to lose weight, was always wet and sore and the people around her grew very concerned. At nine months Tessa was not sitting up, not attempting to make any sounds and she lay listless in her cot with her eyes fixed on one spot. Several bruises appeared which were explained by Jenny as due to Tessa banging herself on the cot. Fingertip bruises around her jaw were taken as the final warning sign and Tessa was placed with foster parents. In her new home she was well cared for and given plenty of attention and affection. She immediately began to put on weight and showed rapid progress in her development, though she remained a little behind the average for her age. Jenny was encouraged to keep up contact with her baby through visiting her at her foster parent's home. The foster mother said she had practically moved in! Jenny began to learn how to care for Tessa through watching someone who was competent and experienced in handling young children (modelling) and through the sensitive way in which the foster mother encouraged Jenny to take over whenever possible and gradually built up her self-confidence. Nursery rhymes, cuddles and the fun of playing together were new experiences for both mother and child. Jenny was being nurtured and growing alongside her baby until

*eventually it was decided that she could take Tessa home. She had come to terms with her
own continuing need for support and with accepting help and advice as Tessa grows up.*

Although change is difficult, Jenny's case shows that just because someone
neglects or abuses a child at one particularly stressful stage of their own lives does not
mean they can never develop the skills of parenting. Jenny fits one of the common
stereotypes of abusing families in which the young, isolated and inexperienced
mother is frustrated by the restrictions that having a child imposes on her life. An
alternative version depicts the disorganized, socially disadvantaged family with low
standards of housekeeping and childcare and high rates of physical punishment. It is
easy to be misled by such stereotypes and important to remember that physical
abuse and neglect can and do occur in all sorts of families and that these two types of
maltreatment do not automatically go hand in hand. In their book, *Battered: The
Abuse of Children*, Jay and Doganis (1987) describe the case of Alia Aziz whose
continued brutal physical abuse went largely unrecognized by social workers
because her mother kept the house spotlessly clean and tidy and because the child
appeared well fed and well cared for.

Neither is it safe to assume that abuse and neglect are exclusively problems of
individual families. The physical abuse of children in schools and other institutions
is unfortunately not unheard of and research has shown that children in some
hospitals and residential homes or nurseries can suffer what amounts to serious
neglect despite being physically well cared for. Children who lack stimulation,
consistent one-to-one attention from a regular caregiver and the magic ingredient
that others have called TLC (tender loving care) show impairment in their mental
development and may become emotionally cold and detached (see, for example,
Goldfarb (1945); Tizard *et al.* (1972); Heywood (1978)).

In this chapter we shall draw on both clinical experience and research to give a
picture of the many and varied effects of physical abuse and neglect. We shall
consider both the immediate impact and the longer-term consequences under two
main headings: physical and neurological consequences; and emotional and
behavioural consequences.

1 Physical and neurological consequences

The immediate consequences of physical abuse are closely related to the nature and
severity of the injuries inflicted. These can range from minor bruising and abrasions
(soft-tissue injuries) which fade away after a few days, to fractured bones which take
much longer to heal. In exceptional cases, severe internal injuries such as damage to
the spleen, liver or kidneys can be brought about by punching or kicking and these
may prove fatal if not treated.

Fractured ribs from excessive squeezing are among the commoner serious
non-accidental injuries in babies and young children, as are twisting fractures of the
long bones of the arms and legs. In a young child a bone may not actually break but
rather crack and distort to give what is known as a greenstick fracture. It was
radiological evidence of long-standing multiple fractures in young children that first
alerted doctors in the 1940s to the possibility of child maltreatment and what was
later termed the 'battered baby syndrome' (Kempe *et al.*, 1962). Most of these
injuries, although horrific at the time, eventually heal leaving little permanent
damage. The two important exceptions are the effect of subdural haematoma
(bleeding into the membranes surrounding the brain) and retinal haemorrhage
(bleeding at the back of the eye). Both of these injuries can be brought about by
blows to the head or can be associated with a fractured skull but they can also result
from violent shaking for which the superficial evidence is minimal – possibly grip
marks on the chest or upper arms. In both cases serious long-term effects are a

possibility. Retinal haemorrhage can lead to blindness and the unrelieved pressure on the brain from a subdural haematoma can lead to permanent brain damage and mental retardation (Schilling and Schinke, 1984).

There is considerable evidence to suggest that children exposed to abusive environments show delays or restrictions in their physical growth as well as in their mental development (Smith, 1975). It may seem obvious to state that children who are neglected and not fed properly will not grow as quickly as normal children and will usually be underweight for their age. What is perhaps less obvious is that other forms of abuse and neglect, including emotional deprivation, may produce similarly stunting effects. In young children this is often referred to as 'failure to thrive' or abuse dwarfism. According to a review of the research by Okell-Jones (1980) between 25 and 35% of all abused children show evidence of poor physical growth and poor nutrition and about half show evidence of neurological abnormalities (mental retardation; visual impairment; speech and language deficits or disorders; perceptual motor dysfunction shown in lack of physical co-ordination, clumsiness and carelessness about physical injury etc.).

Some doctors take the view that the age at which physical abuse or neglect takes place is critical. According to Taitz from the Sheffield Children's Hospital 'failure to thrive' is associated with deficient production of growth hormones that also have a key role to play in the development of the central nervous system.

> From about eighteen months to four years there is the most dramatic change in the infant. You go from an infant who, in developmental skills, is not much different to a chimpanzee baby, to the four year old who has practically all the human cognitive skills inside him. The significance of abuse during this age of accelerated development is part of the medical model that really does need to be understood. (Taitz, quoted in Jay and Doganis, 1987, p. 50)

However, the fact that many children make rapid progress when well cared for in a calm, structured environment (as in the case of Tessa described earlier) has led some authors to suggest that these sorts of problems are not so much due to actual damage to the nervous system as to behavioural adaptation to the abusive environment. There have been some quite remarkable individual cases of children who have achieved average intelligence levels and a reasonable degree of social adjustment despite experience of extreme deprivation and abuse from an early age. For example, a six-year-old girl rescued from total isolation with her deaf mute mother, suffering from malnutrition, lack of speech and apparent mental subnormality (Davis, 1947); twin boys isolated, neglected and cruelly treated from 18 months to seven years who showed severe subnormality and emotional disturbance when discovered (Koluchova, 1972). These and other studies were cited by Clarke and Clarke (1976) to support the alternative view that there is no such thing as a critical period and that good care and educational opportunitites can compensate for bad experiences no matter what the age of the child.

In a review of the developmental effects of child abuse, Toro (1982) drew attention to the poor quality of much of the research. He pointed out that the majority of studies have been based on clinical samples (i.e. children who have come into contact with hospital or psychiatric social work services) which means they tend to be biased towards the more serious end of the abuse spectrum and to include a high proportion of children from socially disadvantaged backgrounds, since they are more likely to come to the attention of welfare agencies for a variety of reasons (see chapter 3). In addition, most studies only cover a relatively short time span and have failed to use control groups of non-abused children from similar backgrounds to establish benchmarks for average development and behaviour in a particular population. One exception to this methodological morass was the long-term follow-up study by Elmer (1977) which included comparison with non-abused but equally disadvantaged children and with a group of children who had suffered accidental injuries. The evidence was not entirely consistent, but, surprisingly, the abused children did not score significantly worse than the others on measures of mental, language and motor development, and what differences existed tended to 'wash out' when the children were followed up eight years later. What was particularly disturbing, however, was the poor overall performance of *all* of the children from low-income families (including the non-abused control group) when compared with the norms for their age, thus confirming that social disadvantage on its own can have devastating consequences for the life chances of children. For many children from socially disadvantaged backgrounds, active abuse or neglect from their parents was just another factor in a generally abusive environment. This argument is developed by Martin Loney in chapter 8.

2 Emotional and behavioural consequences

Children who are subject to a chronic pattern of serious physical abuse and neglect live in a very unpredictable world. They live in fear and have to be continuously vigilant about the moods and reactions of the adults around them. Take the example of Mary which follows.

Mary was admitted to hospital when she was 18 months old with a severe fracture of the upper arm. She couldn't yet talk and faced the world with the classic expression of 'frozen watchfulness'. After speaking with her mother it was discovered that Mary had been abused for some time by her mother's co-habitee and that her mother had been reluctant to face up to this because she was now expecting his baby. Mary's mother clearly loved her and was distressed and cried over her when she was hurt. She had tried to avoid the sort of confrontations that led to forced feeding and physical violence but she had been unable to protect Mary from this man's violent temper. Mary was eventually reunited with her mother after she had taken the painful decision to choose her child over her boyfriend. She is now faced with loneliness and grief over her own personal loss for which she will require continued support.

Children like Mary have to adapt to survive, by, for example, anticipating the mood and actions of their carers and trying to avoid doing anything that will provoke aggression – hence the watchful expression. On the basis of a study of 50 abused children, Martin and Beezley (1977) drew up a list of characteristics of the behaviour of abused children:

- Impaired capacity to enjoy life – abused children often appear sad, preoccupied and listless.
- Psychiatric or psychosomatic stress symptoms, for example, bed-wetting, tantrums, bizarre behaviour, eating problems etc.
- Low self-esteem – children who have been abused often think they must be worthless to deserve such treatment.
- School learning problems, such as lack of concentration.
- Withdrawal – many abused children withdraw from relationships with other children and become isolated and depressed.
- Opposition/defiance – a generally negative, unco-operative attitude.
- Hypervigilance – typified in the 'frozen watchfulness' expression.
- Compulsivity – abused children sometimes compulsively carry out certain activities or rituals.
- Pseudomature behaviour – a false appearance of independence or being excessively 'good' all the time or offering indiscriminate affection to any adult who takes an interest.

Of course, none of these behaviours are a necessary or exclusive characteristic of abused children. How an individual child reacts to being abused will depend on the complex interaction between the child's own personality and predispositions, his or her unique family circumstances and relationships and the nature, severity and duration of the abuse.

Some children react to abuse with fear, anxiety, withdrawal, overcompliance and a general pattern of avoidance behaviours. Others appear to be willing victims and to actively expose themselves to repeated pain and suffering. The case of Frank would be an example of the latter.

From the age of six, Frank had lived in numerous foster homes and children's homes. Before coming into care he had been denied adequate food, tied in his cot and battered by his father. Physical pain always came at the end of a lengthy process of torment. Frank was unable to settle anywhere, he trusted no one and constantly sought to destroy any relationship. By the time he arrived at the boy's hostel aged 13 he saw himself as a victim and was totally unable to recognize that his behaviour invited punishment and pain. The other disturbed boys who lived in the hostel made Frank's life hell and he was constantly crying for help having set himself up for further abuse. A night staff member found herself sitting outside Frank's bedroom to protect him and allow him to sleep after a particularly difficult evening. The other boys seemed compelled to pursue him and the staff member was horrified to find that Frank climbed out of his window to return to the fray.

In contrast as Frude (1988b) points out, 'a high level of aggressiveness would appear to be a dominant characteristic of many abused children'. For example, he cites a study by Straus (1983) which found that 76% of abused children repeatedly and severely assaulted their brothers or sisters compared with only 15% of a comparison group of children who were not physically abused. Further other studies (e.g. Sroufe, 1983) showed that many abused children lacked empathy with the distress of others and had a tendency to respond maliciously.

Kempe and Kempe (1978) estimated that about a quarter of young abused children showed what they described as 'demon' symptoms. They could not settle at anything for long and were continually rushing about; they were heedless of danger to themselves and behaved with unprovoked aggression to others; they appeared immune to any form of disapproval or punishment and held a negative and aggressive stance towards the world in general.

It may seem paradoxical, but it is worth considering to what extent such generally antisocial behaviour might be partly a trigger rather than just an effect of being abused. Saying this is not to blame children for inviting abuse, but it is necessary to explore ways in which it may be the child's behaviour that precipitates an abusive reaction. Child abuse is often the product of long-standing difficulties in the relationship between parent and child and the child's own personality or predispositions or ways of responding may certainly contribute to the pattern of interaction. There is substantial evidence to suggest that some children may be less rewarding to parents or more frustrating and difficult to manage from the outset. This sets the scene for more confrontations and puts them at higher risk of negative, punitive and potentially abusive interactions with their caretakers, which in turn may increase their aggressive behaviour (Frude, 1988b). On the other hand, some abusive parents may positively encourage aggression in children.

The following case illustrates just how children of different predispositions can show different reactions to the same family environment.

Two brothers, Harry aged nine and Malcolm aged five, reacted in different ways to a violent father. Harry was a slight lad who always looked as if he was about to cry and never reacted quick enough to avoid trouble. He was rejected by his father as 'no good at anything boys should be good at' and seemed to invite the same response at school. Malcolm was only half his size but seemed a lot bigger and was a good fighter – a child who rushed into everything fists flying and mouthing obscenities. He was put forward for suspension in his first term at school and his father laughed with pride. The contrast between the two boys was so marked that it was hard to believe that they came from the same family. Intervention allowed some of Malcolm's energy to be more effectively channelled but constant encouragement from his father ensured an aggressive approach to the world. Harry had to be removed from home for his own safety and placed with foster parents.

In the long term there is some evidence to suggest that exposure to violence can have a desensitizing effect on children (Berkowitz, 1962) and that children who have been subjected to severe physical punishment themselves are more likely to use similar methods of discipline as parents, which in turn puts them at higher risk of abusing their own children. In addition, lack of empathy with the suffering of others is a trait which is reported in many abusing parents and which some authors attribute to abusive childhood experiences (Fraiberg, et al., 1975). There have been few systematic long-term studies of abused children but it is clear that not all abused children go on to become abusive adults. Children have proved to be remarkably resilient to all forms of maltreatment and many thousands who have experienced what would be considered abusive childhoods by contemporary standards have become affectionate, caring and sensitive parents.

Conclusions

How are we to make sense of such diverse and paradoxical descriptions of children's behaviour in response to being severely abused? One plausible, if controversial, analysis likens the experience of an abused child to that of adult concentration camp inmates or hostage survivors (Filmore, 1981):

> The abused child, like a camp inmate, is told to love and obey his warders or be injured, but at the same time given the message that he is abhorred and unworthy of love and protection. He is asked to perform acts of loyalty but at the same time psychologically and physically degraded. Most important, he is constantly threatened with life-destroying violence and often receives violence for no consistent reason or for a reason which is patently untrue. To complete the comparison, neither the abused child nor the camp inmate have time limited sentences – there seems no end to their situation. (Quoted in Jones *et al.*, 1987)

Adult survivors of such experiences are often reported to have low self-esteem, guilt and self-blame; to have difficulty coping with anger or depression; to show paradoxical support for their captors and hostility towards their rescuers and to suffer from recurrent fears and anxieties, particularly in new or stressful situations. Jones *et al.* (1987) point out the danger of taking this analogy too far but nevertheless recognize its usefulness.

> The main lesson from this comparison is that the child, especially the adolescent, is unlikely to develop a quick positive relationship with therapists, residential workers, foster parents or other adults. He will expect rejection and sometimes provoke adults to fulfill his fear. He may have no trust in the intentions of his helpers. The process of change will be slow and must not rely exclusively on learning from the relationship. (p. 262)

The self-blame and intense loyalty felt by some abused children is well illustrated by the case of Mike.

At the age of eight, Mike came into care because his younger brother told his teacher that he didn't like Mike being locked in his bedroom. When Mike was discovered he was naked and dirty in a small empty box room with no furnishings or toys. A plate with crumbs, a glass of water and a pot were the only things in the room. The window-ledge was covered with broken glass to prevent him reaching up. Mike stood in a corner. There seemed no explanation; the rest of the house was warm and comfortable, the other children seemed well fed and had toys to play with. Mike spent the next few years in a children's home. He was a persistent bed-wetter but apart from that he caused no trouble. Plans were made for adoption and Mike looked forward to meeting his prospective foster parents.

Suddenly Mike's mother came back into his life. She arrived without notice and asked to take him home, since his father who had abused him had left and she now had a new husband. Mike desperately wanted to go and was allowed home on trial for a weekend but was brought back early because his mother complained she was afraid of him because 'he keeps looking at me'. Mike became very unsettled at school and aggressive with other children in the playground. Plans for adoption were shelved and, despite the uncertainty of the first weekend visit, social workers began working with Mike's family with a view to returning him home permanently.

Mike said he wanted to know how much the other children knew about what had been happening and a meeting was arranged with his two brothers. The atmosphere was highly charged as Mike began to tell them his version of events. 'It started because I bit my nails. Dad used to look at them on a Friday night. Then he would fetch a hammer and hit each finger I had bitten, then put it in a lighted candle. When it didn't stop he took my things away. When that didn't work he wired me up to the car. If I hadn't been naughty he wouldn't have had to do it.' There was total silence. No one in the room had realized the extent of physical cruelty and emotional abuse to which he had been subjected. Mike had come into care because he had been rejected. He still felt that it was his fault.

At 15 Mike is a charming, good-looking, intelligent young man who is very capable when he chooses to be, but he is almost unreachable emotionally.

Helping children who have been severely abused and neglected is thus likely to be a long and emotionally demanding process in which the resources and patience of would-be helpers are tested to the limits.

FURTHER READING
CICCHETTI, D. and CARLSON, V. (eds.) *Child Maltreatment; Theory and research on the causes and consequences of child abuse and neglect*, Cambridge University Press (1989)

24 THE EFFECTS OF CHILD SEXUAL ABUSE

Denise Hevey

Lecturer in Health and Social Welfare, The Open University

Helen Kenward

Principal Social Worker monitoring child abuse, Northamptonshire County Council

When someone mentions the term 'child sexual abuse' (CSA) the most common reaction is to think in terms of anal or vaginal intercourse or attempted intercourse between an adult and a sexually immature child. However, definitions of CSA used in research are much wider than this. The most commonly used definition is that proposed by Schecter and Roberge (1976): 'The involvement of dependent, developmentally immature children and adolescents in activities they do not fully comprehend to which they are unable to give informed consent or that violate the social taboos of family roles.'

As well as including penetration with the finger or other objects, most definitions cover oral sex, masturbation, sexual kissing and fondling with or without clothes as a barrier. Together these practices are referred to as 'contact abuse'. In addition, most researchers have included in their definitions some aspects of involving children in sexual activities inappropriate to their age and stage of development that do not involve physical contact. This could cover inappropriate exposure of the genitals (exhibitionism), watching others perform sexual acts either directly or on video, participating in pornographic photographs or videos, being exposed to erotic magazines or lewd and sexually provocative suggestions etc. There is much less consensus on whether all of these activities warrant the term child sexual abuse. For example, some people might regard the park 'flasher' as a public nuisance rather than a serious offender. But the apparent seriousness of the offence to an outsider is not always related to its impact on the child.

When Rita took a short-cut along an alleyway her parents had told her never to take – although they had not explained why – she was confronted by a man exposing himself. When she ran home she felt so guilty at having disobeyed that she was frightened to tell her mother what had happened to her. These intense feelings of guilt and fear are still triggered for her as an adult, whenever the memory surfaces. This triggering of the feelings associated with an incident of abuse is a common phenomena for sexual abuse victims. No physical harm came to Rita in this case but she still feels the distress and can recall vividly the sight, sound and situation many years later.

Research findings

Obviously, the broader the definition of sexual abuse the more incidents will be included and the higher the estimated rate of CSA. This makes comparison of studies based on different definitions extremely difficult. A further difficulty arises from the different populations studied and the different research methods used. Much of the 'evidence' that we have about the effects of CSA comes from clinical work with children and adults undergoing therapy. They necessarily represent a specially selected sample biased in the direction of those referred for major problems and those that select themselves by coming forward for treatment. Because the primary interest of therapists and psychiatrists is in the treatment of patients rather than research, the 'evidence' is often not collected in a standard way or not compared with evidence from non-abused control groups matched for other background factors such as age, sex, social class, educational experience etc. Large-scale properly controlled research studies based on screening 'normal' populations for previous histories of abuse are few and far between and have separate problems to do with willingness to report and the length of time that may have elapsed since the abuse took place. The stigma and distress associated with CSA may make individuals reluctant to participate in current research or make them refuse to be followed up years after events they would rather forget. In addition, surveys of special populations such as known abusers or prostitutes often reveal a high percentage of sexual abuse, but as Steve Taylor points out (see chapter 3) it is false to assume that, for example, prostitution is a direct effect of a previous history of CSA. Rather it is just one of a number of factors which make people more vulnerable to exploitation.

We therefore need to be cautious in accepting the claims of individual research studies and to be prepared to place more weight on those which have been properly designed and controlled and are consistent with the accumulated wisdom of clinical experience. It is precisely this type of research review exercise that Browne and Finkelhor carried out in 1986 in relation to American research on CSA. In the rest of this chapter we will draw heavily on their work, supplemented with information from recent British-based studies (for example Frude, 1988a).

It should be noted that the majority of research studies of the effects of sexual abuse are based on all-female samples. This is largely because of the much higher *reported* incidence of sexual abuse in girls compared with boys. Very little is actually known about the prevalence or effects of sexual abuse in boys. Some have suggested that the abuse of male children is more common than was formerly imagined (e.g. Hobbs and Wynne, 1986). It can be argued that it is simply more difficult for boys to report such things because it amounts to admitting weakness and vulnerability in a way that runs counter to the stereotype of masculinity.

The gender issue is important in other ways. In the vast majority of cases covered by research studies of abuse both within and outside the family, the abusers have been adult males. While it is true that some children and young people can and do sexually abuse others younger and weaker than themselves, this is relatively unusual unless they themselves have been abused (and as we shall see, the effects of abuse by another child are generally regarded as less serious). It is also true that women can and do sexually abuse children, although again this is comparatively unusual and often at the instigation of a male partner. The evidence to date suggests that child sexual abuse is largely a problem perpetrated by adult men on female children (see chapter 35).

But other than gender, there are no easily identifiable common characteristics of abusers. They can be of any age, any cultural background and come from all walks of life from dockers and farm labourers to doctors and judges. Perhaps most disturbingly though, there is some evidence to suggest that men with paedophilic tendencies are attracted into work or leisure activities or relationships which bring them into regular contact with children, including befriending lone mothers with dependent children.

Evaluating the effects of child sexual abuse

Consistent with Finkelhor, we have decided to use the words 'initial' and 'long-term' to describe the effects of abuse in order to avoid the implication that short-term effects do not last long. Initial effects are those that can be observed immediately but may also persist into the longer term. It should also be noted that there is a large degree of overlap between the initial effects of abuse and what have been called elsewhere the signs and symptoms, since the former become the basis for the latter in many cases (see chapter 18).

The range of initial effects of sexual abuse on children can be classified under three main headings: physical consequences and psychosomatic effects; emotional and psychological reactions; and behavioural effects.

1 Physical consequences and psychosomatic effects

Physical consequences
The initial physical consequences of child sexual abuse depend on the age of the child, the nature of the abuse and the degree of physical force used. Non-contact abuse and less severe forms of contact such as fondling and masturbation usually have no physical consequences. Where penetration has been attempted, physical symptoms can range from reddening and soreness of the anal or vaginal opening through to bleeding, bruising, tearing and other forms of abrasion. Children who have been subject to anal abuse may have dilated anuses or may show spontaneous relaxation or opening of the back passage when the buttocks are gently parted. This physical sign of 'reflex dilatation' was taken as contributory evidence of CSA by paediatricians in Cleveland (Hobbs and Wynne, 1986). In addition to injury, children who have been sexually abused are vulnerable to sexually transmitted diseases such as genital warts, gonorrhoea of the genitals or throat and AIDS, and around 10% of adolescent girl victims become pregnant. Some young children have been known to die as a direct result of the physical effects of sexual abuse, or of the panicked actions of their abusers, for example by choking on semen or through internal haemorrhage, although this is extremely rare. Significantly, several authors have been at pains to point out that the vast majority of sexually abused children do not suffer any adverse physical consequences either immediately or in the long term (e.g. Jones *et al.*, 1987) although many abused children require constant reassurance that their bodies are all right and that they are developing normally throughout the stages of growing up. In this respect, if handled sensitively and efficiently, the medical examination that is normally required after an allegation or suspicion of CSA can be an important source of reassurance and the beginning of the healing process. The child's fear that the abuse has caused permanent physical harm is a real one often connected with the fact that the child may not have fully understood what was happening at the time.

Jody was four when her father physically and sexually abused her. She was taken into care for other reasons and did not tell anyone of the sexual abuse until five years later. Abusive and aggressive in school, she was referred for play therapy. In her first drawing of herself, she painted from the waist down black and placed the eyes on the top of the head, great black tears rolling down the face. Jody explained her drawing quite simply. 'The black is what I am inside, empty and hurt. The tears are the pain coming out, the eyes are on top of the head so they can't see what is happening.'

Jody was convinced she would never be physically normal because of the implements that had been inserted in her vagina and the blood and pain she had seen and felt. A simple medical examination with a doctor able to tell her that she was 'just like any other little girl' lifted a great weight from her mind. Jody began to heal. The effect long term has been a need for constant reassurance at different stages of development that things were normal, that menstruation and physical development were to be expected. All the usual anxieties of adolescent development have been heightened and Jody needed to receive confirmation from her foster mother and social worker that she was fine.

Psychosomatic effects

The term 'psychosomatic' is derived from the combination of psyche (mind) and soma (body). In using it we mean the various physical symptoms and conditions that can be brought about or exacerbated by psychological reactions and mental states, and we hasten to point out that the physical manifestations are no less real for being psychological in origin. A wide range of physical symptoms characteristic of anxiety and distress are commonly reported in the immediate aftermath of abuse. Estimates based on empirical research suggest that in the case of sexual abuse within the family up to one-third of children have difficulty sleeping or sleep disturbance and up to one-fifth may show changes in their eating habits such as going off their food, compulsive eating or digestive disturbances. Anxiety and distress may of course aggravate pre-existing conditions with a psychological component such as asthma, eczema, hives etc. and be the underlying cause of a variety of vague or non-specific symptoms such as abdominal pains and 'tension' headaches which are frequently reported in the clinical histories of abused children.

Many of the psychosomatic effects characteristic of anxiety persist in the longer term or recur in adulthood. For example, Briere (1984) (cited in Browne and Finkelhor (1986)) reported that 54% of the formerly abused adults in his clinical sample experienced anxiety attacks compared with 28% of non-abused, and 72% (compared with 55%) had difficulty sleeping. Studies of college students and community samples generally show lower overall rates of disturbance than clinical populations but still confirm that adults who have experienced CSA are up to twice as likely to report psychosomatic symptoms associated with anxiety than those who have not been abused. Further, recent work in the United Kingdom with patients who have serious eating disorders such as anorexia (not eating) and bulimia (excessive eating binges often followed by self-induced vomiting) has shown that roughly two-thirds have histories of childhood sexual abuse.

Melissa, aged 15, was trying to describe her difficulties after disclosure. 'When I went to secondary school at 11, I didn't think much about what my dad did. I didn't like it but he said I had to learn and every dad did it. In the first term we had a talk and a film about the facts of life. I sat absolutely still, after all I knew all about it but it was obvious the others didn't. During break the others made jokes, I didn't know what to say. If I'd have let on they'd think it was my fault. I decided to say nothing and I stopped having friends and concentrated on my books. They thought I was a swot but they didn't know how sad I felt. I wasn't a child, he'd stolen that from me.'

Melissa became more and more depressed and withdrawn, the teacher became concerned and the school nurse suggested the doctor. Melissa took little care of herself, her hair was dirty, she did not wash, and she became anorexic. Melissa had a very poor image of herself, believing that she was worthless: 'He stole everything from me.'

When Melissa was asked why she had not told someone she said quite simply, 'No one ever asked me.'

For years Melissa had been unable to trust anyone enough to tell them and they did not ask. A social worker visited the family but Melissa felt her father was so powerful, that no one would believe her and that no one cared anyway. On the day of disclosure Melissa sat in utter desolation – an old lady of 90 at 15. The turning-point for her was a sailing expedition some two years later. The owner of the sloop knew only that she came from a poor family. A couple of days aboard and she began to enjoy herself. When asked in an off-hand manner to take the boat out of harbour whilst the rest of the crew hauled up the sails her eyes shone. A little later she confided that 'I couldn't believe it. I was in charge of all those people and that beautiful yacht. He must have thought I was a person and I showed him I could do it.'

2 Emotional and psychological reactions

Initial impact
Estimates vary widely but suggest that around two-thirds of children show some degree of emotional disturbance as an initial consequence of the experience of being sexually abused and that the impact is related to age as well as to the nature of the abuse and the relationship to the abuser. In one of the better-designed studies (Tufts', 1984) the highest incidence of disturbance was shown in the 7–13 age range with 40% rated as seriously disturbed.

Josie was 12, her father had a second wife who had two small sons that Josie was very close to. Josie was assaulted by her father almost every night. 'He would come into my room after everyone had gone to sleep, he had a wet towel which he would hit me with – they don't cause bruises – and then have intercourse. I couldn't make a noise in case I woke the boys. When he left he always said the same thing, "Don't think you would be believed and if you tell I'll kill them both in front of you." '

Josie held onto her fear for 18 months. During that time – 'All the men I met changed before my eyes until they looked exactly like my dad – imagine sitting on a bus when everyone changes so that you're surrounded.' In addition – 'Every car on the street that came towards me became a black Cortina. I felt my dad's presence everywhere, I was so afraid. One day I saw a policeman standing by a shop window, I went up to him and told him how frightened I was that dad was going to kill my brothers.' Josie's problems had only just begun.

Fear is the primary emotion reported in most sexual abuse and even at a very young age children are made aware by the adult's behaviour that what is happening is wrong. The silence of the activity, the secrecy and the responsibility that is put upon the child becomes a heavy burden.

Anger, hostility and depression are also commonly reported. Consistent with clinical experience, feelings of guilt and shame have been found in between one-quarter and two-thirds of cases but it is hard to disentangle how much of this is due to the actual abuse and how much due to responses aroused by disclosure.

Maria was the middle child in a family of five. At 13 she was sexually abused by her father. Her mother abdicated totally so that Maria managed the children, looked after the parents, bought and prepared food. When she was placed in a children's home she spun round like a top. What was she to do all day? Her brothers and sisters became absorbed in other activities, dad was in jail and who would love him. Mum couldn't pay the rent or remember to get milk. Maria sank into a deep depression and finally had to be admitted to a psychiatric unit. Disclosure meant the loss of everything and she felt totally rejected.

Clinical and therapeutic work with adults and children suggests that being abused has a marked effect on self-esteem and that many come to think of themselves as dirty, worthless and unlovable. But research evidence into the initial consequences of abuse is less clear-cut as to whether abused children are significantly different in this respect from their non-abused peers matched on relevant background factors such as social class and educational achievement levels.

Long-term effects
In the long term the most commonly reported emotional consequence of having been sexually abused as a child is undoubtedly depression. In one study by Sedney and Brooks (1984) depressive symptoms were reported by 65% of college women who had been sexually abused compared with 43% of non-abused controls, and the abused group were four times as likely to have been hospitalized for depression. Further, a higher proportion of formerly abused adults have suicidal tendencies or have attempted suicide, although these represent a small minority of abuse

survivors. The evidence for damage to self-esteem is much more substantial in the long term than it is for the short term. One explanation offered is that children do not fully understand what is happening to them at the time and it is only when the full realization sets in that the impact on self-esteem is greatest. The majority of adult women survivors in clinical populations report feeling isolated and stigmatized and have predominantly negative self-images – that is they tend to see themselves as inadequate, worthless and not worth caring about.

Self-esteem seems to be particularly badly effected when the abuser is a father or father figure and in the case of incest victims, estimates of moderate to severe effects range from 60 to 87%

3 Behavioural effects

Initial impact
As we noted earlier, the distinction between emotional, psychosomatic and behavioural effects is in some senses arbitrary, particularly in the case of young children. Sexually abused children are often reported to show sleep disturbances and nightmares, but in addition, if bed- or bathtime have become associated with abuse, they may show more than the normal reluctance to co-operate or be extremely fearful and anxious about going to bed.

Depression and the burden of carrying guilty secrets in order to protect others may actually show in the child's observable behaviour, for example, in terms of lethargy, listlessness and body posture.

Lucy came into the room as if physically handicapped. Each foot lifted as if she had lead boots on, her shoulders were hunched and her head bowed. When it was suggested that she looked as if she was carrying the world on her shoulders she looked up querying. 'Have you read Pilgrim's Progress?' I nodded, 'Well then you know exactly how it is, I'm in the slough of despondency and no one can help me out.'

Lucy surprised everyone by her perception and understanding of what was happening to her. Helping her out became symbolized by each session beginning with her buried in bean bags and allowing one finger to show through a gap – taking hold of her hand and helping her into the world was ritualized and she began to shed her burden. Lucy was surprised that I knew what she was carrying, looking into a mirror helped her see what the world saw. A very different child emerged once she began to work on the abuse she had received from her mother seven years previously.

Clinical experience suggsts that children who are angry cannot take it out on powerful adult abusers so they frequently take it out on themselves, on their environment or on other children and they may become hostile and aggressive at school.

At the age of 11 Claire was a quiet, well-behaved middle child of three. The good child she was became outrageous at 13. She constantly used foul language and was destructive of what had previously been her carefully guarded bedroom and possessions. Her rage exploded against herself when she took a massive overdose and her desolation showed itself when she said, 'If he could do this to me I must be nothing.'

On the other hand, because many children who have been abused feel somehow spoiled, different and ashamed, they may withdraw from all social contact with their friends, they may avoid contact by truanting from school and their isolation can make them vulnerable to bullying and further victimization. There is, however, little research evidence to link these sorts of behaviour specifically to sexual abuse. Other troubled children also act aggressively or truant and become involved in delinquent behaviour. But there is some evidence to suggest that sexually abused children and adolescents are more likely to run away from home. In one study (Herman, 1981) of father–daughter incest, one-third of the subjects had tried to run away compared with only one in 20 of the comparison group. Many others leave home at the first legitimate opportunity, for example through early marriage.

The other way in which sexually abused children typically differ from other troubled children is in their inappropriate sexual behaviour. Children who have been sexually abused have been made aware of sexual feelings, sexual responses and adult-style sexuality at an early age. They may have been taught to respond to all demonstrations of affection in a sexual way or they may have become used to using sexual approaches or favours in order to get their own way. Sexualized behaviour can be seen in different forms at different ages. Whereas it is perfectly normal for young children to explore their own bodies, to masturbate and to show sexual curiosity about others, in abused children these types of behaviour may be extreme. Inappropriate sexual behaviour includes compulsive masturbation, exposure of the genitals in public, acting out the sort of sexual practices to which they have been subject on other children or with toys in their fantasy play or making overtly sexual advances to adults. Research studies suggest that up to 70% of boys and 44% of girls who have suffered CSA showed significantly more sexually problematic behaviour than their peers (Friedrich et al., 1986).

Susie at seven was highly sexualized. She had experienced many forms of sexual activity, had observed adults perform sexual acts – both her parents and those in pornographic videos – and her behavioural responses were sexual. When male friends stopped visiting the foster home it became apparent that they were unable to deal with their responses to Susie climbing on their knee, unzipping their trousers and attempting to masturbate them. When she played out her fears and anger at school, she became isolated. Little boys objected to her pulling down their trousers and trying to use their penises like the handle of a skipping rope. The teacher objected to her masturbating constantly using pencils, rulers and any other object no matter if it caused pain and bleeding. Susie began to withdraw – 'I won't tell you because you won't like me any more', was her cry when an investigation into her behaviour began. Susie felt powerful and powerless in responding to people around her and her lack of communication in anything other than sexual terms frightened her. She responded well to adults who set clear boundaries and offered an understanding of her needs. Gentle correction with regard to touching, kissing and cuddling to make them non-sexual helped her feel safe and able to grow in relationships.

Long-term effects

As one might expect, CSA has been shown to have a lasting effect on adult sexuality and sexual functioning. Many adults do manage to overcome the traumatic effects of their past, but sometimes stressful events in the present or dealing with their own children can reawaken long-forgotten experiences (see, for example, 'Acquittal' by Jacqueline Spring in chapter 26). The evidence of a link between early sexual experience and later sexual activity or prostitution is inconclusive. Although studies of prostitutes show a high proportion with histories of CSA and retrospective studies of abuse survivors report a high incidence of multiple sexual partners, other studies have suggested that the connection is not straightforward. One study cited in Browne and Finkelhor (1986) showed that a history of sexual abuse in childhood was not linked to the number of sexual partners in adulthood but that it was linked to whether the subjects described themselves as promiscuous (Fromuth, 1983). This finding is important because it indicates that the connection may be through the negative self-image of the abuse survivors.

There is no doubt that sexualized behaviour makes abuse victims more vulnerable to further victimization as children and to choosing partners who are more likely to be physically or sexually abusive to them or their children. Studies of older women as opposed to college students show a higher incidence of sexual dysfunction amongst those with a history of CSA. For example, Meiselman (1978) reported that 87% of incest survivors undergoing therapy had a serious problem of sexual adjustment compared with only 20% of a clinical comparison group and Courtois (1979) found that 79% had serious difficulties in relating to men.

CSA survivors may also experience difficulties in other relationships. Their experience has usually involved a betrayal of trust and a misuse of power so they may find it difficult to trust anyone or to let anyone get emotionally close to them. In particular, there is some limited research evidence to support the widely held clinical view that CSA survivors have difficulty in their parenting roles (Goodwin et al., 1981). These authors suggest that because closeness and affection have become associated with physical contact, abused parents may try to distance themselves from their children. This in itself could be the basis of future abuse.

Frank is a successful businessman; he is married with two children. He is sexually inactive because he's afraid he won't please his wife. He's obsessive around the house and highly protective of his children. He's a caring loving father afraid to touch his children in case he abuses them. His wife is confused by his angry outbursts and his fear of failure. Frank has a legacy of 10 years of physical and sexual abuse that he is fighting hard to understand and come to terms with.

Other factors related to effects of abuse
Browne and Finkelhor (1986) drew attention to the problems of making generalizations from the limited research evidence and also because of the complexity of individual cases and the interrelationship between factors. In particular, evidence relating to the age of the child, the severity of the abuse and whether or not the child disclosed what was happening was conflicting and inconclusive. However, on balance the available research supported the following additional generalizations:

- Multiple incidents – the longer the abuse goes on or the more often it happens the more traumatic the effects.
- Father figures – abuse by a father or father figure is usually more serious in its consequences than abuse by other relatives or acquaintances.
- Multiple abusers – when a child is abused by more than one person the effects are more serious.
- Use of force – where force or violence is used this adds significantly to the trauma for the child.
- Sex of offender – very few of the abusers in any of the studies were women, but the limited evidence suggests that the effects of abuse are more serious when the perpetrator is male.
- Age of perpetrator– the age gap does make a difference and abuse by an adult seems to be more serious in its effects than abuse by other children or adolescents.
- Response to disclosure – a positive accepting reaction does not appear to protect a child from the traumatic effects of abuse but a negative response to disclosure definitely makes things worse.

Conclusion
In this chapter we have attempted to draw out the main messages from both clinical experience and recent research evidence into the effects of child sexual abuse, while stressing the limitations of the evidence on which such generalizations are based. At the time of writing (September, 1988) this is still a relatively new area for research. Some people have likened our current level of understanding of CSA to that of physical abuse around the time when Kempe et al. (1962) first coined the term 'battered baby syndrome'. It is important to remember that even in an ideal world

research can never tell us what the precise effects of being abused will be for a particular child in the context of his or her unique personality, personal history and family circumstances. As Frude (1988a) pointed out: 'No uniform picture can be presented of the typical after effects of sexual abuse in childhood. There is no "post-sexual abuse syndrome" and the effects are highly varied.' Frude has also alerted us to the very real danger of overreacting and overdramatizing the likely effects. If we accept a wide definition of sexual abuse, then large numbers of people (some say as many as one in three) have been sexually abused in some way at some stage of their childhoods, and it is patently absurd to look for evidence of significant trauma in all of them. In addition, in stating (as we have) that around two-thirds of sexually abused children suffer some degree of initial emotional disturbance and around the same proportion of adult women survivors suffer from depression or from lowered self-esteem, we are also stating that at least one-third of children *do not* appear to be disturbed emotionally and that one-third of adult survivors *do not* become depressed or think themselves worthless. Referring to what he describes as 'the most extensive review of pertinent research' to date (Powell and Chalkley, 1981) Frude (1988a) says: 'Analyzing the findings of over 50 studies covering intra- and extra-familial abuse, the authors conclude that while the after effects of such assaults are generally assumed to be traumatic and to have lasting effects and wholly deleterious consequences for the victim . . . the evidence . . . does not support this view' (p. 59). This is not meant to give us grounds for complacency but merely to counteract the possible distortion that can arise from focusing on the extreme end of the spectrum as represented in the clinical case studies that we have used to illustrate this article. Of course, absence of proof cannot be taken as proof of absence, and failure to find significant effects may be due to the insensitivity of the measures used to indicate social and emotional adjustment in some studies (such as being married and holding down a job). As Mrazek and Mrazek (1981) rightly point out 'the effects of sexual abuse may be more subtle in nature'.

All forms of sexual abuse are *potentially* traumatizing, and as long as this is so there can be no excuse or justification for exposing children to risk of trauma, nor for ignoring the signs of the effects of sexual abuse of which we are now aware. There is no excuse for failing to respond sensitively with help and support.

FURTHER READING
WYATT, G. E. and JOHNSON-POWELL, G. (eds.) *Lasting Effects of Child Sexual Abuse*, Sage Publications Inc, London. (1988)

25 FOSTERING AN ABUSED CHILD*

Mary Thornley

One hears much about 'the abused child' nowadays. It is a coy euphemism in the main: one which relates less to the child who has been the recipient of blows and more to the child who has, sexually, been treated as an adult.

In the light of current statistics, we who have been fostering for a decade or more might have received, in the past, children whose root cause of unhappiness could well have side-stepped diagnosis by social services. For it is but recently that we have discarded the metaphorical modesty-vest which so effectively restrained enquiry and opinion on all things sexual. We could not, until now, bring ourselves to comprehend that, except in circumstances of unbalanced depravity, any adult would want to masturbate a child or, worse, engineer to have sexual intercourse with him or her. 'Ordinary' abuse, though abhorrent, was at least comprehensible; we've all lost our tempers, felt off-colour, become frustrated by events going on around us, and have thus gone over the top to some measure. But this other thing – no: it's been beyond our reasoning: almost certainly beyond our forgiveness.

On the other hand, here it is, apparently commonplace, in our midst. Apparently one in ten adults in our society can, if persuaded, recount some form of sexual interference experienced as a child. So, how do we, as foster parents, recognise such damaged children, when, even now, 'definite sightings' are missed by professionals involved in care proceedings? How do we behave towards these small beings who may have more 'experience' than we do ourselves? And what precautions would we be wise to take in respect of other, innocent, members of our extended families?

I shall call him Sam. He and his little sister have been living with us for the past year and the placement is on a long-term basis. Sam has just celebrated his tenth birthday. His sister is five. The family background is out of the ordinary on two main points: mother is mentally ill, wildly erratic, extremely loud and a great thrower of dinner plates: father is an upright military man who operates like a pre-set machine, expects instant reaction to any order, pursues fitness to the limit and lives in an old-fashioned fear of God. The children, considered to be 'at risk', were taken into care without opposition.

As the prospective foster mother I was obviously made privy to the basic upsets – the unsuitable domestic picture, the absence of tenderness in everyday care. There was absolutely no mention of sexual abuse, and yet, that there had been such interference was suggested within days of Sam coming to us. At nine he was precocious way beyond his years – we were confronted by a boy whose manner corresponded with that of a mature and awakened young man – one felt him to be

---

*The material contained in this chapter is from *Nursery World*, 7 May 1987.

openly 'flirting': eschewing the games and pastimes of his age group – taking the other children into corners, giggling and whispering, looking round furtively. His social graces were perfect: he was the real 'little gentleman', never forgetting his 'thank you', never answering back, never bolting his food or proving his eyes larger than his stomach. However, he was constantly carping about his figure, whether certain foods made you fat, asking what was the correct weight for his age and build. He spent long hours arranging his hair, sorting and matching his clothes for tomorrow, exercising his biceps and scrubbing his teeth with enormous vigour. He was, shall we say, hugely self-aware, self-referential.

Suffering, as he was in those early days, the loss of his parents and home, his school, neighbours and entire known environment, he could only effect to 'hate' his mother and father (an emotion not borne out when, say, they telephoned him) and his revulsion was effected also towards his small sister.

Sam could also switch off. He only heard what he wanted to hear. This vacuity was much used at school, for in spite of his assumed superiority he did not like work which required effort. If pressed to do some reading, for example, he might say, 'You can ask me all day, but I'm afraid I shall never do it.' Quite calm, quite firm. He was not to be treated, thank you, as other children. He had his secret. He knew about grown-ups.

By and by the facts sidled out. Sam worked on another child in our family; one immediately below him in age, a shy and slightly backward boy who needed much mothering and tender care. Of course, it had to be someone else who pointed out the irregularity – why do we never notice what's going on under our very noses? The boy's had gone to stay with a friend for the weekend, a capable neighbour who had undertaken to teach them to ride. Sam had insisted, while there, that I let him sleep in a sleeping-bag with this younger child, and when this was discouraged he had waited until late and then crept in. Our neighbour had also witnessed much kissing and cuddling over and beyond normal childish affection and had been struck dumb by the explicit words used by Sam while, for example, watching TV. Sam had never been quite as open in his behaviour at home with us – on 'foreign ground' he obviously felt entitled to push the boat out a bit.

So, the younger child had been introduced to masturbation and its attendant secrecy. Brought out into the open, we were able to deal with this by reducing Sam's opportunities to as good as nil by gently 'talking it through' and by the standard channelling of energies elsewhere. We also felt that sessions with a child psychologist could well be beneficial and this was arranged through school where, at the time, the PE mistress was getting fed up with Sam's promiscuous behaviour in the changing room and where there was talk of suspending him from swimming on account of his rivetting interest in his companions' private parts.

Yet, as time passes, Sam is getting younger – aspects of his earlier attitude are being diluted by the taking up of 'ordinary' games and projects. He is not, and perhaps never can be, *the same* as other boys of ten. He knows too much, has played the role of gigolo and has been excited by it – he misses it. However, he has been able to talk, to spill the beans, and to realize that, although we are not cross, it is imperative that certain outlooks must change.

Just now I went upstairs to turn off the reading lamps and settle the boys for the night. The little shy lad puckered up his face and pursed his lips for my goodnight kiss – the book slid off his bed and he curled up like a happy animal under the duvet.

Sam, in his bedroom, lay as always ramrod straight, the covers just-so, no book or comic, and when I bent over him he opened his mouth and provocatively waggled his tongue. He got a quick peck on the cheek.

26 AQUITTAL. EXTRACT FROM *CRY HARD AND SWIM: THE STORY OF AN INCEST SURVIVOR**

Jacqueline Spring

When my daughter was six months old, she loved to sit on the rug surrounded by a few objects, which I tried to make sure were changed each day. I would sit with her quietly in the afternoons, reading and occasionally watching her out of the corner of my eye. She would pick up an object, taste it, feel it with tongue and lips, smell it, pass it repeatedly from right to left hand, put it behind her back, find it again, and repeat the whole performance, meanwhile talking to herself with soft enquiring gurgles. Finally, she would hold it out to me, and I would take it and say, 'Block. It's a block.' – and hand it back to her. Now she had explored everything about this block, including its verbal symbol, which she had checked out with me. She put it away and went on to the next object, for the possibilities of blocks are rather limited.

The possibilities of sex are less limited, but when I consider how my daughter went about exploring her world, it helps me to understand how ordinary small children approach finding out about sex. To the growing toddler blocks and sex are of equal interest, and carry equal emotional weight. Both carry sensual and intellectual information to be processed in the child's brain. Sex only increases in emotional weight when the child, upon holding out her question to the adult, is met with either sudden evasion, or a concrete demonstration of what sex means in adult terms.

This is what must have happened to me as a small child. Along with everything else that called for my attention to be explored, objects, animals, people, places, there was sex, and it was no less, but not more fascinating than anything else in my world. As with the baby and the block, I first of all tested my own physical sensations, as all children do. Then, since it was not a concrete object, but a sensation, I looked for further information, not from left and right hand, but from mother and father, the most obvious sources of information available.

If the left hand gives too little and the right hand too much information, the nature of the object being explored cannot be discovered. Accurate information coming from both hands is needed. But the ability of my parents to convey that information to me in a balanced way was impaired. What's more, the actual information was distorted, for it was geared towards me as if I had been an adult, with an adult's understanding. For a child it was simply inappropriate information. Having no words for it, I could not handle it like a small block, but rather moved within this threatening area which enclosed me.

It could not be put behind my back while other things were being explored, yet the absence of a thing teaches as much about it as its presence. Its importance was

---

*The material contained in this chapter is excerpted from Spring, J., *Cry Hard and Swim: The Story of an Incest Survivor*, Virago, London (1987).

consistently magnified out of all proportion, because of my mother's evasion, and my father's preoccupation with it. As a small child, my mind could not contain this enormous secret message, but only what it must mean about me, whose body somehow did contain it.

The left hand, my mother, gave no information except fear. The right hand, my father, gave far too much information, overwhelmed me, confused me with its wealth of sensual information, till I remembered the message of the left hand, and putting the two together, knew that this thing, childish sexual pleasure, so natural to every baby touching itself before its attention passes on to other things, this thing, for which I had no name, was hugely terrifying and wicked. The thing was wicked, not my father. And because I contained this wicked thing, this feeling that was a part of me, it must be me who was wicked.

I was not allowed to put down this thing which had become impossibly painful to hold. My wickedness was held up to me by my father, and defined by my mother, though neither of them understood what was happening inside me. The only way to handle this huge, hideous block of horror was to perform an almost impossible mental trick, to, as it were, place what was inside of me outside of me, as the baby places the block behind her back. But because I had to do this with what was a part of me, I had to split myself in two. I had to forget. I had to hide this event from consciousness with all its accompanying feelings, so that it would remain forever hidden from view. As far as awareness of sexuality went, the clock stopped for me at the age of six. I was not allowed to find out about sex at my own childish pace. Natural feeling became a thing that was forbidden to me by one parent, and forced on me by the other, and the moment this happened, all possibility of sexual enjoyment came to an end, not only then, but far into the future, far past the time when it should have been mine by right of adult loving commitment.

Tree

This tree I hide behind
displays its weals
where I have peeled the bark
to find larvae.

They burrow deeper in the wood,
escape the air
they dare not breathe outside the bark.
They like it dark.

I hold me still
to sense them in my doubt –
love biting fear.

But have to stand inside myself and out,
wood can't feel care.

I came to Eve as the mother of a child who was troubled, and for whom I was afraid. A great deal of care was taken by the clinic to build up my trust in their ability to handle my child's needs with understanding and skill, so that I could release him to his own play therapist. I could then allow myself to become slowly conscious that I was not only anxious as a parent, but that the hurt I felt for my child was an accurate reflection of the anxious hurt child I also was inside.

By the time the day came when I was able to reveal what had happened to me, I had developed a mental picture of myself which lasted throughout that day, and for a long time following. In my picture I stood as a small child with hands outstretched to Eve, showing her the deep wounds in my palms, which were encrusted with dried blood and pus. Because she did not recoil from this ugliness, I was able to show her other cuts, weals, bruises and grazes all over me, as trustingly as a child to its mother, confident that no matter what needs to be done in order to heal the wounds, and no matter how much that hurts, the mother feels only affection and the desire to make everything better.

I was very tempted in some ways to minimise what happened, and in other ways to exaggerate. This temptation was made still more difficult to control because the memory returned in such a distressing, disjointed way, with abrupt halts and sudden flows of words that left me choking and gasping, as if I had been half strangled all my life. I was filled with exactly the feelings I would have experienced upon trying to tell my mother at the time it actually happened. Split many ways, I wanted to be protected from Eve's horror, shock, anger, disgust, withdrawal. With another part of me, I wanted to protect Eve from the impact of what I was saying, to minimise. And yet I also wanted, silently cried out for her to protect me. I would have given anything in the world just to be taken in her arms and cuddled. I even drew nearer to her after a while, hoping that she would make it easier in this way for me to go on remembering.

Most extreme of all was the fear of her disbelief. On the child level, I was sure she would not be able to accept this torrential pain I was pouring out, any more than my mother could have, that she would downplay everything and accuse me of over-dramatising. On the adult level, her disbelief of the actual event I was remembering, in addition to my own wildly fluctuating self-doubt, self-belief, would have been a direct threat to my sanity.

27 EXTRACTS FROM A DIARY TOWARDS SURVIVING SEXUAL ABUSE

Anonymous

These are four extracts from a journal kept by a young woman during, in her words, her journey from victim to survivor. The first is a letter to her cousin, the wife of the man who abused her, a relative she had known since childhood. The second and third extracts are attempts to make sense of what happened and how she was hurt. The final extract is a prayer.

1 A letter to my abuser's wife, my cousin

I'm not really sure what it is I want to say here. It's not that I want to cause you any harm or trouble but in order to sort out this mess I've got to ask you a few questions.

Firstly – do you know – do you realize how hurt I am – are you aware that I have suffered hell because of the games you and he involved me in. Or were they games? – Games are things to be enjoyed!

Why did it start. . . ? Who decided when – what – where. In order to gain some peace of mind over the years I told myself it was him – but now I have to admit to myself and others that you were in the middle of it all – *and that hurts!*

Did you feel any love for me at all – What about the happy times before your marriage? The holidays – the Sunday lunches? – did all this mean nothing to you? If you felt anything for me why did you let it happen?

I feel like a vase or a piece of china that has been dropped and broken – that somehow I have put the pieces together again – but the cracks are still there – and run deep. I can't even put into words how hurt and broken I actually feel – because somebody that I loved and thought loved me could betray me like you did.

Some have tried to show me how you may have been trapped – the weaker partner – having to go along with him – if only I could believe that. What was it that made you do these things?

Every time I look at you I feel somehow you know what I'm thinking – so if you do why don't you ask – you've never yet asked me. That's another thing – why the silence then and now. How can you face me and look me in the eye as though nothing ever happened – perhaps you think/hope I have forgotten – *never* – even after all the therapy etc. I'll never forget – how could I.

Many times I've felt really sorry for you – genuine sympathy – I know you suffered too – but that doesn't excuse the two of you for making me suffer also.

I really can't find answers to these questions – believe me I've tried – for the past week since realizing you were the silent partner – I have turned all of these questions over and over and over in my mind – hoping – praying for an answer or reason to excuse you for what happened – but I just can't find any way – all there is are more questions.

All I want to be able to do is look at you and be able to say – well what happened

happened – here's why it happened – and here's how I'm coping with it. I just hope that day actually comes 'cause I couldn't cope with feeling like this the rest of my days.

I'm sorry I had to bring all this up now just when you're setting up a decent steady life for you and the kids and if it's any comfort to you – I don't hate you – I couldn't – I don't even wish any harm on you – all I ask is for the hurt to heal – for the cracks to be mended so that I can feel a whole person.

2 Justification

HIM	HER
1 Allowed me to be involved	1 *Allowed me to be involved*
2 Willingly involved me	2 *Willingly involved me*
3 Abused my body	3 *Possibly encouraged abuse to gain kicks for herself*
4 'Stole' from me aspects of loving that I should have	4 *Totally disregarded any feelings I had for her*
5 Gave no thought/concern as to how I would be affected	5 *Ignored the fact that I was part of her family and was such long before he came on the scene*
6 Used me for his perverted pleasure	6 *Didn't think enough of me to protect me in any way*
7 Caused me years of suffering and shame	7 *Didn't think to ever mention it to me or ask if I was OK*
8 Didn't stop to consider my feelings both during and after	8 *Expects me to treat her normally and for me to accept her efforts of conversation etc.*

A lot of opportunities have been missed or fouled up as a result of their combined efforts. Failing 'A' level English Lit. – skipping chances of career that I really wanted to mention but a few. I feel therefore that even though the abuse wasn't all that it could have been – physically – the emotional damage it has caused is cause enough for feelings such as Anger, Hatred and Intense hurt.

3 Going back – resolved

1 I liked him as a person – Looked up to him – Nine year old doesn't recognize faults.
2 I loved her.
3 I loved cars.
4 Enjoyed their impulsive decisions (Newcastle after tea-time etc.) – They had no ties – They decided to go somewhere and just up and went.
5 My love of sport – him bringing me to rugby/hockey matches.
6 I enjoyed being allowed to feel like/being treated like an adult.
7 I didn't appreciate the importance of the price I was having to pay. – if I refused to co-operate the situation would have changed and they would probably have stopped bothering with me.
8 I was prepared/willing to trust both of them but they betrayed my trust.
9 He warned me not to tell my Mum/Dad about what was going on because they would be very cross with me and would punish me.
1 Corinthians 13,v.11 – 'When I was a child, I spoke as a child, I understood as a child, I thought as a child.'

4 Prayer

Lord,
Since starting back to work this week I have experienced 'panic attacks' which

have been quite frightening. I have tried to figure out the source of these and can I suppose think of 2 reasons. The first one simply being that I have had to cope with work! Meeting people and trying to get back into some kind of routine. It hasn't been easy but they're all very good and understanding and I know I'll be able to manage it.

The other reason isn't so straight-forward. It was suggested that the panic was the anger and hurt coming very close to the surface, and I'm not so sure that this isn't true. I just want to say that if at any time during all this that I speak in an unaccustomed manner – I hope you understand. I have been accused of keeping a tight bolt on the door and so I want to do some explaining. I keep these feelings locked away because I fear I might shock myself to utter the words that I feel, but don't you realize Lord that if these feelings aren't expressed then I'm the one ending up hurt.

So all I want to do is to ask you to help me – just let me feel that you understand. At the end of all this I just want to be able to look at these people and feel no bitterness or hatred – but in order for that to be achieved these feelings have got to be let out. Help me Lord that if I need to cry – I won't feel ashamed to – or that if I need to voice my anger – I won't feel guilty because Lord I just can't can't cope with any more shame or guilt. So Lord it all boils down to this – either you understand and will bear with me on this or else you don't – but my prayer is that you will free me from these guilty feelings over venting my feelings so that I can start to move on again.

28 THE HIDDEN CHILD WITHIN US

John Southgate

Introduction – the experience

When people grow up they tend to think that childhood is in the past, leaving only memories, some of which can be recalled – a bit like a family album stored on videotape within the mind. To some degree this is what happens. But when an adult behaves frivolously, or is enchanted by a view, or feels inside like a scolded child, or stifles a scream at a horror movie, or makes a daisy-chain, or plays with a toy train, then she is in touch with her* *inner child*. The inner child is alive, there and then, within the adult body. A person who is out of touch with her inner child has no fun or flair, she is always serious and ponderous. This is because the playful, energetic inner child has been stifled, hidden away or 'made unconscious'.

It can be that another side to the inner child is also hidden from view. This is the child who is sad, miserable, lonely or terrorized. For some adults it is so unbearable to be in touch with these bad feelings that they do not allow them into their consciousness. The price that they have to pay for this is to lack all feelings and emotions, to live in a flat and colourless world. This may have been absolutely necessary in order to survive. In this process of surviving *both* the bad experiences and the good experiences may have been suppressed.

No matter what happens, a baby strives towards gaining love. At this stage to gain love and approval is life itself – it is all the baby has. She has to believe that her caretakers are good. If she is mistreated and there is no one to help her, she has to 'die' – that is, to stifle all the feelings that result from being mistreated, such as anger and rage. She then shuts these feelings out of her consciousness to avoid further hurt. This enables her to pretend and imagine that her caretakers are good – she idealised those who have mistreated her. This process leads the child to build a 'false self' which, apparently, says and does the expected or normal things in life. She may try to build relationships and to some degree succeed. But underneath she may feel empty, and find it difficult to make real emotional contact with other people.

Sometimes close relationships are avoided altogether, in case the lonely, frightened or terrorized inner child bursts forth and overwhelms the person. If the early experience was that love is followed by vulnerability and then terror, closeness to an adult in the present can bring the fear of repetition. Usually the early experiences are not consciously recalled and the person does not know or understand why relationships seem to go wrong.

Traumatic experiences often take place before spoken language has developed. Our earliest language is in the form of body sensations and visual images, as in

---

*Wherever she/her are used in this chapter, he/him should be read as possible alternatives.

dreams. The terror can be symbolized as fleeing from monsters as in a nightmare. In therapy, when a person starts to recover these memories into consciousness, it can feel to her like opening a 'Pandora's box'. Dreams are important as they can describe symbolically the baby's preverbal experience. Dreams and body sensations, in this case, are the 'voice' of the inner child, expressed in the language of the unconscious. Attempts to stifle the unhappy inner child are in vain because she can never simply disappear. Her voice, if it is not heard by the grown-up self, 'speaks' via the languages of the unconscious, through physical sensations, or symptoms, dreams and behaviour in relationships. The body may develop migraine, rashes, asthma, ulcers and, some think, even cancer. Another common 'indicator' is refusing food (anorexia) or gorging and then vomiting food (bulimia). At an unconscious level, starving oneself is like the inner child saying, 'I won't have bad things inside myself, I don't deserve to live, it's all my fault.' Compulsive eating is like the inner child trying to fill up space inside herself to stifle the feelings of pain and terror.

Of course neither 'solution', starving or gorging, is dealing with the real problem and *in extremis* can be life-threatening. Orbach (1979) and Chermin (1985) have written about this subject.

Most disrupting for our intimate sexual and social life is the fact that the unhappy inner child influences relationships. This may cause the grown-up self to repeat an early trauma within a current relationship.

If the early scenario was of abandonment and neglect, the adult may repeatedly choose partners who run away or leave. If there was early physical or sexual violence, the adult may choose partners who are violent and sadistic, or who are passive and masochistic. If the inner child's message is not 'heard' then the 'message' will be repeated over and over again in terms of disruptive feelings, symptoms or behaviour. This can make the adult feel inexplicably compelled by an inner force. This force often seems to say that the inner child is guilty and bad and is to blame for others' unhappiness. The same voice implies that parents (and later parental figures in society) are always right and good. The overall effect is that the inner child takes upon herself all the blame and guilt and shame that really belongs to those who have abused or abandoned the child. For many people the whole process remains within the unconscious for a lifetime.

The child is innocent: the viewpoint of Alice Miller
Alice Miller was a world-famous psychoanalyst and had herself been analysed twice. Whilst painting some pictures she began to get in touch with the hurt little girl inside her who had not been reached before. After much research and investigation she came to the conclusion that all children are born innocent and that this fact is hidden by our culture. She has written books (Miller, 1986, 1987a and 1987b) that are read worldwide and have influenced many people regarding child abuse, therapy, politics and social life. The descriptions in the introduction to this chapter derive largely from her work and from therapists influenced by her. A number of important points lead on from the premise that the child is born innocent, that is, 'not guilty'. Among these Miller includes the following.

- Each child needs among other things: care, protection, security, warmth, skin contact, touching, caressing and tenderness.
- These needs are seldom sufficiently fulfilled: in fact, they are often exploited by adults for their own needs (trauma of child abuse).
- Society takes the side of the adult and blames the child for what has been done to her.
- The victimization of the child has historically been denied, even today.
- This denial has made it possible for society to ignore the devastating effects of the victimization of the child for such a long time.

- The child, when betrayed by society, has no choice but to repress the trauma and to idealize the abuser.
- Repression leads to neuroses, psychoses, psychosomatic disorders and delinquency.
- The therapeutic process can be successful only if it is based on uncovering the truth about the patient's childhood instead of destroying that reality.
- A past crime cannot be undone by our understanding of the perpetrator's blindness and unfulfilled needs.
- New crimes, however, can be prevented, if the victims begin to see and be aware of what has been done to them.
- Therefore, the reports of victims will be able to bring about more awareness, consciousness and sense of responsibility in society at large.

As you can see, Miller believes that neurosis and psychosis, delinquency and addictions are rooted in the mistreatment of children. This implies that forms of child abuse are quite widespread. This is now being accepted more generally as true. If we define 'abuse' widely to include psychological invasion, abandonment and neglect, then almost *everyone* in our culture has suffered abuse. The implications of this view are radical and for many people hard to accept. It means that our families, culture and social system are partly based upon the mistreatment, manipulation, deprivation and exploitation of children. It follows that the unconscious aspects of abuse permeate our thought, ideas and education. The term that has been coined for this process is 'adultism'. This means that the needs, desires, wishes and demands of the adult are, or may be, satisfied *at the expense* of those of the child. An extension of this argument is that adultism is at the root of all situations where the strong cruelly exploit the weak – for example, sexism, racism and imperialism. Throughout recorded history, wars and violence have been endemic in these processes. The thesis here is that the unconscious repetition pattern, where the adult repeats a childhood experience, is the mechanism that passes potential violence down the generations.

The reader may think this is all very well at an abstract historical level, but how does it affect one personally? What about you and me? As a parent have I mistreated my children? Have you mistreated yours? And what about all those who come under our care or control – lovers, friends, students, colleagues, clients, patients or even pets? An understandable reaction is to feel guilty, to blame ourselves or others or to dismiss the theory entirely. Alice Miller's argument is that it is not helpful or relevant to lay blame. She suggests that we unconsciously, unwittingly, and *innocently* repeat compulsively what has been done to us in our childhood. We do this partly as an attempt to exorcize or deal with early experience and partly because our ethical, political, religious and educational beliefs unknowingly collude in this process and make it feel 'natural'.

The obviously abused child who comes to the attention of social workers, doctors and the police is but an extreme example – the 'tip of the iceberg'.

When early abuse is unconscious, people choose different ways of coping with anxiety and body symptoms. For some it can be drink or drugs, for others smoking, gambling, overwork, or even neurosis and psychosis. These are the slightly more visible victims of adultism. There is, therefore, no one reading these words who has not, in a very general sense, suffered abuse as a child – to a greater or lesser degree. So what can be done? Is the process reversible? Miller and those influenced by her work have an optimistic answer. Yes. It *is* reversible though not easily nor without pain. To develop this answer we need to consider in more detail the processes for countering the effects of abuse.

The advocate for the child

In the best of circumstances a baby feels that she is held safely by a warm person who conveys without words that she is beautiful, good and worthwhile. This gives a self-confidence that lasts a lifetime. In time the growing child, and later the teenager, develops an internalized version of this person who nurtures. This internalized figure can be thought of as an inner advocate who supports the child. Consequently, later in life the adult also feels supported and thereby develops a personality that can cope with adversity and feel basically real and true. This person will easily be able to be an outer advocate for a child or grown-up. Each person needs to develop an 'inner advocate' who supports the child inside themselves and also an 'outer advocate' who can support others. Quite often people who are good as outer advocates may be attracted to one of the helping professions – for example, nursing, therapy – or they may be people to whom friends and neighbours frequently turn for help and advice. When someone has never had the chance to develop an inner advocate, they can be helped to do so by an outer advocate/therapist. No matter how bad the experience in early life, for most people some spark of the creative self survives from babyhood. An advocate for the inner child can help this part of the person to grow. As a therapist I sometimes find it hard to believe that a person could survive the experiences that are shared with me. But it can be, and sometimes is, possible to regain health and well-being.

The reason that this is possible is not due to something special about a therapist, but the fact that nature has provided creative and repair cycles that enable us to cure ourselves (with a little help from our friends!).

Nature's two cycles (see Figure 1)

There is a *creative cycle* in nature which we all know even though we may not conceptualize it. Even a mundane task has its elements of nurturing – energizing – peak – relaxing. Take gardening as an example. You may nurture yourself with a cup of tea and reflect upon the task. You prepare tools and materials. You put more energy into working as you dig and prune etc. Then *voilà*! You reach a peak. It's done! You step back and admire your creation. You may now relax and tidy up and ask others to share your pleasure and achievement. An outer advocate or mother helps the inner or actual child through a similar process. First, to nurture, hold and encourage the child, physically and emotionally. It is important that the child's needs take priority – it is possible to over-love or smother. Then, in the energizing part of the cycle the advocate/mother facilitates play and activity. Again it is important that it is play that the child desires and not play the adult decides is for the child's own good. At the peak of pleasure and laughter the advocate is a witness and one who recognizes the child's achievements: for example, where a child builds her first sandcastle and says with joy 'Look what I've made!' In the relaxing phase the advocate/mother encourages rest, day-dreaming and sleep. An adult's own inner advocate can encourage the inner child to enjoy this process, or a therapist/advocate can encourage the child within the adult to do the same. (An excellent example of such advocacy is given in Pinney and Schlachter (1983).) Although one needs to pay attention to the hurt or abused child within a person, it is important to develop the creative child at the same time. Sometimes the experiences to be worked through are so appalling that they cannot be faced without the help of the creative child within the person. The creative cycle was formulated by Randall and Southgate (1980), by a synthesis of the work of Reich (1961) and Bion (1968).

The *repair (mourning) cycle* provides nature's healing and 'repair' for trauma. A lot of work has been done to try to understand the curative process of mourning the death of a loved one; the key researcher in this area is Bowlby (1985). Most of us think of the mourning process as weeping or crying. In fact there is more to it than

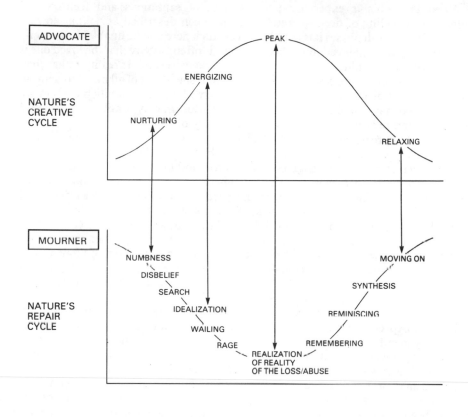

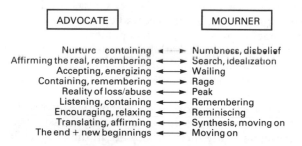

Figure 1. Relationship and process between advocate and mourner

this. Miller describes how mourning is a natural curative process not only for the trauma of bereavement, but for *any* trauma – sexual abuse, violent attack, abandonment or whatever. (Bowlby suggested this many years ago but few people seem to have taken it up until recently.) Below are described the basic elements of mourning (in actual practice there would not be a neat movement from one phase to another).

1 *Traumatic event* Emotional and physical shock galvanize the body and psyche. In bereavement this would be witnessing the moment of death or hearing about it. In abuse it would be the actual moment of the abuse happening or reliving and remembering the event. An immediate reaction may be to scream, shout or wail. It is not usual to remain 'stuck' in this phase, as the sheer physical exhaustion will lead to the following phases.

2 *Numbness* This is experienced as the loss of sensations and feelings and sometimes a feeling of deep depression. It has been described as 'falling down a black hole'. As in all phases it is possible to get stuck here and be unable to move on.

3 *Disbelief* An initial reaction in bereavement is often to deny that the loved one is really dead. Social influences on the person are likely to support reality rather than fantasy. However, in the case of an abused person, she is first of all likely to deny an experience that blames someone loved. And even when other family members are told, they too may disbelieve that it happened. Unfortunately, until recently, social influences and pressures tended to deny the reality of abuse.

4 *Search* In bereavement this is the belief that the lost one is still alive and may be found in the street or some familiar setting. In abuse it may be a search for the good, idealized person who, it is imagined, will protect and look after the child.

5 *Idealization* In bereavement this is where the loved one's good side is remembered and idealized. In abuse the perpetrator is idealized, as described earlier. It is not uncommon to become stuck in this phase. There is enormous social and cultural pressure to 'honour thy father and thy mother'. But the effect is to halt the mourning process and leave the person in a very unhealthy state.

6 *Weeping and wailing* This is the most commonly accepted part of mourning in the case of bereavement. Unfortunately many well-meaning people try to ignore or stop this process. In abuse it happens when the person can really let themselves feel the gravity and awfulness of what happened to them.

7 *Raging anger* Often people are angry that someone has left them by dying. It is helpful to express this with someone they trust. Again, many well-intentioned people try to stifle this phase. In the case of abuse it can be a time when the inner child finally rages back at the perpetrator – encouraged by an inner or outer advocate. It is possible to get stuck in this phase too, often in combination with the previous one – so that active anger is followed by quieter weeping and so on.

8 *Realization of reality – depressive/creative contradictions* In bereavement the person begins to accept the reality of loss. Both the good and bad parts of the person are seen as a whole. Similarly, in abuse, the person feels both the cruelty and the kindness of the other as a whole. But it is contradictory, and a depressive rumination may happen with times of insight and even happiness.

9 *Remembering and reminiscing* In both bereavement and abuse there is a time of recalling all kinds of experience, including those which were previously uncon-scious. It is important to encourage this process and it is helped enormously if there is a good advocate/listener.

10 *Synthesis* In bereavement all parts of the lost one are internalized. The lost one lives on inside the bereaved person. In abuse the person may either be indifferent towards the perpetrators or see them as they are in the present (if alive), i.e. old persons who could not help their behaviour.

11 *Moving on* Mourning is over and life is to be lived. Therapy changes to encouraging creativity and finally finishes altogether.

Therapists as advocates

The Institute for Self Analysis was set up in 1986 to train therapists as advocates for the inner child. Our first inspiration is Alice Miller; our second Karen Horney (1942), who was a pioneer in encouraging people to write a self-analysis with occasional help from a therapist. Many people spontaneously write letters and diaries when trying to deal with anxieties arising from childhood. We have found the combination of face-to-face work with an advocate, plus the exchange of letters, poems and paintings to be an effective way to do therapy (see, for example, the letter of one of our members – what we call a 'LISA', a Live Interactive Self Analysis – in the *Journal of the Institute for Self Analysis*, April 1988).

The most important thing an advocate does is to *listen* and *be* with the person, giving undivided attention. This sounds simple and easy, and although this is true in one sense, people in our culture rarely give or receive such attention. It is important to create a safe place where the inner child can tell her story. This can only happen when considerable trust, confidence and even love has grown between the outer advocate and the inner child. The inner child may 'speak' of preverbal experience so that listening includes messages from the body and the unconscious (as in dreams). Such messages may need 'translating' into ordinary language and this is a skill an outer advocate needs to learn. Another skill is facilitating the person so that the creative and repair cycles described earlier can be encouraged. None of the above will work unless the inner child or infant feels safely held – in the sense of a baby feeling safe in her mother's arms (see Winnicott, 1971; Bowlby, 1988). This is not a skill but a way of *being* and of each person relating to the other. It takes time to build such a relationship. It is very important that the advocate is *never* parental or adultist – even benevolent paternalism is bad for the inner child. Finally, it is crucial for a therapist to be in touch with her own inner child and to have worked through her own abuse and mourning. The function of the advocate for the inner child can be summarized in five roles:

- nurturer;
- witness (accompanying the person as they relive traumas);
- protector against what has been done to the person;
- translator;
- supporter of the person's inner advocate and creativity.

However, it is important that the reader does not conclude that only a specialist can be an advocate. In daily life, at work, at home, at play anyone can, and most of us do, some kind of advocacy. Nurses can be advocates for patients, teachers for pupils, play workers for toddlers and so on, using the principles already discussed. It is only when a person has been severely abused in early life that it is advisable to consult an inner child advocate/therapist.

SECTION SIX

RESPONDING TO CHILD ABUSE

29 FAMILY CENTRES*

Robert Holman

Although some Family Centres are run by local authorities, the majority are run by voluntary bodies. Indeed, Holman (1988) identifies Family Centres as the 'flagship of the voluntary organisations' passage into the community' (p. 115), noting that the National Children's Home, the Children's Society and other similar organizations have responded to changed needs, and to the shift towards *preventing* children entering residential care by offering this kind of service rather than the large orphanages and children's homes of the Victorian era and before.

Family Centres offer a range of different kinds of community-based support for families, which generally include childcare (particularly for the under-fives) but also such services as drop-in facilities for parents, individual counselling, group meetings for specific kinds of problems, training in childcare and child development, toy libraries and so on.

Phelan (1983), in a study of some of the earliest Family Centres initiated by the Children's Society, identified three common features:

- they are usually located in neighbourhoods where there is a marked incidence of the kinds of 'social problems' (such as poor housing and high levels of poverty) that tend to be associated with high rates of receiving children into care;
- they are intended to draw out families' strengths instead of labelling the families as 'problems';
- their services aim to be accessible to local communities, and responsive to people's actual needs.

De'Ath (1985), after reviewing information from 250 Family Centres across the country, added three further common features, the most important of which were: they work with parents as well as children; there is an emphasis upon participation by the people who use the Centre; and there is a commitment to increasing the confidence, competence and self-esteem of parents.

Within these broad characteristics and goals, however, Family Centres vary enormously, depending upon who runs them, what is their ethos and what are their values, upon local needs and circumstances, and upon the people who work in them and use them. To give you some idea of the kind of places they are, here is a description of one Centre, Baron's Close in Bletchley, given by the project leader.

Baron's Close Young Family Centre
'Most families are referred to us through the SSD [Social Services Department]

---

* The description of a Family Centre in this chapter is excerpted from Holman, R. *Putting Families First: Prevention and Child Care*, Macmillan, Basingstoke (1988).

usually while at a crisis or despair point. A lot of these are on the child-abuse register. After the family has been coming here for about 3 weeks, we have a meeting together to work on a contract which is signed by the mother, the key worker from here and the SSD social worker. The first part of the contract is what days they come, what time they come, whether the mother stays with the child. Sometimes we have the mum in for 1½ days with the child and the child in half a day on its own; or the child might come in a day on its own and mum might come in 2 days. The second part may say that mum needs to make friends here to build up her confidence or that we may agree to help mum handle her child who is out of hand.

'We start at 9 o'clock in the morning, when some children come with their parents and some without. The children are all under five and are divided into three groups and their activities go on all the time. The parents do different things on different days and the normal programme is that on Monday morning a group of them go to a skills centre, which is about 3 miles up the road. Monday afternoons we run a mums and toddlers group on the Lake Estate. On Tuesday mornings, in addition to normal activities, we have a toy-library session in one of the schools with two members of staff there. Tuesday afternoons we have a mums and toddlers here. This is open to outsiders and is one of the few activities which take families not referred by the SSD. But the room for this is very small, so we usually take families recommended by health visitors, those who don't fit very easily into the large mums and toddlers groups in the area. Wednesday mornings we have a parents' general activities group, which has been going on since 1979. They have family cookery, keep fit, films, speakers from social security. Thursdays we usually have staff meetings and training sessions. Fridays we have a health programme, about looking after yourself.

'The aim of the centre has always been preventative work. As a day-care centre we probably helped just by giving parents a break from their children. Now we have a more planned system, which is concerned with directly helping the parents as well as the child. One of the hopes is that we will change the parents a little bit by making them into better parents and to help them to understand why their children do things that they do. They can find friends here. We are a new town and there isn't mum or a familiar face around the corner. When I came, I didn't know anybody and I know what it is like. They haven't got anyone to turn to, they are separated from families and they haven't got the money to go off and visit relatives, or the reality is that they have lost contact with them. A lot of families over the years have come to us through Women's Aid. Now they are often very damaged people and they have often come from London because the London Women's Aid hostels are full and they are isolated.

'Families like this can benefit from the parents' groups here. The groups are open; we encourage people to go in but by no means force them. Mostly they enjoy the groups. Films on caring for children are very popular. The police have sometimes brought things like 'Don't Talk To Strangers'. Health care and make-up are always popular. We go off on outings, we like to have fun. Our best discussions are often in somewhere like the park. They talk about what it is like being with children on your own, what it's like not having any money, not having contact with your own family, how nervous you are going into places and meeting people. The sort of things that people share in common. Sometimes they are very hairy: people share terrific confidences, as when they have beaten their children and how guilty they felt and couldn't talk to anybody, and it will come out of the blue, and then somebody else will remember that they had done exactly the same and they can support one another.

'It is much easier to help the children because they are ripe to learn and they are usually quite bright children. If the children need individual sessions, we can give that, usually in the last term before they go to school and make sure they are up to coping with school, and we help them a bit with concentration and learning. But children just enjoy learning and getting together and the freedom of being able to play, learning controls which they often don't get at home. We are practically all of us trained in child care and that's the easy part of our job. It works. We are told very often that where the older brothers and sisters have not had the benefit of this kind of situation, the differences at school between them and the children who have been here is very marked.

'I think the centre has helped many families. In one case a very depressed mum was living with a dad who got hooked on drugs. She ended up in a 'battered wives' hostel not because she was battered but because she had run away. She returned home but the dad deliberately fed his children drugs or left them around where they could pick them up. They took the drugs, both were very ill, and the little one nearly died. Dad got a 4-year sentence for attempted manslaughter. When he was inside, the mother found it very difficult to cope. So the children came to us 2 days a week and mum came on the third day and we kept this up for 2 years. At first we had to collect mum to bring her in on the third day but gradually her confidence built up and in the end she was giving us a lot more than we were giving her. You don't get many pats on the back but one of our staff met mum recently at a workshops' meeting where this mum was actually speaking. This mum, whom everybody said was not fit to look after her children, was on the committee of the workshops and she said, "I would never have coped without the help that the centre gave me", and I know that's true.

'Our efforts have always been helped by a good working relationship with the local authority. I admire them because they are under a lot of pressure from the outside to take children into care. They have often taken a risk and allowed children to be shared between us and the parents where other authorities would have taken the children away and denied them the chance of being kept with their parents. Just lately, after the cases that have been in the papers, they have persuaded mums to let them take children into care just for a short period to give mum a break. But it is better if children come to a place like this, because I feel that once they have been in care, it becomes easier for them to go in again. In some cases it's what was the mum's life when she was young, so it is just history repeating itself.

'We have been to court on several occasions with parents. On one occasion the magistrates were debating as to whether a child should be returned to its parents and they actually came here to see the centre and then decided yes, the child could go home on condition that it came regularly to the centre with its parents; and that family did actually survive, the child is still with mum.

'There are difficulties in the work. We just haven't got the space. And we went through a phase when some of the parents have said such things as "Oh, I'm not going to let my child go there because that's where the battered children go". Up until a short time ago we did take a mixture of children referred by the SSD and voluntary admissions, and that gave a lovely balance. Now they are nearly all referred.'

30 INDIVIDUAL PSYCHOTHERAPY

Elizabeth Ash

I shall begin with a story, not a case history, but a composite picture based upon several women who have come to me with problems arising from their childhood abuse.

Margaret came because of marriage difficulties. She was the mother of three children: one young adult from her first marriage, which ended in divorce, and two of primary-school age by her present husband. Her face reflected her age, late thirties, yet there was the air of a little girl about her, expressed partly in her style of dress and hair, but mostly in her manner. She looked sad, uncared for, her hair long and lank, her clothes shapeless. She loved her children and her husband, was overconscientious towards them and driven by a need to please, yet she found herself resenting their demands and feeling inadequate, particularly in response to her husband's sexual needs. She was anxious about everything and she disliked everything about herself. She had outbursts of rage, triggered by the minor irritations of daily life and directed at her husband and children, at whom she occasionally struck out. At other times, she would sit, immersed in sadness, tears streaming, and think about dying. Her husband had problems at work; one of her children had school phobia; she thought that all of this was her fault and her guilt drove her, on their behalf, to seek help. She desperately wanted to be 'a good wife and mother'.

Her initial recollection of childhood and adolescence was of a mother who was rather child-like, suffered mood swings, and had several men friends, one of whom became her stepfather. She recalled her mother (recently dead) with affection tempered by sadness, remembering that she had always felt responsible for her and somehow sorry. Her father was an absent figure, with whom she was only just beginning to make contact. She also remembered being hit and neglected.

What did individual therapy have to offer her, that her apparently kind husband and sympathetic friends could not? She was intelligent, thoughtful and had considerable understanding of herself. People came to *her* with *their* problems – how had she got so stuck in hers? And how could I help to 'unstick' her? Using her story, I shall try to answer these questions and illustrate, somewhat superficially, the principles of individual psychotherapy, which I believe are fundamental regardless of the 'school'. They draw heavily upon developments of Freud's pioneering work on the 'unconscious' (Jones, 1955).

Psychodynamic psychotherapy is based upon the following general assumptions:
- that certain inner mechanisms govern our feelings, behaviour and response to others; they are protective of our developing selves and their pattern is largely determined in very early childhood, particularly by hostile or negative experi-

ences, such as neglect, loss of a loved one (usually mother) (Bowlby, 1973) or violation through any sort of abuse;

- that in later life we defend ourselves against the painful memories of hurtful early experiences by 'forgetting' them (repression), displacing them onto other situations, into other (often opposite) feelings or projecting the feelings associated with them onto other people – *but they continue to exist*. The more potentially hurtful and unacknowledged these memories are, the more likely they are to interfere in our present-day lives;

- that the mind contains elements not easily accessible to consciousness, that is 'the unconscious', which provides a repository for such repressed memories. The material of the unconscious is accessible via dreams and 'free associations', which, in our everyday lives, we may recognize as 'Freudian slips'. Both dreams and the uncontrolled flow of thoughts and their associations are used in the process of psychotherapy to make contact with the repressed memories of past experiences which are causing present problems. It may demystify the 'unconscious' to think of it, as Malan (1979) suggests, as a continuum from memories that we are unwilling to acknowledge to material of which we are totally unaware.

Many people seek individual therapy for feelings of 'depression', hopelessness, apathy, disinterest in life, sometimes bordering on self-destruction and often associated with acute anxiety attacks, like Margaret. Such feelings are common in adults who have been abused in childhood. The inner mechanism seems to work by protecting the psyche from pain by producing a state of detachment, 'don't careness', to a damaging situation over which the child had no control and in which it was unsafe or impossible to express feelings of rage, hurt or sadness to a necessary and 'loved' adult (see chapter 28 and Miller, 1987b). So the memory of the painful episode has to be quickly suppressed or 'repressed'. The vigilance necessary to maintain such repression, rather like that needed by the army in a harsh totalitarian regime, further depletes energy and adds to the depression. Anxiety is provoked whenever a later situation in life seems, by repeating a pattern of circumstances, to trigger the feelings associated with the painful but repressed memory. Only acknowledgement of the original episode – facing the nightmare upon which the door may have been barred for many years – can stop the early wounds from continuing to fester and from erupting destructively into the present. Paradoxically, the door has to be shut increasingly more tightly, exhausting energy reserves and then resulting in symptoms which cannot be ignored.

Margaret could no longer contain the distress arising from early incidents of abuse, neither could she, at the start of therapy, recall them clearly. All that she realized was that, in certain situations, she felt disproportionately angry or anxious. Important clues were the circumstances in which she felt particularly 'bad'; these related to mothering her twin daughters and her sexual relationship with her husband. Her initial effect upon me as 'the little girl needing attention' was also significant.

Our task was to uncover the childhood incidents in which she had been so badly hurt, so that her sadness and rage could be directed at the source of her unhappiness, not displaced into the present and projected onto her family. Dreams and 'active imagination' – a form of meditative free association developed by Jung (Hannah, 1981) helped her to get in touch with the little girl, who had, we discovered, been emotionally and physically abused by her mother and sexually abused by her older brother and one of her mother's lovers. The process was a slow and difficult one, lasting well over a year of weekly sessions.

My gut reaction to the 'little girl' was, of course, an immediate and intuitive response. She had certain expectations of me, one of which was that I could, in some way, nurture her, be her mother in the healing process. This is common in therapy, particularly when there has been childhood neglect or abuse, when there is likely to be projection of feelings onto the therapist about 'the mother' (or other significant figures), both as an ideal and a painful reality. This can be a very helpful indicator about the source of a problem. This displacement of feelings, known as 'transference', can be a useful tool in the therapeutic process. (How the therapist 'feels', in return, is called 'counter-transference'.) The application of this dynamic emphasizes the distinction between therapist and friend. Transference and projection occur in all relationships, but it takes a trained awareness and skill, enhanced by practice, to recognize *when* and *why* this might be happening and when it would be helpful to comment on or 'interpret' its significance: friends and family are unlikely to have the necessary emotional distance to do this.

Another dynamic in all relationships, of which therapy makes deliberate use, is 'unconscious communication'. This can occur in the retelling of dreams, or be a simple matter of body language or verbal expression in 'coded' messages. Margaret started off with the demeanour of a child. Her 'coded' verbal messages, which contained clues to her childhood, were about her inadequacy in mothering her own children, and their consequent difficulties, and her sexuality. She was only 'turned on' by her husband's anger and physical roughness. It was as if she were telling a parable which, if I 'got it' at the right moment could trigger a further unravelling of the thread leading to her past. Such interpretations, bridging the past and the present, should not be forced. Some therapists eschew them, except in their own notes, as they can be experienced by the client as part of the 'poisonous pedagogy' referred to by Alice Miller (1987a) implying that 'I, the therapist, know best what you were trying to say' – a further abuse of power.

The pace of therapy, especially in problems stemming from abuse in childhood, where self-esteem needs careful nurturing, should be set by the person seeking help *not* by the therapist. This is sometimes difficult, as logistics and finances may dictate the frequency and length of therapy. Sometimes only a few weeks of once-a-week sessions are available, or only one or two sessions after a crisis, such as admission to hospital after an overdose. It is surprising what can be achieved, in such time-limited interactions. It is important to be *clear* about the constraints, agree an agenda and make a contingency plan for later should the need arise. Short-term therapy can also be used to enhance self-confidence in preparation for more in-depth work later. For many people, taking the history involves them in telling their story, possibly for the first time, to a non-judgemental, skilled listener and this can be therapeutic. Acknowledging the 'unspeakable' may be the first step on the road to recovery. This points to another distinction between therapy and friendship: it is difficult to hear someone's distress without wishing to say or do something to 'make it better'; but friendly advice and reassurance is not helpful when it usually masks the pain of the listener by not fully acknowledging that of the teller.

A final point about the therapeutic context relates to the climate of the interaction. Woody Allen jokes about the intimacy between client and therapist which develops over months and often (as in his case) years of weekly or more frequent sessions. Murray Cox (1978) writes sensitively of 'structuring the therapeutic space', a meeting-ground for *two* minds to work on the problems of *one*, in contrast to other personal relationships, where each expects to satisfy their own needs. Psychodynamic therapy has been described as a science by Malan (1979) and others, in that it makes use of the 'medical model' of observation and history-taking. It also draws upon more mysterious and intuitive ways of 'knowing' ourselves and others, particularly in the contribution of 'the unconscious'. Murray Cox worked in prisons, with convicted murderers, and had to share the horrors of their crimes in order to make contact with them as individuals. He describes the 'danger' of contamination by the terrible material he had to work with. Child abuse can have a similar effect, for it draws upon some of the darkest corners of the mind. The therapist, therefore, while engaging with such material, must ensure that emotionally safe boundaries are set. These can be expressed in terms of the structure, physical environment, reliability and availability of the therapist, but more importantly by establishing a climate of confidence, honesty, trust and openness. The journey to recovery is so often distressing for the person abused as a child. It takes courage to face the demons of childhood still lurking in the dark, to examine the unacceptable faces of 'love'. In accompanying someone on such a journey, the therapist's own emotional baggage must not be an impediment, though it is important to acknowledge shared elements of humanity and human frailty.

For some, individual psychotherapy as described above is not helpful. For those who seek, or are driven to explore, the origins of present problems in past abuse, the therapeutic process, though daunting and energy-consuming, can lead to a happier life. For the therapist it is a privilege to be a travelling companion and occasionally a guide on such a journey.

31 GROUPWORK WITH MOTHERS OF SEXUALLY ABUSED CHILDREN

Judy Hildebrand

Clinical Consultant, Institute of Family Therapy

In this country, mothers are assumed to have basic responsibility for parenting their children, so if something goes wrong in the family, it is generally the mother who takes the child for help. Then, all too often, she is seen as primarily responsible for the situation! In cases of child sexual abuse too, although the abuser is punishable by law, the weight of responsibility for rehabilitating the family usually lies with the mother. Offering mothers some support can thus be seen as potentially both supportive and educative for them, as well as making a contribution to the protection of children. In offering such support, it is very important to remember that some mothers have no knowledge whatsoever of the abuse and immediately seek help when they learn about it; others may not pick up the 'clues' surrounding abuse; others may know about it and be fearful of getting help; a very, very few mothers are actively involved in the abuse itself.

Groupwork is an economic method of providing help. It is also an effective way of helping people share their problems, of boosting their low self-esteem and of helping them gain information and insight into what has contributed to their problems. It is because these very issues arise in families where child sexual abuse has occurred that groupwork is such an effective form of treatment. Furthermore, it can suggest new ways of coping in the future. In this chapter I concentrate on my own work with groups of mothers of sexually abused children (see Hildebrand and Forbes, 1987), but I do believe that wherever possible such groups should be part of an overall comprehensive treatment programme (see Bentovim *et al.*, 1988).

The aims of my work are:

- to provide oppportunities for mothers of abused children to share their experiences;
- to acknowledge how the marriage relationship or partnership, as well as the structure and organization of the family, may have contributed to the sexual abuse (this in no way is intended to deny that responsibility for abuse lies with the abuser);
- to consider the nature of the mother's relationship with the abused child, especially where she or he was unable to divulge the secret and ask for help;
- to boost mothers' self-esteem, independence and assertiveness so that they can become more effective at protecting their children;
- to help mothers manage their anger and ambivalent feelings not only towards the abused child and other children in the family but also to the abuser;
- to foster more open communication between mothers and abused children and to help re-establish appropriate parent and child roles and responsibilities;
- where relevant, to help mothers deal with their own experiences of being abused.

Group structure

I think that eight is an ideal number for a group. Meeting weekly for one and a quarter hours over a period of 16–20 weeks seems to offer enough opportunity for everyone to air their problems and to contribute.

Each group is different and will work at a different pace. This reflects the different personalities and experiences of both its members and its leaders. Nonetheless, there are common issues which I believe occur in all such groups, and I have categorized these into three stages: (1) creating the environment; (2) turbulence; (3) consolidation.

Stage 1 How you start sets the tone for future meetings, so it is essential to create a safe context for sharing confidences. I always assume that mothers have mixed feelings about attendance and that many fear they are going to be judged and blamed.

Stage 2 The second stage focuses on trying to understand the context in which the abuse occurred and feeling able to discuss it openly. Mothers frequently want emotional support and practical management advice about how to act with 'difficult' and withdrawn children; they also sometimes need help to cope with the many professionals involved. During this period mothers often make links between their own early history, their current adult/partner relationships and the abuse.

Stage 3 At this stage the task is to consolidate what the participants have learnt and to acknowledge their strengths. Mothers are encouraged to face future possibilities, both positive and negative, and to share ideas about how they might tackle them. For many this is a sad as well as a confirming time since the group is preparing to end and for many mothers this means the end of a safe and often enjoyable context in which they can openly share their feelings and their problems.

I think that the most successful groups are those in which warmth, humour and spontaneity are encouraged and in which the participants themselves offer new ideas and support to each other rather than becoming dependent on the group leader or co-leaders.

It is important to remember that even though these mothers have a common experience in terms of their children being abused, they may have very different histories and they may come from very different backgrounds with very different expectations of marriage, relationships and parenting. Their differing views should be respected but discussed. My experience suggests that well over 50% of mothers of children sexually abused within the family were themselves sexually abused as children. It is because of the likelihood of this cycle repeating itself that so much effort is put into helping mothers improve their self-confidence, so that they feel more entitled to assert themselves for their own children's benefit. Groupwork can be very challenging and co-leaders should recognize that if they dare to be flexible and willing to learn from the group, they will be encouraging the members to do likewise.

32 FAMILY THERAPY

Karl Asen

Senior Registar/Psychiatry, Marlborough Family Service

Introduction

Family therapists argue that in cases of child abuse the whole family is involved – even though this does not, of course, absolve the abuser from being personally responsible for the actual act of abuse. Abusive behaviour is seen to have a 'function' for the family, for instance maintaining the family balance: scapegoating a child may have the effect of minimizing the parents' marital problems as they unite in the face of an apparently 'uncontrollable' child (see chapter 2). In order to get a clear picture of what is going on in a family and to make interventions that can be accepted by all family members, the family therapist has to remain as neutral and as objective as possible. This is not always an easy task, since the worker is faced with a dual role as protector of the child and therapist to the whole family. In this chapter I will focus on the use of family therapy with regard to physical abuse. It is, of course, also used with families when the abuse has been emotional or sexual, or the problems are more complex mixtures of different kinds of mistreatment.

Interventions with physically abusing families

For family therapy to be possible, one needs to have the full co-operation of the family. In child abuse cases families often feel that they are being persecuted by social services departments, and are thus reluctant to accept any help. The first step, therefore, is to enable families to acknowledge that they have a problem managing a child. This can best be achieved by giving the parents the opportunity to state what they want to change about the child's behaviour before spelling out in clear terms, using straightforward examples of observed family interaction, what are the concerns of the professionals. This discussion can then lead to a clear statement of how things need to be different in order for both sides, family and professionals, to be satisfied.

As abusing families often complain about how difficult it is to control their child(ren), the initial family therapy meetings will mostly aim at putting the parents in charge of their children. Getting families to predict and enact (Minuchin and Fishman, 1981) problems is a powerful way of studying and changing the family interactions that habitually result in abuse. If the parents think that they are likely to lose their tempers when a child throws a tantrum because he or she does not get his or her way, then the family is encouraged to demonstrate how this happens. Parents inevitably know how to trigger such an event, for example by raising such simple issues as what chair to sit on, when and how much to eat, when to stop watching television, and so on. During such 'enactments', the worker using a family therapy model can challenge the ways parents and child(ren) interact with one another. He or she can, for instance, comment on the way one parent contradicts and undermines the other when asking a child to do something ('I'm not surprised Johnny doesn't know what to do because he hears one thing through one ear and something else through the other ear. If you don't "get your act together", parents, he'll continue to give you hell'). The therapist can challenge how the parents give in to the child ('How is it that you both believe he is so much stronger than the two of you put together? You allow him to be the boss in the family and then you get cross with him'). The grandparents can be invited to family sessions to address issues from the past that interfere with current parenting ('Granny, your daughter thinks that you are a much better "mother" to her son than you ever were to her. Talk with her about this, because if you don't, she might take it out on your grandson').

By challenging the ways in which families behave, the therapist not only gets families to question themselves but also helps them to experiment with new ways of being with one another. Such family work can be done on a weekly or fortnightly basis, but in more serious cases is probably even more effective in the intense setting of a day unit. Day units for families (Cooklin et al., 1983; Cooklin, 1986; Asen, 1988) deliberately create as many real-life stress situations as possible around familiar issues such as cooking, playing, outings to supermarkets or playgrounds, and so on. This provides good opportunities for working with families to help them find new and more acceptable solutions to the problems thrown up in the course of everyday activities. Such units have the added benefit that up to a dozen abusing families can share their experiences with one another, supporting as well as making criticisms, which cannot be blocked out with 'you don't know what it's like'.

Patterns of physical abuse

In order to make appropriate interventions, family therapists need to recognize a framework within which abuse occurs and recurs. It is for this reason that clinicians have attempted to identify typical sequences of family interaction that result in abuse and these abusive patterns are described in some detail elsewhere (Asen et al., 1988). Two commonly encountered patterns of abuse will be mentioned here and their clinical usefulness illustrated.

In *stand-in abuse* the child is put in the position of a pawn: an attack on the child is a way of getting at the partner. If, for instance, Mary finds there is no way of stopping her husband John going to the pub, Mary may use their daughter Ann's 'naughty' behaviour as a way of controlling John. Mary may say that Ann only behaves well when John is around. In John's absence Mary resorts to excessive physical punishment of her child in an attempt to get John involved in the parenting of Ann. Mary may threaten that she will hit Ann again if John goes to the pub and Ann may well 'learn' that she can stop her parents rowing by playing up. The child quickly becomes an active participant in the family game, uniting the parents around her apparently uncontrollable behaviour. A family therapist will try to help the parents to resolve their own conflicts without the child becoming involved. In a family session the parents might be encouraged to discuss differences in front of their child without allowing themselves to be sidetracked by the child's increasingly provocative attempts to rescue them from arguing. In this way the family gets a new experience upon which the members can subsequently build. Often longstanding parental conflicts need to be addressed at a later stage, frequently without the child being present.

The pattern of *helpless and help-recruiting abuse* can be described in the following terms. Many abusing parents have themselves had very poor experiences of being parented. This has left them with limited ways of dealing with the 'bad' behaviour of their children. The use of excessive physical punishment seems the only 'answer'. Often experiencing their child's behaviour as 'abuse', such parents quickly turn for help to others. Repeated offers of help from friends and professionals may result in reinforcing the parents' helplessness. It now seems as if the continuation of abuse fits with the continuing close involvement of the helpers. The previously socially isolated abusing family now has regular visitors, activated by the frequent crises involving family violence. To such families giving up abusive behaviour might mean losing the visiting helpers. The solution, that is 'help', has become part of the actual problem. Interventions need to aim at putting parents into roles of competence, helping them to enlarge their own childrearing capabilities. The problem of social isolation needs to be tackled at the same time by connecting these families with other families, through lunch-time clubs, self-help groups or mother-and-toddler activities. Disengaging the 'unhelpful' helpers may be necessary in order to allow the parents to find their own solutions, rather than constantly relying on others.

Conclusion

The family approach provides a framework for assessing and treating child-abusing families. It aims to change specifically those family interactions that are known to result in abuse. Using the family therapy model does not mean that one can ignore the very real power differential between an abusing adult and an abused child and this has increasingly become an issue in the treatment of such families. Although there is now some considerable interest in using a family therapy approach for the management of physical abuse (Alexander et al., 1976; Beezley et al., 1976; McKamy, 1977; Dale and Davies, 1985; Dale et al., 1986), there are to date no systematic studies examining which types of families specifically benefit from family therapy.

33 GRACEWELL CLINIC

Ray Wyre

Director, Gracewell Clinic

Gracewell Clinic – a British diversion scheme for male sexual abusers

Gracewell Clinic is a private clinic offering a diversion programme in the United Kingdom similar to those now common in the United States. It works with individuals and families that have experienced abuse as well as with abusers. It seeks to rehabilitate the family or, if this is not possible, reduce the risk of the offender abusing another family. It also offers full-time supervised accommodation for men who have abused.

The residential accommodation which is separate from the clinic enables offenders to have a more normal lifestyle while still offering control and supervision. A team of qualified professionals from social work, probation, education and psychiatric backgrounds with a wealth of experience have been brought together to provide a uniquely therapeutic programme through which offenders identify the deliberateness of their actions and take responsibility for their offending. It is on this foundation that the programme builds thereby reducing the risk of re-offending. The clinic offers the facility of supervised access with regard to family members and therapeutic meetings with children and the abusing father. All such meetings can be recorded on video- and audiotape. Contractual arrangements are made between the offender, the family and the referring agencies involved.

Diversion programme

Where the court is considering Gracewell as an alternative to custody whilst subject to a probation order/parole, it is necessary for the offender not only to agree with probation but also to understand the conditions pertaining to the clinic. The clinic staff guarantee the court that they will fulfil the contract and conditions described below, and will liaise with the probation service and notify them of any breach in the conditions. Behind these criteria is the belief that the courts can be assured that attendance is a direct alternative to custody and also that there is genuine control and support in the community. The clinic recognizes the need for a comprehensive programme in working with offenders and this is reflected in the timetable for treatment and the contract. (The clinic would not accept an individual for treatment other than on a voluntary basis if the nature of the offending behaviour would not have led to imprisonment.)

Condition of residence: requirements

1 The offence is serious enough or repetitive enough that the court is considering imposing a custodial sentence.
2 The offender has no record of overt criminal violence in addition to and remote from his sexual offending.

3 The offender is not psychotic and has no other mental or emotional disturbance which would contravene his ability to participate fully in the diversion programme.
4 The offender candidly acknowledges his responsibility for sexual offending with the victim.

Procedure

1 The court adjourns for four weeks, asking for full reports, and imposes a condition of residence at the Gracewell Clinic (as would be done for a bail hostel – although in some cases a further adjournment may be required). During this period full reports will be prepared together with an assessment as to the offender's suitability for residence. At the next hearing the court will be given the following.

   - The SER prepared by the probation service (for the clinic to accept a residence the probation officer must be requesting probation and be asking for a condition of residence).
   - A full specialist report from the clinic. This report will address sexuality and offending behaviour issues and comment on the offender's performance during the remand period.

2 Contracts will be signed by the offender, the key worker in the clinic, the Clinic Director and where necessary the probation officer and social worker.
3 An outline of the treatment programme and a timetable will be made available to the court. The clinic will send the sentencing court a six-monthly progress report.
4 It will have been made clear to the offender that his stay on remand is no guarantee that the court will not impose a custodial sentence.
5 If probation is imposed the offender will need to accept the following.
   - Signing the contract means that he is willing to abide by the rules of the clinic, and failure to attend or comply with the conditions of the contract will lead to a referral back to the probation service who, after due liaison and agreement with the clinic, will instigate breach proceedings.
   - The terms offered in the diversion contract are not negotiable and must be strictly fulfilled.

Benefits

A diversion scheme like this can offer the following benefits to the offender and his family which would not be available *within* prison:

- it takes the offender out of the home, offering a supportive, therapeutic programme within a residential setting, enabling the child or children to stay at home;
- long-term counselling is available to offenders and family members;
- it prevents the normalizing and justifying that often happens when an offender is sent to prison;
- it marks clearly the fact that the offender is guilty but also recognizes that for many children it is important that the abuser whom they love and hate is receiving help and yet still offers the security and protection the child needs;
- it cuts the cost of children being moved into care and recognizes the fact that sexualized children are extremely vulnerable in existing care facilities;
- it offers control in the community to a level not known in this country;
- it has the safeguard of criminal proceedings should the offender fail to co-operate;
- in some cases where the rehabilitation of the family is impossible it prevents the offender moving to another area, joining a family and possible abusing other children;

- the programme clearly demonstrates how seriously offending is seen. It does not offer a soft option and neither does it ignore punishment issues. The offender is in residential care and his freedom is restricted but – more important – he is daily being faced with the reality of his offending behaviour.

For further information please contact: Gracewell Institute, 25–29 Park Road, Moseley, Birmingham B13 8AH. Telephone 021–442–4994.

34 PARENTLINE
(Parents Anonymous)

Sandra Buck

Clinical Medical Officer in Child Health

'Parentlines' are self-help groups for parents under stress. The groups provide a helpline telephone service run by parents for other parents who are distressed. Some also provide befriending, group meetings for parents or informal drop-in centres.

There are a number of reasons why these groups emerged as they did in the 1970s. Following the tragic death of Maria Colwell and the resulting public outcry, some parents began to reflect on their own violent impulses towards their children. Many parents who felt they too might be reaching breaking-point began to wonder where they could look for help from a more informal network than was available at the time. These parents were all troubled by their feelings and experiences and wanted to reach out to others. At the same time, information about the American and Canadian Parents Anonymous movements began to filter through (Wheat and Lieber, 1979). These groups began as self-help meetings for parents with abuse problems; telephone support to the public followed on from telephone support for group members.

One of our guiding principles is that parents should not undervalue themselves, within the helping role or outside it. Parents often say 'But we don't know all the answers, even with our own children, so how can we help?' But a group of parents who have survived many stresses with their children has a wealth of important experience. When this is shared, for instance in preparation courses for volunteers, and understood, there are much larger resources available to draw upon. The fact that we *are* ordinary parents and *do not* know all the answers is beneficial. Our responses on the telephone will convey that we too have found it difficult being a parent, and this can help callers feel less guilty and more happy about themselves. If professional help is needed, it is easier to ask for if you have sounded out the problem – if someone considers your worries are valid.

When a troubled parent calls a helpline, they talk to another parent. The focus is on them; how they are feeling. No one asks for a name and address. The caller is in control. The listener has time for them and not knowing anything about the caller means there is less room for prejudice about their capabilities. After talking through the stresses he or she has suffered, the caller may be able to see things more clearly.

Does all this help reduce child abuse? We believe it does – at many levels. The availability of a confidential phoneline service means that when stress is building up, parents can reach out for help from people who understand their problems from first-hand experience. This immediately reduces their isolation, which is a major factor in child abuse. And by responding to the parent's need to feel valued and understood, we reduce the pressure on the child to meet those needs. A parent under stress, by using the telephone, can vent his or her anger and frustration on another parent and not the child.

The caller can get practical advice, about alternative ways of responding to children and managing difficult behaviour, from people who have 'been there' themselves – often more acceptable than advice offered by professionals. Guilt may be reduced by discovering that other parents make mistakes and that other children behave badly. Indeed, the fact that such helplines exist is an acknowledgement that many parents have difficulties, and makes asking for help more acceptable than it was.

We have found that there are enormous benefits too for the parents who run the service. Volunteers discover that their own parenting skills improve, and their self-confidence increases when they find they can help others.

'Parentlines' are built on the needs and experiences of parents who have abused or may abuse their children. Not all parents who answer the telephone have had such serious problems, but they feel 'there but for the Grace of God, go I'. They acknowledge that they received support when they needed it, or that their lifeline was 'a friend who cared and made me feel good when I felt I least deserved it'.

In 1988, there were 28 functioning groups in the United Kingdom still using different names, although in the future we expect them to adopt the common name of 'Parentlines'. Over the years, under the umbrella of OPUS (Organizations for Parents Under Stress) groups have shared their experiences and agreed a common code of conduct (*OPUS Manual*, 1986). This covers things like preparation courses, record-keeping, support for volunteers, professional back-up and confidentiality.

The most difficult and hotly debated issue has been about getting help to a child at serious risk. One mother was in tears as she pleaded to the assembly to pass a motion that the child's need for help is what matters most. She said that when she contacted her helpline, she resisted professional help even though her children were considered to be at serious risk. 'I don't dare to think what might have happened if I had been left that night with my children. I will always be grateful to the volunteers who broke confidentiality, although I was too ill to appreciate it at the time.' The motion was carried that OPUS should work from the principle that it is not helping parents if they call for help and we allow a life-threatening situation to continue without getting help for the child. In practice, though, most callers are willing to accept professional help when they are advised that they need it.

No parent should have to bear their problem alone. We need to share our pain and misery before we can find relief and joy. We need people to value and believe in us, not to make us feel worse when we make mistakes. We need people to recognize that being a parent really is one of the toughest jobs in the world.

For further information please contact: PARENTLINE, 106 Godstone Road, Whyteleafe, Surrey CR3 0EB. Telephone: 081–668–4805.

35 FEMINIST SELF-HELP

Jenny Kitzinger

Child Care and Development Group, Department of Paediatrics and Social and Political Sciences Committee, University of Cambridge

> I will not say again
> I sat on his lap. No
> He had me on his lap
> You were not raped: he raped you
> Memory moves as it can, freedom is yours
> To place the verb.

(From 'Let Us Move On', in Randall, 1987)

The women's liberation movement has provided the context for redefining many aspects of our lives including our experiences of male violence. Feminism challenges sexual harassment, battery and rape – not only by strangers but by husbands, brothers, sons, colleagues and 'friends'.

Since the 1970s women have been setting up self-help groups, crisis lines (often run from women's own homes) and education initiatives in the fight against child sexual abuse. Self-help and grassroots political activity were often the only alternatives in the face of widespread professional indifference, disbelief and victim-blaming. Today, largely due to the earlier efforts of the feminist movement, there is more recognition of child sexual abuse both by professionals and the media. However, the radical implications of this issue are still being denied or neutralized as 'the problem' is being defined in liberal democratic terms (Feminist Review Collective, 1988). Survivors of child sexual abuse are still being silenced as 'sympathetic experts' rush to determine their needs on their behalf.

The self-help group – in which survivors get together to discuss what has happened to them and how they are feeling – is an important alternative to 'professional treatment'. By sharing their experiences, women can identify the ways in which their abusers controlled them, acknowledge their own strengths and redefine their reactions to abuse as resistance strategies rather than 'symptoms'. Working together enables women to reject individual or pathological explanations for the abuse, to identify power structures and to find self-worth and outrage.

A self-help group is not right for everyone and is certainly not an easy option but there is a power in self-help that cannot be found in receiving support from 'the experts' or from people who have not experienced childhood sexual abuse.

Self-help is about redefining the meaning of experiences which have left you feeling dirty and ashamed, it is about rejecting the interpretations imposed at the time by the abuser: 'you are my little princess and I am doing this because I love you', 'you are a slut and you deserve this' or, perhaps, 'you are imagining it, nothing is happening'. As Moira summed it up: 'I had absolutely no words for it, all the words I had were the ones he gave me.' The self-help group provides a place to share and to redefine the meanings of such experiences, a space to find your own words for what was done to you.

Meeting regularly and with a common commitment to dealing with the issues is one way of creating a space where this most taboo and painful subject can be confronted rather than avoided:

> Because everyone was there for the same reason I knew that, however difficult it was to talk about it, they would talk about it eventually, and not talk about other things all the time. Being able to get really angry or really upset about it and knowing that they are going to let you be like that if you want, that has been really important. And to see that you can do something about it as well, you don't just have to say 'Oh, my life is terrible, full stop.' There are things that you can do if you want to. When I was going to the self-help group, when it was really good, it felt like I could get on with the rest of the week.

The importance of being in a group with other women who share similar personal experiences cannot be overestimated. As Jaqueline Spring (1987), in her eloquent description of her experience of a self-help group, writes:

> The simple sight of what looked a perfectly ordinary gathering of women, one that could have been picked at random from any city street, mirrored back to me, as nothing else could have, that incestuous experience had not put me at one remove from the rest of the human race. No one there was the freakish alien we had each, in our secret souls, conceived ourselves to be. This was the very first gift we gave to each other, just by sharing our physical presence. (p. 147)

The group can undermine the sense of isolation and freakishness that many abused children grow up with. Members of the group can develop very strong, caring relationships. In part this comes from recognizing their own feelings and reactions in other women. Hearing other women talk about reactions and feelings that you recognize only too well can be very confirming: 'It helped me to stop feeling that I'm intrinsically flawed. My reactions started to make sense, be something I could understand and change, not just be the way I was, and always would be.'

When women first go to a group they often fear being judged, found guilty or disgusting; they fear letting other people too close; they fear self-exposure both to other people and to themselves. Some survivors fear looking too closely at themselves because their abusers have taught them that they are bad. Bettina says she was terrified of going to a self-help group:

> It's very scarey because by doing it you may discover that you are a horrible person. You are very scared that the person you discover inside is somebody that you don't like. That's still there for me, I can't believe that somewhere, in all this, there is anything other than a horrible person.

Often they feel they don't deserve help, they are not worth it, what happened wasn't really bad enough or maybe they are just imagining it all. If you are thinking of joining a group you too may experience such reactions. However, if you *do* join a group you'll probably find that every other woman in the group felt the same thing when she first came.

In theory at least the group is free to set its own agenda, there need be no predetermined goals or definitions of health. In a self-help group you can define yourself as a survivor, reject the label 'victim' and refuse to hand over control to 'the experts'.

Self-help groups can also be organized around other power structures over and above those of men over women, experts over 'clients', or 'non-survivors' over survivors. Some women are active in self-help and campaign groups which are organized autonomously as black survivor groups, lesbian groups, Jewish groups and disabled survivors groups.

Interested in joining a self-help group?
If you are a woman, try ringing the nearest Rape Crisis Centre (the telephone number can be found in your local telephone directory). Although there is not the same tradition of self-help available to men, some male self-help groups are now starting up – try ringing 'Survivors' (071-833 3737) for further information.

Crisis lines are not just for 'crises'! They should be able to put you in touch with an existing local group or link you up with other people who want to meet.

If you want to start your own group some early planning is useful. You should think about what you would like to get out of it; whether it will be a closed group or new people can join at a later date; how long it will meet for (indefinitely or for a fixed period of time) and whether you wish to structure it around any exercises or topics. Some groups, for instance, have found it useful to have a structure that protects each person from feeling overexposed or panicked. Get in touch with an existing group in another area for advice and support.

FURTHER READING
Some survivors have written about the process of working on their experiences of childhood sexual abuse – on their own, with therapists, with friends and/or with a self-help group. You might find the following books or articles a useful starting-point: Anon., 'Experiences of lesbian survivors of incest' (1981), SPRING, *Cry Hard and Swim* . . . (1987), RANDALL, *This is About Incest* (1987). Some of the accounts in anthologies such as those collected in WARD, *Father Daughter Rape* (1984) or ARMSTRONG, *Kiss Daddy Goodnight* (1987) are also relevant to anyone interested in self-help.

It might also be useful to look at books discussing the practice of self-help and some of the leaflets produced by Rape Crisis Centres which have co-ordinated groups: ERNST AND GOODISON, *In Our Own Hands* . . . (1981), SHEFFIELD RAPE COUNSELLING AND RESEARCH GROUP, 'Setting up incest survivors' groups' (1987), OXFORD WOMEN'S LINE, 'Incest survivors' group' (1987), WILSON, *Self-help Groups* . . . (1986). HALL, L. and LLOYD, S. *Surviving Child Sexual Abuse: A Handbook for Helping Women Challenge their Past*, Falmer Press, London (1990).

36 PREVENTION AND PROTECTION

Michele Elliott

*Director of Kidscape**

Introduction

Children are taught from the time that they are very young that there are ways to stay safe from dangers in the world – they take these messages in their stride. Fortunately, most children will not drown, become victims of traffic accidents or fire, yet we teach children about these dangers without a second thought. In the same matter-of-fact manner, children can be taught strategies for staying safe and getting help in case of abuse. These practical ideas are set out in a number of publications cited throughout this chapter.

Although adults are not unduly worried about teaching children how to avoid hazards such as fire or cars, many adults express some concern about teaching children how to avoid abuse. Yet the statistics being accumulated from adults about the abuse they suffered as children, indicate that children have a potentially greater risk of being abused than they have of being in a car accident or drowning or being seriously burned in a fire. Why are adults willing to teach children about some dangers and not about others? In a survey of 534 parents, Finkelhor (1984) found that those who had not talked with their children about keeping safe from abuse gave the following reasons:
– that their children were never going to be at risk (55%);
– that abuse is a difficult subject to talk about (74%);
– that it had not occurred to them to discuss it with their children (65%).

In my own research with 184 parents I found that the reason most parents had not discussed the subject of child abuse with their children was that they felt inadequate to the task. They were extremely concerned about the issue, but could not think of a way to broach the subject. All the parents in this survey had warned their children about strangers, however, and often in a way that would terrify most adults. Yet, abuse of children by strangers is a comparatively rare occurrence. Children are much more likely to be abused by a known adult than a stranger – as shown by police statistics that in 75% of child sexual abuse cases, the perpetrator was known to the child.

It seems that adults are leaving children vulnerable to possible abuse because they do not know how to talk to children or because they think that their children will never be victims of abuse. Warnings about matches, cars and strangers are easier and there is an established body of knowledge to draw on when teaching about these dangers. Until recently, the same could not be said of teaching children about keeping safe from potential abuse.

---

* A national campaign to provide practical strategies to children on how to keep safe.

Within the past ten years, prevention of abuse and protection of children has become a growth industry, with ideas ranging from teaching 'children to mistrust all adults' (Lenett and Crane, 1986) and variations of karate-type self-defence to watching children 24 hours a day. One recent development has been to equip children with bleep-style alarms in case they should wander away (Anon. 1988). Videos abound before which children can be placed to learn how to protect themselves from sexual abuse. Theatre groups are presenting plays about child abuse based upon fairy tales or wild animals to classrooms of children as young as four years old.

Well-intentioned though these efforts are, the reality is that introducing children to the idea of keeping safe from abuse through passive watching of videos or 'hooray for Hollywood' one-off performances makes it easier for adults. We can hide behind the media and the method without having to face the problem directly with the children ourselves. It is *safer* and more comfortable for the adult than talking with children or getting them actively involved in personal safety. Yet many adults say they would talk with children if they knew how. However, there is another group of vociferous and angry adults decrying the trend towards preventing abuse of children because it interferes with the rights of adults and families. This group states that child abuse is the 'flavour of the month' and that do-gooders are teaching children to 'tell on their parents' to the state (Amiel, 1986). One of their arguments is that they have never seen child abuse and that the professionals are making it up to enhance their own reputations (Kenny, 1985).

In the midst of the uncertainty and debates, children are being left vulnerable, while adults analyse the subject until they are paralysed with inactivity.

Prevention

In the meantime, we rely on the traditional methods of 'prevention'. This often means picking up the pieces of hurt children and hoping that other children will not encounter dangers. If they do, we will then talk with them and help them to decide what to do in case there is a next time. Prevention and protection of children has traditionally meant protection *after* some sort of abuse has occurred.

The development of a national telephone helpline just for children came about comparatively recently in the form of 'ChildLine'. The demand for its services, and the increasing pressure on the social services and voluntary organizations such as the Royal Scottish Society for the Prevention of Cruelty to Children (RSSPCC) and the National Society for the Prevention of Cruelty to Children (NSPCC), along with the reported statistics, indicate that today's children are in need of help and protection. But what about helping children through prevention?

Traditionally we have 'prevented' abuse by *following rules to stay safe*. These rules were based on the idea that most of the threats to children came from strangers. So the messages of not talking to strangers, not taking sweets from strangers, not playing in dark places etc. were taught to children. Yet we are now aware that the majority of children who are beaten, sexually abused or suffer burns, bites or other non-accidental injuries, are actually harmed by someone they know. The safety rules were and are useful, but they do not address some of the major threats to children. It is assumed that by adhering to rules, children can avoid people who will harm them. When this does not work, it is because the rules were broken (Elliott, 1988). The guilt is that of the victim, not the offender. The victim then thinks 'if only I had followed the rules, this wouldn't have happened'. Or the parents are blamed for not being all-knowing and all-powerful. After a recent child murder, the media was full of condemnation for the mother because she allowed her child to walk to the bus stop alone. Somehow it was the mother's fault that a person *known* to the child had abducted and murdered the child. What about the guilt of the offender?

What about the problem that prevention has not included warnings and strategies for children about what to do if someone known to them tries to harm them?

If we cannot always be safe by adhering to rules, there is an argument for *locking up people who harm children and throwing away the key*. But this is also based on the premise that it is mostly strangers who harm children, for it becomes problematic to lock up 'Uncle George' or a close relative. It is surprising how quickly society condemns the stranger who attacks children, while finding excuses for the known attacker. There are problems with this approach, the first being that we already have a victim – we have not prevented their victimization. The second is that locking up offenders has not been shown to deter other offenders. It does, however, prevent children being harmed while the offender is in prison. The third and most obvious is that we cannot find all the offenders to lock them up. The fourth is that we are reluctant to lock up the offenders known to the child for a variety of complex reasons and since these offenders are in the majority, most of those who abuse children would not be locked up. Some adults can be forgiven for feeling that perhaps it is children who should be 'locked up' and watched 24 hours a day. The fallacy in any discussion about protecting children is that we cannot watch them 24 hours a day and that children can and do come into contact with people who may harm them – bullies, strangers and adults known to them. Should we be able to live in a society which allows children the freedom to walk to the bus stop without being abducted and murdered? Or allows children the right not to be bullied? Or allows children the right to tell someone if they are frightened, uncomfortable or feel unsafe?

Are we threatened by children who say 'no' to being spanked? To being abused? What if they extend that 'no' to bedtime? Or to eating dinner? Or to going to school? What are the implications of teaching children that they have rights? Do we want assertive children? Does assertiveness mean that we must tolerate unruly, badly behaved children? Why is it that we would not raise such concerns when discussing the right of adults to be safe?

Protection

These questions and concerns as well as years of experience in dealing with hurt children were the basis of setting up the prevention progamme 'Kidscape'. There is nothing magic in the methods used by 'Kidscape'. It is based on active learning involving children, listening to them and giving them strategies for dealing with problems such as getting lost, bullies, strangers and known adults. But the idea of using normal teaching methods to empower children to protect themselves and seek help is a recent innovation.

Inherent in this philosophy is the adult's responsibility to keep children safe, to listen to them and to act should a child tell about a problem. Involving adults means *all* the adults in the community – parents, teachers, police, social services and other professional groups, as well as catering staff, secretaries and anyone who is likely to come into contact with children. This gives children options about who they can tell. So if abuse is happening within the home, children will potentially have several people who are at least prepared to listen.

The messages to children are clear:

- tell someone you trust if you are being hurt in any way by anyone;
- do not keep any kind of touches by anyone secret, even if they feel good;
- hugs and kisses are lovely, but never secret;
- you are allowed to do anything to keep safe: run away, shout, kick, bite, break windows etc. and we will support you.

Attitudes

Underlying all of these messages is the assumption that prevention is *not* just about teaching children to shout. It is about changing our attitudes to children. It is about listening to them, valuing them and doing something if they are in pain. As one head teacher, Linda Frost, wrote (1986) after implementing prevention into the school curriculum:

> When given the opportunity to talk, 80% of the children did. Some revelations were trivial. Others were appalling in their severity. The space, time and opportunity to talk was vital. The important support we could give was to listen and believe them. In most cases, they wanted us to tell their parents, and make them believe too. We followed up and supported every case. It took a whole year. For me, the point of disclosure was hardest. I found it very difficult to control my own feelings of anger, anxiety and depression at what these children had suffered. At this most depressing point, things suddenly got better. The improvement in academic and social terms of the children with the most traumatic experiences suddenly mushroomed. A child who could only write about 20 confused words suddenly wrote a coherent story covering three sides of A4 paper. Another child's reading age improved by three years in a matter of weeks. The rapport with teachers became even closer. Children began using Kidscape strategies for dealing with bullying situations. Some formed their first trusting relationships. Children without bad experiences seemed to be more confident and supportive of each other. The ability to say 'no' won't turn a school into a chaotic madhouse. Pupils won't disintegrate into giggling heaps when private parts of the body are mentioned. It doesn't work that way. It is too important to the children themselves.
>
> If you accept a child's right to say 'no' in respect to his or her rights over their own body, you presuppose the necessity of teaching strategies that develop an independent and an assertive attitude. The compliant, conforming child becomes one who is at risk. The ramifications of this are far reaching. You can't implement Kidscape without thorough preparation and total commitment. But . . . what price a child's peace of mind? (p. 7)

Finally, although we have hundreds of reported cases of 'Kidscaped' children keeping safe from danger and abuse, how can we really know if it was learning the strategies which accomplished their safety?

For example, an 11-year-old boy John was on his way home when he was confronted by two youths with knives. He shouted and ran to a safe place, gave the police a description and went home. He did not tell his mother. The next day, social services rang his mother to offer help for the traumatic experience that John had undergone. 'What traumatic experience?' she replied. John told her that he had been 'Kidscaped' and knew what to do, so he did not feel it necessary to tell her. Keeping safe had become second nature to him.

But would he have done it anyway? How do you measure what you have prevented? What about the five-year-old whose older brother attempted to get her to play secret games involving her touching his penis. She told her mother. Would she have told if she had not had the programme? We will never know, but we do know that all of the reported cases represent prevention *before* abuse had occurred, which must remain the ultimate goal of prevention and protection of children.

Conclusion

Prevention is not the only answer, but it is an important piece in the puzzle of how to stop child abuse. As Dick Krugmann from the Kempe Institute says:

It enables us to stop looking at the problem of child abuse as if it were an ocean which we are trying to bail out with a bucket into a pool behind us. Instead of facing the ocean with complete despair, look at the pool. Each bucket into the pool represents one child we have helped.

And the pool is getting bigger every day.

Further Information
Kidscape is a national charity which aims to introduce child protection (such as sexual assault and bullying) programmes into schools and playgroups, and to enable professionals to acquire the skills and techniques necessary to talk to children about good self-defence. Send a large S.A.E. for details of publications and an information leaflet to:

KIDSCAPE, 152 Buckingham Palace Road, London SW1W 9TR

REFERENCES

ABRAMS, P. and MCCULLOCH, A., *Communes, Sociology and Society*, Cambridge University Press (1976).

ALEXANDER, H., MCQUISTON, M. and RODEHEFFER, M., 'Residential family therapy', in H. P. Martin (ed.), *The Abused Child*, Ballinger, Cambridge, Mass. (1976).

ALLAN, G., *Family Life*, Blackwell, London (1985).

AMIEL, B., 'Teaching children to complain', *Times*, 5 November 1986.

ANON., 'Experiences of lesbian survivors of incest', *Common Lives, Lesbian Lives: A Lesbian Feminist Quarterly*, no. 2 (1981), pp. 62–8.

ANON., 'Mayday badge for children', *Daily Express*, 13 September 1988.

ANTHONY, J., 'Other peoples's children', *Case Conference*, Vol. 5 (1958) [reprinted in R. J. N. Tod (ed.), *Children in Care*, Longman, London (1968)].

ARIES, P., *Centuries of Childhood*, Penguin, Harmondsworth (1973).

ARMSTRONG, L., *Kiss Daddy Goodnight*, Pocket Books, New York (1987).

ASEN, K., 'The Marlborough family day unit', *Bulletin of the Royal College of Psychiatrists*, vol. 12 (1988), pp. 88–90.

ASEN, K., GEORGE, E., PIPER, R. and STEVENS, A., 'A systems approach to child abuse – management and treatment issues', *Child Abuse and Neglect*, vol. 12 (1988).

BAILEY, V. and BLACKBURN, S., 'The Punishment of Incest Act 1908: a case study of law creation', *Criminal Law Review* (1979), pp. 708–18.

BAINHAM, A., 'Protecting the unborn – new rights in gestation', *Modern Law Review*, vol. 50 (1987), pp. 361–8.

BAKER, A. and DUNCAN, S., 'Prevalence of CSA in Great Britain', *Child Abuse and Neglect*, vol. 9 (1986), pp. 457–69.

BALLARD, R., 'South Asian families', in Rapaport, Fogarty and Rapaport (eds) (1982).

BANDURA, A., *Principles of Behaviour Modification*, Holt, Rinehart & Winston, New York (1965).

BARROW, J., 'West Indian families: an insider's perspective', in Rapaport, Fogarty and Rapaport (eds) (1982).

BAUMAN, Z., *Hermeneutics and Social Science*, Hutchinson, London (1978).

BAYLISS, S., 'One way ticket to Paddington', *Times Educational Supplement*, 30 October 1987.

BEAIL, N., 'The role of the father during pregnancy and birth', in Beail and McGuire (eds) (1982).

BEAIL, N. and MCGUIRE, J. (eds), *Fathers: Psychological Perspectives*, Junction Books, London (1982).

BEEZLEY, P. J., MARTIN, H. P. and ALEXANDER, H., 'Comprehensive family-oriented therapy', in R. E. Helfer and C. H. Kempe (eds), *Child Abuse and Neglect: The*

Family and the Community, Ballinger, Cambridge, Mass. (1976).

BEHLMER, G. K., *Child Abuse and Moral Reform in England 1870–1908*, Stanford University Press (1982).

BELL, C., *Middle-class Families*, Routledge & Kegan Paul, London (1968).

BELL, S., *When Salem Came to the Boro*, Pan, London (1988).

BENN, S. and PETERS, R. S., *Social Principles and the Democratic State*, Allen & Unwin, London (1959).

BENTOVIM, A, 'Setting up the treatment programme', in Frude (ed.) (1980).

BENTOVIM, A., ELTON, E., HILDEBRAND, J., TRANTER, M. and VIZARD, E. (eds), *Child Sexual Abuse Within the Family: Assessment and Treatment*, John Wright, London (1988).

BERGER, P. L. and LUCKMANN, T., *The Social Construction of Reality*, Penguin, Harmondsworth (1967).

BERKOWITZ, L., *Aggression: A Social Psychological Analysis*, McGraw-Hill, New York (1962).

BERNARD, J., *The Future of Marriage*, Yale University Press, New Haven (1982).

BERRIDGE, D., *Children's Homes*, Basil Blackwell, Oxford (1985).

BERRIDGE, D. and CLEAVER, H., *Foster Home Breakdown*, Basil Blackwell, Oxford (1987).

BIGGS, V., 'Private fostering', in Ellis (ed.) (1978).

BION, W. R., *Experiences in Groups*, Tavistock, London (1968)

BOULTON, M. G., *On Being a Mother*, Tavistock, London (1983).

BOWLBY, J., *Child Care and the Growth of Love*, Penguin, Harmondsworth (1953).

BOWLBY, J., *Attachment and Loss*, 2 vols, Hogarth Press, London (1969, 1973).

BOWLBY, J., *Attachment and Loss*, vol. 3, Penguin, Harmondsworth (1985).

BOWLBY, J., *A Secure Base. Clinical Applications of Attachment Theory*, Routledge, London (1988).

BREMNER, R. H., *Children and Youth in America: A Documentary History*, vol. 2, Harvard University Press, Cambridge, Mass. (1970).

BRIERE, J., 'The long term effects of childhood sexual abuse: defining a post-sexual abuse syndrome', paper presented at the Third National Conference on Sexual Victimization of Children, Washington D.C., April (1984).

BRITISH MEDICAL ASSOCIATION, *Deprivation and Ill-health* (1987). BMA, BMA House, Tavistock Square, London WC1H 9JP. Telephone: 01-387 4499.

BROWN, G. W. and HARRIS, T., *Social Origins of Depression*, Routledge & Kegan Paul, London (1978).

BROWN, M. and MADGE, N., *Despite the Welfare State*, Heinemann, London (1982).

BROWN, S. R., *Political Subjectivity: Applications of Q Methodology in Political Science*, Yale University Press, New Haven (1980).

BROWNE, A. and FINKELHOR, D., *A Sourcebook on Child Sexual Abuse*, Sage, Beverly Hills (1986).

BRYCE, J. W. and ARMENIAN, H. K. (eds), *In Wartime: The State of Children in Lebanon*, American University of Beirut (1986).

BURMAN, S., 'The contexts of childhood in South Africa: an introduction', in S. Burman and P. Reynolds (eds), *Growing Up in a Divided Society*, Ravan Press, Johannesburg (1986).

CAFFEY, J., 'Multiple fractures in the long bones of children suffering from chronic subdural haematoma', *American Journal of Roentgenology*, vol. 56 (1946), p. 163.

CAIRNS, E., *Caught in Crossfire: Children and the Northern Ireland Conflict*, Appletree Press, Belfast and Syracuse University Press, New York (1987).

CALAM, R. and FRANCHI, C., *Child Abuse and its Consequences: Observational Approaches*, Cambridge University Press (1987).

CAMERON, J. M. *et al.*, 'The battered child syndrome', *Medicine, Society and the Law*, vol. 6 (1966), pp. 2–21.

REFERENCES

CAMPBELL, B., *Unofficial Secrets: Child Sexual Abuse – The Cleveland Case*, Virago, London [1988].

CAMPBELL AND COSANS v. *UNITED KINGDOM* [1982] 4 EHRR 293.

CHERMIN, K., *The Hungry Self: Women, Eating and Identity*, Virago, London (1985).

CHIKANE, F., 'Children in turmoil: the effects of the unrest on township children', in S. Burman and P. Reynolds (eds), *Growing Up in a Divided Society*, Ravan Press, Johannesburg (1986).

CHILD POVERTY ACTION GROUP, *Poverty – The Facts* (1987). CPAG, 1/5 Bath Street, London EC1V 9PY. Telephone: 01-253 3406.

Childright, no. 30 (September 1986), pp. 11–14; no. 39 (July/August 1987), pp. 12–17; no. 42 (November/December 1987), p. 5; no. 43 (January 1988), pp. 7– 10; no. 46 (April 1988), pp. 9–13. Children's Legal Centre, 20 Compton Terrace, London N1 2UN. Telephone: 01-359 6251.

CLARKE, A. M. and CLARKE, A. D. B., *Early Experience: Myth and Evidence*, Open Books, London (1976).

COHN, A. H. and DARO D., 'Is treatment too late: what ten years of evaluative research tells us', *Child Abuse and Neglect*, vol. 11 (1987), pp. 433–42.

COMMITTEE OF INQUIRY INTO CHILDREN'S HOMES AND HOSTELS (NORTHERN IRELAND), 'Report of the Committee of Inquiry into Children's Homes and Hostels' (Hughes), HMSO, Belfast (1986).

COOKLIN, A., 'The family day unit: regenerating the elements of family life', in C. Fishman and B. Rosman (eds), *Evolving Models for Family Change*, Guildford Press, London (1986).

COOKLIN, A., MILLER, A. C. and MCHUGH, B., 'An institution for change: developing a family day unit', *Family Process*, vol. 22 (1983), pp. 453–68.

COOPER, D., *The Death of the Family*, Penguin, Harmondsworth (1972).

COURTOIS, C., 'The incest experience and its aftermath', *Victimology*, vol. 4 (1979), pp. 337–47.

COX, M., *Structuring the Therapeutic Process*, Pergamon Press, Oxford (1978).

CRAFT, A., *Mental Handicap and Sexuality: Issues and Perspectives*, Costello Press, Tunbridge Wells (1987).

CREIGHTON, S. J., Annual update of statistics. National Society for the Prevention of Cruelty to Children (NSPCC), 67 Saffron Hill, London EC1N 8RS. Telephone: 01-242 1626.

CREIGHTON, S. J., *Trends in Child Abuse*, NSPCC, London (1984).

CRETNEY, S., *Elements of Family Law*, Sweet & Maxwell, London (1987).

DALE, P., 'Perpetrators are people', *Community Care*, 4 August 1988.

DALE, P. and DAVIES, M., 'A model of intervention in child abusing families: a wider systems view', *Child Abuse and Neglect*, vol. 9 (1985), pp. 81–7.

DALE, P., DAVIES, M., MORRISON, T. and WATERS, J., *Dangerous Families*, Tavistock, London (1986).

DARBY, J., *Intimidation and the Control of Conflict in Northern Ireland*, Gill & Macmillan, Dublin (1986).

DARWIN, C., *On the Origin of Species by means of Natural Selection*, Murray, London (1859).

DAVEY, T., *A Generation Divided: German Children and the Berlin Wall*, Duke University Press, Durham, North Carolina (1987).

DAVIES, G. M., STEVENSON, Y. and FLIN, R. H., 'The reliability of children's testimony', *International Legal Practitioner*, vol. 11 (1986), pp. 95–103.

DAVIS, K., 'Final note on a case of extreme isolation', *American Journal of Sociology*, vol. 45 (1947), pp. 554–65 [reprinted in Clarke and Clark (1976)].

DAWKINS, R., *The Selfish Gene*, Oxford University Press (1976).

DE'ATH, E., *Self Help and Family Centres* (1985). National Children's Bureau, 8 Wakley Street, London EC1V 7QE. Telephone: 01-278 9441.

DELANEY, J., 'New concepts of the family court', in R. E. Helfer and C. H. Kempe (eds), *Child Abuse and Neglect: The Family and the Community*, Ballinger, Cambridge, Mass. (1976).

DE MAUSE, L. (ed.), *The History of Childhood*, Psychohistory Press, New York (1974).

DENNIS, W., *Children of the Creche*, Appleton-Century-Crofts, New York (1973).

DENZIN, N. K., *Childhood Socialisation*, Jossey-Bass, San Francisco (1977).

DES, 'Report of the Committee of Inquiry into the Education of Handicapped Children and Young People' (Warnock), Cmnd 7212, HMSO, London (1978).

DHSS, *Child Abuse, A Study of Inquiry Reports, 1973–1981*, HMSO, London (1982).

DHSS, *Children and Young Persons on Child Protection Registers Year Ending 31 March 1989*, HMSO, London (1990).

DHSS, *The Family in Society: Dimensions of Parenthood*, HMSO, London (1974a).

DHSS, *The Family in Society: Preparation for Parenthood*, HMSO, London (1974b).

DHSS, *Social Work Decisions in Child Care*, HMSO, London (1985).

DHSS, 'Report of the Inquiry into Child Abuse in Cleveland' (Butler-Sloss), Cmnd 412, HMSO, London (1988).

DINGWALL, R., 'The Jasmine Beckford affair', *Modern Law Review*, vol. 49 (1986), pp. 489–507.

DINGWALL, R., EEKELAAR, J. and MURRAY, T., *The Protection of Children: State Intervention and Family Life*, Basil Blackwell, Oxford (1983).

DOMINELLI, L., 'Father–daughter incest: patriarchy's shameful secret', *Critical Social Policy*, no. 16 (1986).

DORAN, C. and YOUNG, J., 'Child abuse: the real crisis', *New Society*, 27 November 1987.

DRIVER, G., 'West Indian families: an anthropological perspective', in Rapaport, Fogarty and Rapaport (eds) (1982).

DUNHAM, J., 'Staff stress in residential work', *Social Work Today*, vol. 9 (1978), pp. 18–20.

DUNN, S., 'The role of education in the Northern Ireland conflict', *Oxford Review of Education*, vol. 12 (1986), pp. 233–42.

DURKHEIM, E., *The Division of Labour*, Free Press, New York (1933).

DURKIN, R., 'The crisis in children's services: the dangers and opportunities for child care workers', Second National Child Care Workers' Conference, Banff, Alberta, mimeographed paper cited in H. W. Maier, 'Primary care in secondary settings', in L. C. Fulcher and F. Ainsworth (eds), *Group Care Practice with Children*, Tavistock, London (1985).

D V. BERKSHIRE C.C. [1987] 1 All ER 20.

ELLIOTT, M., *Preventing Child Sexual Assault: A Practical Guide to Talking with Children*, NCVO and Child Assault Prevention Programme, Bedford Square Press, London (1985).

ELLIOTT, M., *Keeping Safe. A Practical Guide to Talking with Children*, Hodder & Stoughton, London (1988).

ELLIS, J. (ed.), *West Indian Families in Britain*, Routledge & Kegan Paul, London (1978).

ELMER, E. A., 'Follow up study of traumatized children', *Paediatrics*, February 1977.

ERIKSON, E., *Childhood and Society*, Pelican, Harmondsworth (1963).

ERNST, S. and GOODISON, L., *In Our Own Hands: A Book of Self-help Therapy*, Women's Press, London (1981).

FAHLBERG, V., *Helping Children When They Must Move* (1979). British Association for Adoption and Fostering (BAAF), 11 Southwark Street, London SE1 1RQ. Telephone: 071-407 8800.

REFERENCES

FAMILY RIGHTS GROUP, *Family Advocacy Units – A Proposal from FRG* (1987). FRG, 6–9 Manor Gardens, Holloway Road, London N7 6LA. Telephone: 071-263 4016 and 071-263 9724.

FARSON, R., *Birthrights*, Penguin, Harmondsworth (1978).

FEMINIST REVIEW COLLECTIVE, *Feminist Review*, no. 28 (1988).

FERRI, E., *Stepchildren. A National Study*, NFER–Nelson, Windsor (1984).

FILMORE, A. V., 'The abused child as survivor', unpublished paper presented to the Third International Congress on Child Abuse and Neglect (1981) (cited in Jones *et al.*, 1987).

FINDLAY, C., 'Child abuse: the Dutch response', *Practice*, vol. 4 (1987–8), pp. 474–81.

FINKELHOR, D., *Child Sexual Abuse. New Theory & Research*, Free Press, New York (1984).

FINKLEHOR, D. and HOTALING, G., 'Sexual abuse in the national incidence study of child abuse and neglect', *Child Abuse and Neglect*, vol. 8 (1984), pp. 22–32.

FIRESTONE, S., *The Dialectic of Sex*, Cape, London (1971).

FLECK, E., *Domestic Tyranny: The Making of Social Policy Against Family Violence from Colonial Times To The Present*, Oxford University Press, New York (1987).

FRAIBERG, S., ADELSON, E. and SHAPIRO, V., 'Ghosts in the nursery: a psycho-analytic approach to the problems of impaired mother–infant relationships', *Journal of the American Academy of Child Psychiatry*, vol. 14 (1975), pp. 387–421.

FRANKLIN, A. W. (ed.), *Child Abuse: Prediction, Prevention and Follow-up*, Churchill Livingstone, Edinburgh (1977).

FRASER, M., *Children in Conflict*, Penguin, Harmondsworth (1974).

FREEMAN, M. D. A., *Violence in the Home: A Socio-legal Study*, Gower, Farnborough (1979).

FREEMAN, M. D. A., 'Removing babies at birth – a questionable practice', *Family Law*, vol. 10 (1980a), pp. 131–4.

FREEMAN, M. D. A., 'The rights of children in the International Year of the Child', *Current Legal Problems*, vol. 33 (1980b), pp. 1–31.

FREEMAN, M. D. A., *The Rights and Wrongs of Children*, Frances Pinter, London (1983).

FRIEDRICH, W. N., URQUIZA, A. J. and BEILKE, R., 'Behavioural problems in sexually abused young children', *Journal of Paediatric Psychology*, vol. 11 (1986), pp. 45–57.

FROMMER, E. and O'SHEA, G., 'The importance of childhood experience in relation to problems of marriage and family building', *British Journal of Psychiatry*, vol. 123 (1973), pp. 157–60.

FROMUTH, M. E., 'The long term psychological impact of childhood sexual abuse', unpublished doctoral dissertation, Auburn University (1983).

FROST, L., 'Kidscape – foolhardy but rewarding', *ILEA Contact*, 28 November 1986.

FRUDE, N. (ed.), *Psychological Approaches to Child Abuse*, Batsford, London (1980).

FRUDE, N., 'Sexual abuse: an overview', paper presented at the Annual Conference of the British Psychological Society, Cardiff, April (1988a) (to appear in a forthcoming British Psychological Society publication).

FRUDE, N., 'The physical abuse of children', in Hollin and Howells (eds), *Clinical Approaches to Sex Offenders and their Victims*, Wiley, Chichester (1988b).

FULLER, P., 'Uncovering childhood', in Hoyles (ed.) (1979).

GARBARINO, J. and GILLIAM, G., *Understanding Abusive Families*, Lexington Books, Cambridge, Mass. (1980).

GELINAS, D. J. J., 'The persisting negative effects of incest', *Psychiatry*, vol. 46 (1983), pp. 312–22.

GELLES, R. and CORNELL, C., *Intimate Violence in Families*, Sage, Beverly Hills (1985).

GIARETTO, H., 'A comprehensive child sexual abuse treatment program', in Mrazek and Kempe (eds) (1981).

GIL, D., *Violence Against Children*, Harvard University Press, Cambridge, Mass. (1970).

GIL, D., 'Unravelling child abuse', *American Journal of Orthopsychiatry*, vol. 45 (1975), pp. 346–56.

GIL, D., 'Societal violence and violence in families', in J. M. Eckelaar and S. N. Katz (eds), *Family Violence: an International and Interdisciplinary Study*, Butterworth, Toronto (1978).

GIL, D., *Child Abuse and Violence*, AMS Press, New York (1979).

GILES-SIMS, J. and FINKELHOR, D., 'Child abuse in step-families', *Family Relations*, vol. 33 (1984), pp. 407–13.

GILLICK V. WEST NORFOLK AND WISBECH AREA HEALTH AUTHORITY [1985] 3 WLR 830.

Gitanjali, Macmillan, London (1986).

GLASGOW, D., *Responding to Child Sexual Abuse: Issues, Techniques and Play Assessment* (1987). Customer Relations and Marketing Agency, Mersey Regional Health Authority, Hamilton House, Pall Mall, Liverpool 3.

GOLDFARB, W., 'The effects of psychological deprivation in the family and subsequent stimulation', *American Journal of Psychiatry*, vol. 102 (1945), pp. 18–33.

GOLDSTEIN, J. et al., *Before the Best Interests of the Child*, Free Press, New York (1979).

GOODWIN, J., MCCARTHY, T. and DI VASTO, P., 'Prior incest in mothers of abused children', *Child Abuse and Neglect*, vol. 5 (1981), pp. 87–96.

GORRELL-BARNES, G., 'Infant needs and angry responses – a look at violence in the family', in S. Walrond-Skinner (ed.), *Family and Marital Psychotherapy*, Routledge & Kegan Paul, London (1979).

GOSTIN, L., 'Ammonia up the nose, compressed air in the face: abuse or therapy?', *Social Work Today*, vol. 19 (1987), pp. 16–17.

GOUGH, D., 'The phenomena of child abuse', Report to Scottish Office (1987).

GRAVERSEN, J., 'Denmark: custody reform', *Journal of Family Law*, vol. 25 (1986), pp. 81–9.

GRIFFITHS, D. L. and MOYNIHAN, F. J., 'Multiple epiphyseal injuries in babies ("battered babies")', *British Medical Journal*, vol. i (1963), pp. 1558–61.

HANNAH, B., *Active Imagination as developed by C. G. King*, Sigo Press, Santa Monica (1981).

HARRIS, T., 'The axeman cometh', *Community Care*, 28 January 1988.

HARRISON, M., 'Do parents respond to a supportive rather than a didactic approach?', in G. Pugh (ed.), *Can Parenting Skills be Taught?*, Parenting Paper 4 (1982). National Children's Bureau, 8 Wakley Street, London EC1V 7QE. Telephone: 01-278 9441.

HART, H. L. A., *The Concept of Law*, Clarendon Press, Oxford (1961).

HENRIQUES, F., *Family and Colour in Jamaica*, Eyre & Spottiswoode, London (1953).

HERMAN, J., *'Father–Daughter Incest'*, Harvard University Press, Cambridge, Mass. (1981).

HEWITT, S. E. K., 'The abuse of deinstitutionalised persons with mental handicaps', *Disability, Handicap and Society*, vol. 2 (1987), pp. 127–35.

HEYWOOD, J. S., *Children in Care: The Development of a Service for Deprived Children*, Routledge & Kegan Paul, London (1978).

HILDEBRAND, J. and FORBES, C., 'Groupwork with mothers whose children have been sexually abused', *British Journal of Social Work*, vol. 17 (1987), pp. 285–304.

HIMMELWEIT, S., *In the Beginning*, Unit 1 of D211, M. Loney *et al.* (eds), *Social Problems and Social Welfare*, The Open University, Milton Keynes (1988).

HOBBS, C. and WYNNE, J., 'Buggery in childhood – a common syndrome of child abuse', *Lancet* 4 October 1986.

HOBBS, C. J. and WYNNE, J. M., 'Child sexual abuse – an increasing rate of diagnosis', *Lancet*, (1987) pp. 837–41.

HOFFMAN, L. W. and HOFFMAN, M., 'The value of children to parents', in J. Fawcett (ed.), *Psychological Perspective on Population*, Basic Books, New York (1973).

HOGG, J. and SEBBA, J., *Profound Retardation and Multiple Impairment*, 2 vols, Croom Helm, London (1986).

HOLMAN, R., *Putting Families First: Prevention and Child Care*, Macmillan, Basingstoke (1988).

HOLT, J., *Escape from Childhood*, Penguin, Harmondsworth (1974).

HORNEY, K., *Self-analysis*, W. W. Norton, New York (1942) (paperback, Routledge & Kegan Paul, London, 1962).

HOYLAND, P., 'Girl "raped in home care"', *Guardian*, 30 September 1988.

HOYLES, M. (ed.), *Changing Childhood*, Writers and Readers, London (1979).

HULME, K., *The Bone People*, Hodder & Stoughton, New Zealand (1985).

HUTCHINGS, J., 'The behavioural approach to child abuse', in Frude (ed.) (1980).

ILLICH, I., *Deschooling Society*, Penguin, Harmondsworth (1973).

INGLIS, R., *Sins of the Fathers*, Peter Owen, London (1978).

JAY, M. and DOGANIS, S., *Battered: The Abuse of Children*, Weidenfeld & Nicolson, London (1987).

JOBLING, M., 'Child abuse: the historical and social context', in V. Carver (ed.), *Child Abuse: A Study Text*, The Open University, Milton Keynes (1978).

JONES, D. P. H., 'The untreatable family', *Child Abuse and Neglect*, vol. 11 (1987), pp. 407–20.

JONES, D. P. H., PICKETT, J., OATES, M. R. and BARBOR, P., *Understanding Child Abuse*, 2nd edn, Macmillan Education, Basingstoke (1987).

JONES, E., *Life and Work of Sigmund Freud*, Basic Books, New York (1955).

Journal of the Institute for Self Analysis, vol. 1, nos. 1 (January) and 2 (April) (1988). Institute for Self Analysis, 12 Nassington Road, London NW3. Telephone: 01-794 4306.

KAYE, B., *Bringing up Children in Ghana*, Allen & Unwin, London (1962).

KEAT, R. and URRY, J., *Social Theory as Science*, Routledge & Kegan Paul, London (1975).

KELLMER PRINGLE, M. L., *The Needs of Children*, Hutchinson, London (1974).

KEMPE, C. H. and HELFER, R. E. (eds), *The Battered Child*, University of Chicago Press (1968).

KEMPE, C. H., SILVERMAN, F. N., STEELE, B. B., DROEGEMUELLER, W. and SILVER, H. K., 'The battered child syndrome', *Journal of the American Medical Association*, vol. 181 (1962), pp. 17–24.

KEMPE, R. S. and KEMPE, C. H., *Child Abuse*, Fontana, London and The Open University, Milton Keynes (1978).

KENNY, M., 'Mary Kenny's week', *Sunday Telegraph*, 10 March 1985.

KIERNAN, C. C., 'Communication', in A. M. Clarke, A. D. B. Clarke and J. M. Berg (eds), *Mental Deficiency: The Changing Outlook*, 4th edn, Methuen, London (1985).

KOLUCHOVA, J., 'Severe deprivation in twins: a case study', *Journal of Child Psychology and Psychiatry*, vol. 13 (1972), pp. 107–14 [reprinted in Clarke and Clarke (1976)].

KRUG, D. and DAVIS, P., *Study Findings: National Study of the Incidence and Severity of Child Abuse and Neglect*, DHSS U.S. (1981).

LA FONTAINE, J., *Child Sexual Abuse* (1988). Economic and Social Research Council (ESRC), Cherry Orchard East, Kembrey Park, Swindon, Wilts. Telephone: 0793 513838.

LAING, R. D., *The Divided Self*, Penguin, Harmondsworth (1960).

LA ROSSA, R., *Conflict and Power in Marriage: Expecting the First Child*, Sage, London (1977).

LAW COMMISSION, 'One hundred and fifty thousand children divorced a year: who cares?', summary of working paper on child custody, HMSO, London (1986).

LAWRANCE, K., 'Let the child be heard', *Police Review*, 20 May 1988, pp. 1074–5.

LEACH, E., *A Runaway World*, BBC Publications, London (1967).

LENETT, R. and CRANE, R., *It's O.K. to Say No!*, Thorsons, Wellingborough (1986).

LEVINE, R., 'A cross-cultural perspective on parenting', in M. Fantini and R. Cardenas (eds), *Parenting in a Multicultural Society*, Longman, New York (1980).

LEWIS, J. *et al.*, *No Single Thread: Psychological Health in Family Systems*, Brunner & Mazel, New York (1976).

LONDON BOROUGH OF BRENT, 'A Child in Trust. The Report of the Panel of Inquiry into the Circumstances surrounding the Death of Jasmine Beckford' (Blom-Cooper) (1985).

LONDON BOROUGH OF GREENWICH, 'A Child in Mind' (Blom-Cooper) (1987).

LONEY, M., 'The American way of child abuse', *Community Care*, 23 July 1987.

LORENZ, K., *Studies in Animal and Human Behaviour*, vol. 1, trans. R. Marin, Methuen, London (1970).

LOW PAY UNIT, *Working Children* (1985). Low Pay Unit, 9 Upper Berkeley Street, London W1H 8BY. Telephone: 01–262 7278.

LYNCH, M. and ROBERTS, J., 'Predicting child abuse: signs of bonding failure in the maternity hospital', *British Medical Journal*, vol. 1 (1977), pp. 624–36.

MACLEOD, M. and SARAGA, E., 'Abuse of trust', *Marxism Today*, August 1987, pp. 10–13.

MADDOX, B., *Step-parenting. How to Live with Other People's Children*, Unwin Hyman, London (1975).

MALAN, D. H., *Individual Psychotherapy and the Science of Psychodyamics*, Butterworth, London (1979).

MANTON, J., *Mary Carpenter and the Children of the Streets*, Heinemann, London (1976).

MARRIS, P., *Loss and Change*, Routledge & Kegan Paul, London (1974).

MARTIN, H. P. and BEEZLEY, P., 'Behavioural observations of abused children', *Developmental Medicine and Child Neurology*, vol. 19 (1977), pp. 373–87.

MCCAULEY, R., *Child Behaviour Problems*, Macmillan, London (1977).

MCKAMY, L. R., 'Multiple family therapy: a treatment modality for child abuse cases', *Child Abuse and Neglect*, vol. 1 (1977), pp. 339–95.

MCKEE, L., 'Fathers' participation in infant care: a critique', in McKee and O'Brien (eds) (1982).

MCKEE, L. and O'BRIEN M., (eds), *The Father Figure*, Tavistock, London (1982).

MEISELMAN, K., *Incest: A Psychological Study of Causes and Effects with Treatment Recommendation*, Jossey-Bass, San Francisco (1978).

MICHENBAUM, D., *Cognitive Behaviour Modification: An Integrative Approach*, Plenum Press, New York (1977).

MILL, J. S., *On Liberty*, Longman, London (1859).

MILL, J. S., *On Liberty*, J. M. Dent, London (1910).

MILLER, A., *Thou Shalt not be Aware*, Virago, London (1986).

MILLER, A., *For Your own Good*, Virago, London (1987a).

MILLER, A., *The Drama of being a Child*, Virago, London (1987b).

MINORITY RIGHTS GROUP, 'Children: rights and responsibilities', Report no. 9 (1982). Minority Rights Group, 29 Craven Street, London WC2. Telephone: 01-930 6659.

MINUCHIN, S., *Families and Family Therapy*, Harvard University Press, Cambridge, Mass. (1974).

MINUCHIN, S. and FISHMAN, H. C., *Family Therapy Techniques*, Harvard University Press, Cambridge, Mass. (1981).

MOHAMED V. KNOTT [1969] 1 QB 1.

MORRIS, B., 'Why are we waiting?', *Insight*, 29 January 1988.

MORRISH, I., *The Background of Immigrant Children*, Allen & Unwin, London (1971).

MOSS, P., Report on child care and equality of opportunity (1988). Summary available from the Commission of the European Communities, 8 Storey's Gate, London SW18 3AT.

MOUNTJOY, P. T., 'Some early attempts to modify penile erection in horse and human', *Psychological Record*, vol. 24 (1974), pp. 291–308.

MRAZEK, P. B. and BENTOVIM, A., 'Incest and the dysfunctional family system', in Mrazek and Kempe (eds) (1981).

MRAZEK, P. B. and KEMPE, C. H. (eds), *Sexually Abused Children and Their Families*, Pergamon Press, New York (1981).

MRAZEK, P. B. and MRAZEK, D. A., 'The effects of child sexual abuse: methodological considerations', in Mrazek and Kempe (eds) (1981).

NATIONAL INSTITUTE FOR SOCIAL WORK, 'A Positive Choice: Report of the Independent Review of Residential Care' (Wagner), HMSO, London (1988).

NATIONAL SOCIETY FOR THE PREVENTION OF CRUELTY TO CHILDREN, *Annual Report* (1969). NSPCC, 67 Saffron Hill, London EC1N 8RS. Telephone: 01-242 1626.

NAVA, M., 'Cleveland and the press: outrager and anxiety in the reporting of child sexual abuse', *Feminist Review*, vol. 28 (1988), pp. 101–21.

NELSON, B. J., *Making An Issue of Child Abuse: Political Agenda Setting For Social Problems*, University of Chicago Press (1984).

NELSON, S., *Incest, Fact and Myth*, Stramullion, Edinburgh (1987).

NEUSTATTER, A., 'The wicked stepfather', *Guardian*, 10 June 1986.

NEWBERGER, E., 'The myth of the battered child syndrome', *Current Medical Dialog*, vol. 40 (1973), pp. 327–30.

NEWSON J. and NEWSON, E., *Seven Years Old in the Home Environment*, Allen & Unwin, London (1974).

NEWSON, J. and NEWSON, E., *Infant Care in an Urban Community*, Allen & Unwin, London (1963).

NEWSON, J. and NEWSON, E., 'Cultural aspects of childrearing in the English-speaking world', in Richards (ed.) (1978).

OAKLEY, A., *Subject Women*, Fontana, London (1982).

OAKLEY, R., 'Cypriot families', in Rapaport, Fogarty and Rapaport (eds) (1982).

OKELL-JONES, C., 'Children after abuse', in Frude (ed.) (1980).

ONG, B., 'The paradox of "wonderful children": the case of child abuse', *Early Child Development and Care*, vol. 21 (1985), pp. 91–106.

OPUS MANUAL (1986). PARENTLINE–OPUS, 106 Godstone Road, Whyteleafe, Surrey CR3 0EB. Telephone: 01-645 0469.

ORBACH, S., *Fat is a Feminist Issue*, Hamlyn, London (1979).

OSWIN, M., *They Keep Going Away*, a critical study of short-term residential care services for children who are mentally handicapped, King Edward's Hospital Fund for London (1984).

OXFORD WOMEN'S LINE, 'Incest survivors' group' (1987), unpublished account of a group that was organized and led by Rape Crisis workers.

PARENTS' AID HARLOW, *101 Questions and Answers*, 4th edn (1987). Parents' Aid, 66 Chippingfield, Harlow, Essex CM17 0DJ.

PARTON, N., *The Politics of Child Abuse*, Macmillan, London (1985).

PAWSON, R., *Measure for Measures: A Realist Manifesto for Empirical Sociology*, Routledge, London (1988).

PETERS, S. D., WYATT, G. E. and FINKELHOR, D., 'Prevalence', in D. Finkelhor (ed.), *A Sourcebook on Child Sexual Abuse*, Sage, Beverly Hills (1986).

PFOHL, S. J., 'The discovery of child abuse', *Social Problems*, vol. 24 (1977), pp. 310–23.

PHELAN, J., *Family Centres* (1983). The Children's Society, Edward Rudolf House, Margery Street, London WC1X 0JL. Telephone: 01-837 4299.

PHILLIPS, M., 'A case of bad treatment for social work', *Guardian*, 11 December 1987, p. 21.

PHILPOT, T., 'What social work must learn from Carlile', *Community Care*, 7 January 1988.

PIACHAUD, D., *Poor Children – A Tale of Two Decades*, Child Poverty Action Group, London (1986).

PINCHBECK, I. and HEWITT, M., *Children in English Society*, 2 vols., Routledge & Kegan Paul (1969, 1973).

PINNEY, R. and SCHLACHTER, M., *Bobby, The Story of an Autistic Child*, Harvill, London (1983).

PLATT, S., 'Councils must sell homes at loss', *New Society*, 27 November 1987.

POLLOCK, L. A., *Forgotten Children*, Cambridge University Press (1983).

POWELL, G. and CHALKLEY, A. J., 'The effects of paedophile attention on the child', in B. Taylor (ed.), *Perspectives on Paedophilia*, Batsford, London (1981).

PRINGLE, M. K., *The Needs of Children*, Hutchinson, London (1975).

PUGH, G. and DE'ATH, E., *The Needs of Parents*, Macmillan Education, Basingstoke (1985).

QUINTON, A., 'On punishment', *Analysis*, vol. 14 (1954), pp. 133–42.

QVORTRUP, J., 'Childhood as a social phenomenon – implications for future social policies', *Eurosocial Newsletter*, no. 46 (1987).

RANDALL, M., *This is About Incest*, Firebrand, New York (1987).

RANDALL, R. and SOUTHGATE, J., *Co-operative and Community Group Dynamics, or Your Meetings Needn't Be So Appalling*, Barefoot Books, London (1980).

RANULF, S., *Moral Indignation and Middle Class Psychology*, Munksgaard, Copenhagen (1938).

RAPAPORT, R. N. and RAPAPORT, R., 'British families in transition', in Rapaport, Fogarty and Rapaport (eds) (1982).

RAPAPORT, R. N., FOGARTY, M. P. and RAPAPORT, R. (eds), *Families in Britain*, Routledge & Kegan Paul, London (1982).

REAVLEY, W. and GILBERT, M. T., 'The behavioural treatment approach to potential child abuse – two illustrative cases', *Social Work Today*, vol. 7 (1978), pp. 166–8.

RE B [1975] Fam. 36.

RE D [1977] Fam. 158.

REICH, W., *The Function of the Orgasm*, Farrar, Straus & Giroux, New York (1961).

RICHARDS, M. P. M. (ed.), *The Integration of a Child into a Social World*, Cambridge University Press (1974).

RILEY, D., *War in the Nursery*, Virago, London (1983).

ROBERTS, H., *The Patient Patients*, Pandora, London (1984).

RODERTSON, F. E., *The Family: Change or Continuity?*, Macmillan, London (1986).

REFERENCES

ROBINSON, M., 'Step-families: a reconstituted family system', *Journal of Family Therapy*, vol. 2 (1980), pp. 45–69.

ROKEACH, M., *Beliefs, Attitudes and Values: A Theory of Organisation and Change*, Jossey-Bass, San Francisco (1968).

ROSE, N., *The Psychological Complex*, Routledge & Kegan Paul, London (1985).

ROWE, J. and LAMBERT, L., *Children who Wait* (1973). Association of British Adoption Agencies, London.

RUSCH, R. G., HALL, J. C. and GRIFFEN, H. C., 'Abuse-provoking characteristics of institutionalized mentally retarded individuals', *American Journal of Mental Deficiency*, vol. 90 (1986), pp. 618–24.

RUSH, F., *The Best Kept Secret*, Prentice-Hall, Englewood Cliffs (1981).

RUTTER, M., *Maternal Deprivation Reassessed*, Penguin Books, Harmondsworth (1972).

RUTTER, M. and MADGE, N., *Cycles of Disadvantage*, Heinemann, London (1976).

R V. HOPLEY [1860] 2 F and F 202.

RYAN T. and WALKER, R., *Making Life Story Books*, BAAF, London (1985).

SAIFULLAH KAHN, V. (ed.), *Minority Families in Britain*, Macmillan, London (1979).

SALZER, E. M., 'To combat violence in the child's world: Swedish efforts to strengthen the child's rights', *Current Sweden*, no. 229 (1979).

SAVOLAINEN, M., 'Finland: more rights for children', *Journal of Family Law*, vol. 25 (1986), pp. 113–26.

SCHECHTER, M. D. and ROBERGE, L., 'Sexual exploitation', in R. E. Helfer and C. H. Kempe (eds), *Child Abuse and Neglect: The Family and the Community*, Ballinger, Cambridge, Mass. (1976).

SCHEPER-HUGHES, N. (ed.), *Child Survival: Anthropological Perspectives on the Treatment and Maltreatment of Children*, Reidel, Dordrecht (1987).

SCHILLING, R. F. and SCHINKE, S. P., 'Maltreatment and mental retardation', in J. M. Berg (ed.), *Perspectives and Progress in Mental Retardation*, vol. 1, University Park Press, Baltimore (1984).

SCHORSCH, A., *Images of Childhood*, Mayflower, New York (1979).

SEDNEY, M. A. and BROOKS, B., 'Factors associated with a history of childhood sexual experience in a non-clinical population', *Journal of the American Academy of Child Psychiatry*, vol. 23 (1984), pp. 215–18.

SGROI, S. M., *Handbook of Clinical Intervention in Child Sexual Abuse*, Lexington Books, Cambridge, Mass. (1982).

SHARRON, H., 'Parent abuse', *New Society*, 13 March 1987.

SHEFFIELD RAPE COUNSELLING AND RESEARCH GROUP, 'Setting up incest survivors' groups' (1987). SRCR, P.O. Box 34, Sheffield S1 1UD. Telephone: 0742 757130.

SHELDON, B., 'The psychology of incompetence', in *After Beckford?*, Department of Social Policy and Science, Royal Holloway and Bedford New College, University of London, Egham, Surrey (1987).

SILVERMAN, F., 'The roentgen manifestations of unrecognised skeletal trauma in infants', *American Journal of Roentgenology*, vol. 69, no. 3, (1953), pp. 413–27.

SINASON, V., 'Smiling, swallowing, sickening and stupefying, the effect of abuse on the child', *Psychoanalytic Psychotherapy*, vol. 3 (1988).

SKINNER, B. F., *Science and Human Behaviour*, Collier Macmillan, Basingstoke (1953).

SKINNER, B. F., 'Punishment: a questionable technique', in R. H. Walters, J. A. Cheyne and R. K. Banks, *Punishment*, Penguin Books, Harmondsworth (1972).

SMELSER, N., 'The Victorian family', in Rapaport, Fogarty and Rapaport (eds) (1982).

SMITH, S. M., *The Battered Child Syndrome*, Butterworth, London (1975).

SPOCK, B., *Baby and Child Care*, W. H. Allen, London (1979).

SPRING, J., *Cry Hard and Swim: The Story of an Incest Survivor*, Virago, London (1987).

SROUFE, L. A., 'Infant–caregiver attachment and patterns of adaptation in pre-school: the roots of maladaptation and competence', in M. Perlmutter (ed.), *Minnesota Symposium on Child Psychology*, vol. 16, Erlbaum Associates, New Jersey (1983).

STAPLETON, P., 'Living in Britain', in Ellis (ed.) (1978).

STEARN, J., 'An expensive way of making children ill', *Roof*, September/October 1986.

STONE, L., *The Family, Sex and Marriage in England 1500–1800*, Harper & Row, New York (1977).

STOLL, C. F., 'Images of man and social control', *Social Forces*, vol. 47 (1968), p. 119.

STRAUSS, M. A., 'Ordinary violence, child abuse and wife beating: what do they have in common?', in D. Finkelhor, R. J. Gelles, T. T. Hotaling and M. A. Strauss (eds), *The Dark Side of Families*, Sage, Beverly Hills (1983).

STRAUSS, M. A. et al., *Behind Closed Doors*, Anchor Doubleday, New York (1981).

SUAREZ-OROZCO, M. M., 'The treatment of children in the "dirty war": ideology, state terrorism and the abuse of children in Argentina', in Scheper-Hughes (ed.) (1987).

SZASZ, T., *Ideology and Insanity*, Penguin, Harmondsworth (1970).

TAYLOR, S., *Durkheim and The Study of Suicide*, Macmillan, London (1982).

TAYLOR, S., 'Researching child abuse', in R. Burgess (ed.), *Investigating Society*, Longman (1988).

THORNLEY, M., 'Fostering an abused child', *Nursery World*, 7 May 1987.

TIZARD, B., COOPERMAN, O., JOSEPH, A. and TIZARD, J., 'Environmental effects on language development: a study of young children in long stay residential nurseries', *Child Development*, vol. 42 (1972), pp. 337–58.

TORO, P. A., 'Developmental effects of child abuse: a review', *Child Abuse and Neglect*, vol. 6 (1982), pp. 423–31.

TOWNSEND, P., 'Current conflicts over the future of the welfare state, in thought and action in social policy', *Eurosocial Occasional Papers*, no. 12 (1985).

TOWNSEND, P., 'A theory of poverty and the role of social policy', in M. Loney et al. (eds), *Social Problems and Social Welfare*, The Open University, Milton Keynes (1988).

TOYNBEE, P., 'The openness with which step-parents confessed to violent hate of children took my breath away', *Guardian*, 8 July 1985.

TREDINNICK, A. and FAIRBURN, A., 'Left holding the baby', *Community Care*, 10 April 1980a, pp. 22–5.

TREDINNICK, A. and FAIRBURN, A., 'The baby removed from its parents at birth – prophylaxis with justice', *New Law Journal*, vol. 130 (1980b), pp. 498–50.

TUFTS' NEW ENGLAND MEDICAL CENTRE, DIVISION OF CHILD PSYCHIATRY, 'Sexually exploited children: service and research project', Final Report of the Office of Juvenile Justice and Delinquency Prevention, U.S. Department of Justice, Washington D.C. (1984).

UNITED NATIONS, 'The UN Declaration of the Rights of the Child', in B. Gross and R. Gross, *The Children's Rights Movement*, Doubleday, New York (1977).

WAGNER, G., *Children of the Empire*, Weidenfeld & Nicolson, London (1982).

WALKER, A. and WALKER, C. (eds), *The Growing Divide, A Social Audit 1979–1987*, Child Poverty Action Group, London (1987).

WALLER, W., 'Social problems and the mores', *American Sociological Review*, vol. 1 (1936), pp. 922–33.

REFERENCES

WARD, E., *Father Daughter Rape*, Women's Press, London (1984).

WATSON, G., 'Sexual attitudes and knowledge of children with mild and moderate learning difficulties', in G. Campbell (ed.), *Health Education and Youth*, Falmer Press, London (1984).

WEINREICH, P., 'Ethnicity and adolescent identity conflicts: a comparative study', in Saifullah Kahn (ed.) (1979).

WEST, S., 'Acute periosteal swellings in several young infants of the same family, probably rachitic in nature', *British Medical Journal*, vol. i (1888), pp. 856–7.

WESTWOOD, S. and BACHU, P., *Enterprising Women*, Routledge, London (1988).

WHEAT, P. and LIEBER, L., *Hope for the Children – A Personal History of Parents Anonymous*, Winston Press, New York (1979).

WHYTE, B., *The Yellow on the Broom*, Futura, London (1979).

WILLER, D. and WILLER, J., *Systematic Empiricism: A Critique of a Pseudo-science*, Prentice-Hall, Englewood Cliffs (1973).

WILLS, D., *Spare the Child*, Penguin, Harmondsworth (1971).

WILSON, B., *Religion in Sociological Perspective*, Oxford University Press, London (1982).

WILSON, J., *Self-help Groups: Getting Started – Keeping Going*, Longman, Harlow (1986).

WINNICOTT, D. W., *Playing and Reality*, Penguin, Harmondsworth (1971).

WOLFENSBERGER, W. and ZAUHA, H. (eds), *Citizen Advocacy and Protective Services for the Impaired and Handicapped*, National Institute on Mental Retardation, Toronto (1973).

WOOLLEY, P. V. and EVANS, W. A., 'The significance of skeletal lesions in infants resembling those of traumatic origin', *Journal of the American Medical Association*, vol. 158, no. 7 (1955), pp. 539–44.

WYMER, N., *Father of Nobody's Children: A Portrait of Dr Barnardo*, Hutchinson, London (1954).

Index